US IMMIGRATION HANDBOOK

● A Survival Handbook ●

David Hampshire & Sid Rizvi

D1301448

Survival Books ● London ● England

First published 2010

Copyright © Survival Books 2010
Cover photograph © Steven Troell (🖳 www.dreamstime.com)
Illustrations, cartoons and maps © Jim Watson

Survival Books Limited
9 Bentinck Street, London W1U 2EL, United Kingdom
☎ +44 (0)20-7788 7644, 🖷 +44 (0)870-762 3212
✉ info@survivalbooks.net
🖳 www.survivalbooks.net

British Library Cataloguing in Publication Data
A CIP record for this book is available
from the British Library.
ISBN: 978-1-907339-12-7

Printed and bound in India by Ajanta Offset

Acknowledgements

Our sincere thanks to all those who contributed to the successful publication of this book. We would particularly like to thank Atif, Joe and Ozz of Visas4America.com, David Woodworth for his help with chapters 2, 6 and 9; Peter Read for general editing and research: Di Bruce-Kidman for desktop publishing and photo selection; Chris Nye for proof-reading; Lilac Johnston for research; and Jim Watson for the cover design, illustrations and maps. Also a special thank you to the many photographers (listed on page 316).

What Readers and Reviewers Have Said About Survival Books:

"If I were to move to France, I would like David Hampshire to be with me, holding my hand every step of the way. This being impractical, I would have to settle for second best and take his books with me instead!"

Living France

"We would like to congratulate you on this work: it is really super! We hand it out to our expatriates and they read it with great interest and pleasure."

ICI (Switzerland) AG

"I found this a wonderful book crammed with facts and figures, with a straightforward approach to the problems and pitfalls you are likely to encounter. The whole laced with humour and a thorough understanding of what's involved. Gets my vote!"

Reader (Amazon)

"Get hold of David Hampshire's book for its sheer knowledge, straightforwardness and insights to the Spanish character and do yourself a favour!"

Living Spain

"Rarely has a 'survival guide' contained such useful advice – This book dispels doubts for first time travellers, yet is also useful for seasoned globetrotters – In a word, if you're planning to move to the US or go there for a long term stay, then buy this book both for general reading and as a ready reference."

American Citizens Abroad

Important Note

U S immigration is a complex subject and the rules and regulations are constantly changing. You also need to bear in mind that each of the 50 states and Washington DC (the nation's capital, formally known as the District of Columbia) has different laws encompassing a wide range of subjects. The authors and publisher cannot recommend too strongly that you check with an official and reliable source (not always the same) before making any major decisions or taking an irreversible course of action. You may also wish to consult a immigration lawyer. However, don't believe everything you're told or read – even, dare we say it, herein!

Useful addresses and references to other sources of information have been included in all chapters and in **Appendices A, B** and **C** to help you obtain further information and verify details with official sources. Important points have been emphasized, in **bold** print or boxes, some of which it would be expensive, or even dangerous, to disregard. **Ignore them at your peril or cost!**

Note

Unless specifically stated, the reference to any company, organisation or product in this book doesn't constitute an endorsement or recommendation. None of the businesses, products or individuals mentioned in this book have paid for an endorsement.

Contents

Authors' Notes

◆ The United States of America (USA) is generally referred to in this book as 'the US', and both 'US' and 'American' are used to mean 'pertaining to the United States of America'.

◆ All times are shown using am (ante meridiem) for before noon and pm (post meridiem) for after noon. Most Americans don't use the 24-hour clock. All times are local, so check the time difference when making inter-state and international telephone calls (see **Time Zones** on page 15).

◆ The costs and fees quoted in this book are in $US (unless otherwise stated) and don't include state and city sales taxes (if applicable), which are almost never included in listed prices in the US. All prices are subject to change and should be taken as estimates only. (See 🖳 www.xe.com to make currency conversions.)

◆ His/he/him also means her/she/her (please forgive us ladies). This is done to make life easier for both the reader and (in particular) the authors, and isn't intended to be sexist.

◆ Most spelling is – or should be – American English and not British English. This is to help readers familiarize themselves with US spelling and terminology. The authors apologize in advance for any English spellings and terminology that may have crept in.

◆ Warnings and important points are shown in **bold** type.

◆ The following symbols are used in this book: ☎ (telephone), 📄 (fax), 🖳 (Internet) and ✉ (email).

◆ Lists of **Useful Addresses**, **Further Reading** and **Useful Websites** are contained in **Appendices A**, **B** and **C** respectively.

◆ A list of Citizenship Questions is contained in **Appendix D** and Immigration Forms are listed in **Appendix E**.

◆ A comprehensive glossary of immigration terms and words used by the US immigration authorities is contained in **Appendix F**.

◆ For those unfamiliar with the metric system of **Weights & Measures**, conversion tables are included in **Appendix G**.

◆ A physical map of the US is contained inside the front cover and a map showing the 50 states inside the back cover.

Introduction

In recent years the US has made it increasingly difficult for foreigners to enter the country (even as tourists) and live or work there, either temporarily or permanently. Nevertheless, it still accepts more immigrants than any other country and issues some 30m temporary visas (such as tourist and student visas) and one million Green Cards (for permanent residents) annually. This is unlikely to change as the US requires a constant source of labor – whether it's farm workers or medical professionals, entrepreneurs or IT experts – to keep the wheels of commerce and industry turning.

If you wish to visit, live or work in the US, then this book was written for you. Irrespective of whether you're going to America on business or holiday, planning to study or work there for a few years, or wish to become a permanent resident or a US citizen, the *US Immigration Handbook* is guaranteed to smooth your path. It's also the only immigration book printed in color.

Unlike most US immigration books, it isn't written by a lawyer but by an experienced non-fiction writer (David Hampshire) – author of *Living and Working in America* and *Culture Wise America* – aided by a US immigration lawyer. **It's written in everyday English (rather than legalese) that a layman can understand without a law degree and the aid of a dictionary!**

That's not to say you won't need to hire a lawyer for some visa applications. Although the procedure for applying for many nonimmigrant visas is straightforward – and US immigration officials, embassies and consulates all provide free advice – you'll probably need the services of a lawyer when applying for some nonimmigrant visas; for example, for temporary workers (e.g. H-1B) and entrepreneurs (e.g. E-1/2, L-1), and some immigrant visas, including most employment-based immigrant visas. However, studying this book before hiring a lawyer will ensure that you're forearmed – and forewarned – and will know the rights questions to ask.

The *US Immigration Handbook* provides comprehensive information for those wishing to know how to immigrate to the US and which category of visa they may qualify under. However, although this book will answer many questions and minimise the frustrations, it doesn't contain all the answers (most of us don't even know the right questions to ask!). It will, however, help you make informed decisions and calculated judgements, instead of uneducated guesses and costly mistakes. **Most importantly, it will help save you time, trouble and money, and repay your investment many times over.**

Although you may find some of the information a bit daunting and difficult to understand, don't be discouraged. The majority of would-be immigrants eventually get their visas, although sometimes it can be a long wait. We trust this book will help you avoid the pitfalls of US immigration and smooth your way to a happy and rewarding future in the US.

Good luck!

David Hampshire & Sid Rizvi

July 2010

Statue of Liberty, New York

1.

WELCOME TO AMERICA

So you want to live in the USA? Unless you already have a good reason to choose a particular state or city, for example, you have family or friends in America, your first task will be to choose the region, state and city where you would like to live. Deciding where to live can be difficult – the US is a BIG country – and will depend on whether you're looking for a job, planning to start a business or are a student. There's a huge difference (and distance) between life in New York, Miami, Houston, San Francisco and Chicago!

The USA is a vast country with a wide range of landscapes, including desert, farmland, prairie, semi-desert, scrub, temperate and sub-tropical forests, mountain ranges, tundra and wetlands. It also has several climatic zones as well as numerous micro-climates (see below), making your choice of location less than straightforward. Unlike most Western countries, large areas of the US are still largely uninhabited.

CLIMATE

Because of its vast size and varied topography, ranging from sub-tropical forests to permanent glaciers, from deserts to swamps, the US's climate varies enormously. The range of weather in the contiguous states is similar to what is experienced in Europe from northern Finland to the south of Spain, with a few cyclones, hurricanes and tornadoes (twisters) thrown in for good measure. Temperatures in the Midwest prairies range from 104°F (40°C) in summer to -40°F (-40°C) in winter. A high of 134°F (57°C) has been recorded in California's Death Valley, while in Montana and Alaska the temperature has dropped to -70°F (-56.5°C) and -80°F (-62°C) respectively. Fortunately, not too many people live in these inhospitable areas. Not surprisingly, the northern states are referred to as the Frostbelt, while the warm southern states are known as the Sunbelt. The cities in the Pacific coastal region have the smallest annual temperature swings (between the highest and lowest), while the largest variations are experienced in the Midwest away from the Great Lakes.

In winter, it's cold or freezing everywhere except in the Sunbelt. However, even in Florida (which has the highest annual average temperatures) and California, the temperature occasionally drops below freezing between December and February, although southern cold spells never last long and can be followed by a heat wave. In all the northern states winters are severe, with heavy snow, ice storms and blizzards. Indeed most of the world's snowfall records are held by North America. Temperatures are often reduced considerably by the wind, known as the 'wind chill factor' where a temperature of 10°F (-12°C) combined with a wind of 25mph (40kph) results in a wind chill factor of -29°F (-34°C). The wind chill factor can cause temperatures to drop as low as -60°F (-51°C), when people (not surprisingly) are warned to stay at home.

The coldest areas include the plains, Midwest and northeast, where temperatures may remain well below freezing (32°F/0°C) for weeks on end. If you're a keen skier you will welcome some snow, but you won't perhaps be so enthusiastic when snowdrifts make roads impassable, engulf your home and cut you off from the outside world for days on end. In some areas, summer snowfalls are also fairly common. Torrential rain and violent thunderstorms are frequent in many regions, often creating floods and mudslides.

A long, hot summer is normal throughout the US, with the exception of northern New England, Oregon and Washington state. The most temperate regions in summer are the Pacific Northwest, Maine and the upper Great Lakes region of Minnesota, Wisconsin and Michigan, although it can be hot and humid even here. Everywhere else it's hot to sweltering (heat waves are common and occasionally cause many deaths), particularly in the southwest, with its many desert areas. The east coast, south and the Midwest are often extremely humid, making it feel even hotter. Smog is a problem in many cities, e.g. Los Angeles, where it's at its worst in August and September. Insects can also be a problem in many states during the summer and many homes have screens to keep them out.

Spring and fall (autumn) are usually fairly mild and are generally the most pleasant seasons, although temperatures can vary considerably from week to week. Spring and fall are warm and sunny in most regions and humidity is low, although it can be very wet in some areas (particularly in the Pacific Northwest). Hurricanes are fairly common in summer until late fall along southern parts of the east coast and around the Gulf of Mexico. Spring (April to June) is the tornado season in the Midwest, between the

Appalachians and the Rockies, when winds can reach 300mph/483kph.

Forest fires and earthquakes (along the San Andreas fault line) are a constant threat in California and there have been a number of earthquakes in recent years (although they're still nervously awaiting the 'BIG ONE', which could be America's worst natural disaster). Severe flooding was experienced in California and Texas in 1992 (after record rainfall caused the worst floods since 1938) and in 1993 the Mississippi and Missouri rivers broke their banks and flooded some 23m acres. The last decade or so has been a bad time for natural disasters in many regions, where it's said (only half-jokingly) that they have four seasons: fire, flood, drought and hurricanes. The frequency and force of severe weather, particularly hurricanes, is increasing and two major hurricanes in 2005, Dennis and Katrina, caused widespread death and destruction in Florida and the Gulf Coast. Hurricane Katrina devastated New Orleans, causing flooding in 80 per cent of the city and damage estimated at $80bn.

 Caution

Hailstones in the US can be the size of baseballs and can severely damage your car, while sleet often refers to small hailstones rather than frozen rain.

American meteorologists are constantly on the alert for severe weather patterns indicating hurricanes, tornadoes and thunderstorms. Warnings are issued if a hurricane, tornado or storm is expected, and storm alerts are broadcast on television and radio and sometimes via sirens. Some radios have a national weather service band. Travel advice is broadcast when road conditions are expected to be bad due to ice, snow, high winds or fog.

Americans usually overreact to extremes of climate with freezing air-conditioning in summer and sweltering heating in winter. Because most buildings are too hot or too cold, it's often a problem knowing what to wear and many people dress in layers that they take off or put on, depending on the indoor or outdoor temperature. Most people use humidifiers to counteract the drying effect of powerful air-conditioning.

The American fascination with statistics is highlighted in weather forecasts. These may include pollution or air quality indexes, pollen counts, ultraviolet (UV) forecasts (to help people avoid potentially dangerous exposure to the sun's rays), record high and low temperatures, and heating (winter) and cooling (summer) 'degree days' (the number of degrees by which the average temperature deviates from 65°F/18°C). The likelihood of rain may be expressed as 'a 40 per cent chance of precipitation' (or 'precip'), which is often used to refer to rain and snow.

Frequent weather forecasts are given on TV, radio and in daily newspapers, and there's even a 24-hour cable TV Weather channel. Radios can be purchased that are programmed to automatically tune to the nearest weather station. A number of newspapers and other sources provide telephone weather forecasts for some 650 US cities and online weather forecasts are

popular, which include 🖳 www.weather.com and www.nws.noaa.gov.

The average daytime temperature range (in Fahrenheit) for selected major cities is shown below.

TIME ZONES

The 48 continental US states are divided into four time zones: Eastern Standard Time (EST), Central Standard Time (CST), Mountain Standard Time (MST), and Pacific Standard Time (PST), which are often marked on maps and shown in telephone

Average Daytime Temperature (°F)				
City	**Jan–Mar**	**Apr–Jun**	**Jul–Sept**	**Oct–Dec**
Chicago	32 – 45	59 – 81	76 – 84	35 – 65
Los Angeles	67 – 69	71 – 77	83 – 84	68 – 78
Miami	76 – 89	83 – 88	88 – 90	77 – 85
New Orleans	62 – 70	78 – 90	77 – 85	64 – 80
New York	39 – 48	61 – 81	77 – 85	41 – 67
San Francisco	59 – 60	61 – 65	64 – 69	57 – 68

A quick way to make a rough conversion from Fahrenheit to Centigrade is to subtract 30 and divide by two (see also **Appendix C**).

Time Zones		
Zone	**Major Cities**	**Difference from GMT**
EST	Atlanta, Boston, Cleveland, Miami, New York, Washington	Minus 5 hours
CST	Chicago, New Orleans	Minus 6 hours
MST	Denver, Houston, Phoenix	Minus 7 hours
PST	Los Angeles, San Francisco, Seattle	Minus 8 hours

When driving from one time zone to another, the local time zone may be indicated by a sign at the roadside. When telephoning someone in a different time zone (not to mention a different country), bear in mind the time difference, as you may not be terribly popular if you wake someone at 4am.

Daylight Saving Time (DST) is observed in all states except Arizona, Hawaii and parts of Indiana (which can make life confusing for residents). Clocks are put one hour ahead in spring, usually on the last Sunday in March or the first Sunday in April, and one hour back in fall (autumn), usually on the last Sunday in October (remember: 'spring forward, fall back'), when the change officially takes effect at 2am local time.

directories. The major cities included in each zone and the difference between local time and Greenwich Mean Time (GMT) are shown in the table above.

When it's noon in New York (Eastern), it's 11am in Chicago (Central), 10am in Denver (Mountain) and 9am in Los Angeles (Pacific). Time zone boundaries don't always coincide with state boundaries and ten states have two time zones: North and South Dakota, Kansas, Kentucky, Idaho, Indiana, Nebraska, Oregon, Tennessee and Texas. Alaska has four time zones: Pacific Standard Time (Juneau and Ketchikan), Alaska Standard Time (Anchorage and Fairbanks), Bering time and Yukon time. The time in Hawaii is GMT minus ten hours.

When stating the time, Americans say 'twenty of three' for 'twenty minutes to three' or 2.40. Similarly 'twenty after three' is 'twenty minutes past three' or 3.20. Times are commonly written with a colon, e.g. 2:40 or 3:20. Americans don't usually use the 24-hour clock and on transport timetables (bus, rail, air) am and pm times are often shown as 'A' or 'P', or pm times may simply be indicated in bold print.

GEOGRAPHY

The USA covers an area of 9,360,000km² (3,615,000mi²), including Alaska and Hawaii, and is the fourth-largest country in the world, after Russia, Canada (most of which is uninhabited) and China. The USA is a federal republic comprising 50 states and the District of Columbia, the nation's capital (which isn't a state or part of a state).

Forty-eight states (the 'contiguous' states) make up the mainland USA, stretching some 4,023km (2,500mi) from east to west from the Atlantic to the Pacific. The country measures around 1,931km (1,200mi) north to south, from the Canadian border to the Gulf of Mexico. The remaining two states are Alaska and Hawaii. Alaska joined the union as the 49th (and largest) state in 1959, having been purchased from Russia a century earlier for around 5 cents per acre. Alaska is situated northwest of Canada and separated from Russia by the Bering Strait. Hawaii joined the union in 1960 as the 50th state and comprises a group of islands in the mid-Pacific Ocean some 3,700km (2,300mi) from continental USA. The US also administers over 2,000 islands, islets and atolls in the Pacific and Caribbean, including American Samoa, Guam, Puerto Rico and the US Virgin Islands.

Geographically, the contiguous states consist roughly of the highland region of Appalachia in the east, the Rocky Mountains in the west and the Great Plains in the centre. The highest point in the USA is Mount McKinley (6,193m/20,320ft) in Alaska and the lowest Death Valley in California (86m/282ft below sea level).

The USA is divided into a number of geographical regions, although regional terms are often vague and can be confusing and overlap. The only thing you can be sure of when discussing geographical regions is that most Americans disagree (as is obvious below). If you ask an American where he's from, the answer is usually a city or a town first, a state second and a region last, if at all.

The nation's capital, Washington in the District of Columbia, is usually referred to as Washington DC, to distinguish it from Washington state, which isn't usually referred to simply as Washington for the same reason. Similarly, the city of New York (known affectionately as the 'Big Apple') is often referred to as New York City to distinguish it from the state of New York, which is referred to as New York State or upstate New York.

The states and Washington DC can be roughly divided into the following four regions:

East

Connecticut, Delaware, District of Columbia, Maine, Maryland, Massachusetts, New Hampshire, New Jersey, New York, Pennsylvania, Rhode Island, Vermont and West Virginia.

South

There are various opinions about which states constitute the South and there isn't even agreement on the favoured term for this grouping of states in the southeast and south-central USA, which are known

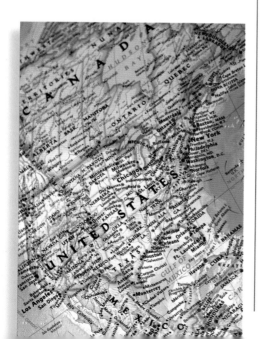

variously as the South, the Southern States, the American South, Dixie and the Deep South (although the last term is used most frequently to describe the most southerly of the Southern states – see below).

The views about how many states should constitute the region range from 11 to 16 (plus Washington DC). The 16 are as follows: Alabama, Arkansas, Delaware, Florida, Georgia, Kentucky, Louisiana, Maryland, Mississippi, Missouri, North Carolina, Oklahoma, South Carolina, Texas, Virginia and West Virginia. Delaware, however, is rarely considered to be part of the South, while Maryland, Missouri and Oklahoma only sometimes are. Those who regard the South as 11 states do so because this was the original number in the Confederacy (Virginia and West Virginia were one state at the time, called Virginia).

Midwest

The Midwest consists of twelve states in the north-central USA: Illinois, Indiana, Iowa, Kansas, Michigan, Minnesota, Missouri, Nebraska, North Dakota, Ohio, South Dakota and Wisconsin. These are sometimes subdivided into the Great Lakes States (Illinois, Indiana, Ohio, Michigan, Minnesota, New York, Pennsylvania and Wisconsin – New York and Pennsylvania, however, aren't part of the Midwest) and the Great Plains States (Iowa, Kansas, Missouri, Nebraska, North Dakota and South Dakota,

which differ from the Plains States – see below). Although there's a fair consensus that these 12 constitute the Midwest, Missouri is sometimes regarded as part of the South and Oklahoma is sometimes regarded as a Midwestern rather than a Southern state.

West

Alaska, Arizona, California, Colorado, Hawaii, Idaho, Montana, Nevada, New Mexico, Oregon, Utah, Washington and Wyoming.

Sub-regions

The following sub-regions are also widely referred to:

New England

Six states in the northeast USA: Connecticut, Maine, Massachusetts, New Hampshire, Rhode Island and Vermont. The region is so-called because it was the site of many of the first English settlements in the 'New World'.

Northeast

New England states (see above) plus Delaware, Maryland, New Jersey, New York, Washington DC and eastern Pennsylvania.

Deep South

Alabama, Georgia and Mississippi, perhaps including Louisiana, South Carolina and northern Florida.

Plains

Kansas, Nebraska, North Dakota and South Dakota, and maybe Colorado, Montana, Oklahoma and Wyoming.

Rockies or Mountain West

Colorado, Idaho, Montana, Wyoming and usually Utah.

Southwest

Arizona, New Mexico and possibly southern California, Nevada, Texas and Utah.

Northwest

Oregon, Washington and maybe northern California and Idaho.

West Coast or Far West

California, Oregon and Washington.

Bible Belt

This is an informal, vague term for the central and southern region of the US most under the influence of conservative evangelical Protestantism. There aren't any firm boundaries to the Bible Belt, but it's generally thought to cover parts or all of the following states: Alabama, Arkansas, Florida, Georgia, Kansas, Kentucky, Louisiana, Mississippi, Missouri, North Carolina, Oklahoma, South Carolina, Texas, Virginia and West Virginia.

STATES

The 50 states and Washington DC are described below. The per capita personal income rankings given come from the Department of Commerce, Bureau of Economic Analysis (2009). State populations are broken down into the majority percentages of white, black, Asian or Native American (as applicable); Hispanic Americans can be white or black. Many cities are part of larger metropolitan areas, in which case population figures are given for both.

Alabama

Alabama is in the Deep South, covering 135,775km² (52,423mi²), which makes it the 30th-largest state. Tennessee lies to the north, Georgia to the east, Mississippi to the west and Florida and the Gulf of Mexico to the south. It's home to around 4.7m people, the 23rd most populous state, around 72 per cent white and 26 per cent black. The capital city is Montgomery (pop. 204,000, 470,000 in the metropolitan area) and the largest city is Birmingham (230,000, 1.19m in the metropolitan area).

Alabama is one of the poorest states (41st on the per capita personal income list), where important industries include aerospace, banking, education, healthcare and a range of heavy industries, including mineral extraction, steel production and vehicle manufacturing. Unemployment in April 2010 was 11 per cent.

The state has a humid subtropical climate, with long, draining, very hot summers (among the country's hottest), mild winters and high rainfall throughout the year. Alabama is prone to tropical storms and hurricanes, and has more thunderstorms than anywhere else in the country.

Alabama

Government: Alabama Interactive, 3 South Jackson Street, Suite 200, Montgomery, AL 36104 (☎ 1-866-353-3468, 🖥 www.alabama.gov).

Business: 🖥 www.alabama.gov (>Online Services>Business Services), www.bcatoday.org, www.businessalabama.net and www.sba.gov (>Local Resources and select the state from the map).

Employment: 🖥 www.al.com/jobs, www.alabamajobs.com and https://joblink.alabama.gov/ada.

Tourist Office: Alabama Tourism Department, 401 Adams Avenue, Suite 126, PO Box 4927, Montgomery, AL 36103-4927 (☎ 1-800-252-2262/334-242-4169, 🖥 www.alabama.travel.org).

Alaska

Alaska is situated in the extreme northwest of the North American continent and is the country's largest state (by a large margin), covering 1,717,855km² (663,267mi²). It's one of only two US states not bordered by another state (Hawaii is the other), has more coastline than all the other US states combined, is larger than all but 18 sovereign nations and has 3.5m lakes of 20 acres or larger. Alaska is bordered by the Canadian provinces of Yukon and British Columbia to the east, and by ocean to the west, north and south.

Despite its immense size, Alaska is home to a mere 698,000 people (the 47th most populous state), 75 per cent of whom are white and 16 per cent Native American or Inuit (Alaska is one of the more racially diverse states). The capital is Juneau (population 31,000), the only state capital inaccessible by land (access is via the sea or air), and the most populous city is Anchorage (280,000, 360,000 in the metropolitan area).

Alaska is one of the country's wealthier states (9th in the per capita personal income list) with one of the lowest individual tax burdens in the US – it's one of the few states with no individual income tax or state sales tax (although some municipalities levy a local sales tax). However, it also has its problems: Alaska has long had a significant amount of alcohol abuse and experiences a brain drain of its brighter young people to other states. Over 80 per cent of the state's income comes from oil extraction, and the government and resource extraction are

Alaska's leading employers. Tourism is of growing importance to the economy, based on the state's great natural beauty and vast areas of pristine wilderness (it's one of the planet's last great wilderness areas). The difficulty of road travel means that the state has well-developed air services. Unemployment in April 2010 was 8.4 per cent.

The north of Alaska has an Arctic climate, with long, very cold winters and short, cool summers. The interior has an extreme, sub-arctic climate (warm, occasionally hot summers and cold or very cold winters), while Juneau and the southeast panhandle have a maritime, wet climate, rarely very cold in winter (it's been compared with a cooler Seattle or Vancouver).

Alaska

Government: Alaska State Capitol Building, Third Floor, PO Box 110001, Juneau, AK 99811-0001 (☎ 1-907-465-3500, 🖥 www.alaska.gov).

Business: 🖥 www.alaska.gov (>Business), www.thealaskadir.com, www.commerce.state.ak.us/occ, www.pbsjobs.com and www.sba.gov (>Local Resources and select the state from the map).

Employment: 🖥 www.alaskajobs.com, www.alaskajobfinder.com and www.jobs.state.ak.us.

Tourist Office: Alaska Travel Industry Association, 2600 Cordova Street, Suite 201, Anchorage, AK 99503 (☎ 1-800-327-9372, 🖥 www.travelalaska.com).

Arizona

Arizona sits in the southwest, covering 295,254km² (113,998mi²), which makes it the 6th-largest state. It borders New Mexico, Utah, Nevada, California, Colorado and Mexico, and is home to around 6.6m people, 77 per cent of whom are white and 6 per cent Native American, while over a quarter of the population is Hispanic. The capital and largest city is Phoenix, with a population of around 1.56m (4.2m in the metropolitan area).

Arizona is 43rd in the per capita personal income table; its economy depends on cattle, copper, cotton and tourism, and it's popular with retirees. Unemployment in April 2010 was 9.5 per cent.

Over half of the state comprises mountains and plateaus, and much of the rest is desert or semi-desert; it's home to the Grand Canyon, one of the country's most popular tourist attractions. Arizona is known for its dry, desert climate and landscape, and much of it experiences very hot summers and mild winters. As in many desert climates, there's often a large diurnal temperature range (the difference between the highest and lowest temperature in a 24-hour period).

Arizona

Government: Governor's Office, 1700 West Washington, Phoenix, AZ 85007 (☎ 1-602-542-4331, 💻 *www.az.gov*).

Business: 💻 *www.az.gov (>Business)*, www.azbop.com, www.azcommerce.com and www.sba.gov (>Local Resources and select the state from the map).

Employment: 💻 www.arizonajobs.com, http://arizona.jobing.com and www.job-hunt.org/jobs/arizona.shtml.

Tourist Office: Arizona Tourism Office, 1110 West Washington Street, Phoenix, AZ 85007-2957 (☎ 1-602-230-7733, 💻 www.arizonaguide.com).

Grand Canyon, Arizona

Arkansas

Arkansas is a state of forests, plains, mountains and cave systems in the South, covering 137,002km² (53,179mi²), making it the 29th-largest state. It shares borders with Louisiana, Texas, Oklahoma, Tennessee, Mississippi and Missouri. Arkansas is home to 2.88m people (82 per cent white and 16 per cent black) and is the 32nd most populous state. The capital and largest city is Little Rock (population 190,000, 675,000 in the metropolitan area).

Arkansas

Government: State Capitol Room 250, Little Rock, AR 72201, (☎ 1-501-682-2345, 🖥 www.state. ar.us/government.php).

Business: 🖥 www.arkansasbusiness. com, www.goarkansas.com, http:// portal.arkansas.gov (>Business), www. sba.gov (>Local Resources and select the state from the map) and www. sosweb.state.ar.us/corp_ucc.html.

Employment: 🖥 www.arkansasjobs. com, www.ark.org/arstatejobs/index. php and www.arjoblink.arkansas.gov.

Tourist Office: Arkansas Dept. of Parks and Tourism, 1 Capitol Mall, Little Rock, AR 72201-1087 (☎ 1-501-682-1191, 🖥 www.arkansas.com).

Arkansas is a lowly 45th in the table of per capita personal income and the economy is based on agriculture (notably poultry), paper products, tourism and vehicle parts manufacturing. Unemployment in April 2010 was 7.8 per cent.

The state has a humid subtropical climate, influenced by the Gulf of Mexico, with very hot, humid summers and mild, drier winters. Arkansas is prone to thunderstorms and tornadoes.

California

California lies along the Pacific coast in the Far West of the continental USA, covering 410,000km² (158,302mi²), which makes it the third-largest state. It's bordered by Oregon to the north, Nevada to the east, Arizona to the southeast, Mexico to the south and the Pacific Ocean to the west. California is the country's most populous state, home to around 37m people, 78 per cent white (over half Hispanic), 13 per cent Asian and 7 per cent black – it has the USA's highest minority population. California has the highest number of non-US citizens per capita (around 15 per cent) of any state.

The capital city is Sacramento (population 464,000, 2.13m in the metropolitan area) and the four largest cities are Los Angeles (3.9m, 13m in the metropolitan area), San Diego (1.279m, 3.001m in the metropolitan area), San Jose (948,000, 7.3m in the metropolitan area) and San Francisco (809,000, 4.2m in the metropolitan area).

California has one of the country's highest per capita personal income figures (it ranks 10th, despite areas of inner city deprivation) and the state's GDP (gross domestic product) is larger than all but nine of the world's countries.

California's largest industry by far is agriculture (the Central Valley is one of the world's most productive agricultural areas), followed by aerospace, entertainment (notably television and film), music production, computer hardware and software manufacturing, and borax mining. The state is known for its car culture and has an extensive system of expressways, freeways and highways, although they haven't stopped it from being prey to some of the worst traffic congestion in the world. Unemployment in April 2010 was 12.6 per cent (the nation's third-highest).

California

Government: State Capitol Building, Sacramento, CA 95814 (☎ 1-916-445-2841, 🖥 www.ca.gov).

Business: 🖥 www.ca.gov (click on 'Business'), www.californiafind.com, www.ptsearch.sos.ca.gov, www.sba.gov (>Local Resources and select the state from the map) and www.sos.ca.gov/business.

Employment: 🖥 www.caljobs.ca.gov, www.californiajobs.com, www.californiajobport.com and http://caljobsource.com.

Tourist Office: Sacramento Convention and Visitors' Bureau, 1608 I Street, Sacramento, CA 95814 (☎ 1-800-292-2334, 🖥 www.discovergold.org).

California has a diverse geography, including rugged coastline, forests, high mountains and deserts. It's noted for its earthquakes, caused by numerous fault lines (notably the San Andreas Fault) and is also prone to droughts, fires, floods, high winds, landslides and even

Big Sur, California

tsunamis. The state has a range of climates, from Mediterranean to desert to sub-arctic, but much of California has broadly Mediterranean conditions, with warm or hot, dry summers and cool or warm, rainy winters. Summers are much hotter inland than along the coast and winters are colder. California's Death Valley has recorded the Western Hemisphere's highest temperature (56.6°C/134°F in 1913).

Colorado

Colorado is in the Rocky Mountains in the West, covering 269,837km² (104,185mi²), making it the 8th-largest state. It's one of

is the 22nd most populous state. The capital and largest city is Denver (population 598,000, 2.5m in the metropolitan area). Colorado is one of the wealthier states (15th in the list of per capita personal income), its economy based on the federal government, financial services, food processing, high technology industries, livestock, mineral extraction and tourism (including for the state's excellent skiing industry). Unemployment in April 2010 was 8 per cent.

three states (with Utah and Wyoming) that have only lines of latitude and longitude for boundaries. Wyoming is to the north, Kansas and Nebraska are to the east, Utah is to the west and New Mexico lies to the south.

Colorado's varied topography causes local climatic variations, but much of the state is cool and generally dry, with periods of extreme weather, notably lightning and thunderstorms. Despite its dry climate, the plains are liable to flooding, while the mountains experience heavy snowfalls.

Colorado

Government: The Governor's Office, 136 State Capitol, Denver, CO 80203 (☎ 1-303-866-2471, 🖥 www.colorado.gov).

Business: 🖥 www.cobizmag.com, www.colorado.gov (>Business) and www.sba.gov (>Local Resources and select the state from the map).

Employment: 🖥 www.coworkforce.com, www.coloradojobs.com and www.coloradojobs.net.

Tourist Office: Colorado Tourism Office, 1625, Broadway, Denver, CO 80202 (☎ 1-303- 892-3840, 🖥 www.colorado.com).

Colorado is home to 5m people (92 per cent white, including many Hispanics) and

Connecticut

Connecticut is in the New England region of the northeast. It covers 14,356km² (5,543mi²), making it the 48th-largest state – only two are smaller (Delaware and Rhode Island). New York State is to the west, Long Island Sound to the south, Massachusetts to the north and Rhode Island sits to the east.

Connecticut is home to 3.5m people (87 per cent white), making it the 29th most populous state and the fourth most densely populated. The capital is

Hartford (population 125,000, 1.2m in the metropolitan area) and the largest city is Bridgeport (138,000, 305,000 in the metropolitan area). Connecticut is renowned for its wealth (it has the country's highest per capita personal income) and its economy is based on agriculture, aircraft production, financial and insurance services, pharmaceuticals, tourism and transport equipment. The state boasts Yale University, one of the world's great seats of learning. Unemployment in April 2010 was 9 per cent.

Connecticut's climate is moderated by its long coastline on the Long Island Sound (which has also bequeathed it a long maritime tradition), with warm or hot, humid summers and cold winters, although milder than much of the rest of the northeastern USA.

Delaware

Delaware is a flat state on the Atlantic coast of the northeast and covers a mere 6,452km² (2,490mi²) – only Rhode Island is smaller. To the north lies Pennsylvania, to the east, New Jersey and the Atlantic Ocean, and to the west and south, Maryland. Delaware's population of 885,000 people (74 per cent white and 21 per cent black) is only the country's 45th-largest, but it's the sixth most densely populated state. The capital is Dover (population 36,000) and the largest city Wilmington (73,000).

Connecticut

Government: Office of the Governor, State Capitol, 210 Capitol Avenue, Hartford, CT 06106 (☎ 1-860-566-4840, 🖥 www.ct.gov).

Business: 🖥 www.ct.bbb.org, www.ct-clic.com, www.ct.gov (>Doing Business), www.ctport.com and www.sba.gov (>Local Resources and select the state from the map).

Employment: 🖥 www.connecticutjobs.com, www.ctjobs.com and www.jobsinct.com.

Tourist Office: Connecticut Commission on Culture and Tourism, 1 Constitution Plaza, 2nd Floor, Hartford, CT 06103 (☎ 1-860- 256-2800, 🖥 www.ctvisit.com).

Delaware

Government: Dover Government Office, Tatnall Building, William Penn Street, 2nd Floor, Dover, DE 19901 (☎ 1-302-744-4101, 🖥 www.delaware.gov).

Business: 🖥 www.delaware.gov (see 'Business' menu), www.delaware.sbdc.org, www.ledgerdelaware.com, www.resourcelinks.net/indexde.htm and www.sba.gov (>Local Resources and select the state from the map).

Employment: 🖥 www.delawarejobs.com, www.delawarestatejobs.com and www.jobopenings.net/jobs_by_state.php?state=de.

Tourist Office: Delaware Tourism Office, 99 Kings Highway, Dover, DE 19901 (☎ 1-866-284-7483, 🖥 www.visitdelaware.com).

Delaware comes 17th in the list of per capita personal income and the state's largest employers are banking, education, farming (especially fruit), the government, insurance, pharmaceuticals and vehicle manufacturing. Unemployment in April 2010 was 9 per cent.

Delaware is in a transitional zone between continental and humid subtropical climates, and the weather is rather milder in the south than the north. Summers are quite hot and humid, winters cool or cold.

Florida

Florida is a low-lying state in the far southeast, with the Gulf of Mexico to the west, the Caribbean to the south, the Atlantic Ocean to the east and Georgia and Alabama to the north. It covers 170,304km² (65,795mi²), the 22nd-largest state, and is home to 18.5m people (80 per cent

Florida

Government: Governor's Office, PL-05 The Capitol, Tallahassee, FL 32399 (☎ 1-850- 488-4441, 🖳 www. myflorida.com).

Business: 🖳 www.fbba.com, www. floridatrend.com/small_biz.asp, www. myflorida.com (>Business), www. stateofflorida.com/doinbusinfla.html and www.sba.gov (>Local Resources and select the state from the map).

Employment: 🖳 www.floridacareers. com, www.floridajobs.com, www. floridajobs.org and www.job-hunt.org/ jobs/florida/shtml.

Tourist Office: Tallahassee Florida Visitors' Bureau, 106 E Jefferson Street, Tallahassee, FL 32301 (☎ 1-850-606-2305, 🖳 www. visittallahassee.com).

white and 16 per cent black) and the fourth most populous state. The capital is Tallahassee (population 172,000, 357,000 in the metropolitan area), the largest city Jacksonville (807,000, 1.31m in the metropolitan area), while the largest metropolitan area is Miami (5.4m, 390,000 in the city).

Florida ranks 24th in terms of per capita personal income and tourism is the largest economic sector, with the state attracting around 60m visitors a year – the amusement parks are a major attraction, especially those in the Orlando area. Agriculture is the second-largest sector, especially citrus fruits (particularly oranges) and phosphate mining the third-largest. Florida is popular with retirees and is one of the few states that doesn't impose personal income tax. Unemployment in April 2010 was 12 per cent.

Most of Florida has a humid subtropical climate (only the far south is truly tropical), with long, hot, sticky summers and short, mild or warm winters. Despite Florida's nickname of 'The Sunshine State', it's often prey to extreme weather: central Florida has the country's highest incidence of lightning strikes, thunderstorms are common throughout the state, it's menaced by hurricanes from June to November (it's the most hurricane-prone state) and cold snaps blowing in from the north occasionally devastate the state's citrus crop.

Georgia

Georgia is in the Deep South, covering 154,077km² (59,422mi²), making it the 24th-largest state. The terrain is varied, comprising mountains, plateaus and plains. To the south is Florida, to the east the Atlantic Ocean and South Carolina, to the west Alabama, while Tennessee and North Carolina are to the north. Georgia is home to 9.8m people (65 per cent white and 30 per cent black) and is the 9th most populous state. The capital and largest city is Atlanta (population 537,000, 5.37m in the metropolitan area), generally regarded as the South's commercial centre.

Georgia lies 39th in the table of per capita personal income (rural areas are much poorer than the cities) and the state's economy is based around agriculture, the communications industry, food processing, real estate and tourism. Unemployment in April 2010 was 10.4 per cent.

Much of Georgia has a humid subtropical climate. Summers are hot and humid (except in the highest areas) and rainfall is high. Winters are mild, with some cold snaps, which are rarer in the south, where the weather is similar to Florida and drier than the rest of the state.

Georgia

Government: State Capitol, 206 Washington Street, Downtown, Atlanta, GA 30334 (☎ 1-404-656-2844, 🖥 www.georgia.gov).

Business: 🖥 www.georgia.gov (>Business, Labor & Employment), www.georgia.org, www.georgiatrend. com and www.sba.gov (>Local Resources and select the state from the map).

Employment: 🖥 www.dol.state. ga.us/js/job_info_system.htm, www. georgiacareers.com and www. georgiajobs.com.

Tourist Office: Atlanta Tourist Office, Convention and Visitors Bureau, 233 Peachtree Street NE, 30303 Atlanta, GA (☎ 1-404-521-6688, 🖥 www. atlanta.net).

Hawaii

Hawaii is a volcanic archipelago in the central Pacific Ocean, 3,700km (2,300mi) from the continental USA. It consists of hundreds of islands, of which eight are considered to be the 'main' islands'; the state covers a total area of 29,311km² (10,931mi²) and is the 43rd-largest. Hawaii is the most southerly state and the second most westerly (after Alaska). Along with Alaska, it's the only state not to share a border with any other US state, and, except for Easter Island, Hawaii is further away from land than any other landmass.

Hawaii

Government: State Capitol, Room 415, Honolulu, HI 96813 (☎ 1-808-586-0222, 🖳 www.hawaii.gov).

Business: 🖳 www.business-brokers.com, www.hawaii.bizhwy.com, www.hawaii.gov/dbedt and www.sba.gov (>Local Resources and select the state from the map).

Employment: 🖳 www.hawaiicareers.com, www.hawaiijobs.net and www.jobs.careerbuilder.com/al.ic/hawaii.

Tourist Office: Hawaii Visitors and Convention Bureau, 2270 Kalakaua Avenue, Suite 801, Honolulu, HI 96815 (☎ 1-800-464-2924, 🖳 www.gohawaii.com).

Hawaii is home to 1.3m people (making it the 42nd most populous state), 27 per cent white and 15 per cent Hawaiian or Pacific Islander. Most of the rest are Asian-American, the largest percentage of any US state. The capital and largest city is Honolulu (population 380,000, 910,000 in the metropolitan area). Hawaii has a fairly high state tax burden and ranks 11th in terms of per capita personal income. The economy relies heavily on tourism (which is the state's largest employer and revenue generator) and the public sector,

which is more important to Hawaii's economy than in any other state. Other notable industries are agriculture (especially flowers, macadamia nuts and papaya), film and television production, and manganese mining.

Hawaii's climate is tropical, with temperatures and humidity moderated by the constant trade winds from the east. The weather is warm or very warm throughout the year, with no extremes of cold or heat. Tourist areas are concentrated on the leeward regions of the islands, which are sunnier and drier than the windward areas. Hurricanes are rare in the Hawaiian Islands.

Idaho

Idaho is a Rocky Mountain state in the northwest, covering 216,632km² (83,642mi²) and is the 14th-largest state. It has a rugged landscape, a wealth of natural resources and is one of the country's most unspoiled areas. To the north is the Canadian province of British Columbia, to the west Washington and Oregon, to the east Montana and Wyoming, with Nevada and Utah to the south. Idaho's population is 1.54m (95 per cent white) – it's the 39th most populous state – and the capital and largest city is Boise (population 205,000, 600,000 in the metropolitan area).

Idaho

Government: Government Office, 999 Main Street, Suite 910, Boise, ID 83702 (☎ 1-208-332-0102, 🖳 www.accessidaho.org).

Business: 🖳 www.accessidaho.org/business, www.idahobizhelp.org, www.idahosbdc.org and www.sba.gov (>Local Resources and select the state from the map).

Employment: 🖳 http://idaho.jobs.com, www.labor.idaho.gov and www.job-hunt.org/jobs/idaho/shtml.

Tourist Office: Boise Convention and Visitors Bureau, 312 South 9th Street, Suite 100, Boise, ID 83702 (☎ 1-800-635-5240, 🖳 www.boise.org).

Idaho is a lowly 48th in terms of per capita personal income. Science and technology is the biggest contributor to the state's economy (over 25 per cent of its income) while other important industries are chemicals, electronics manufacturing, food processing, mining, tourism and wood products. Unemployment in April 2010 was 9.1 per cent.

Idaho has a varied climate. The Pacific Ocean is 560km (350mi) from the state's western border and has a moderating influence, especially in winter, when it's not as cold as might be expected for a northern, elevated state. Summer days are hot, but humidity is low and evenings are cool.

Illinois

Illinois is the most diverse and populated of the midwestern states, covering 140,998km² (59,918mi²), which makes it the 25th-largest state. Lake Michigan and Indiana sit to the east, Wisconsin to the north, Missouri and Iowa to the west, and Kentucky in the south. Much of Illinois is flat plains with some rugged land in the north.

Illinois is home to around 13m people (the fifth most populous state), 65 per cent white and 15 per cent black. The capital is Springfield (population 117,000, 200,000 in the metropolitan area) and the largest city Chicago (2.85m, 9.6m in the metropolitan area). Illinois is often regarded as a microcosm of the US, the 'most average state' (according to an Associated Press analysis of 21 demographic factors).

The state ranks 14th in terms of per capita personal income and has a broad-based economy, including agriculture (especially soybeans and corn), chemical manufacturing, fabricated metals, financial services, petroleum refining and transport equipment. Unemployment in April 2010 was 11.2 per cent.

Illinois has a varied climate, generally humid continental, with hot, humid summers and cool or cold winters, which are more moderate in the south. The state is prone to thunderstorms and around 35 tornadoes hit Illinois each year – the country's deadliest recorded tornado occurred mainly in Illinois in 1925, killing 695 people, 613 in Illinois.

Illinois

Government: Office of the Governor, 207 Statehouse, Springfield, IL 62706 (☏ 1-217-782- 0244, 🖳 www.illinois. gov).

Business: 🖳 www.business.illinois. gov, www.ibjonline.com, www.illinois. bizhwy.com and www.sba.gov (>Local Resources and select the state from the map).

Employment: 🖳 www.illinoisjobs.com, www.work.illinois.gov and www.job-hunt.org/jobs/illinois.shtml.

Tourist Office: Springfield Convention and Visitors Bureau, 109 North 7th Street, Springfield, IL 62701 (☏ 1-217-789-2360, 🖳 www.visit-springfielddillinois.com).

Indiana

Indiana is a Midwestern state covering 94,321km² (36,418mi²), the 38th-largest.

Michigan and Lake Michigan sit to the north, Ohio is to the east, Illinois lies to the west and Kentucky is to the south. Indiana has few large urban areas and is probably best known for the Indianapolis 500 (a motorsports race), which is the world's largest one-day sporting event (held on Memorial Day, the last Monday in May).

Indiana's population is 6.4m, 88 per cent white and 9 per cent black – it's the 16th most populous state. The capital and largest city is Indianapolis (population 798,000, 1.7m in the metropolitan area). The state is 40th in terms of per capita personal income and much of its economy is based on the manufacturing sector, notably electrical equipment, pharmaceuticals, petroleum and coal products, steel and vehicles; farming is also important. Unemployment in April 2010 was 10 per cent.

Indiana

Government: Indiana State Government Center, 402 West Washington Street, Indianapolis, IN 46204 (☏ 1-317-233-0800, 🖳 www. in.gov).

Business: 🖳 www.in.gov/core/business. htm, www.indiana.bizhwy.com, www.ibrc. indiana.edu, www.onlineindiana.com and www.sba.gov (>Local Resources and select the state from the map).

Employment: 🖳 www.indianajobs.com, www.indianacareerconnect.com and www.jobs.careerbuilder.com/al.ic/indiana.

Tourist Office: Indianapolis Convention and Visitors' Association, 30 South Meridian Street, Suite 410, Indianapolis, IN 46204 (☏ 1-317-639-4282, 🖳 www. visitindy.com).

(population 198,000, 556,000 in the metropolitan area). Iowa is 27th in the list of per capita personal income and its economy is based around agriculture (the state is an important cattle, pig and soybean producer), insurance and industry, notably chemical products, food processing, machinery manufacturing and metals. Unemployment in April 2010 was 6.9 per cent.

Iowa has a humid continental climate, with hot, sticky summers and cold, snowy winters. Tornadoes are common in the spring and summer, with around 35 a year.

The state has a humid continental climate, with hot, humid summers and cool or cold winters, which are milder in the south. Indiana receives its fair share of thunderstorms and winter storms, and is occasionally hit by tornadoes.

Iowa

Iowa is a Midwestern state, covering 145,743km² (56,272mi²), and is the 26th-largest. Minnesota lies to the north, Missouri to the south, Nebraska to the west, and Illinois and Wisconsin to the east. Iowa is an area of gently rolling plains and has the country's highest average radon concentrations – many of the state's cities have legislation that radon-resistant construction techniques must be used in new homes.

Iowa is home to some 3m people (96 per cent white and 2 per cent black) and is the 30th most populous state. The capital and largest city is Des Moines

Iowa

Government: State Capitol, 1007 East Grand Avenue, Des Moines, IA 50319 (☎ 1-515-281-5211,🖥 www.iowa.gov).

Business: 🖥 www.iowa.gov/state/main/business.html, www.iowaabi.org, www.iowalifechanging.com/business and www.sba.gov (>Local Resources and select the state from the map).

Employment: 🖥 www.iowajobs.org, www.iowajobs.net and www.jobs.careerbuilder.com/al.ic/iowa.

Tourist Office: Iowa Tourism Office, 200 East Grand Avenue, Des Moines, IA 50309 (☎ 1-515-725-3083, 🖥 www.traveliowa.com).

Kansas

Kansas is a Midwestern state, situated in America's 'Heartland', with Midwestern and southern cultural influences. It covers 213,096km² (82,277mi²), the 15th-largest state, and one of the most agriculturally productive. The eastern third of Kansas is noted for its rolling hills and forests, while most of the rest is fairly flat. To the north is Nebraska, Missouri lies to the east, Colorado in the west and Oklahoma to the south.

Kansas has a population of 2.8m (91 per cent white and 6 per cent black) and is the 33rd most populous state. The capital city is Topeka (population 123,000), the largest city is Wichita (345,000) and the largest metropolitan area Kansas City (2.1m). Kansas is one of the slowest-growing states where the economy is based on agriculture (especially cattle, sunflowers and wheat), oil and natural gas production, and a variety of manufacturing industries, including aircraft production, chemical products, food processing and transport equipment. It's 23rd in terms of per capita personal income. Unemployment in April 2010 was 6.5 per cent.

The climate is humid continental in the east, with hot summers and cold winters; semi-arid steppe in the west, with hot or very hot summers and cool or cold winters; and humid subtropical in the far southeast, with long, hot summers, short, mild winters and more rainfall than the rest of the state. Kansas is the ninth-sunniest US state, but is also vulnerable to thunderstorms and prone to tornadoes: around 50 hit each year.

Kansas

KANSAS

Government: Office of the Governor, Capitol, 300 SW 10th Avenue, Suite 2128, Topeka, KS 66612, (☎ 1-785-296-3232, 🖥 www.kansas.gov).

Business: 🖥 www.kansas.bizhwy.com, www.kansas.gov/business and www.sba.gov (>Local Resources and select the state from the map).

Employment: 🖥 www.job-hunt.org/jobs/kansas.shtml, www.jobs.ks.gov and www.kansasjobs.net.

Tourist Office: Kansas Travel and Tourism Division, 1000 S.W. Jackson Street, Suite 100, Topeka, KS 66612 (☎ 1-785-296-2009, 🖥 www.travelks.com).

Kentucky

Kentucky is located in east central USA, sometimes regarded as a southern state, sometimes in the Midwest. It covers 104,749km² (40,444mi²), making it the 37th-largest state. West Virginia is to the east, Virginia lies to the southeast, Tennessee to the south, Missouri to the west, Illinois and Indiana in the northwest, while Ohio sits to the north and northeast.

Kentucky is one of four US states known as a Commonwealth (along with Massachusetts,

Pennsylvania and Virginia). This has no constitutional impact, but is to emphasize that they have a 'government based on the consent of the people', as opposed to one legitimized through their former royal colony status, derived from Great Britain. Kentucky is home to 4.3m people (91 per cent white and 8 per cent black) and is the 26th most populous state. The capital is Frankfort (population 30,000) and the largest city Louisville (713,000, 1.25m in the metropolitan area).

Kentucky is renowned for thoroughbred horses, horse racing, bluegrass music, tobacco, bourbon distilleries and for having the country's most productive coalfield, but, despite these assets, it's one of the poorest states, 46th in terms of per capita personal income. Agriculture is significant to the economy, notably cattle, corn, horses and tobacco, while other important industries include chemical products, coal, food processing, tourism and transport equipment. Unemployment in April 2010 was 10.6 per cent.

Kentucky's climate is humid subtropical, with four pronounced seasons and weather that tends to vary considerably from year to year. The state often experiences a wide diurnal range (the difference between the highest and lowest temperature in a 24-hour period).

Kentucky

Government: Governor's Office, 700 Capitol Ave, Suite 100, Frankfort, KY 40601 (☎ 1-502-564-2611, 🖳 www.kentucky.gov).

Business: 🖳 www.kentucky.bizhwy.com, http://kentucky.gov/business, www.sba.gov (>Local Resources and select the state from the map), www.sos.ky.gov/business and www.thinkkentucky.com.

Employment: 🖳 www.kentuckyjobs.com, www.job-hunt.org/jobs/kentucky.shtml and www.oet.ky.gov.

Tourist Office: Kentucky Department of Tourism, Capital Plaza Tower 22nd Floor, 500 Mero Street, Frankfort, KY 40601 (☎ 1-502-564-4930, 🖳 www.kentuckytourism.com).

Louisiana

Louisiana is located in the Deep South covering an area of 134,382km² (51,885mi²) – the 31st-largest state. Texas lies to the west, Arkansas to the north, Mississippi to the east, and the Gulf of Mexico to the south. The coastal part of the state is low and swampy, with some higher ground in the north, but Louisiana is one of the country's lowest-lying states.

Louisiana is home to 4.5m people (65 per cent white and 33 per cent black), the 25th most populous state, with a unique multicultural and multilingual heritage; many people speak Cajun French and Louisiana Creole French. French is an official language and the state has a unique legal system based on the Napoleonic code. The capital is Baton Rouge (population 227,000, 774,000 in the metropolitan area) and the largest city New Orleans (336,000, 1.1m in the metropolitan area), which is a major tourist destination for its festivals and historic architecture.

Louisiana is 32nd in terms of per capita personal income. Its economy is dominated by the oil and gas industry, and its subsidiary industries of oil refining and transport. Agriculture (notably cotton) and fishing are important (Louisiana is the world's largest producer of crayfish), as is tourism. Unemployment in April 2010 was 6.7 per cent.

The state's climate is humid subtropical (arguably the country's most archetypal), with long, hot, humid summers and short, mild winters. It's wet throughout the year, with thunderstorms common in summer. The state is hit by around 25 tornadoes a year and tropical cyclones frequently threaten Louisiana. It's also vulnerable to hurricanes, sometimes with devastating consequences, such as the

damage and loss of life caused by hurricane Katrina in August 2005, when New Orleans was virtually inaccessible until October.

Louisiana

Government: Governor's Office, PO Box 94004, Baton Rouge, LA 70804 (☎ 1-225-342-7015, 💻 www.louisiana. gov).

Business: 💻 www.louisiana. gov/business, www. louisianaeconomicdevelopment.com, www.resourcelinks.net/indexla.htm and www.sba.gov (>Local Resources and select the state from the map).

Employment: 💻 www.jobs. careerbuilder.com/al.ic/louisiana, www. job-hunt.org/jobs/louisiana.shtml and www.louisianajobs.com.

Tourist Office: Baton Rouge Area Convention and Visitors' Bureau, 359 3rd Street, Baton Rouge, LA 70801 (☎ 1-800-527-6843, 💻 www. visitbatonrouge.com).

New Orleans, Louisiana

Maine

Maine covers the most northerly part of New England in the far northeast of the country. It's the largest New England state, around the size of the other five put together. Maine covers 86,542km² (33,414mi²), the 39th-largest state, and is renowned for its seafood (especially lobster and clams) and landscape: a rocky, jagged coastline, low mountains and a thickly-forested interior. To the north and northeast is the Canadian province of New Brunswick, to the northwest is the Canadian province of Quebec, while the Atlantic Ocean is to the south and southeast. Maine is the only US state to border only one US state – New Hampshire – which lies to the west.

Maine's population is 1.32m (98 per cent white), the 40th most populous state. The capital is Augusta (population 19,000) and the largest city Portland (63,000, 513,000 in the metropolitan area). Maine ranks 28th on the list of per capita personal income, where the economy is based around agriculture

Maine

Government: Office of the Governor, #1 State House Station, Augusta, ME 04333 (☎ 1-207-287-3531, 🖳 www.maine.gov).

Business: 🖳 www.maine.gov/portal/business, www.mainebusinesslisting.com and www.mainesbdc.org and www.sba.gov (>Local Resources and select the state from the map).

Employment: 🖳 http://jobsinmaine.com, www.jobsinme.com, www.maine-job.com and http://mainejobs.mainetoday.com.

Tourist Office: Maine Office of Tourism, 111 Sewall Street, Augusta, ME 04330 (☎ 1-207-287-5711, 🖳 www.visitmaine.com).

(including apples, cattle, dairy products and maple sugar), industry (mainly electronics, paper, lumber and wood products, and shipbuilding) and, increasingly, tourism – it's a popular fishing, hunting and outdoor sports

destination. Unemployment in April 2010 was 8.1 per cent.

Maine's climate is humid continental, with warm rather than hot summers and cold, snowy winters (especially in the north). The state has fewer thunderstorms than any other state east of the Rockies and tornadoes are rare, with an average of fewer than two a year.

Maryland

Maryland is situated roughly halfway down the Atlantic coast of the USA, covering 32,133km² (12,407mi²) – the 42nd-largest state. It has northern and southern characteristics (reflecting its geographical position), the urban areas being more northern, while rural areas have the feel of the south. Maryland has varied topography, giving rise to its nickname of 'America in Miniature', which includes marshland, sand dunes, gentle hills and mountains. To the north sits Pennsylvania, to the west is West Virginia, to the east Delaware and the Atlantic Ocean, and to the south lie West Virginia and Virginia.

Maryland's population is 5.69m (65 per cent white and 30 per cent black), making it the 19th most populous state. The capital is Annapolis (population 37,000) and the largest city Baltimore (637,000, 2.7m in the metropolitan area). Maryland is one of the wealthiest states (4th) in terms of per capita personal income. Transportation is important to the economy and there's a large food production industry centred around the

Port of Baltimore; commercial fishing and computer and electronics' manufacturing are significant. Unemployment in April 2010 was 7.5 per cent.

Maryland has a wide range of microclimates for its size (around the same as Belgium), depending on elevation and proximity to water. The east has a humid subtropical climate, with hot, humid summers and short, mild or cool summers, while the west of the state has a humid continental climate, with milder summers and cold, snowy winters. Precipitation is high throughout the state. Maryland's Atlantic position makes it vulnerable to tropical cyclones and it experiences around 35 thunderstorms and six tornadoes a year.

Maryland

Government: The Governor's Office, 100 State Circle, Annapolis, MD 21401 (☎ 1-410-974-3901, 🖳 www. maryland.gov).

Business: 🖳 www. annapolisbusinessassoc.com, www. ci.annapolis.md.us (>Doing Business), www.maryland.gov (>Working) and www.sba.gov (>Local Resources and select the state from the map).

Employment: 🖳 www.maryland.gov (>Working), www.marylandjobs.com and www.job-hunt.org/jobs/maryland/shtml.

Tourist Office: Maryland Office of Tourism Development, 401 East Pratt Street, 14th Floor, Baltimore, MD 21202 (☎ 1-866-639-3526, 🖳 www. mdisfun.org).

Massachusetts

Massachusetts is a Commonwealth (for a definition, see Kentucky) in New England in the northeast. To the north lie New Hampshire and Vermont, to the west New York State, to the south Connecticut and Rhode Island, and to the east the Atlantic Ocean. Massachusetts is a small state (the 44th-largest), covering 27,336km² (10,555mi²), but is the country's third most densely populated (the eastern half of the state is mainly urban and suburban). The population is 6.59m (88 per cent white and 8 per cent black), the 15th-largest, over two-thirds of whom live in the Boston Metropolitan Area (Boston is the capital and largest city, home to 620,000).

Massachusetts has played an important role in US history and was the site of some of the earliest English settlements. The Boston area is known as the 'Cradle of Liberty' due to its role in fermenting the Revolution and American Independence. Massachusetts was the first state to abolish slavery and has provided a number of

Massachusetts

Government: Office of the Governor, Massachusetts State House, Room 280, Boston, MA 02133 (☎ 1-617-725-4005, 🖳 www.mass.gov).

Business: 🖳 www.bostonbusiness.com, www.bostoncatalog.com, www.mass.gov (>For Businesses), www.msbdc.org and www.sba.gov (>Local Resources and select the state from the map).

Employment: 🖳 www.boston.com/jobs, www.boston-online.com/employment, www.massachusettsjobs.com and www.massachusetts-job.com.

Tourist Office: Massachusetts Office of Travel and Tourism, 10 Park Plaza, Suite 4510, Boston, MA 02116 (☎ 1-617-973-8500, 🖳 www.massvacation.com).

prominent politicians, notably members of the Kennedy family. Massachusetts's economy relies on finance, healthcare, high technology, higher education (it's the site of Harvard University and the Massachusetts Institute of Technology or MIT) and tourism. It ranks 3rd in terms of per capita personal income, headed only by nearby Connecticut and New Jersey.

Massachusetts has a humid continental climate, with warm summers and cold, snowy winters. It's prone to winter storms and experiences around 30 thunderstorms a year, mostly in the summer; it's also vulnerable to tornadoes and hurricanes.

Michigan

Michigan is found in central northeastern USA, bounded by four of the five Great Lakes (Erie, Huron, Michigan and Superior), which gives it the world's longest freshwater coastline. It's the only state to consist entirely of two peninsulas – the Lower and Upper – which are connected by the 5mi-long Mackinac Bridge. Both contain plenty of marshes, lakes and offshore islands. Michigan covers 253,793km² (97,990mi²) and is the 11th-largest state. To the north are the Great Lakes, to the south Ohio and Indiana, to the west is Wisconsin, and to the east the Canadian province of Ontario.

Michigan's population is 9.9m (the country's 8th-largest), 80 per cent white and 14 per cent black. The capital is Lansing (population 114,000, 455,000 in the metropolitan area) and the largest city Detroit (913,000, 4.4m in the metropolitan area). Michigan ranks 37th on the list of per capita personal income, with a diverse economy which includes car manufacturing, engineering, fruit growing, information technology, life sciences and tourism (visitors are drawn to the remote hinterland, half of the state being covered by forest, and thousands of miles of beaches). Unemployment in April 2010 was 14 per cent (the highest in the country).

The climate is humid continental, although part of the Lower Peninsula has a warmer climate than the rest of the state, which experiences long, cold winters and warm, humid, quite short summers. Much of Michigan experiences heavy snowfall and there are around 15 tornadoes and 30 thunderstorms each year.

Michigan

Government: Governor's Office, PO Box 30113, Lansing, MI 48909 (☎ 1-517-373-3400, 🖥 www.michigan.gov).

Business: 🖥 www.michiganbusiness.us, www.michigan.gov/business, http://ref.michigan.org/medc/services/startups and www.sba.gov (>Local Resources and select the state from the map).

Employment: 🖥 www.job-hunt.org/jobs/michigan.shtml, www.flipdog.com/jobs/lansing, www.michigan.gov/jobs and www.michiganjobs.com.

Tourist Office: Greater Lansing Michigan Convention and Visitors' Bureau, 500 E. Michigan Avenue, Suite 180, Lansing, MI 48912 (☎ 1-888-252-6746, 🖥 www.lansing.org).

Minnesota

Minnesota is in the northern Midwest, covering 225,365km² (87,014mi²), the 12th-largest state. The Canadian provinces of Ontario and Manitoba are to the north, Iowa to the south, Michigan and Wisconsin to the east, and North and South Dakota to the west. Minnesota is known as the 'Land of 10,000 Lakes' and is renowned for its outdoor recreation opportunities, which are eagerly taken up by the locals: the state has the country's highest percentage of residents who exercise regularly.

Minnesota

Government: Office of the Governor, 130 State Capitol, 75 Rev. Dr. Martin Luther King Jr. Boulevard, Saint Paul, MN 55155 (☏ 1-651-296-3391, 🖥 www.governor.state.mn.us).

Business: 🖥 www. minnesotabusiness.com, www. minnesota.bizhwy.com, www. positivelyminnesota.com, www.sba.gov (>Local Resources and select the state from the map) and www.state.mn.us (>Business & Jobs).

Employment: 🖥 http://minnesotajobs. com, http://minnesotajoblist.com and www.job-hunt.org/jobs/minnesota. shtml.

Tourist Office: Explore Minnesota Tourism, 121 7th Place E, Metro Square, Suite 100, Saint Paul, MN 55101 (☏ 1-651-296-5029, 🖥 www. exploreminnesota.com).

The population is 5.3m (the 21st-largest), 88 per cent white and 4 per cent black. Many of Minnesota's inhabitants are of Nordic or German descent; its population is one of the USA's healthiest and best educated, and the state is regarded as culturally and politically liberal. The capital is Saint Paul (population 295,000, 3.5m in the metropolitan area) and the largest city is Minneapolis (390,000, 3.5m in the metropolitan area). Some 60 per cent of Minnesotans live in the Minneapolis-Saint Paul Metropolitan Area, which is considered

to have one of the country's best qualities of life (despite its frigid winters).

Minnesota's economy used to be dominated by raw materials production, but it's become much more diverse in recent times. Agriculture is important, especially corn, peas and sugar beet, as are biomedical products, food processing, forestry, heavy industry and technology. The state comes an impressive 13th in terms of per capita personal income. Unemployment in April 2010 was 7.2 per cent.

Minnesota's climate is 'extreme' continental, with hot summers and long, cold or very cold winters. The record high and low span is a massive 174°F/96°C (from -60 to 114°F/-51 to 45°C). Its weather encompasses torrential rain, snow, blizzards, thunderstorms, hail, derechos (wind storms), tornadoes and high-velocity straight-line winds.

Mississippi

Mississippi is a heavily forested state in the Deep South, on the Gulf of Mexico. To the north is Tennessee, to the east Alabama, to

the west Louisiana and Arkansas, and to the south Louisiana and the Gulf of Mexico. It covers 125,443km² (48,434mi²) and is the 32nd-largest state.

Mississippi's population is 2.95m (62 per cent white and 37 per cent black) and is the 31st most populous state. The capital and largest city is Jackson (population 174,000). Mississippi has the country's lowest per capita personal income but also one of the lowest costs of living, and consistently ranks as one of the most generous in per capita charitable contributions (reinforcing the view that people who have the least tend to be the most eager to help others). Obesity is a particular problem in Mississippi, with more than a third of the state's residents classified as obese. Agriculture (notably cotton) used to be the largest contributor to the state's economy, but now it's manufacturing. Cotton, rice and soybeans continue to be important, as are chemicals and plastics, fishing and seafood processing, petroleum and natural gas. Unemployment in April 2010 was 11.5 per cent.

Mississippi

Government: Governor's Office, PO Box 139, Jackson, MS 39205 (☎ 1-601- 359-3150, 🖳 www. mississippi.gov).

Business: 🖳 http://mississippi.bizhwy. com, www.mississippi.gov (>Business in Mississippi), www.mississippi.org, http://msbusiness.com and www.sba. gov (>Local Resources and select the state from the map).

Employment: 🖳 www.mdes.ms.gov, www.job-hunt.org/jobs/mississippi. shtml and http://jobs.careerbuilder. com/al.ic/mississippi.

Tourist Office: Division of Tourism Development, PO Box 849, Jackson, MS 39205 (☎ 1-601-359-3297, 🖳 www.visitmississippi.org).

Mississippi has a hot, humid, subtropical climate, with long, hot summers and short, mild winters. Late summer and fall often see hurricanes arrive from the Gulf of Mexico, sometimes with devastating consequences. The state also has around 25 tornadoes a year.

Missouri

Missouri is a Midwestern state, where the blend of urban and rural culture is often regarded as mirroring the country's demographic, economic and political makeup, meaning it has long been seen as a political bellwether state. As befits its location, it has Midwestern and Southern cultural influences: Iowa is to the north, Illinois, Kentucky and Tennessee to the east, Arkansas to the south, and Oklahoma, Kansas and Nebraska to the west. Missouri's geography is diverse – a mixture of plains and mountains – and it covers 180,533km² (69,704mi²), the 21st-largest state.

Missouri

Government: Office of the Governor, PO Box 720, Jefferson City, MO 65102 (☎ 1-573-751-3222, 🖳 www.mo.gov).

Business: 🖳 www.business.mo.gov, www.missouri.bizhwy.com, www.missouribusiness.net, www.mo.gov/business and www.sba.gov (>Local Resources and select the state from the map).

Employment: 🖳 www.job-hunt.org/jobs/missouri/shtml, www.jobs.net/missouri.htm and www.missourijobs.com.

Tourist Office: Missouri Division of Tourism, PO Box 1055, Jefferson City, MO 65102 (☎ 1-573-751-4133, 🖳 www.visit.mo.com).

Missouri is home to some 6m people (86 per cent white and 12 per cent black), the 18th most populous state. The capital is Jefferson City (population 41,000) and the largest city Kansas City (475,000, 2m in the metropolitan area, which is split between Missouri and Kansas). Missouri ranks 30th in terms of per capita personal income and key industries include aerospace, agriculture (especially beef, corn, dairy products and hay), beer production, chemical manufacturing, food processing, mining (notably lead and limestone), printing and publishing, and transport equipment. Unemployment in April 2010 was 9.4 per cent.

The climate is humid continental, with hot, humid summers and cold winters. It's warmer in the south of the state, bordering on humid subtropical. Missouri's inland location, away from a moderating maritime influence, makes it prey to extreme temperatures.

Montana

Montana is a Great Plains state in the Mountain West, sometimes called 'Big Sky Country'. Around 60 per cent of it is prairie, with mountains in the centre and west (part of the northern Rockies). To the north are the Canadian provinces of British Columbia, Alberta and Saskatchewan, to the east are North and South Dakota, to the south is Wyoming, and to the west sits Idaho. Montana covers 381,156km² (147,165mi²), the 4th-largest state, but its population is only around 1m (93 per cent white and 7 per cent Native American), the 44th most populous state with the third-lowest population density. The capital is Helena (population 29,000, 73,000 in the metropolitan area) and the largest city Billings (104,000, 180,000 in the metropolitan area).

Montana ranks 38th in terms of per capita personal income and the economy is based mainly on agriculture (it's one of the leading ranching states), lumber and mineral extraction and mining (notably coal), while tourism is also important – visitors are attracted to Glacier and Yellowstone National Parks and the site of the Battle of Little Bighorn. Unemployment in April 2010 was 7.1 per cent.

Montana has a varied climate, generally continental, but with a Pacific influence in the west, which creates milder winters and cooler summers. Montana has recorded the continental USA's lowest temperature: -70°F, in 1954.

Montana

Government: Office of the Governor, Montana State Capitol Bldg, PO Box 200801, Helena, MT 59620 (☎ 1-406-444-3111, 🖥 www.governor.mt.gov).

Business: 🖥 http://mt.gov/business.asp, www.mtbusiness.com, www.businessresources.mt.gov, www.sba.gov (>Local Resources and select the state from the map) and www.sbdc.mt.gov.

Employment: 🖥 www.job-hunt.org/jobs/montana.shtml, http://mt.gov/statejobs/statejobs.asp and www.montanajobs.com.

Tourist Office: Montana Office of Tourism, PO Box 200533, Helena, MT 59620 (☎ 1-406-841-2870, 🖥 www.visitmt.com).

Nebraska

Nebraska is a Great Plains state, covering 200,520km² (77,421mi²), the 16th-largest in the US. To the north lies South Dakota, to the east are Iowa and Missouri, to the south is Kansas, to the southwest Colorado, and to the west is Wyoming. Nebraska is home to 1.8m people (93 per cent white and 5 per cent black) and is the 38th most populous state. The capital is Lincoln (population 252,000, 292,000 in the metropolitan area) and the largest city is Omaha (439,000, 838,000 in the metropolitan area).

Nebraska

Government: Office of the Governor, PO Box 94848, Lincoln, NE 68509 (☎ 1-402-471-2244, 🖥 www.nebraska.gov).

Business: 🖥 http://nebraska.bizhwy.com, www.nebraska.gov (>for Businesses), www.neded.org, http://nbdc.unomaha.edu and www.sba.gov (>Local Resources and select the state from the map).

Employment: 🖥 www.jobs.net/nebraska.htm, www.nebraskajobs.com and www.employmentspot.com/state/ne/htm.

Tourist Office: Nebraska Division of Travel and Tourism, 301 Centennial Mall South, PO Box 98907, Lincoln, NE 68509 (☎ 1-402-471-3796, 🖥 www.visitnebraska.gov).

Nebraska ranks 22nd in terms of per capita personal income, and its economy relies on agriculture (especially beef, corn, pork and soybeans), freight transport, information technology, insurance and telecommunications. Unemployment in April 2010 was just 5 per cent (the third-lowest).

Eastern Nebraska has a continental climate, with hot summers and cold winters, while the west has a semi-arid steppe climate. The state experiences wide seasonal temperature and precipitation variations (it was one of the 19 dust bowl states, which suffered a severe drought in the 1930s), and is prone to thunderstorms and tornadoes.

Nevada

Nevada is situated in the southwest of the USA and much of the north of the state is in the Great Basin Desert, while the south is in the Mojave Desert; there are also some high mountains. It covers an area of 286,367km² (110,567mi²) and is the 7th-largest state. Oregon and Idaho are to the north, California to the west, Utah to the east and Arizona in the southeast.

Nevada is home to 2.64m people (84 per cent white and 9 per cent black) and is the 35th most populous state. The capital is Carson City (population 55,000) and the largest city Las Vegas (558,000, 1.8m in the metropolitan area). Nevada ranks 20th in terms of per capita personal income and is one of the few states with no personal or corporate income taxes (it attracts a lot of retirees). The state has the second-highest (after California) number of non-US citizens per capita and the largest increase in non-citizen population between 2000 and 2008. Around 12 per cent of its residents weren't US citizens in 2008 (compared with 15 per cent in California).

The economy relies on agriculture (alfalfa, cattle, hay, onions and potatoes), electronic equipment, food processing, gold mining, machinery, printing and tourism (the state's largest earner) – resorts such as Lake Tahoe, Las Vegas, Laughlin and Reno draw millions of visitors annually, as does the presence of gaming and the fact that prostitution is legal in parts of the state. Unemployment in April 2010 was 13.7 per cent (the second-highest).

Most of Nevada has a desert climate (it's the driest state, despite having a ski resort – Lake Tahoe – and some large lakes), the north

experiencing hot summers and freezing winters; the south has very hot summers and less cold winters, while there are slightly greener, wetter areas in the east.

Nevada

Government: Office of Governor, State Capitol, 101 N. Carson Street, Carson City, NV 89701 (☎ 1-775-684-5670, 🖥 www.nv.gov).

Business: 🖥 www.business.nv.gov, www.nevadabusiness.com, http://nv.gov/doingbusiness_nevada.htm, www.nsbdc.org and www.sba.gov (>Local Resources and select the state from the map).

Employment: 🖥 www.detr.state.nv.us, www.job-hunt.org/jobs/nevada/shtml and www.nevadajobs.com.

Tourist Office: Nevada Commission on Tourism, 401 N. Carson Street, Carson City, NV 89701 (☎ 1-775-687-6779, 🖥 www.travelnevada.com).

New Hampshire

New Hampshire is in the New England region of the northeast and is the country's second most forested state (after its neighbour Maine) in terms of the percentage of land covered by trees; the north is mountainous. The Canadian province of Quebec is to the north and northwest, Maine and the Atlantic Ocean to the east, Vermont to the west, and Massachusetts in the south. New Hampshire covers a mere 24,217km² (9,350mi²) and is the 46th-largest state.

New Hampshire

Government: Office of the Governor, State House, 25 Capitol Street, Concord, NH 03301 (☎ 1-603-272-2121, 🖥 www.nh.gov).

Business: 🖥 www.concord.bbb.org, www.nh.gov/business, www.nhbia.org, www.nheconomy.com, www.nhbr.com and www.sba.gov (>Local Resources and select the state from the map).

Employment: 🖥 www.ci.concord.nh.us, www.cnhesinc.com and www.nhjobs.com.

Tourist Office: Division of Travel and Tourism, PO Box 1856, 172 Pembroke Road, Concord, NH 03302 (☎ 1-603-271-2665, 🖥 www.visitnh.gov).

The state is well known for the New Hampshire primary, which is the first primary in the four-yearly US presidential election cycle. It's home to 1.33m people (97 per cent white) and is the 41st most populous state. The capital is Concord (population 43,000) and the largest city is Manchester (109,000). New Hampshire doesn't levy personal state income tax and ranks 8th in terms of per capita personal income. The economy consists of agriculture (especially apples, cattle, dairy products and eggs), electrical equipment, machinery, plastic and rubber products, and tourism. Unemployment in April 2010 was 6.7 per cent.

New Hampshire's climate is humid continental, with warm, humid summers and cold, wet winters. The climate in the southeast is moderated by the Atlantic and is milder and wetter than the rest of the state. Winters can be severe in most of New Hampshire (especially the north), very cold and snowy (but great for winter sports fans).

New Jersey

New Jersey is on the Atlantic coast of the northeast. It covers 22,608km² (8,729mi²) and is the 47th-largest state. To the north is New York State, to the east the Atlantic Ocean, to the southwest Delaware, and to the west lies Pennsylvania. It's home to 8.71m people (78 per cent white and 15 per cent black) and is the 11th most populous and the most densely populated of the US states – it's the only one where all the counties are deemed to be 'urban' (many residents commute into New York City). The capital is Trenton (population 83,000) and the largest city Newark (282,000, 2.2m in the metropolitan area).

New Jersey is one of the most ethnically and religiously diverse states, with (by percentage) the second-highest Jewish population (after New York), the second-largest Muslim population (after Michigan), the third-highest Asian-American population and the third-highest Italian-American population.

New Jersey

Government: Office of the Governor, 125 West State Street, Trenton, NJ 08608 (☎ 1-609-292-6000, 🖥 www.state.nj.us).

Business: 🖥, www.nj.com/business, www.njbia.org, www.njbiz.com, www.sba.gov (>Local Resources and select the state from the map) and www.state.nj.us/njbusiness.

Employment: 🖥 www.newjerseyjobs.com, www.job-hunt.org/jobs/newjersey/shtml, www.nj.com/jobs and www.jobs.net/newjersey.htm.

Tourist Office: Division of Travel and Tourism, PO Box 460, Trenton, NJ 08625 (☎ 1-609-292-2470, 🖥 wwww.visitnj.org.)

Although Camden and Newark are two of the USA's poorest cities, New Jersey as a whole has the country's second-highest

Princeton University, New Jersey

balloons in Albuquerque, New Mexico

per capita personal income. The state's strategic location means that it's at a crossroads for commerce, which is aided by its extensive transportation system. New Jersey's lake and seaside resorts (such as Atlantic City) make it the fifth-largest earner from tourism of all US states. Other important sectors of the economy are agriculture (fruit, horses and vegetables), chemical and pharmaceutical products, electrical equipment, financial services, food processing, oil refining, printing and publishing, and seafood. Unemployment in April 2010 was 9.8 per cent.

New Jersey has a humid continental climate, somewhat tempered by its proximity to the Atlantic coastline. Summers are hot and humid, winters cold, sometimes with heavy snowfalls.

New Mexico

New Mexico is located in the southwest, covering 315,194km² (121,665mi²) and is the 5th-largest state. Despite its image as little but arid desert, a fair portion of New Mexico is covered by heavily forested mountains, especially in the north. To the north sits Colorado, to the east is Oklahoma, to the south lie Texas and Mexico, and to the west is Arizona.

New Mexico is home to just over 2m people (84 per cent white and 9 per cent Native American) – the 36th most populous state and the 6th most sparsely inhabited. It has one of the highest percentages of Hispanic Americans (over 44 per cent of the population) and the second-highest of Native Americans (after Alaska), mostly Navajo and Pueblo people. New Mexico's capital is Santa Fe (population 73,000), while the largest city is Albuquerque (522,000, 846,000 in the metropolitan area).

The state ranks a lowly 42nd in terms of per capita personal income and the economy is based on coal and petroleum products, defence-related industries, electrical equipment, farming (especially cattle, dairy produce and sheep), high technology, lumber mills, mineral extraction (especially copper, manganese ore, potash, tin and uranium ore), and tourism. Unemployment in April 2010 was 8.7 per cent.

The climate is arid and sunny, with very hot summers (cooler at altitude) and cold or cool winters. As in many desert-like climates, New Mexico experiences wide diurnal ranges (i.e. the difference between the highest and lowest temperatures in a 24-hour period) and offers excellent skiing in winter.

New York is home to 19.5m people, the third most populous state; its population is one of the country's most cosmopolitan, including a higher proportion of Italian-Americans than any other state and significant African-American, Irish-American and German-American communities. New York has a high proportion of Catholic residents at over 40 per cent. The capital is Albany (population 95,000, 1.1m in the metropolitan area) and the largest city New York City (8.3m, 18.8m in the metropolitan area), which dominates the state due to its huge global importance as a cultural, financial, manufacturing and transportation centre.

New Mexico

Government: Office of the Governor, 490 Old Santa Fe Trail, Room 400, Santa Fe, NM 87501 (☎ 1-505-476-2200, 💻 www.newmexico.gov).

Business: 💻 www.edd.state.nm.us, http://new-mexico.bizhwy.com, www.newmexico.gov/business.php, www.nmsbdc.org/santafe and www.sba.gov (>Local Resources and select the state from the map).

Employment: 💻 www.job-hunt.org/jobs/newmexico.shtml, www.excelstaff.com and www.newmexicojobs.net.

Tourist Office: New Mexico Tourism Department, 491 Old Santa Fe Trail, Santa Fe, NM 87501 (☎ 1-505-827-7400, 💻 www.newmexico.org).

New York

New York State is in the northeast of the country, and, as well as being home to one of the world's great cities – New York City – also has plenty of mountains and remote areas. In fact, most of the state consists of farms, forests, lakes, mountains and rivers. It covers 141,205km² (54,529mi²), the 27th-largest state, and is bordered by Vermont, Massachusetts, Connecticut, New Jersey, Pennsylvania and the Canadian provinces of Quebec and Ontario.

New York

Government: Office of the Governor, State Capitol, Albany, NY 12224 (☎ 1-518-474-8390, 💻 www.state.ny.us).

Business: 💻 www.bcnys.org, www.crainsnewyork.com, www.empire.state.ny.us, www.nybdc.com, www.nyssbdc.org, www.sba.gov (>Local Resources and select the state from the map) and www.state.ny.us (>Business).

Employment: 💻 www.cs.state.ny.us/jobs.htm, www.labor.state.ny.us, www.newyorkjobs.com and www.statejobsny.com.

Tourist Office: New York State Division of Tourism, 1 Commerce Plaza, Albany, NY 12245 (☎ 1-518-474-4116, 💻 www.iloveny.com).

New York's gross state product ranks third (behind California and Texas) and it's 5th in terms of per capita personal income. The economy is varied and vibrant, based on banking, communications, finance, diverse manufacturing, publishing, scientific instruments and tourism. The state is also a major agricultural producer (in the USA's top five), notably of apples, cherries, dairy produce, grapes, maple syrup, potatoes and wine. Unemployment in April 2010 was 8.4 per cent.

New York's climate is broadly humid continental, with some diversity due to the influence of the Great Lakes, Atlantic ocean, and mountains and rivers. Summers in the mountains are cool, but hot or very hot and it's sometimes uncomfortably humid in coastal areas. Winters can be long and cold, with plenty of snow, although the New York Metropolitan Area has milder winters than 'upstate' New York.

North Carolina

North Carolina is on the USA's mid-southern Atlantic seaboard and has a wide range of elevation, from sea level to over 2,000m (6,500ft) in the mountains. It covers an area of 139,059km² (53,865mi²) and is the 28th-largest state. South Carolina is situated to the south, Georgia to the southwest, Tennessee in the west, Virginia to the north and the Atlantic Ocean in the east.

North Carolina is home to 9.38m people (75 per cent white and 22 per cent black) and is the tenth most populous state. The capital is Raleigh (population 393,000) and the largest city is Charlotte (688,000, 2.3m in the metropolitan area).

The state ranks 35th in terms of per capita personal income and the economy relies on agriculture and farming (cattle, poultry, soybeans, sweet potatoes and tobacco), biotechnology, chemical production, electrical equipment, financial services, paper production and textiles. Unemployment in April 2010 was 10.8 per cent.

The state's coastal climate is similar to Georgia and South Carolina (humid subtropical), while in the mountains it resembles New England or the upper Midwest (humid continental). North Carolina experiences around 20 tornadoes a year, a tropical storm every three or four years and a hurricane once a decade.

North Carolina

Government: Office of the Governor, 20301 Mail Service Center, Raleigh, NC 27699 (☎ 1-919-733-4240, 🖥 www.ncgov.com).

Business: 🖥 www.blnc.gov, www.businessnc.com, www.nccommerce.com/en/businessservices, www.ncgov.com (>to do business), http://north-carolina.bizhwy.com and www.sba.gov (>Local Resources and select the state from the map).

Employment: 🖥 www.job-hunt.org/jobs/northcarolina.shtml, www.northcarolinajobs.net and www.north_carolina.jobopenings.net.

Tourist Office: North Carolina Tourism Services, 301 N. Wilmington Street, Raleigh, NC 27601 (☎ 1-919-733-4151, 🖥 www.visitnc.com).

North Dakota

North Dakota straddles the Midwest and the West. The western half of the state consists of hilly Great Plains, there's prairie

North Dakota has a continental climate, with extremes of temperature during the cold winters and hot summers. The state can be very windy and is prey to hail, snow, thunderstorms and tornadoes.

North Dakota

Government: The Governor's Office, 600 East Boulevard Avenue, Bismarck, ND 58585 (☎ 1-701-328-2200, 💻 www.nd.gov).

Business: 💻 www.business. nd.gov, www.nd.gov (>Business), www.ndbusinesswatch.com, www. ndsbdc.org and www.sba.gov (>Local Resources and select the state from the map).

Employment: 💻 http://jobsnd.com, www.northdakotajobs.com and www. job-hunt.org/jobs/northdakota.shtml.

Tourist Office: North Dakota Tourism Division, Century Center, 1600 East Century Avenue, Suite 2, PO Box 2057, Bismarck, ND 58502 (☎ 1-701-328-2525, 💻 www.ndtourism.com).

---

and plateau in the centre, while in the east lies the flat Red River Valley. North Dakota covers 183,272km² (70,762mi²) and is the 19th-largest state. South Dakota is to the south, the Canadian provinces of Saskatchewan and Manitoba to the north, Minnesota to the east and Montana in the west.

North Dakota's population is 647,000 (93 per cent white and 5 per cent Native American), the third-smallest state population. The capital is Bismarck (population 60,000, 105,000 in the metropolitan area) and the largest city is Fargo (99,000, 196000 in the metropolitan area). Most North Dakotans are of north European descent, particularly German, Norwegian and Irish. The state has one of the country's highest life expectancies and lowest crime rates.

North Dakota ranks 20th in terms of per capita personal income; agriculture is the largest industry – the state is the USA's largest producer of barley, durum wheat, farm-raised turkeys and sunflower seeds – while food processing, mining and petroleum are also important. Unemployment in April 2010 was just 3.8 per cent (the nation's lowest).

Ohio

Ohio is situated in the Great Lakes (Rustbelt) region and occupies a strategic position, linking the northeast and the Midwest, with obvious economic advantages: much business and cargo traffic passes through the state. Ohio is within a one-day drive of half of North America's population and 70 per cent of its manufacturing capacity. It covers 116,096km² (44,825mi²) – the 34th-largest state – much of which consists of plains, with rugged terrain in the southeast. Pennsylvania lies to the east, the Canadian province of Ontario to the north, Michigan to the northwest, Indiana in the west, Kentucky to the south, and West Virginia in the southeast.

Ohio

Government: Governors' Office, Riffe Center, 30th Floor, 77 South High Street, Columbus, OH 43215 (☎ 1-614-466-3555, 🖥 www.ohio.gov).

Business: 🖥 http://business.ohio.gov, www.ohiobiz.com, www.ohiobusinessmagazine.com, http://ohiomeansbusiness.com and www.sba.gov (>Local Resources and select the state from the map).

Employment: 🖥 www.columbus.employmentguide.com - United States, www.columbus.careerboard.com and www.ohiojobs.com.

Tourist Office: Ohio Division of Travel and Tourism, PO Box 1001, Columbus, OH 43216 (☎ 1-800-BUCKEYE, 🖥 www.discoverohio.com.)

Ohio's population is 11.5m (83 per cent white and 12 per cent black), the seventh most populous state. The capital and largest city is Columbus (population 755,000, 1.77m in the metropolitan area). Ohio ranks 33rd in terms of per capita personal income and the economy is based on agriculture (especially corn), automobile and machine production, processed foods, steel, and tyre and rubber products. Unemployment in April 2010 was 10.9 per cent.

The state's climate is humid continental, except in the far south, which is humid subtropical. Summers are hot and humid throughout Ohio, while winters are cool or cold. Severe weather is quite common, as for much of the year the state is a confluence for cold Arctic air and warm Gulf air.

Oklahoma

Oklahoma is located in south-central USA, mostly in the Great Plains region, with small mountain ranges and some prairie and forests in the east. It covers 181,196km² (69,898mi²) and is the 20th-largest state. Arkansas and Missouri lie to the east, Kansas to the north, Colorado in the northwest, New Mexico to the west and Texas in the south.

It's home to 3.68m people (78 per cent white, 8 per cent Native American and 8 per cent black), the 28th most populous state. The capital and largest city is Oklahoma City (population 552,000, 1.27m in the metropolitan area). Oklahoma is very much part of the Bible Belt, with a widespread following of evangelical Christianity and conservative social views.

Oklahoma ranks only 34th in terms of per capita personal income, but has one of the country's lowest costs of living. The state also has one of the fastest-growing economies and is a major producer of food, natural gas and oil. Aviation, biotechnology, energy

and telecommunications are also important to the economy, while the federal government is a major employer. Unemployment in April 2010 was 6.6 per cent.

The state's climate has temperate and continental influences, and Oklahoma is particularly prone to severe weather (it was the centre of the dust bowl drought of the 1930s). It lies in 'Tornado Alley' and experiences around 50 a year, one of the world's highest rates. The southeast of the state has humid, subtropical weather.

Oregon

Oregon is in the Pacific Northwest, covering 255,026km² (98,466mi²), making it the 9th-largest state. It has one of the country's most diverse landscapes, known for its scenic coastline, dense forests, glaciated Cascade Mountains, volcanoes, deserts, prairies and semi-arid scrub. The Pacific Ocean lies to the west, Idaho is to the east, Washington sits to the north, and California and Nevada are to the south.

Oregon's population is 3.82m (93 per cent white and 4 per cent Asian), the 27th most populous state. The capital is Salem (population 154,000, 383,000 in the metropolitan area) and the largest city is Portland (582,000, 2.15m in the metropolitan area).

Agriculture is important to the state's economy, including apples, cattle, dairy products, hazelnuts, hops, peppermint, potatoes and wheat. Logging, timber and wine production are significant sectors, while the high technology and service industries are big employers. Oregon also has one of the world's largest salmon

---

Oklahoma

Government: Office of the Governor, State Capitol Building, 2300 N. Lincoln Blvd, Room 212, Oklahoma City, OK 73105 (☎ 1-405-521-2342, 🖳 www.ok.gov).

Business: 🖳 www.okcommerce.gov, www.ok.gov (>Business), www.okc.biz, www.osbdc.org and www.sba.gov (>Local Resources and select the state from the map).

Employment: 🖳 www.alloklahomajobs.com, www.oklahomajobs.com and www.job-hunt.org/jobs/oklahoma.shtml.

Tourist Office: Convention and Visitors' Bureau, 189 West Sheridan Avenue, Oklahoma City, OK 73102 (☎ 1-405-297-8912, 🖳 www.okccvb.org).

Cascades, Oregon

Oregon

Government: Governor's Office, 160 State Capitol, 900 Court Street, Salem, OR 97301 (☎ 1-503-378-4582, 🖥 www.oregon.gov).

Business: 🖥 www.licenseinfo.oregon. gov, www.oregon.gov (>Business), www.oregonbusiness.com, www. oregonbusinessplan.org, www. oregon4biz.com and www.sba.gov (>Local Resources and select the state from the map).

Employment: 🖥 www.employment. oregon.gov, www.employmentspot. com/state/or.htm and www. workinginoregon.org.

Tourist Office: Oregon Tourism Commission (Travel Oregon) 670 Hawthorne Avenue SE, Suite 240, Salem, OR 97301 (☎ 1-503-378-8850, 🖥 www.travel.salem.com).

fishing industries. The state ranks 31st in terms of per capita personal income. Unemployment in April 2010 was 10.6 per cent.

Oregon's climate is influenced by the Pacific Ocean and is generally mild with periods of extreme heat and cold (especially in the east). Precipitation varies greatly across the state; parts of the west are very wet, while much of the east is very dry.

Pennsylvania

Pennsylvania is a Commonwealth (see the entry on Kentucky for a definition) in the northeast, covering 119,283km² (46,055mi²), the 33rd-largest state. It has diverse geography, with a mountainous interior, and is bordered by New York State to the north, New Jersey to the east, Ohio to the west, and West Virginia, Maryland and Delaware to the south.

Pennsylvania's population is 12.6m (87 per cent white and 11 per cent black) and it's the 6th most populous state. The capital is Harrisburg (population 47,000, 529,000 in the metropolitan area) and the largest city is Philadelphia (1.54m, 5.83m in the metropolitan area). Pennsylvania is famous for its Amish community, who are descendants of Dutch settlers who shun most of the trappings of modern life. Manufacturing is important to the state's economy, as are agriculture (e.g. Christmas trees, mushrooms and wine production), finance and insurance. It ranks 18th in terms of per capita personal income. Unemployment in April 2010 was 9 per cent.

The state has a humid continental climate, with humid subtropical characteristics in the south. Winters are much colder in the mountains than elsewhere and the west gets a lot of snow.

Rhode Island

Rhode Island is in the New England region of the northeast, a mostly flat state with no mountains. It's the smallest state by area, covering a mere 3,144km² (1,214mi²), but, perhaps as compensation, has the longest official name of any state: the State of Rhode Island and Providence Plantations. Despite its name, most of the state of Rhode Island is on the mainland (to which 'Providence Plantations' refers), while 'Rhode Island' was the old name for Aquidneck Island (the largest island in Narragansett Bay). To the north and east is Massachusetts, to the west, Connecticut, and to the south, Rhode Island Sound and the Atlantic Ocean.

The state is home to 1.05m people (90 per cent white and 7 per cent black) and is the 43rd most populous state. The capital and largest city is Providence (population 172,000, 1.6m in the metropolitan area). Rhode Island ranks 16th in terms of per capita personal income and much of the state's economy is based on services, especially education and healthcare. Tourism is also important and there's some manufacturing, including boats and ships, electrical equipment, jewellery, metal products and textiles. Unemployment in April 2010 was 12.5 per cent.

Rhode Island has a humid continental climate, with hot, wet summers and cold, snowy winters.

Pennsylvania

Government: Governor's Office, Room 225, Main Capitol Building, Harrisburg, PA 17120 (☎ 1-717-787-2500, 🖥 www.state.pa.us).

Business: 🖥 www.newpa.com, www.pachamber.org, www.paopen4business.state.pa.us, www.pasbdc.org, www.sba.gov (>Local Resources and select the state from the map) and www.state.pa.us (>Work>Doing Business).

Employment: 🖥 www.pennsylvaniajobs.com, www.pennsylvaniajobs.net and www.job-hunt.org/jobs/pennsylvania.shtml.

Tourist Office: Pennsylvania Tourism Office, 4th Floor, Commonwealth Keystone Building, 400 North Street, Harrisburg, PA 17120 (☎ 1-717-787-5453, 🖥 www.visitpa.com).

Rhode Island

Government: Office of the Governor, State House Room 115, Providence, RI 02903 (☎ 1-401-222-2080, 💻 www.ri.gov).

Business: 💻 www.mbe.ri.gov, www.pbn.com, http://rhode-island.bizhwy.com, www.ri.gov/business, www.riedc.com/business-services, www.risbdc.org and www.sba.gov (>Local Resources and select the state from the map).

Employment: 💻 www.job-hunt.org/jobs/rhodeisland/shtml, www.dlt.ri.gov/Jobsri/statejobs.htm and www.rhode.island.jobs.com.

Tourist Office: Rhode Island Tourism Division, 315 Iron Horse Way, Suite 101, Providence, RI 02908, (☎ 1-800-250-7384, 💻 www.visitrhodeisland.com).

South Carolina

South Carolina is situated on the southern Atlantic coast, covering 82,965km² (34,726mi²) and is the 40th-largest state. The coastline is dotted with salt marshes and estuaries, while the interior is hilly. To the north is North Carolina, to the south and west Georgia, and to the east lies the Atlantic Ocean. South Carolina suffers the occasional earthquake, particularly in the southeast.

The state is home to 4.56m people (69 per cent white and 30 per cent black) and is the 24th most populous state. The capital and largest city is Columbia (population 127,000, 728,000 in the metropolitan area). South Carolina is placed a lowly 47th in terms of per capita personal income and its economy consists of agriculture (especially cattle, hogs, poultry, soybeans and tobacco), chemical production, machinery, paper products, textiles and tourism. Unemployment in April 2010 was 11.6 per cent.

South Carolina

Government: Governor's Office, 1301 Gervais Street, Suite 710, Columbia, SC 29201 (☎ 1-803-734-9900, 💻 www.sc.gov).

Business: 💻 www.sc.gov (>Business), www.scbos.sc.gov, www.scbusinessweek.com, www.sciway.net/bus, www.sba.gov (>Local Resources and select the state from the map) and www.scsbc.org.

Employment: 💻 www.sciway.net/jobs, www.job-hunt.org/jobs/southcarolina.shtml and www.southcarolinajobs.net.

Tourist Office: SC Department of Parks, Recreation and Tourism, 1205 Pendleton Street, Columbia, SC 29201 (☎ 1-803-734-1700, 💻 www.discoversouthcarolina.com).

The climate is humid subtropical, although higher areas are noticeably less subtropical. Summers in most of the state are hot and humid, but there's more varied winter weather, when coastal areas are mild, while inland regions are cool or cold. Precipitation is high throughout the year in most of the state, which is prone to tropical cyclones. It experiences around 50 days of thunderstorms and 15 tornadoes a year.

South Dakota

South Dakota is a Midwestern state in north-central USA, covering 199,050km² (77,116mi²) and is the 17th-largest. Although it's geographically in the Midwest, it's also part of the Great Plains and is sometimes regarded as more correctly part of the West. South Dakota was traditionally an agricultural state with a rural lifestyle, much of it being temperate grasslands (except the Black Hills, a place of great religious significance to Native Americans and the site of Mount Rushmore). North Dakota (not surprisingly) sits to the north of South Dakota, Nebraska is to the south, Iowa and Minnesota lie east, and Wyoming and Montana are in the west.

South Dakota

Government: Office of the Governor, 500 E. Capitol Avenue, Pierre, SD 57501 (☎ 1-605-773-3212, 🖥 www.sd.gov).

Business: 🖥 www.sba.gov (>Local Resources and select the state from the map), www.sdchamber.biz, www.sdreadytowork.com and www.usd.edu/sbdc.

Employment: 🖥 www.job-hunt.org/jobs/southdakota.shtml, http://south.dakota.jobs.com and www.southdakotajobs.com.

Tourist Office: Office of Tourism, Capitol Lake Plaza, 711 East Wells Avenue, c/o 500 East Capitol Ave, Pierre, SD 57501 (☎ 1-605-773-3301, 🖥 www.travel.sd.com).

South Dakota's population is just 812,000 (87 per cent white and 8 per cent Native American), making it the 46th most populous state. The capital is Pierre (population 14,500) and the largest city Sioux Falls (155,000, 233,000 in the metropolitan area). The state ranks 25th in terms of per capita personal income, with the service industry (primarily finance, healthcare and retail) the largest contributor to the economy; agriculture is important, particularly beef, corn, pork, poultry, soybeans, sunflowers, wheat and wool. Tourism

is also significant and one of the state's largest single employers is Ellsworth Air Force Base. Unemployment in April 2010 was 4.7 per cent (the second-lowest).

South Dakota has a continental climate with four distinct seasons. Summers are hot (although summer nights are usually mild or cool) and winters are cold. The northwest of the state is semi-arid, while the southeast is semi-humid. South Dakota is prey to many summer thunderstorms, while the east of the state is situated in Tornado Alley.

Tennessee

Tennessee is located in southern USA, covering 109,247km² (42,169mi²). It's the 36th-largest state and a mixture of plains and mountains. To the north are Kentucky and Virginia; to the south Georgia, Alabama and Mississippi; to the east, North Carolina and to the west Arkansas and Missouri.

Tennessee is home to just over 6m people (81 per cent white and 17 per cent black) and is the 17th most populous state. The capital is Nashville (population 626,000, 1.6m in the metropolitan area) and the largest city Memphis (670,000, 1.28m in the metropolitan area). Tennessee ranks 36th in terms of per capita personal income and the economy is dominated by cattle, chemicals, cotton, electricity, food processing and textiles. The state is strongly associated with country and western music, with Nashville a world centre and an important tourist attraction (as is Elvis Presley's Graceland mansion in Memphis). Unemployment in April 2010 was 10.5 per cent.

Most of Tennessee has a humid subtropical climate, except in the higher mountains, which have humid continental conditions. Summers are hot throughout the state, winters cool or mild, with plenty of precipitation throughout the year. Tennessee has around 15 tornadoes and 50 thunderstorms annually, while fog is a frequent problem in some areas.

Tennessee

Government: Governor's Office, Tennessee State Capitol, Nashville, TN 37243 (☎ 1-615-741-2001, 💻 www. tennesseeanytime.org).

Business: 💻 www.sba.gov (>Local Resources and select the state from the map), www.tennesseeanytime.org/ business and www.tsbdc.org.

Employment: 💻 www.job-hunt. org/jobs/tennessee.shtml, www. tennesseejobs.com and http://jobs. careerbuilder.com/al.ic/tennessee.

Tourist Office: Tennessee Department of Tourist Development, William Snodgrass/Tennessee Tower, 312 Rosa L. Parks Avenue, 25th Floor, Nashville, TN 37243 (☎ 1-615-741-2159, 💻 www.tnvacation.com).

Texas

Texas is in south-central USA, covering 678,051km² (261,797mi²) – the second-largest state after Alaska. Its geography and

include aerospace, agriculture (cabbages, cattle, corn, cotton, spinach, watermelons and wheat), defence manufacturing, financial services, information technology, petrochemicals and timber, while Houston is one of the world's leading ports. Texas doesn't levy personal state income tax. Unemployment in April 2010 was 8.3 per cent.

In the same way that Texas's huge size makes it difficult to categorize culturally, economically and geographically, the same is also true of its climate, and it has a variety of climatic zones. Conditions are humid subtropical in the east, temperate semi-arid steppe in the northwest and subtropical steppe in the south, verging on a desert climate in some regions. Tornadoes are common, with around 140 per year (the most of any state).

character are varied, with parts resembling the Midwest (especially the Panhandle in the north), while other areas are similar to the southwest and some like the south. New Mexico lies to the northwest, Mexico to the southwest, Oklahoma sits to the north, Arkansas is in the northeast, Louisiana in the east and the Gulf of Mexico to the southeast.

Texas has a population of 24.7m people (70 per cent white and 12 per cent black, with Hispanics comprising around 35 per cent of the population), the second most populous state (after California). The capital is Austin (population 757,000, 1.65m in the metropolitan area), while the largest city is Houston (2.24m, 5.72m in the metropolitan area).

Texas has the country's second-largest economy and is home to the second-highest number of Fortune 500 companies (the top 500 American public corporations, measured by gross revenue) after New York, yet ranks a relatively modest 29th in terms of per capita personal income. It's noted for its energy and aeronautical industries; the state's known oil deposits are around a third of the US total. Other important industries (some regional)

Texas

Government: Office of the Governor, PO Box 12428, Austin, TX 78711 (☎ 1-512-463-2000, 🖳 www.texasonline.com).

Business: 🖳 www.commerce-chamber.com, www.sba.gov (>Local Resources and select the state from the map), http://texas.bizhwy.com, www.texasonline.com (>Business) and www.txbiz.org.

Employment: 🖳 www.job-hunt.org/jobs/texas.shtml, www.employmentspot.com/state/tx.htm and www.texasjobs.com.

Tourist Office: Office of the Governor, Economic Development and Tourism, Texas Tourism, PO Box 12428, Austin, TX 78711 (☎ 1-512-936-0101, 🖳 www.travel.state.tx.us).

Utah

Utah is situated in the southwest, covering 219,887km² (84,889mi²), making it the 13th-largest state. It has a diverse geography, including stony desert, green river valleys and snowy mountains. To the north are Idaho and Wyoming, to the east Colorado, to the southeast is New Mexico, to the south lies Arizona, and to the west is Nevada.

Utah is home to 2.78m people (95 per cent white) and is the 34th most populous state, and the capital and largest city is Salt Lake City (population 182,000, 1.1m in the metropolitan area). Large expanses of Utah are virtually uninhabited and nearly 90 per cent of Utahns live in an urban area called the Wasatch Front (centred on Salt Lake City).

Over half of the state's population claim to be Mormons (members of The Church of Jesus Christ of Latter-day Saints), which makes it one of the most religiously homogenous states. Mormonism has a

Monument Valley, Utah

Utah

Government: Government Office, 30 East Broadway, Suite 300, Salt Lake City, UT 84111 (☎ 1-801-983-0275, 🖥 www.utah.gov).

Business: 🖥 www.alpinebusinessbrokers.com, www.commerce.utah.gov, www.sba.gov (>Local Resources and select the state from the map), www.utah.bizhwy.com, www.utah.gov/business, www.utahbusiness.com and www.utahsbdc.org.

Employment: 🖥 www.job-hunt.org/jobs/utah.shtml, www.jobs.careerbuilder.com/al.ic/utah and http://jobs.utah.gov.

Tourist Office: Utah Office of Tourism, Council Hall/Capitol Hill, 300 N. State Street, Salt Lake City, UT 84114 (☎ 1-801-538-1030, 🖥 www.travelutah.gov).

significant influence on the state's culture and daily life, including the restrictive attitude towards alcohol and gambling, and the high birth rate – the country's highest of any state. Utah's economy is based on cattle ranching, government services, information technology, mining, petroleum production and refining, salt production, tourism (especially for outdoor recreation) and transportation. It's a lowly 49th in terms of per

capita personal income. Unemployment in April 2010 was 7.3 per cent.

Much of Utah is high in elevation and arid. Winters are cold in most of the state – very cold in some areas. Summers are hot or very hot. Unlike in most of the western US, thunderstorms are relatively rare – occurring on around 40 days a year – and there's an average of just two tornadoes annually.

Vermont

Vermont is in the New England region of the northeast, covering 24,923km² (9,620mi²), the 45th-largest state. It's the only New England state without an Atlantic coastline and is noted for the Green Mountains in the west, Lake Champlain in the northwest and its beautiful fall foliage. Massachusetts lies to the south, New Hampshire to the east, New York State in the west and the Canadian province of Quebec to the north.

Vermont is home to just 622,000 people (98 per cent white) and is the second least-populous state. The capital is Montpelier (population 8,300, the least populous state capital) and the largest city Burlington (40,000). More than 20 per cent of Vermont's population identify themselves as non-religious, tying with Oregon as having the second-highest percentage of non-religious people in the USA; only Washington State has a higher percentage.

Dairy farming is Vermont's main agricultural activity and the state also manufactures and sells 'artisan' foods such as beer, butter, cheese, chocolates and ice cream, as well as producing wine. IBM is one of the state's largest commercial employers, while other important sectors include electronic equipment, insurance, machine tools and tourism, the latter being Vermont's largest industry, notably for its fishing, hiking, and some of New England's best cross-country and downhill skiing. The state ranks 21st in terms of per capita personal income. Unemployment in April 2010 was low, at 6.4 per cent.

Vermont's climate is moist continental, with warm, humid summers and cold winters, particularly at higher elevations and in the north.

Vermont

Government: Governor's Office, 109 State Street, Pavilion, Montpelier, VT 05609 (☎ 1-802-828-3333, 💻 www.vermont.gov).

Business: 💻 www.sba.gov (>Local Resources and select the state from the map), www.thinkvermont.com, www.vermont.gov/portal/business, www.vermontbiz.com, www.vermontbusinessbrokers.com and www.vtsbdc.org.

Employment: 💻 www.jobs.careerbuilder.com/al.ic/vermont, www.humanresources.vermont.gov, http://jobsinvermont.com and www.vermontjobs.net.

Tourist Office: Tourism and Marketing Department, National Life Drive, Montpelier, VT 05620 (☎ 1-802-828-3676, 💻 www.vermontvacation.com).

Virginia

The Commonwealth (see the entry for Kentucky for a definition) of Virginia is on the central southeast Atlantic coast, covering 110,785km² (42,774mi²), making it the 35th-largest state. Despite its central geographical position, Virginia is traditionally and culturally part of the South. To the north are Maryland and the District of Columbia, to the east Chesapeake Bay and the Atlantic Ocean, in the south are North Carolina and Tennessee, and to the west lie Kentucky and West Virginia.

Virginia's population is 7.88m people (72 per cent white and 21 per cent black), making it the 12th most populous state. The capital is Richmond (population 200,000, 1.2m in the metropolitan area) and the largest city Virginia Beach (434,000, 1.79m in the metropolitan area). Virginia comes an impressive 7th in terms of per capita personal income and has a diverse economy, with many federal and military employees – it's home to the world's largest naval base at Norfolk – while the 'Historic Triangle' of Jamestown, Yorktown and Colonial Williamsburg is one of the USA's most popular tourist destinations. The technology sector is important, as are cattle, chemicals, communications, computer chips, coal, federal agencies, peanut farming, software, tomatoes, tobacco and wine production. Unemployment in April 2010 was 7.2 per cent.

Most of the state east of the Blue Ridge Mountains has a humid subtropical climate and it's humid continental in the mountains. The state is hit by around 85 tornadoes each year and the coast is sometimes struck by hurricanes.

Virginia

Government: Government Office, East Main Street, Suite 901, Richmond, VA 23219 (☎ 1-804-796-4718, 🖥 www.virginia.gov).

Business: 🖥 www.dba.virginia.gov, www.sba.gov (>Local Resources and select the state from the map), www.virginia.gov (>Business), www.virginiabusiness.com and www.yesvirginia.org.

Employment: 🖥 www.virginia.jobopenings.net, http://jobs.virginia.gov, www.jobs.careerbuilder.com/al.ic/virginia and www.localvirginiajobs.com.

Tourist Office: Virginia Tourism Corporation, 901 E. Byrd Street, Richmond, VA 23219 (☎ 1-800-847-4882, 🖥 www.virginia.org).

Washington

Washington is a state in the far northwest of the continental USA – usually referred to as Washington State so as not to be confused with the nation's capital, Washington DC – on the Pacific coast. It covers 184,827km² (71,342mi²), making it the 18th-largest state. To the north is the Canadian province of British Columbia, to the south Oregon, to the east Idaho, and to the west the Pacific Ocean.

Supreme Court, Washington DC

Washington

Government: Office of the Governor, PO Box 40002, Olympia, WA 98504 (☎ 1-360-902-4111, 🖥 access.wa.gov).

Business: 🖥 http://access.wa.gov/business, www.awb.org, www.dol.wa.gov/business, www.sba.gov (>Local Resources and select the state from the map) and www.wsbdc.org.

Employment: 🖥 www.wa.gov/esd/employment.html, www.washjob.com and www.careers.wa.gov.

Tourist Office: Washington Tourism Office, PO Box 42500, Olympia, WA 98504 (☎ 1-360-725-5050, 🖥 www.experiencewa.com).

Washington is home to 6.66m people (88 per cent white and 8 per cent Asian) and is the 13th most populous state. The capital is Olympia (population 44,000) and the largest city Seattle (602,000, 3.34m in the metropolitan area). The state ranks 12th in terms of per capita personal income and it doesn't levy personal income tax. Important sectors of the economy include aluminium production, biotechnology, computer software development (Microsoft is based in the Seattle area), the design and manufacture of jet aircraft (Boeing), electronics, hydroelectric power generating, lumber, mining and tourism. Washington is also an important agricultural state for apples, grapes, hops, lentils, potatoes, raspberries and spearmint oil. Unemployment in April 2010 was 9.2 per cent.

The area west of the Cascade Mountains (which contain several active volcanoes) has a maritime west coast climate, with cool or mild, wet winters and mild, dry summers. The coast has areas of dense forest, some of which have a temperate rainforest climate (wet and mild). East of the Cascades, the climate is semi-arid steppe – dry and with more extreme temperatures in summer and winter – with the odd area of desert.

Washington DC (District of Columbia)

Washington DC isn't a state (or part of one) but a district, the national capital and centre of all three branches of the US government (executive, judicial and legislative). It covers

177km² (68.3mi²) and sits on the banks of the Potomac River, with Virginia to the west and Maryland to the north, east and south. The city has a population of 599,000 (56 per cent black and 36 per cent white), while the metropolitan area/district is home to 5.3m (the 8th-largest in the USA).

Washington DC

Government: Executive Office of the Mayor, 1350 Pennsylvania Avenue NW, Suite 316, Washington, DC 20004, (☎ 1-202-727-2980, 🖥 www. dc.gov).

Business: 🖥 www.brc.dc.gov, www. dc.gov (>Business), www.dcchamber. org, www.sba.gov (>Local Resources and select the state from the map), www.sbnow.org and http://washington. bizjournals.com.

Employment: 🖥 www.washingtondc. employmentguide.com, www. dcjobsource.com and www.dcjobsite. com.

Tourist Office: Destination DC, 901 7th Street NW, 4th Floor, Washington, DC 20001 (☎ 1-202-789-7000, 🖥 www.washington.org).

Washington DC's economy has been diversifying in recent years, with less reliance on federal government jobs – other significant activities include architecture, education, healthcare, insurance, law, media, public relations and real estate. Away from Washington's impressive, government-dominated city centre are

some of the country's worst areas of urban deprivation (with a high crime rate). Unemployment in April 2010 was 11 per cent.

The District of Columbia has a humid subtropical climate typical of the mid-Atlantic USA, with four distinct seasons, including hot, humid summers (with lots of thunderstorms), and cool or cold winters.

West Virginia

West Virginia is located roughly half way down the eastern coast of the USA, covering 62,809km² (24,244mi²), making it the 41st-largest state. It's entirely within the Appalachian Mountain range and is one of the Border States (between the North and South), regarded as part of the South because most of it is below the Mason-Dixon Line (the demarcation line between Pennsylvania, Maryland, Delaware and West Virginia), which is the symbolic division between the North and South.

West Virginia's geographical location means that some parts of the state resemble the northeast, others are like the Midwest and some areas have the feel of the south. To the north sits Pennsylvania, to the north and west Ohio, to the west Kentucky, to the north and east Maryland, and to the east and south Virginia. The state is noted for its natural beauty.

It's home to 1.81m people (96 per cent white) and is the 37th most populous state. The capital and largest city is Charleston (population 50,000, 310,000 in the metropolitan area). West Virginia has one of the USA's most fragile economies and ranks 44th in terms of per capita personal

West Virginia

Government: Governor's Office, 1900 Kanawha Boulevard E, Charleston, WV 25305 (☎ 1-888-438-2731, 🖥 www.wv.gov).

Business: 🖥 www.business4wv.com, www.charlestonareaalliance.org, www.sba.gov (>Local Resources and select the state from the map), www.sbdcwv.org, http://west-virginia.bizhwy.com and www.wv.gov/business.

Employment: 🖥 www.charleston.wv.jobs.com, www.job-hunt.org/jobs/westvirginia.shtml and www.westvirginiajobs.com.

Tourist Office: West Virginia Department of Tourism, 2101 Washington Street East, Charleston, WV 25305 (☎ 1-304-558-2200, 🖥 www.wvtourism.com).

income. Coal is a major resource and there's some farming, although it's limited by the mountainous terrain. There's also some heavy industry, including chemicals and metallurgy (especially steel), while the state has become a popular tourist destination (notably for outdoor leisure and sports). Unemployment in April 2010 was 9.2 per cent.

West Virginia's climate is borderline humid subtropical in the lower areas of the southwest, with hot, humid summers and fairly mild winters. The rest of the state experiences humid continental conditions, with warm or hot, humid summers and cold winters.

Wisconsin

Wisconsin is a Great Lakes state, covering 169,790km² (65,498mi²) – the 23rd-largest. It's a region of lowlands, forests (which cover nearly half of the state) and rugged uplands. To the north is Michigan, to the east lies Lake Michigan, to the south is Illinois, and to the west are Iowa and Minnesota. It's home to 5.6m people (91 per cent white and 6 per cent black) and is the 20th most populous state. The capital is Madison (population 229,000, 543,000 in the metropolitan area) and the largest city Milwaukee (605,000, 1.74m in the metropolitan area). Over 40 per cent of the population has German ancestry and a large

number has a Scandinavian background, especially Norwegian.

Wisconsin is 26th in terms of per capita personal income and its economy is based on agriculture, healthcare and manufacturing, while tourism is also significant. Major agricultural products include cranberries, corn, dairy (notably butter, cheese and milk), ginseng, maple syrup, oats, potatoes and sweet corn, while food processing is an important part of the manufacturing sector. Wisconsin also makes a lot of beer, as well as machinery and transportation equipment. Unemployment in April 2010 was 8.5 per cent.

The state has an extreme continental climate, with warm or hot summers and cold or very cold winters.

Wyoming

Wyoming is in western USA, covering 253,348km² (97,818mi²), making it the 10th-largest state. It's dominated by rangelands and the Rockies, although the east is high altitude prairie (part of the Great Plains). Montana lies to the north, South Dakota and Nebraska to the east, Colorado in the south, Utah to the southwest, while Idaho sits to

---

Wisconsin

Government: Office of the Governor, 115 East State Capitol, Madison, WI 53702 (☎ 1-608-266-1212, 🖥 www.wisconsin.gov).

Business: 🖥 www.sba.gov (>Local Resources and select the state from the map), http://wisconsin.bizhwy.com, http://wisbusiness.com, www.wisconsin.gov (>Business), www.wisconsinsbdc.org and www.wwbic.com.

Employment: 🖥 http://wisconsin.jobing.com, www.employmentspot.com/state/wi.htm and www.cityofmadison.com/employment.

Tourist Office: Wisconsin Department of Tourism, 201 West Washington Avenue, PO Box 8690, Madison, WI 53708 (☎ 1-800-432-8747/1-608-266-2161, 🖥 www.travelwisconsin.com).

Wyoming

Government: Governor's Office, State Capitol, 200 West 24th Street, Cheyenne, WY 82002 (☎ 1-307-777-7434, 🖥 www.wyoming.gov).

Business: 🖥 http://allwyoming.uwyo.edu, http://gowyld.net/wyoming/business.html, www.sba.gov (>Local Resources and select the state from the map), http://wyoming.bizhwy.com, www.wyoming.gov/business, www.wyomingbusiness.org and www.wyomingbusinessreport.com.

Employment: 🖥 www.job-hunt.org/jobs/wyoming.shtml, www.wyomingatwork.com and www.wyomingjobs.com.

Tourist Office: Wyoming Travel and Tourism, 1520 Etchepare Circle, Cheyenne, WY 82007 (☎ 1-307-777-7777, 🖥 www.wyomingtourism.org).

the west. Wyoming is the least populous US state, home to just 545,000 people (96 per cent white and 3 per cent Native American). The capital and largest city is Cheyenne (population 56,000).

The state ranks a creditable 6th in terms of per capita personal income and its economy is powered by tourism and mineral extraction, especially coal, gas, methane, oil, trona and uranium. Cattle ranching and tourism are also important.

Unemployment in April 2010 was 7.1 per cent.

Wyoming's climate is semi-arid continental, drier and windier than most of the USA, with notable temperature extremes. Summers are hot at lower levels, cooler with altitude; summer nights are cool everywhere. Winters are cold or very cold. Wyoming gets more hail damage than most states and the southeast is prone to tornadoes.

2.

IMMIGRATION HISTORY & DEMOGRAPHICS

Since its early days, North America has been a country of immigrants, although where the first arrivals came from isn't generally agreed upon. Some think that the antecedents of native Americans arrived from Asia via a land bridge in the region of the Bering Strait sometime between 20,000 and 11,000BC, while others believe that the first Americans came from Polynesia, South Asia or even Europe. It is, however, now widely agreed that the Vikings landed in North America around the year 1000, but they aren't believed to have left any ancestors.

Almost since the arrival of Columbus in 1492, America has been a magnet for travelers seeking a better life. The first settlers began arriving from Europe in the 16th century, with Spain, Britain, France and the Netherlands leading the way. They brought with them slaves from Africa, and were followed by many more waves of immigrants; Germans, Irish and Scandinavians in the early 19th century, settlers from eastern and southern Europe and Asia in the late 19th century to, most recently, migrants from Latin America and Asia. By the 21st century, every nation on Earth has at least one community somewhere within the 50 states and the US remains the number-one destination for many would-be immigrants from across the globe. As a result of the sustained waves of immigration, the US contains a highly diverse population and ethnic and racial diversity – the so-called 'melting pot' – which is celebrated as a core element of the American ideology.

Immigration has been a major source of population growth and cultural change in the US, as it has throughout the new world. The economic, social, and political aspects of immigration have sparked controversy about the influence on many aspects of American society and its way of life, such as ethnicity, religion, crime, economic benefits, job benefits and opportunities, the environmental impact, social mobility, politics, and family and moral values, to name but a few. Nevertheless, despite the logistical problems assimilating millions of immigrants, the US has hugely benefitted from the influx of new 'Americans' who have constantly revitalized the country and made it what it is today: the most powerful and successful nation the world has ever seen.

As a result of such sustained immigration, the US is one of the most culturally diverse nations in the world. Americans are fiercely proud of their heritage – or their heritages – and of the fact that their 'land of opportunity' offers newcomers a crack at *'the American Dream'* – the belief that through hard work and determination, immigrants can achieve a better life, particularly in terms of financial prosperity and enhanced personal freedom.

Whether your stay in the US is short or long – and whether or not you live the Dream – the experience is sure to be unforgettable.

THE US POPULATION: OVERVIEW

The US is the third most populous nation in the world after China and India. The population, which is expanding at the rate of around 1 per cent a year, passed the 300m mark in 2007 and in June 2010 stood at 310m, of which some 38m (around 12.5 per cent) were foreign-born residents, with over half coming from Latin America.

It's estimated that the population will reach 400m by the 2040s, and, if current birth rate and immigration rates were to remain constant for another 70 to 80 years, the population would double to some 600m. The Census Bureau's estimates go even further and predict that there'll be a billion Americans by 2100, compared with just one million in 1700 and 5.2m in 1800. Immigration is what keeps America growing, as the US birth-rate is below the 'replacement' rate required to maintain the current population.

The increase is largely due to the influx of migrants from Central and South America in recent decades and the high birth rate among Hispanics, who are the fastest-growing population group (accounting for around half the population growth) and in 2010 were believed to outnumber African-Americans .The largest Spanish-speaking communities are Mexicans in the south-west (Arizona, California, New Mexico, Texas), Cubans in the south-east (Florida) and Puerto Ricans in New York City. In 2010, some 38m Americans were foreign-born, the highest proportion since the '30s.

The population density of the US is around 80 people per mi² (30 per km²), compared with around 600 per mi² in the UK and almost 850 per mi² in Japan. Some 75 per cent of Americans live in urban areas and are concentrated in just 2.5 per cent of the country's land area. There are some 40 metropolitan areas with a population of over 1m, comprising a total of 150m inhabitants or around half of the total population. The US has some of the world's largest urban areas, including greater Los Angeles, which stretches almost 100mi (160km) along the west coast and around 50mi (80km) inland. The east coast from Boston to Washington DC (taking in New York City and Philadelphia) is virtually a continuous 250mi (400km) long urban sprawl. New

York is the largest city, with around 8.4m inhabitants (over 1.5m in Manhattan alone), followed by Los Angeles (3.8m), Chicago (almost 2.9m) and Houston (2.2m). Washington, DC, the nation's capital, has a population of around 600,000.

Despite its huge metropolitan areas, 97.5 per cent of the US is classified as rural, where the population density may be just a few people per square mile.

Between the major population centers in the east and west are the huge sparsely populated areas of the wheat belt and Great Plains in the Midwest, the Rocky Mountains, and the desert lands of Colorado, Nevada, New Mexico and Utah. However, only Alaska can be defined as true wilderness, where most of the state has a population density of less than two people per square mile.

Although the most densely populated region remains the northeast, population growth there is slowing as people move to the west and the Sunbelt, lured by 'sunrise', high-tech industries and newly booming centers such as Atlanta and Las Vegas. In the decade 1990-2000, the population of the northeast rose by just 2.8m compared with increases of 10.4m in the west and 14.8m in the south. As a result, Texas has overtaken New York as the US's second most populous state after California, whose population (almost 34m) is larger than that of the 21 least populous states combined! Wyoming has the smallest population, with fewer than half a million inhabitants – even Alaska has more. The states with the largest population increases in percentage terms are Nevada (66 per cent) and Arizona (40 per cent), but in absolute terms California, Texas and Florida have grown the most (by more than 3m people each) in the last decade.

> Like other Western countries, the US is faced with the problem of an ageing population due to a declining birth rate (the average number of children per family is 2.1) and an increasing life expectancy: 72 for men and 78 for women.

In 1960, over 35 per cent of the population was under 18, which had fallen to 26 per cent by 2000. During the same period, the number of people over 65 doubled to around 35m. The number of people over 50 rose from 33m in 1950 to 77m in 2000 and is expected to increase to 100m by 2020 as the 'baby boomers' (those born in the decade after the second world war) reach retirement age.

IMMIGRATION HISTORY

For centuries, the US has attracted migrants from all corners of the globe in search of a share of the 'American Dream'. In fact, the history of the US is one of immigration. In 1620 the Pilgrim Fathers left England for America seeking religious freedom and landed near Plymouth, Massachusetts. Little did they realize it, but they were to become trailblazers for waves of European migration to North America, which hitherto had been inhabited only by native Americans for thousands of years.

The flow of immigrants to the US was at first a trickle, but accelerated after the French Revolution and during the 19th century, as people were driven by ethnic, political and religious persecution, wars and famine – or were simply in search of a better life. Throughout the 19th and 20th Centuries, American ports welcomed millions of immigrants, not least from China, Germany, Ireland, Italy, Poland and Russia; between 1836 and 1914 over 30m Europeans emigrated to the US.

The US government practiced an open door immigration policy until 1882, but at the end of the century, it began to control immigration by excluding prostitutes, criminals, alcoholics, and Chinese, among others, from coming to the country.

Under the national origins quota system, established in 1921, admission to the US largely dependent upon an immigrant's country of birth, and some 70 per cent of all immigrant 'quotas' were allotted to citizens of just three countries: the UK, Ireland and Germany. However, these were mostly unused, while there were long waiting lists for the small number of visas available to those born in eastern and southern Europe.

> A little known fact is that Americans of German ancestry are the country's largest single ethnic group, comprising around 50m people or some 17 per cent of the population as a whole.

The history of American immigration history can be viewed in four eras: the colonial period, the nineteenth century, the early twentieth century and post-1945. Each era brought distinct national groups – and races and ethnicities – to the US. The 19th century saw an influx, initially largely from northern Europe; the late 19th and early 20th centuries mainly from Southern and Eastern Europe; and post-1965 mostly from Latin America and Asia.

The Colonial Period

The original people of north America, who made up several distinct groups of native Americans, went into decline (and now constitute a minority of the population) after the arrival of settlers and even more importantly the diseases they brought with them, to which the natives had no natural resistance. The early settlers came predominantly from the British Isles. Large numbers of black Africans were subsequently 'imported' as slaves to work the plantations of the Americas, while millions of Europeans in search of political freedom and economic opportunity constituted a third stage of immigration.

The US originated in a revolution, which won it independence from the British Crown. The constitution, drafted in 1787, established a federal system with a division of powers which has remained unchanged since its inception.

19th Century

The early 19th century saw mainly immigration from the countries of Western Europe; largely from the Protestant countries of Britain, Germany and Scandinavia, along with Catholics from Ireland; this period became known as one of 'old immigration'. However, in 1870 what became known as a flood of 'new immigration' began, with new arrivals from eastern and southern Europe plus Asia, Russia and Japan.

Early 20th Century

The early 20th century saw mass immigration to the US peak in 1907, with almost 1.3m immigrants entering the country; this compares with under a 1m immigrants in the 17th and 18th centuries combined. By 1910 there were 13.5m first generation immigrants living in the US. In 1921 an Emergency Quota Act and in 1924 an Immigration Act were enacted to limit the overall numbers of immigrants arriving, and to keep their nationalities in proportion to those already in the US. The ten year economic depression of the 1930s marked the end of that period of mass immigration, as more people left the US than arrived.

Post–1945 Period

Immigrants coming to the US after 1945 were more likely to be refugees and more highly skilled than previously – and the majority were female. From 1945 to 1965, most European immigrants were from northern and Western European countries, but by the '70s, southern and eastern European countries provided the bulk of European immigrants.

In 1965, nationality origin quotas were abolished, which heralded a new era of mass immigration, particularly from Mexico and Latin America. The liberalization of immigration policy in 1965 and subsequent legislation opened the floodgates for a vast new wave of immigrants, one that brought millions of people to the US from parts of the world from where entry was previously denied or severely limited. After 1965 an important shift was apparent, with third

Great Hall, Ellis Island, NY

In the most recent decade, the 10m immigrants that settled in the US represent an annual growth rate of around one-third of 1 per cent (as the US population grew from 249m to 281m). In comparison, the highest previous decade was 1901-1910 when 8.8m people arrived, increasing the total US population by 1 per cent per year as the population grew from 76 to 92m during that decade. Specifically, almost 15 per cent of Americans were foreign-born in 1910, while in 2002 the US Census Bureau pegged the country's foreign-born population at 11.5 percent.

The racial and ethnic identity of the US is – once again – being remade. The 2000 Census (at the time of going to press results of the 2010 census were yet to be announced) counted some 28m first-generation immigrants, which was the highest number in history (often cited by anti-immigration lobbyists). However, it wasn't the highest percentage of the foreign-born in relation to the overall population; in 1907 the figure was 15 per cent, while today it's around 10 per cent.

Immigration to the US has grown from just 250,000 in the 1930s, to 2.5m in the 1950s, 4.5m in the 1970s, 7.3m in the 1980s and around 10m in the 1990s. Since 2000, immigrants to the US have numbered around one million annually, of whom some 600,000 are 'Change of Status' immigrants already in the US. In addition, illegal immigration may be as high as 1.5m a year, with a net of around 700,000 arriving each year to join the 12m (or more) already there.

As mentioned above, the proportion of the population born outside the US was higher in 1910 (about 15 per cent) than it is today (about 10 per cent). A number of factors may be attributed to the decrease in the representation of foreign-born residents in the US. Most significant has been the change in the composition of immigrants. Prior to 1890, some 80 per cent of immigrants came from north and Western Europe, while from 1891 to 1920 the percentage dropped to 25 per

world nations replacing Europe as the major source of immigrants, and by the late '70s the vast majority of new arrivals were from the third world.

US Immigration Today

The US accepts more immigrants as permanent residents than all other countries of the world combined. Since the liberalization of immigration policy in 1965, the number of first- generation (foreign born) immigrants living in the US has quadrupled, from 9.6m in 1970 to around 38m in 2007, and a record 1,046,539 people were naturalized as US citizens in 2008. The leading countries of birth of new citizens were Mexico, India and the Philippines.

Current immigration rates are moderate, although the US admitted more immigrants (between 10 and 11m) from 1991 to 2000 than in any previous decade.

cent, with a rise in immigrants from east, central, and southern Europe. Animosity towards these different and more 'foreign' immigrants led to legislation to limit immigration.

Contemporary immigrants settle predominantly in seven states: California, Florida, Illinois, New Jersey, New York, Pennsylvania and Texas. These are all states with a high percentage of foreign-born people and together comprise around 45 per cent of the population as a whole. The combined total immigrant population of these seven states is much higher in proportion than elsewhere in the country, totaling 70 per cent of the foreign-born population in 2000. Of those who immigrated between 2000 and 2005, almost 60 per cent were from Latin America.

Until the 1930s, the gender imbalance among immigrants was quite sharp, with most being male. However, from the '90s women accounted for just over half of all immigrants, indicating a shift away from the male dominated immigration of the past. Contemporary immigrants tend to be younger than the average age of the native population of the US, with those aged between 15 and 34 substantially overrepresented; immigrants are also more likely to be married and less likely to be divorced than native-born Americans of the same age.

Immigrants are likely to move to areas populated by people with similar backgrounds, a tendency which has remained constant throughout the history of the US. Some 75 per cent of immigrants plan to make the US their permanent home and 80 per cent of immigrants are happy with their decision and would do it again.

Around half of new immigrants say the government has become tougher on enforcing immigration laws since 9/11 (the terrorist attacks on the World Trade Center in New York on September 11, 2001) and some 30 per cent have personally experienced discrimination.

Public attitudes towards immigration have been heavily influenced by the aftermath of the 9/11 attacks. Half of all Americans believe that tighter immigration

controls would do 'a great deal' to enhance US national security.

Today, Asians from the Pacific rim and Hispanics from Central and South America are among those seeking to be part of 'the American Dream'. However, despite relative prosperity in recent years, the gap between rich and poor remains vast. Over 35m Americans live below the official poverty line, with a disproportionate percentage of these being African-Americans and Hispanics.

Impact of Immigration on the US

A high rate of immigration, whether legal or illegal, is a mixed blessing to the US. Positive aspects include a constant source of healthy young workers which reduces the average age of American workers and provides a high proportion of economically productive people, many of whom are prepared to work for lower wages than native-born Americans. On the other hand, unskilled and semi-skilled American workers (in particular) blame the influx of new immigrants for lowering wages, reducing job opportunities and increasing unemployment. However, public opinion surveys suggest that Americans see both the good and bad arguments of immigration, and the proportion in favor and against are roughly equal.

A fast-growing population also has an impact on the environment. California is growing by around half a million people a year, and the California Department of Water Resources has estimated that if new water sources aren't found by 2020 there'll be a shortfall of water as large as the total amount used today. Adding to the population of the US has other undesirable effects; although it comprises less than 5 per cent of the world's population, the country generates 25 per cent of the world's CO_2 and 30 per cent of the world's wealth, and despite possessing just 3 per cent of the world's oil reserves it uses some 25 per cent of its energy resources.

Demographics

Full country name: United States of America

Capital city: Washington, DC

Population: 310m

Population density: 31 people per km² (80 per mi²). New York City has a population density of 10,300 per km² (26,700 per mi²).

Largest cities: There are nine cities with a population exceeding 1m – New York City (8.3m), Los Angeles (3.8m), Chicago (2.8m), Houston (2.2m), Philadelphia and Phoenix (1.5m), and Dallas, San Antonio and San Diego (1.3m).

Foreign population: 38m people were born outside the US. Of these, 52 per cent are from Latin America, 27 per cent from Asia and 15 per cent from Europe. The remainder are from Africa, Oceania – and Canada.

Largest expatriate groups: Mexicans, Puerto Ricans, Cubans

State religion: The US is a secular country – the First Amendment to the Constitution guarantees the right to freedom of religion.

Most popular religion: Just over 75 per cent of Americans are Christian, while other religions such as Judaism, Islam, Buddhism and Hinduism account for less than 4 per cent; some 14 per cent of people claim no religion.

A POTTED HISTORY

Although man has lived on American soil for thousands of years, there's a distinct line between the history of the country's indigenous people and modern recorded history – which was drawn late in the 15th century, when the continent was 'discovered' by Columbus. A colossal amount of change has taken place at a breathtaking pace in just over 500 years, the main events of which are listed below:

Indigenous People

ca 20,000 BC – Man begins migrating to the North American continent from Asia on a land bridge across the Bering Strait. This first wave of immigration by Asiatic people to the New World continues without pause until the route is cut off by a rise in sea levels at the end of the last Ice Age, some 11,000 years ago.

2500 BC – The demise of the hunter-gatherer as agriculture is developed.

1200 BC – Emergence of the first ancient cultural groups, such as the Anasazi in south-west America and the Adena in the east.

1000 AD – Arrival of the first Europeans as the Vikings, under Leif Ericson, establish a short-lived settlement on what is today Newfoundland.

From Early Settlers to the Birth of the United States

'Discovery' of the New World (1492) – Columbus sails west in search of a new route to the Far East. Instead, he lands at Hispaniola (now Haiti) and, shortly after (allegedly) lands on American soil. The following year, Pope Alexander VI 'gifts' the Americas to Spain, on the condition that the natives are converted to Christianity.

Authors' Note
The items in blue text in this section relate to immigration.

1500 – The first permanent European settlements are founded by the Spanish in modern-day Florida in St Augustine in 1565, which is the oldest continuously-occupied European established city and the oldest port in the continental US.

1607 – English settlers found the colony of Jamestown on an island off Virginia. It later relocates to Williamsburg.

1614 – Dutch settlers buy an island from local Indians for just 60 guilders and name it New Amsterdam. The British will later capture this prize and rename it New York.

1620 – Pilgrim Fathers aboard the ship *Mayflower* land at Cape Cod in Massachusetts and set up the Plymouth Colony, named after their port of departure in England. Other Puritan exiles follow, escaping religious persecution, to settle around Boston.

1692 – Witch hunts take place in Salem, New England and 19 'witches' are hanged.

1773 – The Boston Tea party. Protestors dump over 300 chests of tea into the sea in the first act of defiance by the new settlers against Britain. This action leads to the American Revolution.

1775-1783 – The American Revolution: The original 13 settlements gain their independence from the British Empire. What began as a protest against taxes escalates into armed conflict. The revolutionaries, or 'Patriots', are led by such notables as George Washington and Thomas Jefferson.

4th July 1776 – The Declaration of Independence is signed by the 13 colonies which become the first 'United States'.

1788 – The new US Constitution is ratified.

1789 – George Washington becomes the first President of the United States.

1790 – The federal government requires two years of residency for naturalization.

1791 – The Bill of Rights guarantees the freedom of the individual.

Slavery

From the early 17th century through to its abolition in 1865, slavery was legal and an accepted part of life. The vast majority of slaves were Africans, shipped to the west to be put to work farming cotton, sugar and tobacco, although some Native Americans were also held as slaves. A census in 1860 revealed that there were almost 4m slaves in the 15 states where the practice was still legal, accounting for a third of the total population. By the early 1800s, many Americans were uncomfortable with the idea of slavery and the best-selling book in the 19th century (after the Bible) was *Uncle Tom's Cabin*, by Harriet Beecher Stowe, which revealed the cruelty of slavery and helped fuel the abolitionists' cause.

19th Century

1803 – The Louisiana Purchase of 828,000mi² (2,140,000km²) of territory from France, for a sum of $15m, effectively triples the size of the nation at a stroke.

1808 – Congress bans the importation of slaves.

1815 – The first great wave of immigration begins, bringing 5m immigrants between 1815 and 1860.

1818 – Liverpool becomes the most popular port of departure for Irish and British immigrants.

1819 – Congress establishes reporting on immigration.

1820 – The US population is around 9.6m and some 151,000 new immigrants arrive in 1820 alone.

1825 – Great Britain decrees that England is overpopulated and repeals laws prohibiting emigration. The first group of Norwegian immigrants arrive.

1830-1900 – Settlers move westward, claiming land and control over the US, as the number of states rises to 45. This increases conflict with Native American tribes over land and resources, and spells disaster for the American buffalo (bison) which are hunted almost to extinction – up to 40m are slaughtered for their skins and meat and to prevent them from delaying trains on the ever expanding railroad network.

1845 – The potato crop fails in Ireland sparking the Potato Famine which kills one million and prompts almost 500,000 to immigrate to America over the next five years.

1845-47 – Crop failures throughout Europe lead to mortgage foreclosures, sending tens of thousands of the dispossessed to the US.

1846-1848 – Victory in the Mexican War sees the US acquire more land from its southern neighbor, including California.

1848 – German political refugees emigrate following the failure of a revolution.

1849 – The California Gold Rush sparks the first mass immigration from China.

1860 – Poland's religious and economic conditions prompt immigration of around 2m Poles by 1914.

1860 – Slavery abolitionist Abraham Lincoln is elected President.

1861 – The Southern Confederacy ratifies a new Constitution and elects Jefferson Davis as the first Confederate president. The Civil War begins with Confederate soldiers firing upon Fort Sumter.

1861-1865 – The American Civil War: America is divided as the Confederate States in the south under Jefferson Davis take on Lincoln's Unionists in the north. Victory for the north effectively abolishes slavery throughout the country, 60 years after its eradication in the northern states. Lincoln is assassinated in 1865.

1862 – The American Homestead Act allows any male over the age of 21 and the head of a family to claim up to 160 acres of land and improve it within five years or to purchase the land at a small fee.

1875 – First limitations on immigration. Residence permits required by Asians.

1880 – The US population is 50,155,783. More than 5.2m immigrants enter the country between 1880 and 1890.

1882 – Russia's (anti-Semitic) May Laws severely restrict the ability of Jewish citizens to live and work in Russia. The country's instability prompts over 3m Russians to immigrate to the US over three decades.

1882 – The Chinese Exclusion Act of 1882 suspends immigration of Chinese laborers under penalty of imprisonment and deportation.

Four American presidents have been assassinated – Lincoln, James A Garfield, William McKinley and John F Kennedy – and a further 12 have been the targets of unsuccessful assassinations attempts. The job should clearly come with a federal health warning!

1868 – Japanese laborers arrive in Hawaii to work in the sugar cane fields.

1876 – California Senate committee investigates the 'social, moral, and political effect of Chinese immigration.'

1877 – US Congress investigates the criminal influence of Chinese immigrants.

1880 – Italy's troubled economy, crop failures, and political climate begin the start of mass immigration with almost 4m Italian immigrants arriving in the US.

1890 – The last battle between the US and Native Americans takes place at Wounded Knee Creek, when a stand off between the Lakota Sioux and the 7th Cavalry Regiment ends in a bloodbath. More than 300 Sioux are killed. The incident, which is later recorded as a massacre, ends over 250 years of fighting – the Indian Wars – in which the settlers slowly but surely took the land from the Native Americans.

1890 – New York is home to as many Germans as Hamburg, Germany.

1890 – The states turn control of immigration over to the Federal Government. The US Congress appropriates $75,000 to build the first Federal immigration station on Ellis Island. While the new immigration station was under construction, the Barge Office on the Battery on the tip of Manhattan was used for immigration reception. During 1891, 405,664 immigrants, or about 80 per cent of the national total, were processed at the Barge Office.

1891 – The Bureau of Immigration is established. Congress adds health qualifications to immigration restrictions.

1892 – The federal immigration station opens on Ellis Island in New York and becomes the traditional door to America (replacing Castle Garden, Manhattan). That first day, three large ships were waiting to land and 700 immigrants passed through Ellis Island; in the first year, almost 450,000 immigrants passed through the Island. (By the time it closes

in 1954, some 12m individuals had passed through its doors.)

1894-96 – To escape Moslem massacres, Armenian Christians emigrate to the US.

1898 – Victory for the US in the Spanish-American War ends Spain's empire in the Caribbean and Pacific. The Treaty of Paris, marking the end of hostilities, hands control of Puerto Rico, the Philippines and Guam to America.

1900 – Congress establishes a civil government in Puerto Rico and the Jones Act grants US citizenship to island inhabitants. US citizens can travel freely between the mainland and the island without a passport.

1900 – The US population is 75,994,575. More than 3,687,000 immigrants were admitted in the previous ten years.

Early 20th Century

1906 – The Bureau of Immigration is established.

1907 – The US and Japan form a 'Gentleman's Agreement' in which Japan ceases to issue passports to laborers and the US agrees not to prohibit Japanese immigration.

1907 – The peak year at Ellis Island, with 1,004,756 immigrants received. The all-time daily high was on April 17, when 11,747 immigrants were processed.

1910 – The Mexican Revolution sends thousands to the US seeking employment.

1911 – The Dillingham Commission identifies Mexican laborers as the best solution to the southwest labor shortage. Mexicans are exempted from immigrant 'head taxes' set in 1903 and 1907.

1914-18 – World War I halts a period of mass migration to the US.

1917 – Having stayed neutral since the outbreak of the First World War in 1914, the US joins the Allied Powers. This is a pivotal point in their victory and the first hint of the power that the US will wield in the new century.

1920 – Alcohol is outlawed under the Prohibition Law, and the gangster culture grows out of the trade in illegal booze. In the same year, women get the vote.

1921 – Post-war immigration is quickly revived and 560,971 immigrants passed through Ellis Island. The first Immigration Quota Law passes the US Congress, adding to the administration problems at Ellis Island. It provided that the number of any European nationality entering in a given year could not exceed 3 per cent of foreign-born persons of that nationality who lived in the US in 1910. Nationality was to be determined by country of birth, and no more than 20 per cent of the annual quota of any nationality could be received in any given month. The total number of immigrants admissible under the system was set at nearly 358,000, but numerous classes were exempt

1922 – The Supreme Court rules in Ozawa v. United States that first-generation Japanese are ineligible

for citizenship and cannot apply for naturalization. The Japanese Immigration Act of 1924 (National Origins Act) establishes fixed quotas of national origin and eliminates Far East immigration. The Border Patrol is established.

1924 – Indigenous people finally gain the right to become American citizens.

1929 – The Wall Street Crash. The US stock market plummets and this, combined with a rise in debt and a series of crop failures, leads to the Great Depression, an economic slump affecting not just America but the whole world. President Franklin D. Roosevelt puts the US back on track in 1933, with his New Deal recovery program, creating public works and relegalizing alcohol.

1929 – Congress makes annual immigration quotas permanent.

The Dust Bowl

Between 1930 and 1936, drought and dust storms devastated the Great Plains region, from Kansas to Texas, as a result of bad farming techniques. This drove many farmers and sharecroppers off the land, exacerbating the effects of the Great Depression. Their dreadful plight was immortalized in John Steinbeck's novel, *The Grapes of Wrath*.

1940 – The Alien Registration Act calls for the registration and fingerprinting of all aliens. Approximately 5m aliens register.

1941 – A shock attack by the Japanese on Pearl Harbor in Hawaii pulls America into the Second World War. Ironically, the increased production for the war effort creates jobs and is a major factor in ending the economic slump.

1942 – Congress allows for the importation of agricultural workers from within North, Central and South America. The Bracero Program allows Mexican laborers to work in the US

1943 – The Magnuson Act of 1943 repeals the Chinese Exclusion Act of 1882, establishes quotas for Chinese immigrants, and makes them eligible for US citizenship.

1945 – Japan surrenders after the US drops atomic bombs on Hiroshima and Nagasaki.

Post-1945

1945 – The War Bride Act and the G.I. Fiancées Act allows the immigration of foreign-born wives, fiancé(e)s, husbands, and children of US armed forces personnel.

1947 – America turns against communism, and the Cold War begins.

1948 – The US admits those fleeing persecution in their home countries, allowing 205,000 refugees to enter within two years.

1950 – Senator Joseph McCarthy's crusade to root out communists in the government and public life spawns the word McCarthyism – the campaign lasts until 1954 and targets many famous people, including Charlie Chaplin and Orson Welles (most of whom weren't communists). Meanwhile, America is back at war, this time aiding the South Koreans against communist China and North Korea.

1952 – The Immigration and Nationality Act allows individuals of all

races to be eligible for naturalization. The act also reaffirms national origins quota system, limits immigration from the Eastern Hemisphere while leaving the Western Hemisphere unrestricted; establishes preferences for skilled workers and relatives of US citizens and permanent resident aliens; and tightens security and screening standards and procedures.

1953 – Congress amends the 1948 refugee policy to allow for the admission of 200,000 more refugees.

1954 – Ellis Island closes, marking an end to mass immigration.

1955 – A tired black woman called Rosa Parks refuses to give up her seat to a white passenger on an Alabama bus. Her actions are seen as the first act of non-violent civil disobedience, which will characterize the Civil Rights movement in the coming decade.

1959 – Fidel Castro's Cuban revolution prompts the mass exodus of more than 200,000 people to the US within three years.

1960 – Democrat John F. Kennedy is elected the 35th President of the United States.

1961 – The Cuban Refugee Program handles the influx of immigrants to Miami with 300,000 immigrants relocated across the US during the next two decades.

1961-1962 – America teeters on the brink of war with the Soviets after the Bay of Pigs invasion, a US-backed plan by Cuban exiles to invade the island, backfires. A communist missile base so close to US soil sends shivers down America's spine, until Kennedy forces the Soviets to back down.

1963 – Kennedy is assassinated in Dallas. His killer, Lee Harvey Oswald, is arrested but then shot dead by Jack Ruby.

1964-1973 – The Vietnam War: One of America's darkest 'hours'. The US steps into the Vietnam conflict, backing the republican

south against the communist north. Support at home soon dwindles as the bodies of young conscripts return home. The war claims 58,000 American lives, a small fraction of the 2m-plus Vietnamese (soldiers and civilians) who perish in the conflict.

1964 – The Civil Rights Act becomes law, promising to end racial discrimination.

1965 – The Immigration Act of 1965 abolishes the quota system in favor of new quota systems with 20,000 immigrants per country limits. Preference is given to the immediate families of immigrants and skilled workers.

1965 – The 'Freedom flight' airlifts begin for Cuban refugees assisting more than 260,000 people over the next eight years.

1966 – The Cuban Refugee Act allows more than 400,000 people to enter the US.

1968 – Civil Rights leader Martin Luther King is assassinated in Memphis, Tennessee, sparking race riots in more than 60 cities across America. Later that year, presidential candidate and the brother of the late John, Robert F. Kennedy, is assassinated by Palestinian Sirhan Sirhan.

1969 – America regains its pride vis-à-vis its Soviet rivals in the Space Race on July 20, when astronauts Neil Armstrong and Buzz Aldrin become the first men on the Moon. More than 700m viewers watch the event on television.

> 'That's one small step for man, one giant leap for mankind.' Neil Armstrong (astronaut, as he became the first man to set foot on the Moon in 1969)

1974 – A break-in at the Watergate hotel in Washington DC reveals the illegal activities of President Nixon's staff and, given the certainty of his impeachment (charging a public official with misconduct in office), Nixon resigns from office. Such is the impact of Watergate that the suffix '–gate' has been tagged to many subsequent political scandals.

1976 – Ellis Island is opened to the public for visits and over 50,000 people visit the island.

1979 – The hostage crisis at the American embassy in Iran marks the first downturn in relations between the US and the Islamic world. The hostages are finally released after 444 days, ironically on the day of President Ronald Reagan's inauguration in early 1981.

1980 – The Refugee Act redefines criteria and the procedures for admitting refugees.

1981-1989 – The Reagan Years: The Republican ex-movie star serves two terms as one of America's most popular and successful presidents, boosting the economy and presiding over the end of the Cold War. His ability to deflect criticism earns him the nickname the 'Teflon President'.

1986 – The Immigration Reform and Control Act (IRCA) legalizes illegal aliens residing in the US unlawfully since 1982.

1986 – The space shuttle Challenger explodes, killing all on board and halting the space program for two years.

1988 – George H. W. Bush, Reagan's vice-president, is elected President.

1991 – The Gulf War. A coalition force led by the US and mandated by the United Nations, liberates Kuwait after the small oil-rich state is invaded by Iraq.

1992 – Democrat Bill Clinton is elected president.

1993 – A truck bomb parked below the North Tower of New York's World Trade Center explodes, killing six and injuring over 1,000, in a chilling foretaste of the September 11 attacks eight years later.

1998 – Bill Clinton is the second serving American president to be impeached by the House of Representatives following evidence that he lied before a grand jury when he denied having sexual relations with White House intern Monica Lewinsky. Clinton is acquitted the following year and ends his term of office as one of America's most popular presidents.

The Waco 'siege' in 1993, and the Oklahoma City bombing in 1995, proved that terrorists and anti-government insurgents also exist on American soil and don't always have Arab surnames. Waco was the home of the Branch Davidian cult, whose leader David Koresh held out against the Federal Bureau of Investigation (FBI) for 51 days. The siege ended in a fire, in which 76 people died, including Koresh, following a controversial FBI assault on the compound. Two years later, an explosion at a government building in Oklahoma City killed 168 people – the worst ever act of terrorism on American soil – until 9/11. It was the work of ex-US soldier Timothy McVeigh, who claimed his anti-government feelings were fired by events at Waco and his experiences during the Gulf War. He was executed in 2001.

21st Century

2000 – George W Bush (Bush Junior) narrowly beats Al Gore in a disputed vote (who can ever forget the drama of the 'hanging chads') to snatch the presidency back for the Republicans.

9/11 – On September 11, 2001, terrorists hijack four passenger planes and succeed in flying them into both towers of the World Trade Center and the Pentagon; the fourth plane crashes in Pennsylvania. The death toll reaches 2,998 (not including the terrorists) with over 6,000 injured. The attacks are identified as the work of al-Qaeda, led by Osama Bin Laden. The US launches its war on terrorism to bring those who planned the attacks to justice, beginning with an offensive to liberate Afghanistan from the ruling Taliban.

2002 – Bush makes his 'axis of evil' speech, naming Iraq, Iran and North Korea among America's most dangerous enemies.

April-May 2003 – Iraq War: On suspicion that Iraq is producing weapons of mass destruction, Bush turns his attention to Saddam Hussein and orders an invasion of the country. The initial skirmishes are brief. American forces advance into Baghdad in early April, and on May 1, Bush declares that the main part of the war is over. However, the 'peace' will prove more elusive.

2004 – The US suffers fall-out from the Iraq war, amid allegations of mistreatment of prisoners at Guantánamo Bay, and Senate reports claiming that the US and its allies went into the war on 'flawed' information.

2005 – In August, hundreds of people are killed and thousands left homeless when Hurricane Katrina hits the Gulf Coast states. One of the worst-affected cities is New Orleans.

2006 – Plans to criminalize illegal immigrants lead to mass protests. Meanwhile, the only man to be charged in connection with the 9/11 attacks, Zacarias Moussaoui, is sentenced to life in prison. In November, the Democrats win control of the Senate and the House of Representatives in mid-term elections.

2007 – President Bush announces that more troops will be sent to increase security in Baghdad. Despite public protest, Congress later approves more funding for the ongoing conflict in Iraq.

August 2007 – Start of the 'credit crunch' as the sub-prime mortgage crisis leads to a downturn in the housing market, and raises the threat of US – and worldwide – recession.

2008 – Election year kicks off. John McCain wins the Republican ticket, while Hillary Clinton and Barack Obama battle to represent the Democrats, boosting the prospect of the first female or black American president.

March 2008 – The 4,000th American soldier is killed in Iraq. Estimates of the death toll among Iraqi civilians are over 100,000.

June 2008 – Barack Obama is declared the Democrats' presidential candidate.

September 2008 – The credit crunch bites hard and the US faces its biggest financial crisis since the Great Depression of the '30s, as major investment bank Lehman Brothers collapses and other large US financial institutions are taken over by rivals. The government bails out the bankers with a $700bn rescue plan, but the crisis is far from over.

November 2008 – Barack Obama is elected the 44th President and the first African-American to hold the post.

2009 – Congress approves a $787bn stimulus package in the face of strong opposition from Republicans.

2010 – Democrats in the House of Representatives narrowly vote to adopt the Senate version of health care reform, thus sidestepping Republican opposition in the Senate.

AMERICA TODAY & TOMORROW

In June 2010, the US population was almost 310m (source: population clock – see box), which is approximately 4.5 per cent of the world's population. The US is an urbanized society, with over 80 per cent of people living in cities and suburbs (the worldwide urban rate is around 50 per cent). California and Texas are the most populous states with 37m and 25m respectively (2009 estimates): the mean center of the US population has consistently shifted westward and southward with the influx of immigrants from Mexico and South America.

Population Clock

The US Census Bureau calculates a 'Population Clock' (🖥 www.census.gov/population/www/popclockus.html) based on the latest births, deaths and immigration statistics. In June 2010, it was estimated that there was:

One birth every...	7 seconds
One death every...	13 seconds
One international migrant every...	36 seconds
A net gain of one person every...	11 seconds

Population Breakdown by Ancestry

Ancestry is a broad concept that can mean different things to different people. The Census Bureau (🖥 www.census.gov) defines ancestry as a person's ethnic origin, heritage, descent, or 'roots', which may reflect their place of birth, the place of birth of their parents or ancestors, and ethnic identities that have evolved within the US. Many people list more than one area of ancestry. The figures in the table below are from the 2000 census, when around 500 different ancestries were reported.

Most common ancestries in the United States

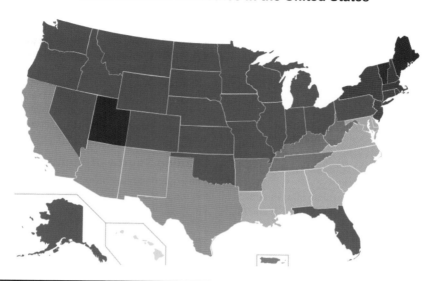

Nationality	Percentage of Population
German	15.2
African American	12.9
Irish	10.9
English	8.7
Mexican	7.3
Italian	5.6
French	3.9
Hispanic	3.6
Polish	3.2
Scottish	1.7
Dutch	1.6
Norwegian	1.6
Native American	1.5
Swedish	1.4
Puerto Rican	1.2
Russian	0.9
Chinese	0.9

Source: 2000 census

Map Key

- German
- American
- Mexican
- Irish
- African
- Italian
- English
- Japanese
- Puerto Rican

To put the figures in the table into perspective, almost 11 per cent of the US population in 2000 were of Irish ancestry, which – based on the 2010 US population of 310m – amounts to some 31m people, compared with the population of Ireland, which is just 6.2m people (4.5m in Eire and 1.7m in Northern Ireland). The number of Americans of German ancestry in 2000 in New York City alone, matched the population of Hamburg in 1890!

The US Census (🖳 www.census.gov), which is conducted every ten years, is the most authoritative source of information about the US population. The information in this book is based on the 2000 census (a new census was conducted in 2010, but the results were unknown at the time of going to press).

Racial & Ethnic Breakdown

The US is a diverse country, both racially and ethnically, where six main racial groups are recognized: White, American Indian and Alaska Native, Asian, Black or African American, Native Hawaiian and Other Pacific Islander. People of mixed race (two or more races) are referred to as 'Some

Racial Group	Percentage of Population (2008)
White (not including Hispanic and Latino Americans)	75
Hispanic	15.4
African-American	12.4
Some other race alone	4.9
Asian alone	4.4
Two or more races	2.3
Native American*	0.8
Native Hawaiian/Pacific	0.14

* Native Indian or Alaskan Native alone

Source: US Census Bureau

other race', which is also used in the census and other surveys, but isn't official. Americans are also classified as 'Hispanic or Latino', which identifies Hispanic and Latino Americans as a racially diverse ethnicity that comprises the largest minority group in the nation.

The figures in the table (left) add up to more than 100 per cent because Hispanic and Latino Americans are distributed among all the races, and are also listed as an ethnic category, resulting in a double count.

Leading Source of Migrants

The countries that currently (2010) provide the most immigrants are Mexico, China, the Philippines, India, Vietnam, Cuba, El Salvador, the Dominican Republic, Canada and South Korea. Other leading countries include refugees from Iraq and Afghanistan, while in 2005, more people (nearly 100,000) from Muslim countries became legal permanent residents than in any year in the previous two decades.

ILLEGAL IMMIGRATION

The Illegal immigrant population – that is anyone who enters the US illegally or overstays their visa or visa waiver – in the US in 2008 was estimated by the Center for Immigration Studies (🖳 http://cis.org) to be around 11m people, down from 12.5 million people in 2007. Other estimates are much higher and put the figure at somewhere between 15 and 20 million (not surprisingly, those opposed to immigration make the highest estimates).

According to a Pew Hispanic Center (🖳 http://pewresearch.org) report, in 2005 almost 60 per cent of illegal immigrants were from Mexico; 24 per cent were from other Latin American countries, primarily from Central America; 9 per cent were from Asia; 6 per cent from Europe; and 4 per cent from the rest of the world.

Illegal immigrants continue to outpace the number of legal immigrants – a trend that's held steady since the '90s. While the majority of illegal immigrants continue to concentrate in places with existing large communities of Hispanics, increasingly illegal immigrants are settling throughout the rest of the country.

Consequences of Illegal Immigration

It's always been easy – and widespread practise – for people to blame the problems in their society on the most recent wave of immigrants. For example, in 1876 the Californian Senate looked into the social, moral, and political effect of Chinese immigration, and the following year Congress investigated the criminal influence of Chinese immigrants.

Folklore has it that present day US illegal Hispanic immigrants create a huge rise in the crime rate, although this has been contradicted by a number of recent academic studies which have shown that in fact illegal immigrants are four times **less** likely to be jailed than members of the general population.

The studies did, however, show that the children of immigrants are more likely to turn to crime, especially gang-related behavior, which is attributed to immigrants being less tolerant of their poverty and poor living conditions than their parents. According to Bureau of Justice statistics, a few years ago 4 per cent of Hispanic men in their twenties and thirties were in prison or jail, compared with less than 2 per cent of white men.

The banking crisis of 2007 is generally put down to the inability of the US banking industry to weather the collapse of the sub-prime mortgage market – loans made to 'poor' people irrespective of their ability to repay the money. Many of these loans were made to Hispanic borrowers and there were claims in the press, subsequently refuted, that many of them had been made to illegal

immigrants, which would have made them ultimately responsible for the worldwide economic recession.

Until recently, illegal workers have been unofficially tolerated, as they did poorly paid domestic jobs as gardeners and cleaners or unskilled farm work such as fruit picking, which are shunned by most Americans. However, in a time of recession some American-born workers resent illegal workers for taking 'their' jobs and driving down wages, although many economists believe that, on the contrary, they enable the creation of a whole new level of jobs that otherwise wouldn't exist. The current state of affairs – that is mass illegal immigration – also exploits the illegals themselves, who often work for well below the minimum wage in appalling conditions, without social security benefits or any job security. (Not surprisingly illegals are beloved by employers and families who employ domestics.)

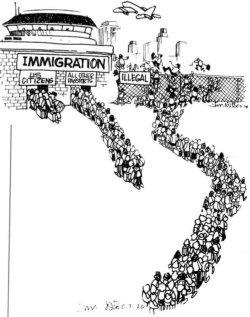

Many analysts believe that costs, delays, and inefficiencies in processing visa applications contributes to the number of illegal immigrants. In mid-2010, there was a backlog of well over one million Green Card applications, with the waiting times for some categories over ten years.

Plans to Curb Illegal Immigration

Stricter enforcement of the borders around cities has failed to significantly curb illegal immigration, instead pushing the flow into more remote regions and increasing the cost to taxpayers. In 2006, the US began construction of a controversial barrier (also know as the border fence or border wall) along the US-Mexico border designed to prevent illegal movement across the border. In January 2010, the barrier (21ft/6.4m high) had been completed from San Diego (California) to Yuma (Arizona), from where it continues into Texas. At the same time as constructing the barrier, the US planned to grant an 'earned path to citizenship' (amnesty – see 🖥 www.usamnesty.org) to the approx. 12m illegal aliens in the US, although there's a lot of opposition and it has not yet been passed in mid-2010.

Opponents claim the barriers are an ineffective deterrent and jeopardize the health and safety of those seeking illegal entry into the US, as well as destroy animal habitat, prevent animals from reaching water, disturb animal migration patterns, and otherwise damage the environment.

In a summit of North American Leaders in 2009, President Obama gave his opinion on the direction immigration reform should take: "With respect to immigration reform, I continue to believe that it is also in the long-term interests of the United States. We have a broken immigration system. Nobody denies it. And if we continue on the path we're on, we will continue to have tensions with our Mexican neighbors; we will continue to have people crossing the borders in a way that is dangerous for them and unfair for those who are applying legally to immigrate. We're going to continue to have employers who are exploiting workers because they're not within a legal system, and so oftentimes are receiving less than the minimum wage, or don't have overtime, or are being abused in other ways. That's going to depress US wages. It's causing ongoing tensions inside the United States. It's not fair and it's not right, and we're going to change it."

President Obama's proposal is to not to give a blanket instant pardon to illegal workers in the US, but to create a way that would enable them to eventually earn citizenship: they would be sent to the back of the queue for entering illegally, but at least they would be in the queue. This policy would be allied with strengthened immigration checks and border security.

New Arizona Law

Arizona probably has the greatest proportion of illegal workers, where it's estimated that 10 per cent of the population are illegal Latino workers, for whom the state has become the main entry point to the US. In April 2010, the Governor (Jan Brewer) enacted some of the fiercest anti-immigration laws yet introduced in the US in the hope of stemming the flood of illegals across the vast desert border with Mexico.

The new laws oblige people to carry proof of their legal status and permit the police to detain anyone suspected of being in the US illegally (historically Americans have been free to go about their business without any form of ID). The clampdown approaches the farcical when it's denied that the authorities will use racial profiling to select people to check (it's suspected that people with blonde hair won't be overburdened by police stop and searches). Although the majority of Arizona residents supported these measures, at the time of going to press they were facing opposition from civil rights activists and President Obama alike. Opponents have called it an open invitation for harassment and discrimination against Hispanics, irrespective of their status.

POPULATION TRENDS

The fertility rate in the US in 2009 was estimated to be 2.05 children per woman, which is roughly the replacement level. The US population growth rate is among the highest in industrialized countries, as the vast majority of Western countries have below-replacement fertility rates, while the US also has higher levels of immigration. Accordingly, the US Census Bureau (🖳 www.census.gov) estimated a population increase of between 0.85 and 0.89 per cent for the 12 months ending in 2009, which although high by industrialized country standards is below the world average annual rate of 1.19 per cent. In comparison, in most European countries – especially Germany, Russia, Italy and Greece – and in Asian countries such as Japan and South Korea, the population is slowly declining.

In 2007, people aged under 20 made up over a quarter of the US population and those aged 65 and over comprised one-eighth, with the average age almost 37. Racially, the US has a majority white population, with minorities comprising just over one-third of the total (102.5m in 2007);

Hispanic and Latino Americans and African Americans are the largest minority groups. The average Hispanic woman gives birth to three children in her lifetime, and the Census Bureau projects that by 2050, 25 per cent of the population will be of Hispanic descent.

Currently, population growth in the US is fastest among minorities as a whole, and the Census Bureau estimated in 2005 that 45 per cent of American children under the age of 5 belonged to minority groups and Hispanic and Latino Americans accounted for almost half (1.4m) of the national population growth of 2.9m between July 1, 2005, and July 1, 2006. Immigrants and their US-born descendants are expected to provide most of the US population gains in the coming ahead.

The American population more than tripled during the 20th century, from around 76m in 1900 to 281m in 2000. It reached the 200m mark in 1967 and the 300m milestone on October 17, 2006.

The Census Bureau projects a US population of 439m in 2050, while the United Nations projects a total of 402m: either way immigrants and their US-born descendants are expected to provide most of the US population gains in the decades ahead.

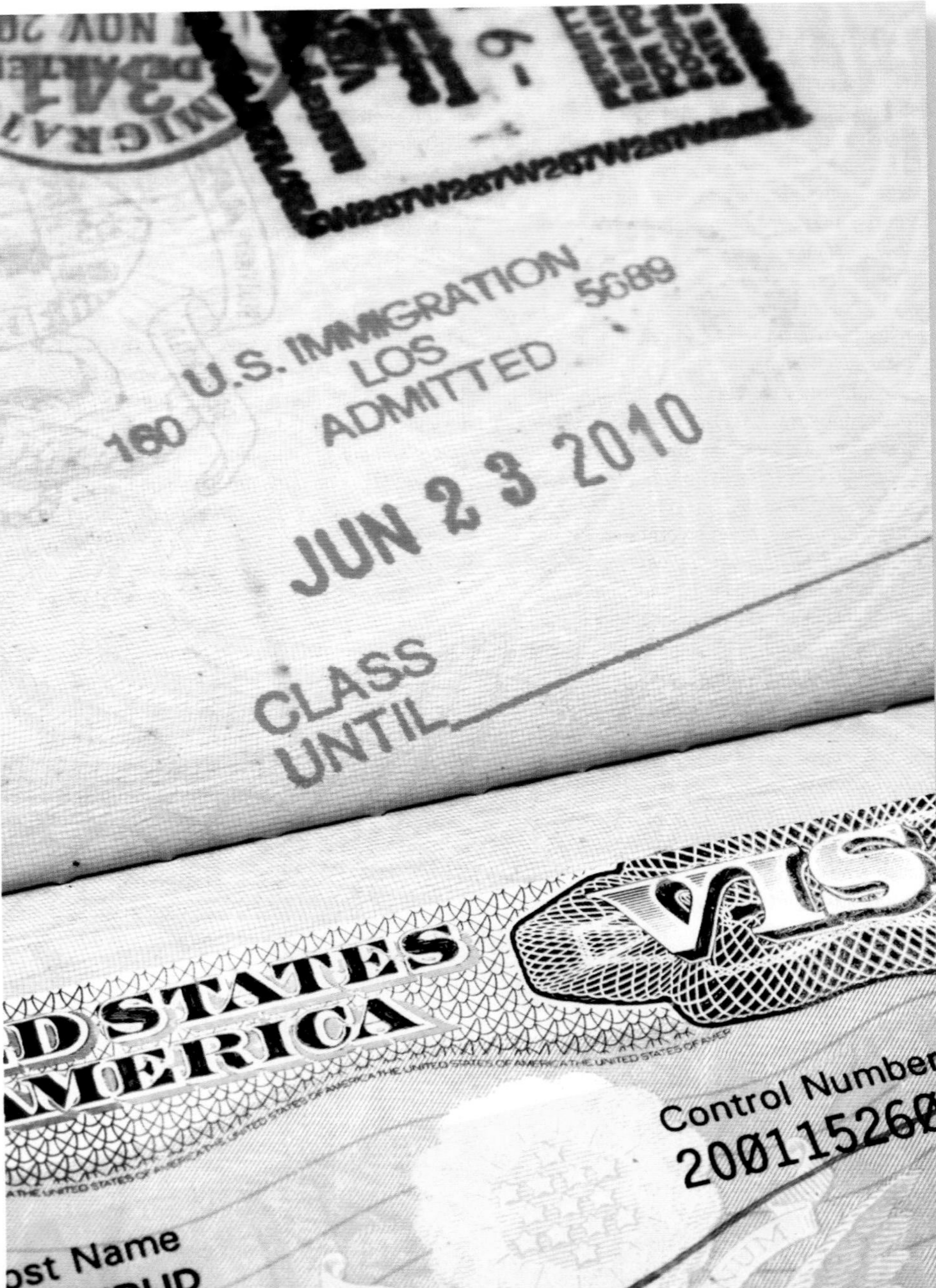

160 U.S. IMMIGRATION 5689
LOS
ADMITTED

JUN 2 3 2010

CLASS
UNTIL

D STATES VIS
MERICA

Control Number
200115260

ost Name
HMDLIR

3.
WHICH VISA?

With the exception of visitors who qualify for the Visa Waiver Program (see page 120), all non-resident foreigners wishing to enter the US require a visa, even those in transit to another country. The US issues a bewildering range of visas, which are broadly divided into immigrant (permanent resident) and nonimmigrant (temporary resident) visas.

An immigrant visa gives you the right to travel to the US, to live and work there (and change jobs freely) on a permanent basis, with the possibility of qualifying for US citizenship after five years' residence. A nonimmigrant visa allows you to travel to the US on a temporary basis, e.g. from six months to five years, and in certain cases to accept employment. Only holders of visas permitting employment can work in the US. Holders of other categories of visa may not accept employment, even informal work in a household as a nanny, au pair or mother's helper. Work permits aren't issued, as the appropriate visa serves the same purpose.

A visa doesn't give you the right to enter the US, only to travel there for a specified purpose. This is because visas are issued by the consular section of the Department of State, which has the authority only to pre-approve foreigners for travel, whereas immigration is handled by Customs and Border Protection.

Possession of a visa isn't a guarantee of entry into the US. Anyone who doesn't comply with immigration requirements (including being able to prove that their visit is in compliance with the terms of their visa) can be fined, jailed or deported. In general, the US attempts to restrict the entry of 'undesirables', i.e. anyone who is a threat to the health, welfare or security of the US.

Your passport must usually be valid for a minimum of six months after the termination of your planned stay; if it's close to its expiry date you should renew it before traveling to the US. (Many countries automatically extend passport validity for an additional six months after expiration – see 🖳 www.state.gov/documents/organization/104770.pdf.)

US GOVERNMENT DEPARTMENTS

For many years, the US immigration and naturalization laws were enforced by the Immigration and Naturalization Service (INS) of the US Department of Justice. After the 2001 terrorist attacks, however, the Department of Homeland Security (DHS) was created to coordinate the various services involved in national security.

On March 1, 2003, the DHS created three new departments, which together provide the basic governmental framework for regulating the flow of visitors, workers and immigrants into the US:

◆ Customs and Border Protection (CBP, 🖳 www.cbp.gov): patrols the borders and entry points; CBP is responsible for the admission of all people seeking entry into the US, and for determining the length of their authorized stay.

♦ US Citizenship and Immigration Services (USCIS, ☎ 1-800-357-2099, 🖳 www.uscis.gov): determines a person's immigration status and issues permits. The USCIS is responsible for the approval of all immigrant and nonimmigrant petitions, the authorization of permission to work in the US, the issue of extensions of stay, and the change or adjustment of a person's status while he's in the US (and much more).

♦ Immigration and Customs Enforcement (ICE, 🖳 www.ice.gov): ICE is responsible for immigration-related investigations, detentions, deportation, and the new registration system for students and exchange visitors.

Once foreigners are admitted into the country by the CBP, it's the job of the USCIS and the ICE to register and track them, ensure that they comply with the terms of their visas, and (especially) that they leave the US when their visa expires. Like the old INS, the USCIS maintains four regional service centers and over 60 local offices throughout the US.

USCIS Service Centers

When you or someone in the US needs to lodge a petition, or you need to make an application regarding an existing visa, e.g. to extend a visa or apply for a change of status, you must apply to the USCIS service center with jurisdiction over the state where you're resident or are staying temporarily. The USCIS has four service centers serving different states, as shown below:

♦ **California:** Arizona, California, Guam, Hawaii and Nevada.

♦ **Nebraska:** Alaska, Colorado, Idaho, Illinois, Indiana, Iowa, Kansas, Michigan, Minnesota, Missouri, Montana, Nebraska, North Dakota, Ohio, Oregon, South Dakota, Utah, Washington, Wisconsin and Wyoming.

♦ **Texas:** Alabama, Arkansas, Florida, Georgia, Kentucky, Louisiana, Mississippi, New Mexico, North Carolina, Oklahoma, South Carolina, Tennessee and Texas.

♦ **Vermont:** Connecticut. Delaware, District of Columbia, Maine, Maryland, Massachusetts, New Hampshire, New Jersey, New York, Pennsylvania, Puerto Rico, Rhode Island, Vermont, Virgin Islands, Virginia and West Virginia.

For a list of the applications and petitions accepted by service centers, see the USCIS website (🖳 www.uscis.gov). Note that all service centers with the exception of Vermont use separate box numbers and zip codes – listed on the USCIS website – for different forms.

The addresses shown below are generally for overnight delivery (Federal Express, UPS, etc.) or bonded courier delivery **only**.

♦ **California:** USCIS, California Service Center, 24000 Avila Road, 2nd Floor, Room 2326, Laguna Niguel, CA 92677.

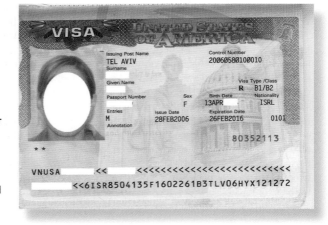

- **Nebraska:** USCIS, Nebraska Service Center, 850 S Street, Lincoln, NE 68508.

- **Texas: USCIS, Texas Service Center**, 4141 St. Augustine Road, Dallas, TX 75227.

- **Vermont:** USCIS, Vermont Service Center, 30 Houghton Street, St. Albans, VT 05478-2399.

Information

There's a wealth of information about US immigration and visas, including numerous websites and books (although few are as comprehensive and up-to-date as this one!). Before making any plans to travel to the US – for whatever reason – you should investigate the visa requirements (and possibilities if you wish to live or work there) via official websites such as the Bureau of Consular Affairs (🖳 http://travel.state. gov), the US Citizenship and Immigration Services (🖳 www.uscis.gov), the US Department of Homeland Security (🖳 www.dhs.gov) and the Transport Security Administration (🖳 www.tsa.gov).

US embassies (see 🖳 www.usembassy. gov), such as the US embassy in London, UK (🖳 www.usembassy.org.uk), also provide a wealth of information, much of which is available online, including up-to-the-minute information on visa issues affecting travelers to the US. Many US embassy websites also contain a handy 'Visa Wizard' feature to help you decide which visa to apply for. Note, however, that not all US consular posts issue visas.

There's also a plethora of commercial visa websites, most of which contain useful information, although many also contain misleading or even false information (some are deliberately designed to look like official website). **Always double check any information you obtain from an unofficial source with a US government department.**

> ⚠ Caution
>
> Many unofficial websites try to sell you information that you can obtain free from official websites (those ending in '.gov') such as ESTA approval (see page 123), entry into the Green Card Lottery (officially called Diversity Immigrants – see page 204) and official forms.

HEALTH REQUIREMENTS

Travelers to the US who've been afflicted with a disease of public health significance; a mental disorder associated with a display of harmful behavior; or are a drug abuser or addict may be ineligible to receive a visa. If you're ineligible, you'll require a waiver from the US Department of Homeland Security and will need to submit a letter from a doctor, specialist and/or other professional person who's familiar with your case.

Medical conditions which may prevent travel to the US include communicable diseases of public health significance such as Chancroid, Gonorrhea, Granuloma inguinale, Human Immunodeficiency Virus (HIV) infection; infectious Leprosy, Lymphogranuloma venereum, infectious stage Syphilis and active Tuberculosis. In such cases, you must apply for a visa and aren't eligible to travel visa-free under the Visa Waiver Program.

In addition, travelers with a physical or mental disorder and a history of behavior associated with the disorder that may pose or has posed a threat to their property, safety or welfare or that of others, and those where the behavior is likely to recur or lead to other harmful behavior, are also required to apply for visa.

If you're HIV-positive and seeking to travel to the US, you usually require a waiver of ineligibility, with the possible exception of B-1/B-2 visa applicants seeking to enter the US for less than 30 days. If you've have been arrested or convicted for driving under the influence of alcohol (DUI), you may be required to undergo a medical examination by a US government (USG) panel physician following your formal visa interview.

TYPES OF VISAS

Anyone who isn't eligible to enter the US visa-free under the Visa Waiver Program (see **Chapter 4**), is exempt from the visa requirement or whose registration has been denied under ESTA (see page 123), requires a visa to enter the US. (A visa consists of a stamp in your passport or a label glued to a page of you passport.) There are two basic types of US visas:

♦ A **nonimmigrant visa** (see below) is required for a temporary stay (with a time limit), which applies to visitors and anyone who isn't planning to become a permanent resident.

♦ An **immigrant visa** (see page 112) is for permanent residence without any time limitation.

The type and category of visa you require is based on the purpose of your travel.

Apart from visitors exempted under the Visa Waiver Program, certain visitors aren't required to obtain a visa, including Canadian citizens with a valid Canadian passport (with certain exceptions) and Bermuda nationals (who are citizens of the British Overseas Territories of Bermuda) with a valid Government of Bermuda passport. Citizens and permanent residents of Mexico generally must have a nonimmigrant visa or a Border Crossing Card (BCC – also known as a 'laser visa'). The BCC (form DSP-150) is a biometric, machine readable card that's a combined visitor B1-B2 visa and BCC.

Travelers born in the US, naturalized citizens and those holding dual citizenship with the US must enter and depart the US using their American passports.

☑ SURVIVAL TIP

If you need a visa to visit the US, you should apply well in advance of your trip and shouldn't finalize your travel plans or buy a non-refundable ticket until your visa has been issued.

NONIMMIGRANT VISAS

A nonimmigrant visa (there's no hyphen after 'non' in US English) gives a person the right to come to the US temporarily, e.g. from a few days up to five years, and in certain cases to work, study or carry out some other activity. There are over 20 categories (see below) of nonimmigrant visa and many sub-categories, many of which are valid for a limited or maximum period, often at the discretion of the immigration officer at the port of entry. There's no limit to the number of nonimmigrant visas issued each year.

The validity of visas varies considerably, e.g. from 1 to 120 months (e.g. tourist visas), and not all visas allow multiple entries (some allow only a single entry). Most nonimmigrant visas are of the multiple-entry type, allowing you to enter and leave the US as often as you wish during the visa's validity period. However, the period for which you're allowed to remain in the US may be affected by the validity of your passport. For example, for certain nationalities, if you have a nonimmigrant visa that's valid for three years, but your passport is valid for only three months, you're admitted for just three months. The visa's validity period is recorded on your I-94 (Arrival-Departure Record).

If you have a valid nonimmigrant visa and obtain a new passport, you should retain your old passport and take it with you when traveling to the US, as the visa

will remain valid. You must never remove a visa from the old passport, as this invalidates it.

The application fee for all nonimmigrant visas is $131. There may also be a visa issue fee, which is based on reciprocity, i.e. if your country of citizenship imposes a visa fee for US citizens, then the US will also impose a fee. For more information, see **Visa Fees** on page 218.

Many nonimmigrant visas don't allow you to adjust status to an immigrant (permanent resident) visa.

A visa is issued by a US embassy or consulate and entitles the holder to travel to the US and apply for admission; it **doesn't** in itself guarantee entry. An immigration inspector at the port of entry determines a visa holder's eligibility for admission into the US.

Questions about filing a petition, qualifications for various classifications, or conditions and limitations on employment should be made by the prospective employer or agent in the US to the nearest USCIS office. Questions about filing a visa application at a consular section abroad should be addressed to the appropriate consular office abroad. US Immigration law is highly complex and it's often advisable to seek the advice of a competent immigration lawyer (lawyers in the US are

known as attorneys). Inquiries about visa cases in progress overseas should be made to the appropriate US embassy or consulate handling the case.

Petitions

Some nonimmigrant visas (see table), for example certain work visas or to get married in the US, require a petition to be filed by someone in the US, known as the petitioner. The petition is filed by the prospective employer, US citizen or resident fiancé(e). When the petition has been approved, you must apply obtain a visa (see below) before traveling to the US.

See also **Petitions** on page 207.

Petition-based Visas	
Category	**Application**
H	temporary workers and trainees
L	intra-company transferees (except for companies with an approved blanket petition)
O	aliens with extraordinary ability
P	athletes, artists and entertainers
Q	international cultural exchange visitors
R	religious occupations

Nonimmigrant Visa Applications

All applicants for nonimmigrant visas filing at a US embassy or consulate (i.e. outside the US) must complete a for DS-160 (Nonimmigrant Visa Application), which can be done on a paper form that can be downloaded or obtained from a US embassy, or completed online (see below).

> ### ☑ SURVIVAL TIP
>
> Note that the form DS-156 (and forms DS-157 and DS-158) has now been replaced by form DS-160 (Nonimmigrant Visa Electronic Application) in many countries, although the information required remains the same.

The questions are fairly straightforward, although you should be careful to answer the questions honestly, as US embassies and consulates maintain meticulous records and can easily check whether you've previously had a visa refused or cancelled. Most visa applicants now require an interview with a consular visa official, although it may last just a few minutes if everything is in order.

There are also supplementary forms for certain students, exchange program participants and potential investors. Keep a copy of the forms for your own records and bring them with you when entering the US. A separate form must be completed for each visa applicant, including your spouse and children. There's a fee for a nonimmigrant visa, currently $131, which is usually payable in the local currency.

The documentation required to support an application for a nonimmigrant visa varies according to the category. For certain categories, e.g. tourist, student and exchange visitor, you should be prepared to provide proof that you intend to return to your country of residence after your legal stay in the US has ended. Certain nonimmigrant visas – for example those entitling you to work or get married in the US – require a petition (see above) to be filed by someone in the US, known as the petitioner. If you're accompanied by your spouse and children, you may need to provide a marriage certificate and a birth certificate for each child, as well as passports for your spouse and children, plus a number of passport-size photographs (see below).

Children under the age of 14 and adults aged 80 may be eligible to apply for a visa by courier. Applicants must be physically present in the country where they're applying and must use the embassy appointed courier company. Note that a consular officer reserves the right to request that you appear in person for an interview, after reviewing the visa application.

Applicants eligible to submit their visa application by courier or those who have been notified that they're required to submit additional documents for the application to be processed, are required to use the services of the embassy's appointed courier company. Before contacting the courier company, you should ensure that you're in possession of all the documents and forms required to apply for a visa.

Applicants who check 'yes' on the visa application form to any of the questions regarding specific categories of people who may be inadmissible to the US are required to provide explanatory documentation. Examples include a police certificate issued within six months of the date of the visa interview, previous visas, and immigration or medical records.

When applying for certain nonimmigrant visas, it's recommended that you use an immigration lawyer.

Online Electronic Visa Applications

The new DS-160 Nonimmigrant Visa Electronic Application replaced the previous nonimmigrant application forms (e.g. DS-156, 157 and 158) and other related forms, such as the DS-156E and 156K from 2009. In summer

2010, when this book went to press, most countries were using the DS-160 form. Check with your nearest US embassy or consulate.

The new DS-160 is a fully integrated online application form that's used to collect the necessary application information for nonimmigrant visas. It's submitted electronically to the Department of State via the Internet and consular officers use the information to process the visa application, combined with a personal interview, to determine your eligibility for a nonimmigrant visa.

For further information, see the US Department of State, Consular Electronic Application Center website (🖥 https://ceac. state.gov/genniv).

Visa Photographs

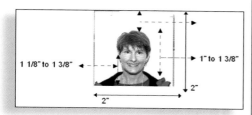

1 1/8" to 1 3/8"   1" to 1 3/8"   2"   2"

All applications for a nonimmigrant visa must be submitted with one or more photographs (check with your nearest US embassy or consulate how many are required). The US requirements for 'passport photographs' are somewhat different from those for other countries. For example, you cannot use photographs taken in DIY booths but must go to a photographer who's familiar with the requirements (see 🖥 http:// travel.state.gov/passport/guide/guide_2081.html).

Visas photos must meet the following specifications:

♦ They must have been taken within the last six months;

♦ They measure 2in (5cm) square, with the head centered in the frame. The head (measured from the top of the hair to the bottom of the chin) should measure between 1 & 1 3/8in (25mm to 35mm) with the eye level between 1 & 1/8in to 1 & 3/8in (28mm and 35 mm) from the bottom of the photograph (see photo);

♦ They must be in color against a white or off-white background. Photographs taken in front of busy, patterned or dark backgrounds aren't acceptable;

♦ They must be unmounted, full face, with the face covering around 50 per cent of the area of the photograph. In general, the head of the applicant, including both the face and hair, should be shown from the crown of the head to the tip of the chin on top and bottom, and from hair-line side-to-side. It's preferable that the ears are exposed;

♦ Head coverings and hats are only acceptable due to religious beliefs, and even then they may not cover any portion of the applicant's face.

♦ Sunglasses or other wear which detracts from the face aren't acceptable unless they're required for medical reasons (an eye patch, for example);

♦ A photograph depicting a person wearing a traditional facemask or veil that doesn't permit adequate identification isn't acceptable.

♦ Photos of military, airline, or other personnel wearing hats aren't acceptable, neither are wearing tribal, national costume or other headgear that isn't specifically religious in nature.

♦ Head-coverings are acceptable only when the applicant's face is completely exposed.

♦ Digitally reproduced photographs must be reproduced without discernible pixels or dot patterns. Photocopied photographs aren't accepted.

♦ A photo may contain a small (one quarter inch) white border on one side.

You need to staple or glue a photograph to the form DS-160 in the designated space. If the photograph is stapled, the staple should be placed as far away as possible from the applicant's face. If you apply online (🖥 https://ceac.state.

gov/genniv) you must provide an electronic copy of your photo (you can test your photo prior to beginning the application).

Visa Application Forms

Most visa application forms listed are available from embassy websites (and from the US Bureau of Consular Affairs' website (⌨ www.forms.gov) in PDF format. You need Adobe Acrobat Reader to view them, which can be downloaded free (see ⌨ http://get.adobe.com/uk/reader).

For a complete list of immigration forms, see **Appendix E**.

Nonimmigrant Visa Application Forms

Form Number	Description
DS-156	Nonimmigrant Visa Application
DS-156e	Supplemental Application for Treaty Traders & Investors
DS-156k	Supplemental Application for K Visa Applicants
DS-157	Supplemental Nonimmigrant Visa Application
DS-158	Contact Information and Work History For Nonimmigrant Visa Applicant
DS-160	Web-based Nonimmigrant Visa Application
DS-230-I Part 1	Biographic Data Form for Immigrant and K Visa Applicants
DS-2000	Evidence Which May Be Presented to Meet the Public Charge Provisions of the Law by Applicants for a K Visa
DS-2001	Applicant's Declaration of Qualification for Immigrant Visa Interview
G-325A	USCIS Biographic Information
I-129F	Petition for Alien Fiancé(e) & K-3 Visa Applicant
I-130	Petition for Alien Relative
I-134	Affidavit of Support for K Visa Applicants
I-140	USCIS Petition for Employment Immigrants
I-360	Petition for Amerasian, Widow(er) or Special Immigrants
I-526	Immigrant Petition for Alien Entrepreneur
I-765	Application for Employment Authorization
I-864	Affidavit of Support Package for Family Based Immigrant Visa Applicants
IV-15K	Document Checklist for K Visa Applicants
IV-18	Immigrant Visa Appointment Letter
IV-19	Fiancée Visa Appointment Letter
NIV-30a	Credit Card Payment Form for Visa Issuance Fee
MIV-30b	Credit Card Payment Form for MRV Fee by Mail
NIV-30c	Credit Card Payment Form for I-601 IV waiver applications
NIV-30d	Credit Card Payment Form for DS-117
NIV-30ins	Credit Card Payment Form for Immigrant Visa Petition, form I-130
VCU-01	Personal Data Sheet

Visa Interviews

With a few exceptions (see box), nonimmigrant visa applicants aged 14 to 79 must make an appointment for an interview with a US consular officer. **Embassies don't accept walk-in applications.** Applicants under the age of 14 and 80 or over may be eligible to apply for a visa through an embassy approved courier service.

Interview Exceptions

Applicants aged 14 to 79 applying for diplomatic (A-1 & A-2), international organization (G-1, G-2, G-3, G-4,) or NATO 1, 2, 3, 4, 5, & 6 visas aren't required to appear in person for an interview with a consular officer. C-3 visa applicants who are accredited officials are also exempt from the interview process.

An appointment for an interview must be scheduled by telephoning your nearest US embassy or consulate's operator assisted information service, which is usually available Monday to Saturdays (business hours vary – contact your nearest embassy or consulate for information). Family or married couples applying for visas at the same time may schedule one appointment per family or couple. A parent can apply on behalf of a child aged under 14, who doesn't need to attend an interview. **If the interview appointment date provided isn't early enough for your intended travel, you can request an expedited appointment.**

The visa application fee (see page 218) must be paid by credit or debit card (e.g. Visa, MasterCard or American Express) when scheduling an interview, when you must also provide a local address. Confirmation of the appointment date and time will be sent by email, together with a receipt for the MRV (machine readable visa) application fee. You'll be required to present the nonimmigrant visa interview confirmation letter and copy of the MRV fee receipt on the day of the interview. **Failure to do so will result in the cancellation of the appointment.**

The MRV application fee is non-refundable and non-transferable, and there's no refund irrespective of whether the visa is ultimately issued or refused. The receipt is valid for one visa application within 12 months of the date ofp payment. If you're unable to attend the interview you may reschedule an appointment for any time within the 12-month period. If you're unable to attend for any reason, you should phone to reschedule. There's no refund of the fee if you schedule an appointment, cancel it and don't reschedule within 12 months. In many countries you're required to pay for the return of your passport by courier or special delivery mail.

Interview Procedure

It used to be the case that if you were called in to a US embassy or consulate for an interview, there was something wrong with

(or suspicious about) your visa application. With increased security concerns, however, nearly everyone requiring a visa must now appear in person at the nearest US embassy or consulate before a visa is issued, although in most cases the interview lasts only a short time (however, embassies recommend that you allow two to three hours!). You're much more likely to be subjected to a lengthy interview in countries where there's a lot of visa fraud or where governments are believed to be supporting known terrorist groups rather than, for example, in a Western European country.

Interviewers are aware that some people travel to the US on a visitor's or student visa while planning to work illegally or remain beyond the permitted period and, depending on the category of visa you've applied for, they may ask questions about your employment or occupation, education and qualifications, finances, living circumstances, personal background, and the extent of your financial and familial links with your country of residence/nationality.

Note that different embassies have different interview procedures, which may differ form those outlined here.

If you're prohibited from working in the US, you must not imply that you may look for work, otherwise your visa application may be rejected (attending interviews with prospective employers is a permitted use of the B1/B2 visa and the visa waiver – but not working). If you're unemployed or don't have permanent full-time

employment, or have recently left school or university, your application will be closely scrutinized as the consular official may suspect that you're planning to look for work in the US (unless you have a specific reason for your visit and can prove it). If you're going to the US as a bona fide visitor, you must have a return ticket, firm plans regarding your travels and what you intend to do after your holiday.

You may also be required to prove that you won't become a 'public charge', i.e. that you have sufficient funds to support yourself in the US, sometimes includng proof of medical insurance. You require documentary evidence (in duplicate) that you have sufficient funds to provide for yourself and your family, or that you'll have employment in the US that will provide an adequate income. The proof required varies, but includes bank statements and a letter from your bank, ownership of property or investments, and income from investments or royalties. If applicable, your sponsor must have executed an 'Affidavit of Support' (see page 208).

When you pass the interview and (where required) the medical examination and are aged over 14, you'll be finger-printed electronically (those under 14 are finger-printed within 30 days of their 14th birthday). If you have a cut or blister on a finger or thumb, your application won't be processed until it has healed and you'll be required to reschedule an appointment for a later date.

Visa Processing

The time required to process nonimmigrant visa applications varies considerably according to the category of visa, the country, and the particular embassy or consulate where you apply. Most nonimmigrant visas are issued by US embassies and consulates within three or four days (you may be able to display the waiting times for different nonimmigrant visas on your 'local' US embassy's website). However, certain visas, e.g. some employment visas, require a petition, which must be approved by the USCIS before the visa application can be processed.

The State Department's goal is visa delivery within 30 days from the time of application, although cases that require 'administrative processing' can take much longer. When administrative processing is required, the timing is based on the individual circumstances of each case. Therefore before making inquiries about the status of administrative processing, you may need to wait at least 90 days from the date of your interview or the submission of supplemental documents, whichever is later. You may be able to check the 'administrative processing status' online to see whether a visa has been processed.

Note that even when a visa has pre-approval from the USCIS, the consular officer may ask for more information, conduct an interview or even deny the visa application, despite the fact that the USCIS approved the petition. This is unusual at the US embassy in London and at other US embassies in Western countries, and is more likely at embassies with a high refusal rate relating to fraud.

A Premium Processing Service is available for certain employment-based petitions, with a guaranteed 15-day processing period (rather than a number of months) for an additional fee of $1,000. A form I-907 (Request for Premium Processing Service) must be filed with the USCIS, who will then determine whether they can meet the 15-day processing period.

> ⚠️ **Caution**
>
> You should apply for a visa as far in advance as possible and shouldn't make any final travel plans until the visa has been issued and you're in receipt of your passport (with the visa).

All 'visa'd' passports may be returned to applicants by courier, in which case you're required to purchase an envelope for the return of your passport when your visa processing has been completed. A visa isn't issued on the day of the interview and therefore it isn't possible to receive your passport with the US visa immediately after your interview. **Bear this in mind if you need your passport to travel abroad in the next few weeks!**

There 's no appeals process for visa refusals (only for petition denials), although you're usually free to re-apply as often as you wish.

Visa Fees

The application fees for nonimmigrant visas were increased on June 4, 2010, when the fee for all non-petition-based, nonimmigrant visas was increased to $140. There may also be a visa issue fee, which is based on reciprocity, i.e. if your country of citizenship imposes a visa fee for US citizens, then the US will also impose a fee. For example, in the UK the only issue fee levied is $105 for an E-2 or L-2 visa. You can check the issue fees by country on the Bureau of Consular Affairs' website (http://travel.state.gov/visa/frvi/reciprocity/reciprocity_3272.html).

The payment procedure for visas fees may vary from embassy to embassy. For example, at many Western embassies you can pay by bank draft or international money order in dollars (payable to the 'US Disbursing Officer') or complete and sign a

'Credit Card Payment Form' authorizing an embassy to charge the fee to a credit card.

The application fee for petition-based visas is $150, which includes the following categories:

Petition-based Visas

Category	Application
H	temporary workers and trainees
L	intracompany transferees
O	aliens with extraordinary ability
P	athletes, artists and entertainers
Q	international cultural exchange visitors
R	religious occupations

The application fee for K visas for the fiancé(e)s of US citizens is $350 and the fee for E visas for treaty-traders and treaty-investors is $390.

For information about fees for immigrant visas, see page 218.

Visa Extensions & Change of Status

Many nonimmigrant visas can be extended, provided your status remains unchanged and the period of admission originally granted hasn't expired, as stated on your form I-94 (see page 115). Applications for extensions must usually be made not more than 60 days before the expiry date and you must show that you acted 'in good faith', i.e. that you didn't plan to stay longer than originally permitted.

An application for an extension of a non-employed category visa is made with form I-539 (Application to Extend/Change Nonimmigrant Status), which must be accompanied by a copy of your I-94 card and supporting evidence, if applicable, e.g. form I-129 for employment categories. You must file your application at a USCIS service center or online, for which the filing fee is $300. If you file your application on time, you may remain in the US for up to 120 days while awaiting a decision, even if your authorized stay has expired.

It's possible to switch from one nonimmigrant visa to another after arrival in the US, or even to 'adjust status' and obtain a Green Card. If you plan to do this, don't apply for a change of visa immediately after arrival, as the authorities may think (correctly!) that you had a 'preconceived intent' and deny your request.

Visa Denial

Grounds for denial (or ineligibility) of a visa include – but aren't limited to – health, criminal or security reasons; public charge, i.e. a risk of you being a burden on the public purse; a previous illegal entrance or immigration violation; failure to produce the requested documents; being ineligible for citizenship (upon application); and having previously been removed from the US.

The most common reasons for visa denial or ineligibility include:

◆ **Denied entry:** If you have been denied entry into the US by a Customs and Border Protection (CBP) officer, you should bring a copy of the report of the incident (form I-877) to your visa interview.

◆ **Deportation or Removed:** If you have been deported or removed, you may be prohibited from reapplying for a visa for up to ten years (depending on the circumstances). In certain cases a waiver of this ineligibility may be available.

◆ **Overstays:** If you have overstayed on the Visa Waiver Program (VWP) or violated the terms of a previous visa, you'll be refused entry to the US unless you apply for a visa with full details of your overstay prior to a subsequent entry. Violating the terms of the VWP or a previously issued US visa can render an individual ineligible for a visa and a waiver of this ineligibility may be required. For more information, see **Exceeding Your Authorized Stay** below.

If you were denied entry into the US, deported or removed or overstayed the length of your authorized stay by more than 60 days, you're required to schedule an appointment with an embassy 'Visa Coordination Officer'. You must allow sufficient time for your case to be reviewed, as your application will be subject to greater scrutiny.

You must bring the following documents to the interview, as applicable:

♦ a completed 'Personal Data Form' (VCU-1);

♦ a copy of the 'Record of Sworn Statement' form (I-877) given to you by the CBP officer who denied you entry into the US;

♦ a copy of removal proceedings or any documentation relating to your deportation/removal.

Applicants for nonimmigrant visas have a responsibility to prove that they're going to return abroad (i.e. to their country of residence or citizenship) before a visa is issued. US immigration law requires consular officers to view every nonimmigrant visa applicant as an intending immigrant (i.e. someone who intends to remain permanently in the US), until the applicant proves otherwise. Most cases are decided after a brief interview and a review of whatever evidence of ties an applicant presents.

Proof of Ties Abroad

A common reason for a visa denial concerns the requirement that applicants possess a residence abroad that they have no intention of abandoning. All visa applicants except those applying as officials (A/G), treaty traders/investors (E-1/E-2), temporary workers (H-1B), intra-company transferees (L1), aliens of extraordinary ability (O1), or religious workers (R), must provide evidence to show that they have a residence abroad to which they intend to return at the end of their stay in the US.

You must prove the existence of such a residence by demonstrating that you have strong ties abroad that would compel you to leave the US at the end of your temporary stay. The law places the burden of proof on the applicant. Strong ties differ from country to country, city to city and individual to individual, but examples include a job (with a career) or business, a house, a family and a bank account. 'Ties' are the various aspects of your life that bind you to your country of residence: your possessions, employment, social and family relationships.

Examples of such evidence may include a letter from your employer indicating how long you've been employed, your position and salary, accompanied by recent payslips and/or tax records; a letter from your school/college/university confirming that you're an enrolled student with a confirmed place at the institution to return to. Unemployed applicants might be required to provide documentation to show how long they have been unemployed and the extent of the benefits they receive, e.g. income, housing,

children's allowance, disability living allowance, a job offer in their country of residence or citizenship, etc., while other evidence may include proof of ownership of a business, property ownership, tenancy agreements, etc.

A consular officer will reconsider a case (on a subsequent application) if you can show further convincing evidence of ties outside the US. In this case you should contact the embassy or consulate to find out about the reapplication procedure. Unfortunately, some people won't qualify for a nonimmigrant visa irrespective of how many times they re-apply, until their personal, professional or financial circumstances change. You may be able to get a friend or relative in the US to provide a letter of invitation or support, although this won't guarantee a visa will be issued as you must qualify for a visa according to your own circumstances, not on the basis of an American sponsor's assurance.

If you're considered to be ineligible for a visa, you'll be advised whether or not a waiver of ineligibility is available from the Department of Homeland Security (DHS).

Exceeding Your Authorized Stay

Staying unlawfully in the US beyond the date Customs and Border Protection (CBP) officials have authorized – indicated on your I-94 card (see page 115) – even by one day, results in your visa being automatically voided (cancelled). Overstaying a visa is officially termed as being 'out-of-status', in which case you're required to reapply for a new nonimmigrant visa, generally in your country of nationality or residence, not in the US.

If you overstay on the Visa Waiver Program (VWP) or violate the terms of a previously issued US visa, you may be refused entry to the US in future, unless you apply for a visa with full details of your overstay prior to subsequent entry. Violating the terms of the VWP or a previously issued visa can render you ineligible for a visa and a waiver of this ineligibility may be required.

If you violate the terms of a visa (called 'status violation'), such as working, studying or getting married when it's prohibited, then you may have to appear before an immigration judge which may result in your visa being voided and you being deported. The USCIS may, at its discretion, merely exclude you from entering the US without summary removal, which means that you're sent home on the next flight but aren't barred from further entry. However, if you have a valid nonimmigrant visa, you're entitled to a hearing before an immigration judge.

Delays beyond your control, such as cancelled or delayed flights and medical emergencies requiring a doctor's care (etc.) aren't considered to be unauthorized overstays. However, it's advisable to bring proof of the reason for your overstay next time you travel to the US, in order for your records to be updated (if this isn't done before you leave the US). For airline delays, you should ask the airline for a letter confirming the delay or a copy of your cancelled boarding pass.

See also **I-94 Card Not Returned on Leaving US** on page 115.

NONIMMIGRANT VISA CATEGORIES

There are around 20 categories of nonimmigrant visas, each designated by a letter – the main categories are shown in the table below.

Note that there's no visa category for retirees and it isn't possible to qualify for immigration on the basis of retirement alone. Retirees may remain in the US for up to six months a year with a B-2 visa (see page 132), or permanently with a

Nonimmigrant Visas	
Category	Description
A-1,2,3	Ambassadors, diplomats, accredited officials and employees of foreign governments, and their immediate families, plus their personal attendants, servants and employees.
B-1, B-2	Business visitors and tourists.
C-1, C-2	Foreign travelers in transit through the US.
D-1, D-2	Crew members of aircraft and ships who must land temporarily in the US.
E-1,E-2	Treaty traders and investors and their immediate families.
E-3	Australian professional specialty.
F-1	Academic or language students and their immediate families.
G-1-5	Representatives of foreign governments coming to the US to work for international organizations and NATO employees and their immediate families.
H	Temporary workers such as registered nurses, those working in specialized occupations, temporary agricultural workers, trainees and their immediate families.
I	Foreign media representatives.
J-1	Exchange visitors and their immediate families.
K-1-3	Fiancé(e)s of US citizens coming to the US to get married and their unmarried children.
L	Intra-company transferees and their immediate families.
M-1	Vocational or other non-academic students (such as language students) and their immediate families.
NATO 1-6	National representatives and international staff employed by the North Atlantic Treaty Organization (NATO) and their immediate family members.
O	Workers with extraordinary abilities in the sciences, arts, education, business or athletics and their immediate families, and essential support staff.
P	Internationally recognized athletes, entertainers (including those in culturally unique groups) and artists and their immediate families.
Q	Exchange visitors in international cultural exchange programs and their immediate families.
R	Religious workers and their immediate families.
V	Family members of lawful permanent residents.

Green Card if they qualify for one (see page 112).

Category A: Diplomats & Foreign Government Employees

Career diplomats, certain other accredited and accepted officials, and employees of recognized foreign governments and their immediate families are issued with a category A visa if their visit to the US is on behalf of their national government, and is to engage solely in official activities for that government. With the exception of a head of state or government, who qualifies for an A-1 visa irrespective of the purpose of his visit to the US, the type of visa required by a diplomat or other government official depends upon his reason for entering the US. Certain holders of category A visas have diplomatic immunity.

A-1 and A-2 visas are issued on the basis of reciprocity and are valid for the duration of the holder's assignment or five years. To qualify for an A-1 or A-2 visa, you must be traveling to the US on behalf of your national government to engage solely in official activities for that government. The fact that there may be government interest or control in a given organization is not in itself the defining factor in determining whether or not you qualify for an A visa. The particular duties or services to be performed must also be of an inherently governmental character or nature. Local government officials representing their state, province, borough or other local political entity don't qualify for 'A' visa status and require a B-1/B-2 visitor's visa (see **Chapter 4**).

Government officials traveling to the US to perform non-governmental functions of a commercial nature or traveling as tourists require the appropriate H, L or B visa, or if qualified, travel visa-free under the Visa Waiver Program (see page 120); they don't qualify for diplomatic visas. Foreign officials who intend traveling to the US on official business **must** obtain an 'A' visa **prior** to their entry and cannot travel on tourist visas or visa-free under the Visa Waiver Program.

Immediate family members are defined as the spouse and unmarried sons and daughters of any age who are members of the household. Partners who are recognized as the principal alien's dependant by the sending government, while not eligible for derivative A visas, may apply for B-1/B-2 visas, if otherwise qualified. B-1/B-2 visa applicants are required to pay visa application and reciprocal issue fees, if applicable.

A-3 visas are issued to attendants, servants and personal employees of a principal A-1 or A-2 visa holder, and the immediate family members of A-3 visa holders (who cannot work in the US under the A-3 dependant category). An A-3 visa is initially issued for a period of two years and can be extended for periods of two years.

For more information, see 🖳 http://travel.state.gov/visa/temp/types/types_2637.html.

Category B: Visitors

Anyone who wishes to visit the US on holiday or business and doesn't qualify for visa-free travel (see **Visa Waiver** on page 120) or, if he does, wishes to remain longer than 90 days must apply for a category B visa. Visitors' visas aren't required by Canadian citizens and most foreign residents of Canada (landed immigrants) who enter the US as visitors, or by Mexican nationals with a US border crossing card. B-1 visas are granted to visitors on business and B-2 visas to tourists, although combined B-1/B-2 visas are also issued.

For more information, see **Chapter 4**.

Category C: Transit

Category C visas are for travelers (aged over 16) in transit through the US to another country. There are three categories:

♦ **C-1:** Foreign travelers passing through the US to another country and foreign travelers passing through the US to change to another visa classification such as D-1 (see below).

♦ **C-1/D:** A special visa for aircraft and ship crew (see below) members who transit through the US regularly

♦ **C-2:** Foreign nationals traveling to the UN on their official work, UN officials passing through the US to another country and the immediate family members of C-2 visa holders.

♦ **C-3:** Foreign government officials passing through the US to another country and the immediate family members of C-3 visa holders.

You must have a ticket or other evidence of transportation from the US to your final destination; a valid visa to the onward destination or evidence that a visa isn't required; and evidence of adequate funds to cover the cost of your transit journey.

> ☑ **SURVIVAL TIP**
>
> Individuals from visa waiver countries (see page 120) don't require a C-1 Transit Visa; neither do those with a valid B-1 business or B-2 tourist visa (see Chapter 4). However, other nonimmigrant visas cannot be used to transit through the US.

A category C visa allows you to remain in the US for up to 29 days, during which time you can tour the country, shop, and visit friends and family. However, you must leave the US on the proposed flight or ship of departure and the visa cannot be extended.

For more information, see 🖳 http://travel.state.gov/visa/temp/types/types_4383.html.

Category D: Aircraft & Ship Crew

Category D visas are issued to foreign crew members serving aboard aircraft and on ships that will land in the US. There are two types of category D visas:

♦ **D-1:** Crew members or employees serving on a commercial ship or aircraft whose services are required for normal operation of the ship or aircraft, including pilots, flight attendants, scientists, electricians, waiters, cooks, entertainers, barbers, lifeguards and salespersons, plus anyone traveling to the US as passengers to join a commercial ship or aircraft.

♦ **D-2:** Crew members or employees serving on fishing vessels (e.g. captains, stewards, seamen, or employees whose services are required for normal operation of the vessel) with its home port or operating base in the US and anyone traveling to the US as passengers to join such a fishing vessel.

Both D-1 and D-2 visas allow only a single entry into the US and you must reapply for the D-1 visa each time you enter the country as the visa expires the moment you leave. However, a C-1/D visa (see above) is available for crew members who transit through the US regularly, which is valid for up to 29 days at a time. A D-2 visa allows for a stay in the US for a period of up to six months (no extensions are permitted).

For more information, see 🖥 www.ukvisas. gov.uk/en/doineedvisa/visadatvnationals.

Category E: Treaty Traders & Investors

Category E visas are termed Treaty Trader (E-1) and Treaty Investor (E-2) visas and are issued to people wishing to invest in or trade with a company in the US. They're issued subject to certain conditions, but there's no restriction on the number issued each year. As the name suggests, category E visas are available only to citizens of countries with which the US has a commerce treaty. An E-3 visa was introduced in 2005 and currently applies only to Australian nationals who are employed in a specialty occupation (see page 139). For more information about category E visas, see **Chapter 6**.

It's also possible for investors who are investing a minimum of $500,000 in a commercial enterprise to obtain an immigrant (permanent residence) EB-5 visa. For information, see page 165.

Category F: Academic or Language Students

Category F-1 visas are issued to students who have been accepted for a full-time course of study at an approved school, although you may visit the US as a tourist to inspect prospective schools. You must continue in full-time education for the visa to remain valid.

An F-2 visa is issued to the spouse and children of F-1 visa holders who wish to visit or accompany a foreign national studying in the US. For more information, see page 179.

Category G: Foreign Government Representatives

Category G visas are granted to the employees of international organizations, e.g. the United Nations (UN), and their immediate families if their visit to the US is in pursuit of official duties. There are five different sub-categories:

♦ G-1: Principal representatives of recognized foreign governments entering the US to work for a United Nations organization or an international mission, the staff of principal representatives of recognized foreign governments and the immediate family members of G-1 visa holders.

♦ G-2: Accredited representatives of recognized foreign governments entering the US to work for a United Nations organization or an international mission, the staff of principal representatives of recognized foreign governments and the immediate family members of G-2 visa holders.

♦ G-3: Representatives of unrecognized foreign governments entering the US to work for a United Nations organization or an international mission, the staff of principal representatives of unrecognized foreign governments and the immediate family members of G-3 visa holders.

♦ G-4: Officials and employees of international organizations and the immediate family members of G-4 visa holders.

♦ G-5: attendants, servants and personal employees (employed in a domestic capacity and paid by the principal) of G-1 to G-4 visa holders and the immediate family members of G-5 visa holders.

Immediate family members are defined as the spouse and unmarried sons and daughters of any age who are members of the household. Partners who are recognized as the principal alien's dependant by the sending government, while not eligible for derivative A visas, may apply for B-1/B-2, if otherwise qualified.

Holders of G category visas may stay in the US indefinitely, provided the Secretary of State continues to recognize their visa status.

For more information, see 🖳 http://travel.state.gov/visa/temp/types/types_2638.html.

Category H: Temporary Workers

If you wish to work in the US for a number of years, you may qualify for a category H visa, some of which are valid (with extensions) for up to six years. In general these visas are based on a specific offer of employment from a prospective employer in the US, which must be approved in advance by the USCIS on the basis of a petition (form I-129), filed by the American employer. There are six sub-categories of H visa; H-1B (workers in specialized occupations), H-1C (registered nurses), H-2A (seasonal agricultural workers), H-2B (workers filling jobs that cannot be filled by US citizens or residents), H-3 (trainees), and H-4 (the immediate families of H-1, H-2 and H-3 visa holders). Australians should see also the E-3 visa.

For more information, see page 158.

Category I: Foreign Media Representatives

Category I visas are issued to representatives of foreign information media, representatives of a foreign tourist bureau, or film crew members holding professional journalism credentials and planning to work on news or non-commercial documentaries. Visas are issued only to those involved in the news gathering process; those involved in associated activities, such as research, aren't eligible. All journalists must have an I visa when entering the US to work, even if they're from a Visa Waiver Program country and staying for less than 90 days. Visas are issued on the basis of reciprocity and include spouses and unmarried children under 21. They're issued for up to five years at a time and are renewable. It isn't possible for a foreign journalist to change employers in the US without prior permission from the USCIS.

Applicants must submit a letter from the foreign media organization stating their name, position/job title and the purpose of their visit to the US; the intended duration of stay; and the nature of the material to be produced or distributed. Freelance journalists and employees of independent production companies are only considered for an I visa when they're under contract to a media organization. If the project is of a commercial or entertainment nature, rather than informational or educational, a P visa may be more appropriate.

For more information, see page 149.

Category J: Exchange Visitors

Category J-1 visas (known as nonimmigrant cultural exchange visas) are issued to foreign exchange visitors including students, scholars, trainees, teachers, professors, medical graduates, research assistants and specialists or leaders in a field of specialized knowledge or skill, who wish to enter the US temporarily as a participant in an approved program. The kind of work that may be performed includes teaching, instructing or lecturing, studying, observing, conducting research, consulting, demonstrating special skills or receiving training. Programs also allow those aged between 18 and 25 to work as au pairs for up to a year. Foreign students may also be eligible for an F-1 or M-1 visa.

For more information, see page 179.

Category K: Fiancé(e)s

A category K-1 visa is granted to a fiancé(e) who's planning to marry a US citizen within 90 days of entering the US. After the wedding, the foreign spouse can apply for a Green Card, although if the intended wedding doesn't take place within 90 days, he or she must leave the country. A K-1 visa holder may leave the US and return during the 90-day period before the marriage takes place, but there's no provision for extending the visa period or obtaining another category of visa. A couple must have met and seen each other within the past two years, unless this is prohibited under the doctrines of their religion, in which case they must show that arranged marriages are a family or religious custom.

The first step in applying for a fiancé(e) visa is for the US citizen (the petitioner) to file a petition (form I-129F) with the USCIS office with jurisdiction over his place of residence in the US. The petition can only be filed with the USCIS in the US and cannot be filed at a US embassy or consulate abroad.

If a US citizen living abroad marries an alien, he or she can file a form I-130 (Petition for Alien Relative) for a Green Card at the US consulate or embassy with jurisdiction over the petitioner's country of residence; however, they must wait until the Green Card is issued before the alien spouse can enter the US. Alternatively, they can file for a K-3 nonimmigrant visa (see below), which allows the couple to enter the US and apply for a Green Card there. Note that it usually takes 6 to 12 months for a Green Card application to be processed, which is much longer than it takes to obtain a K-1 visa for a fiancé(e) or a K-3 visa for an alien spouse.

It can take three to six months (sometimes longer) to obtain a K-1 visa and most couples simply get married, in the US or abroad, and apply directly for a Green

Card or apply for a K-3 visa abroad if they qualify (see below). However, it's illegal to enter the US as a visitor with the intention of getting married. It's also illegal to enter into marriage purely for the purpose of remaining in (or entering) the US and there are stringent checks for 'marriages of convenience' (satirized in the film *Green Card*, starring Gérard Depardieu).

⚠ **Caution**

You may not enter the US as a tourist or nonimmigrant worker with the intention of marrying a US citizen, for which there are serious penalties if you're discovered.

If you're legally in the US and meet and marry a US citizen, you can apply to adjust status and become a permanent resident. You shouldn't, however, leave the US before receiving your Green Card without permission from the USCIS, as you must then apply for a visa to re-enter the country, which can take many months.

A K-3 visa can be granted to the spouse of a US citizen, allowing him or her to enter the US to wait while completing the immigration process; it's valid for two years and can be extended indefinitely provided the marriage on which it's based isn't dissolved. A K-4 visa is granted to unmarried children aged under 21 accompanying a K-3 visa holder. The American spouse must have started the immigration process by filing the necessary petitions in the US, and the K-3 visa application must be made in the country where the wedding took place. The K-3 visa then allows the foreign spouse to join the husband or wife in the US while waiting for the Green Card application to be processed. On arrival, the foreign spouse can also apply to the USCIS for permission to work, as can his or her children with K-4 visas.

You aren't eligible for a K visa to marry a non-US citizen who's a lawful permanent resident (Green Card holder). If you marry a foreign Green Card holder, you're subject to the quotas for family-sponsored immigrants (see page 200) and must usually wait a number of years for a Green Card. However, if the Green Card holder becomes a US citizen, you immediately become eligible for a Green Card.

Foreign same-sex partners of US citizens aren't currently recognized by the USCIS and accordingly cannot be sponsored for a K visa or for permanent resident status, which means that many 'families' based on a same-sex relationship are forced to live outside the US if a different kind of visa cannot be procured. This leads to many foreign same-sex partners residing in the US illegally. There's an act before congress – the Uniting American Families Act (see 🖳 http://en.wikipedia.org/wiki/Uniting_American_Families_Act) – which would create a new family category, 'Permanent Partner', allowing foreign partners recognition by the USCIS.

A K-1 or K-3 visa holder can apply to work immediately after arriving in the US, subject to permission being granted by the USCIS. The unmarried children aged under 21 of a fiancé(e) receive K-2 visas and can accompany him or her to the US or follow within one year. If they don't follow within one year, a separate visa petition is required. K-2 and K-4 visa holders may study in the US but aren't permitted to work.

For more information, see 🖳 http://travel.state.gov/visa/immigrants/types/types_1315.html. See also **Chapter 8** for information about Green Cards for alien spouses.

Category L: Intra-company Transferees

Category L-1 visas are granted to intra-company transferees. These are people employed abroad who are transferred to a branch, subsidiary, affiliate or joint venture partner of the same company in the US, which must be at least 50 per cent owned by the foreign company. To qualify you must have served in a managerial or executive capacity or possess specialized knowledge necessary to the US business, and be transferred to a position within the US company at either of these levels, although not necessarily in the same position. You must also demonstrate that the company has procured premises to house the new 'branch'.

For more information, see page 167.

Category M: Non-academic Students

There are three categories of visa for foreign students: category F for full-time academic and language students; category J-1 for students coming to the US on exchange visits; and category M-1 for vocational and non-academic students. M-1 visas are issued for the estimated length of time it will take you to complete your proposed studies up to a maximum of five years, although visas aren't usually approved for longer than 18 months at a time.

For more information, see page 192.

Category NATO: NATO Representatives & Staff

NATO visas are issued to national representatives and international staff employed by the North Atlantic Treaty Organization (NATO) and their immediate family members. An interview isn't usually required (although a consular officer can request one) and applicants for NATO1-6 visas are exempt from the fingerprint scan requirement. However, personal employees, attendants and servants of NATO visa holders, i.e. applicants for NATO-7 visas, are required to be interviewed and fingerprinted.

Many armed forces personnel are exempt from passport and visa requirements if they're attached to NATO Allied Headquarters in the US, and are traveling on official business or entering the US under the NATO Status of Forces Agreement. In the case of the later, they must carry official military ID cards and NATO travel orders.

For more information, see 🖥 http://travel. state.gov/visa/temp/types/types_1279.html.

Category O: People of Extraordinary Ability

Category O-1 visas are for people of extraordinary ability in the fields of science, art, education, business and athletics, and workers in film and television whose work has earned them 'sustained national or international acclaim'. O-2 visas are issued to the support staff and crew of O-1 visa holders, e.g. a film or television production crew, but only if they possess skills and experience that isn't available in the US. The immediate families of O-1 and O-2 visa holders receive O-3 visas. There's no annual quota for O visas. An O-1 visa can be issued for up to three years with an indefinite number of one-year renewals permissible.

For more information, see page 149.

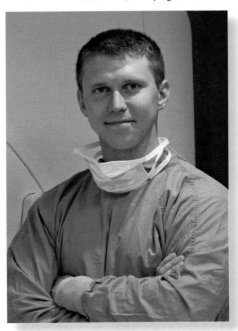

Category P: Athletes & Entertainers

Category P visas are issued to internationally recognized athletes, entertainers and artists, and to their essential support personnel. Individual athletes and teams are eligible for P-1 visas, which may be valid for five years in the case of individual athletes or six months for a team. P-2 visas are issued for individuals or groups involved in a reciprocal exchange program between the US and one or more foreign countries, and P-3 visas are for performers (individuals or groups) in a culturally unique program.

P-4 visas are granted to the spouse and unmarried children under 21 of those granted P-1, P-2 and P-3 visas. Dependants aren't allowed to work, although they're permitted to study. The qualifications necessary for P visas aren't as stringent as for O visas (see above), although there's a significant overlap between the uses and qualifications for O and P visas.

For more information, see page 149.

Category Q: Cultural Exchange Visitors

Category Q visas are for those involved in international cultural exchange programs. Programs must be designed to provide practical training, employment or opportunities for sharing with US citizens the history, culture and traditions of your home country. The Q visa is an alternative to the J-1 visa, but unlike the J-1 visa prior approval from the USCIS and a two-year home residence aren't necessary. Registration with the SEVIS program (see page 178) isn't required either. However, Q visas are issued for only 15 months at a time, unlike J visas which may be valid for up to five years. There's no provision for the issue of visas to the spouse and unmarried children aged under 21 of Q visa holders and dependants must qualify for visas in their own right.

For more information, see page 151.

Category R: Religious Workers

Category R-1 visas are for workers who have been members of recognized religious groups for at least two years and are coming to the US to work for an affiliated religious organization (in any capacity). The term 'worker' includes counselors, social workers, health-care workers for religious hospitals, missionaries, translators and religious broadcasters, but not, for example, janitors or fund-raisers. A petition isn't required for an R-1 visa, which is granted for an initial maximum of three years. The spouse and unmarried children aged under 21 of R-1 visa holders are granted R-2 visas, but aren't permitted to work. Religious workers may also apply for a Green Card under the 'special' immigrant category (see **Chapter 8**).

For more information, see page 151.

Category V: Family Members

Category V visas were created under the Legal Immigration and Family Act of 2000 (the 'LIFE' act) in order to reunite families separated while waiting for their immigrant visa applications to be processed. Those eligible for V visas were the spouse and unmarried children aged under 21 of lawful permanent residents who had been waiting at least three years for their immigrant visa applications to be processed. The spouse could work and the children could attend public schools, international travel was permitted, and the visa remained valid as long as the underlying immigrant petition was valid.

Over a million spouses/minor children of lawful permanent residents have been waiting for immigrant visas for up to eight years, without being allowed to live with their spouses/parents in the US.

The act was designed to relieve those who applied for immigrant visas on or before December 21, 2000. While the V visa is still available to those who satisfy the conditions, it's effectively no longer of any use as it isn't available to the spouses and minor children of lawful permanent residents who applied after December 21, 2000. Similar bills have been proposed (the latest in 2009) but have made little progress, as they are seen by many legislators as a back door to increasing immigration numbers, particularly from countries such as China, India, Mexico and the Philippines.

IMMIGRANT VISAS

An immigrant visa bestows upon the holder the status of a permanent resident. In general, to be eligible to apply for an immigrant visa, an alien must be sponsored by a US citizen relative, a US lawful permanent resident or by a prospective employer, and be the beneficiary of an approved petition. Immigrant visas give you the right to live and work in the US (and change jobs freely) on a permanent basis and confer eligibility to apply for US citizenship after three years (for the spouses of US citizens) or five years (for all others).

The main difference between the rights of a permanent resident and those of a US citizen is that a permanent resident, although having all the responsibilities of a US citizen, is ineligible for certain welfare benefits, including some Medicaid and Social Security insurance benefits, and cannot vote in federal elections or serve on a jury. Green Cards are valid for ten years and cannot be withdrawn (except voluntarily), provided you don't abandon your US residence for more than a year or commit certain crimes.

There are two main ways most people can obtain a Green Card: through blood ties (or marriage), i.e. as an immediate or close relative of a US citizen or permanent resident, and through employment.

An immigrant visa consists of a stamp in your passport by an American embassy or consulate (as with nonimmigrant visas), which allows you to enter the US to take up permanent residence. Holders of immigrant visas are issued with an Alien Registration Card, commonly referred to as a Green Card, consisting of a plastic identification card with your photo, thumb print and signature on the front. With the exception of immediate relatives, Green cards are issued on a preferential basis (i.e. with quotas) and you may therefore have to wait many years as only a limited number are issued annually. A Green Card serves as a US entry document for permanent residents returning to the US after a period abroad.

For comprehensive information about immigrant visas, see **Chapter 8**.

ARRIVAL-DEPARTURE FORM

Nonimmigrants (with a visa) and visa-free visitors arriving in the US by air or sea are given an Arrival-Departure card by the airline or shipping company. (Crewmen/women must complete an I-95 'Crewman Landing Permit'). There are two types of I-94 cards – ensure that you receive the correct one:

◆ **I-94 Arrival/Departure Record** (white) for nonimmigrants with a visa;

◆ **I-94W Nonimmigrant Visa Waiver Arrival/Departure Form** (green) for visitors arriving under the Visa Waiver Program (see page 120).

If you enter the US by road from Canada or Mexico, you must complete the I-94 form at the frontier and pay a fee of $6. Canadians traveling to the US as tourists or on business generally aren't required to complete an I-94 form and Mexicans with a nonresident alien

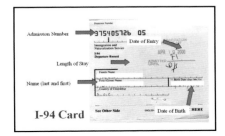

I-94 Card

Mexican Border Crossing Card (commonly known as a laser visa) may also not need to complete an I-94 form.

The I-94/I-94W card is divided into two parts, an 'Arrival Record' (items 1–13 or 1-11 on the I-94W) and a 'Departure Record' (items 14–17) and contains the following sections:

I-94/I-94W Form

Top section of form:

1. Family name
2. First (given) name
3. Birth date (day/month/year)
4. Country of citizenship
5. Sex (male or female)
6. Passport number
7. Airline and flight number (if applicable)
8. Country where you live – lawful permanent residence
9. City where you boarded (if applicable)
10. City where visa was issued – I-94 only
11. Date issued (day/month/year) – I-94 only
12. Address while in the us (house number and street)
13. City and state

Bottom section of form:

14. Family name
15. First (given) name
16. Birth date (day/month/year)
17. Country of citizenship

You must complete the form in blue/black ink in block capitals and in English. If you make a mistake and correct it, you may be asked to complete a new card. If you don't have an address while in the US (item 10 or 12), it's wise to enter the name of a hotel in an area or city where you're heading or write 'touring', rather than leave it blank. If you're entering the US by land, enter 'LAND' under 'Airline and Flight Number' (item 7) or 'SEA' if you're entering the US by ship. You need to complete both the 'Arrival' and 'Departure' parts before arrival.

On the reverse are a number of questions (A-G); you should tick the 'NO' box for all these questions otherwise you may be refused entry! You must complete the four fields (below) after the list of questions and sign and date the form at the bottom where indicated.

Family Name

First Name

Country of Citizenship

Date of Birth

On arrival in the US, hand the I-94 card with your passport to the Customs and Border Protection (CBP) officer. After taking your photograph and fingerprints, the officer will retain the 'Arrival' part of the card and staple the 'Departure' part in your passport and return it to you.

You're authorized to remain in the US until the date stamped on your I-94 card, entered by the immigration officer when you arrive. This is normally the date specified when your visas expires or the maximum stay permitted by your visa or after 90 days is you have an I-94W card, although a Customs and Border Protection (CBP) officer may stamp your I-94 card with a date that precedes the expiry of your visa or the maximum period permitted. If this happens you can apply for an extension of up to 60 days and not less than 15 days before the date on your I-94 card becomes due. However, if you enter the US under the Visa Waiver Program, you cannot obtain an extension of the 90-day limit.

☑ SURVIVAL TIP

If you're refused entry to the US and have a nonimmigrant visa, you're entitled to a hearing before an immigration judge, However, if you're refused entry under the Visa Waiver Program, you have no right of appeal and must leave the country (unless you're applying for asylum).

Most nonimmigrant visas are of the multiple-entry type, which allow you to enter and leave the US as often as you wish during the visa's validity period. However, the period that you're allowed to remain also depends on the expiration date of your passport. The Departure Record is stapled into your passport and must be carried at all times.

When you leave the US, the card is removed from your passport by an official of the transport, e.g. airline or shipping, company or you can drop it in a container for I-94 cards at some airports. If you leave the US via a land border to Canada or Mexico and intend to remain outside the US for more than 30 days, you should surrender your I-94 card to a official at the border.

All I-94 cards are recorded on a computer, which makes it easy for immigration officials to check whether you failed to return your card or overstayed your departure date. If you lose your Departure Card, you should replace it at the nearest USCIS office. A list can be obtained by calling the USCIS National Service Center (☎ 1-800-375-5283) or online from the USCIS website (🖥 www.uscis.gov).

Make sure that your Departure Record is surrendered when you leave the US; if you fail to do surrender it a future entry may be delayed or you may even be refused entry (see below).

On arrival in the US you must also complete a Customs Declaration form (6059B), which are distributed by airlines and shipping lines (and also provided at airports and ports). One form must be completed per family or couple, although if there's more than one surname in your family group then you'll need a separate form for each family surname.

Lost or Mutilated I-94 Card in US

If you lose your I-94 departure card from your passport or it's mutilated or destroyed, you'll need to file form I-102 (Application for Replacement/Initial Nonimmigrant Arrival-Departure Document) at the USCIS office with jurisdiction over where you're temporarily located in the US (offices are listed on the USCIS website, 🖥 www.uscis.gov). There's a filing fee of $320!

You will need to submit a copy of the I-94 form (it's highly unlikely that anyone will have a copy!) or a copy of the biographic/photo page of your passport and a copy of the passport page that was stamped by the CBP officer when you entered the country. If you cannot submit any evidence of your legal admission to the US – for example, your passport has been stolen – submit a full explanation and proof of your identity.

If your application for a replacement arrival-departure document is denied, you'll receive a letter informing you why. You cannot appeal a negative decision to a higher authority, but you may submit a motion to reopen or a motion

to reconsider with the same office that made the unfavorable decision. By filing these motions, you may ask the office to reexamine or reconsider their decision. A motion to reopen must state the new facts that are to be provided in the reopened proceeding and must be accompanied by affidavits or other documentary evidence.

A motion to reconsider must establish that the decision was based on an incorrect application of law or USCIS policy, and further establish that it was incorrect based on the evidence in the file at the time the decision was made.

I-94 Card Not Returned on Leaving US

Travelers to the US must return their I-94 or I-94W departure record card to the airline, shipping line or a land border officer before departing the US. If you fail to do so you may be recorded as overstaying your visit. I-94 cards are usually removed from passports by airline or shipping line staff. If the card isn't surrendered, the next time you apply to enter the US your visa may be subject to cancellation and/or you may be denied entry. Visitors who remain beyond their permitted stay in the US under the Visa Waiver Program must obtain a visitor's visa to re-enter the US.

If you leave the US without surrendering your I-94 or I-94W card, you must complete the back of the card listing the port and date of departure from the US and the carrier/flight information. The card should then be sent together with a letter of explanation and evidence of your departure (see below) to the following address:

DHS-CBP SBU,
PO Box 7125
1084 South Laurel Road
London
Kentucky 40742-7125
USA

The evidence of your departure may consist of any of the following:

♦ the original boarding pass you used to depart the US;

♦ entry or departure stamps in your passport to indicate that you entered another country after you departed the US (copy the relevant passport pages and include the biographic page containing your photograph);

♦ dated pay slips or vouchers from your employer to indicate that you worked in another country after you departed the US;

♦ dated bank records showing transactions in your home country to indicate that you were in another country after your left the US;

♦ school records showing your attendance at a school outside the US to indicate that you were in another country after you left the US;

♦ dated credit card receipts with the credit card number deleted for purchases you made after you departed the US to indicate that you were in another country after you left the US.

You should send legible copies or the original materials where possible. If you send originals, you should retain a copy for your records as they won't be returned to you. It will assist the CBP if you include an explanation letter.

If you left the US with the I-94 card in your possession, but no longer have it, you should write to the address above with the following information:

♦ Name;

♦ date and place of birth;

♦ country of citizenship;

♦ date of arrival in the US;

♦ date of departure from the US;

♦ airline or carrier departed on;

♦ flight number or name of vessel.

If the departure was via a land border, enter 'land' instead of carrier information. You must also include evidence of your departure as listed above.

You should retain a copy of everything you send to the DHS-CBP and take it with you the next time you enter the US, in case the CBP officer has any questions about your eligibility. If there's a problem, this will allow your record to be corrected at the time of entry, e.g. if for some reason the CBP head office hasn't updated your departure record.

If you have problems entering the US due to incorrect arrival and departure information, you can request a review of the information by writing to the: US Customs and Border Protection (CBP), Office of Public Affairs, Customer Service Center, Room 3.4A, 1300 Pennsylvania Avenue, N.W., Washington, DC 20229 (☎ 703-526-4200). You'll be required to submit evidence of your departure from the US, as listed above.

bald eagle, US national bird

4.

VISITORS

Anyone who wishes to visit the US on holiday or business (or is in transit) and doesn't qualify for visa-free travel (see Visa Waiver Program below) or wishes to remain as a visitor for longer than 90 days, must apply for a category B nonimmigrant visa; B-1 visas are granted to visitors on business and B-2 visas to tourists or those visiting the US for medical treatment. If you wish to combine a business trip with tourism, you should apply for a B-1 visa.

Visitors' visas aren't required by Canadian citizens but permanent residents (aka landed immigrants) of Canada must have a nonimmigrant visa unless they are nationals of a country that participates in the Visa Waiver Program (VWP), meet the VWP requirements, and are seeking to enter the US for 90 days or less under that program. Bermuda nationals (at the discretion of the US Department of Homeland Security) who enter the US as visitors and Mexican nationals with a Border Crossing Card also don't require a visitor's visa.

Under US immigration law, it's assumed that every visitor visa applicant is an intending immigrant. Therefore, applicants for visitor visas must demonstrate:

♦ that the purpose of their trip is to enter the US for business, pleasure, or medical treatment;

♦ they plan to remain for a specific, limited period;

♦ they have sufficient funds to cover expenses in the US;

♦ evidence of compelling social and economic ties abroad; and

♦ that they have a residence outside the US as well as other binding ties that will insure they return abroad at the end of their visit.

Students, temporary workers, journalists and those planning to travel to the US for a purpose other than those permitted with a visitor visa, must apply for a different nonimmigrant visa (see **Chapter 3**) in the appropriate category.

> ## ⚠ Caution
>
> You may be asked to provide evidence of onward travel or other documentation regarding the purpose of your stay in the US, and you may also need to prove that you have strong ties abroad. Failure to do so could mean that you're refused a visitor's visa (see **Visa Denial** on page 100).

For general information about nonimmigrant visas, see **Chapter 3**.

VISA WAIVER PROGRAM (VWP)

Nationals of certain countries – listed in the table below – can visit the US for the purposes of tourism or business (or in transit – see below) without a visa under the Visa Waiver Program (VWP), although eligible travelers may apply for a visa if they prefer to do so. If you're a citizen of one of the VWP countries (see box), you don't usually require a visa to visit the US, provided:

♦ Your visit is for business, pleasure or medical treatment.

♦ Your stay is for a maximum of 90 days.

♦ You have a valid passport issued by a participating country and are a citizen of that country (not just a resident). Your passport must usually be valid for at least six months beyond your expected stay in the US. Passports issued on or after October 26, 2005 must be machine readable, i.e. have a strip of standardized characters on the main photograph page (see **VWP Passport Requirements** below).

♦ If you're entering the US by air or sea, you must have a return or onward non-transferable ticket for a destination outside the US, issued by a participating carrier (i.e. most major airlines and shipping lines), which is non-refundable except in the country of issue or your home country. Travelers with onward tickets terminating in Mexico, Canada, Bermuda or the Caribbean Islands must be legal permanent residents of these countries. If you enter the US by land from Canada or Mexico, the return ticket requirement isn't applicable. You aren't usually permitted to use the VWP if you enter the US on a private or official aircraft or vessel or by other non-VWP approved carriers.

♦ If you're entering the US by land from Canada or Mexico, you must have a completed form I-94W, issued by the immigration authorities at the port of entry, and pay a $6 fee.

♦ You aren't a journalist entering the US to do any form of work-related activity, who must have the appropriate visa (see page 141), even if you're from a Visa Waiver country and otherwise meet all the VWP requirements.

Visa Waiver Countries		
Andorra	Hungary	the Netherlands
Australia	Iceland	New Zealand
Austria	Ireland	Norway
Belgium	Italy	Portugal
Brunei	Japan	San Marino
Czech Republic	South Korea	Singapore
Denmark	Latvia	Slovakia
Estonia	Liechtenstein	Slovenia
Finland	Lithuania	Spain
France	Luxembourg	Sweden
Germany	Malta	Switzerland
Greece	Monaco	United Kingdom

♦ There are no 'grounds of exclusion' or reasons why you shouldn't be admitted to the US.

♦ You must be In possession of a completed form I-94W (Nonimmigrant Visa Waiver Arrival/Departure form), obtainable from airline and shipping companies (see page 115).

♦ You must have a valid authorization through the Electronic System for Travel Authorization (ESTA) prior to travel (see below).

You should be aware that if you enter the US under the Visa Waiver Program, you cannot obtain an extension of the 90-day limit and you waive your rights to a hearing if you're refused admission at the port of entry (except when applying for asylum). Likewise, if you're later found to have violated the conditions of admission under the Visa Waiver Program, you don't have the right to contest a removal.

For further information, see 🖳 http://travel.state.gov/visa/temp/types/types_1265.html or check with a US embassy or consulate in your home country (see 🖳 www.usembassy.gov).

IMPORTANT NOTE

Since 12th January, 2009, Electronic System for Travel Authorization (ESTA) approval has been required prior to travel to the US under the Visa Waiver Program (see below).

VWP Exceptions

Some travelers may be ineligible to enter the US under the VWP, including those who have been arrested, even if the arrest didn't result in a criminal conviction; those with criminal records; people with certain serious communicable illnesses; those who have been refused admission into or have been deported from the US; and those who have previously overstayed a visit to the US on the VWP. Such travelers must apply for a visa and in certain circumstances a waiver of inadmissibility/ineligibility. If they attempt to travel to the US without a visa they're likely to be refused entry.

British passport holders should note that if their passport indicates that they're a British Subject, British Dependent Territories Citizen, British Overseas Citizen, British National (Overseas) Citizen, or British Protected Person, they don't qualify for travel to the US under the VWP. A passport which states that the holder has the right of abode or indefinite leave to remain in the United Kingdom also doesn't qualify for visa-free travel.

Visa-free travel doesn't include those who plan to study, work or remain longer than 90 days in the US. Such travelers need visas. If an immigration official has reason to believe that a visa-free traveler is going to study, work or stay longer than 90 days, he'll refuse to admit the traveler.

VWP Passport Requirements

Visa-free travelers entering the US under the Visa Waiver Program (VWP) require individual machine-readable passport (MRP). If a passport was issued, renewed or extended between October 25, 2005 and October 25, 2006 it must contain a digital photograph, and if it was issued, renewed or extended on or after October 26, 2006, it must be electronic.

Electronic passports (also called e-passports or smart passports) include an integrated circuit chip capable of storing the biographic information from the data page, a digitized photograph and other biometric information. **Diplomatic and official passports** are exempted from digital photo and electronic chip requirements, but must be machine-readable. Temporary and emergency passports must meet the electronic passport requirement.

e-passport

Machine-readable passports allow data in the passport to be scanned automatically by a machine. There are two lines of letters, numbers and '>>>>' printed at the bottom of the personal information page (see image), which is the page with your photograph and personal details. If you're in any doubt as to whether your passport is machine-readable, you should check with the passport issuing authority of your country.

The majority of VWP countries issue passports with a digital photo integrated into the data page. Visitors can tell whether their passport meets these requirements, as it will contain a digital photograph that's printed on the page, not glued or laminated into the document.

If you don't have a machine-readable passport you'll either be required to apply for a B-1 (business) or B-2 (tourist) visa, or

if you wish to continue traveling visa-free under the VWP, obtain a new passport which is machine readable.

Digital Photograph

If you're a national of a country that doesn't issue passports with digital photographs and your passport is issued on or after October 26, 2005, you'll be required to apply for either a B-1 (business) or B-2 (tourist) visa. If your passport is issued before this date, the digital photograph requirement won't apply to you.

Nationals of the Czech Republic, Estonia, Hungary, Latvia, Lithuania, Malta, the Republic of Korea and the Slovak Republic must have an e-passport with an integrated chip in order to travel under the Visa Waiver Program.

Because they aren't part of the VWP, requirements for machine-readable or biometric passports don't apply to nationals of Canada, Mexico or Bermuda. However, it should be noted that some nationals of Canada and Bermuda traveling to the US require a nonimmigrant visa.

Machine-readable zone

VWP Transit Travelers

Travelers who qualify for visa-free travel under the Visa Waiver Program (VWP) are eligible to transit the US. If transiting the US to a destination in Canada, Mexico or the adjacent islands, travelers may re-enter the US on the return journey using any mode of transport, provided the total visit, including the periods spent in transit and in Canada, Mexico or the adjacent islands, doesn't exceed 90 days.

If you're transiting to a destination outside Canada, Mexico or the adjacent islands, the return journey must be on a participating carrier. However, it doesn't need to be within 90 days, as you're required to make a new application for admission and complete a new arrival/departure form (I-94W). Travelers transiting the US to take up residence in Mexico, Canada, Bermuda or the Caribbean Islands, must be legal permanent residents of these countries/areas.

Note that if you're a VWP transit traveler, you must obtain ESTA authorization (see below).

ELECTRONIC SYSTEM FOR TRAVEL AUTHORIZATION (ESTA)

Electronic System for Travel Authorization
U.S. Department of Homeland Security

Since January 12, 2009, all nationals who qualify to travel to the US under the Visa Waiver Program (VWP) – and entering the US by air or sea – have been required to obtain authorization prior to travel via the Electronic System for Travel Authorization (ESTA). Until March 20, 2010, travelers who failed to register under ESTA were allowed to complete an I-94 card on arrival in the US if they hadn't registered online. However, since March 20, 2010, airlines who board passengers without an ESTA have been fined and travelers who fail to register can also be fined and refused entry.

ESTA is a free (although a fee may be introduced), fully automated, electronic screening system that determines the eligibility

of visitors to travel to the US (see 🖳 *https://esta.cbp.dhs.gov* – click on 'Apply' at the bottom left of the screen to apply for an ESTA). Accompanied and unaccompanied children, irrespective of age, must obtain an independent ESTA authorization. **If you have a valid US visa, you aren't required to register under ESTA.**

▲ Caution

Since March 20, 2010, airlines have refused to board passengers without an ESTA. It may be possible to get one at the airport via the internet, but don't count on it as it can take up to 72 hours for it to be approved!

The ESTA application requires the same information that's entered on the Nonimmigrant Visa Waiver Arrival/Departure form (I-94W – see page 115). ESTA applications may be submitted at any time prior to travel, although it's recommended that you apply when you begin to prepare your travel plans, and no later than 72 hours before you're due to travel. You can apply well in advance and update your travel details later. In most case, you'll receive almost immediate determination of eligibility. Therefore if you need to travel at the last minute you may still be able to obtain an ESTA (or update an existing ESTA), **but don't rely on it as it can take much longer.**

ESTA Authorization

Response	Action
Authorization Approved	You may board an approved US air or sea carrier under the VWP
Authorization Pending	you need to check the ESTA website for an update within 72 hours to receive a final response
Travel Not Authorized	you're must apply for a visitor's visa (see **ESTA Denied** below)

There are three possible responses to an application for an ESTA shown in the table above.

You aren't required to print the ESTA authorization and carry it with you as your airline or shipping company will have received confirmation that you're authorized to travel, and you aren't required to present evidence of your ESTA registration when you check in. However, you're advised by US Homeland Security to print a copy for your records because if you need to update your information in future you'll need to enter your application number (along with your date of birth and passport number) and it may also be advisable to carry a copy with you when traveling in the US. Your ESTA also shows its validity period. If you don't keep a note of your application number it isn't possible to retrieve your registration and you must re-register, when the old number is automatically cancelled and a new number is generated.

An ESTA authorization is generally valid for up to two years – or until your passport expires – and for multiple entries. If your itinerary changes (address, flight number, etc.) you can update the information through the ESTA website. If you obtain a new passport, change your name, date of birth, citizenship, or gender, you cannot amend an existing registration, but must apply for a new ESTA.

If you're entering the US by land from Canada or Mexico you don't require travel authorization under ESTA, but you require ESTA authorization if you're a transit traveler (see above).

Note that having an ESTA isn't a guarantee that you'll be admitted to the US. ESTA approval only authorizes a traveler to board a carrier for travel to the US under the VWP. An immigration inspector at the port of entry will determine your eligibility for admission into the US (which also applies to visitors with a visa).

 Caution

There's no fee for an ESTA and companies and websites that charge a fee are unofficial and aren't approved by or operated on behalf of the US government.

ESTA Information

You're required to provide the same information as requested on the form I-94W (Arrival/Departure form), i.e. your biographical data including your name, birth date, and passport information, as well as travel information such as your flight number, destination and address in the US. You're also required to answer VWP eligibility questions regarding subjects such as communicable diseases, arrests and convictions for certain crimes, and your past history of visa revocation or deportation, among others. The information must be provided in English and you must complete the form yourself. The details required are listed in the table below:

> ## ESTA Details
>
> Name
> Date of birth
> Country of citizenship
> Country of current residence
> Gender
> Email address
> Phone number
> Passport number, issuing country, date of issue, date of expiration
> travel information – departure city, flight number, carrier, address while in the us
> VWP eligibility questions

ESTA Denied

If your registration under ESTA is denied, you should ensure that you're eligible under the Visa Waiver Program and that you've completed the ESTA application correctly. If you think that you may have made a mistake you may submit a new registration, but you must wait 24 hours before doing so. This is advisable even if you're certain that you entered the correct information, as there could have been a system 'error'.

If you believe that you have been incorrectly denied authorization to travel, you should contact the Department of Homeland Security through their Travel Redress Inquiry Program (TRIP – 🖳 www. dhs.gov/files/programs/gc_1169673653081. shtm). However, there's no guarantee that a request for redress through DHS TRIP will resolve the issue and a US embassy or consulate is unable to provide information about ESTA denials or resolve an issue that caused the ESTA denial.

If you qualify under the VWP but are denied an ESTA, you must apply for a visitor's visa.

Approval to travel under ESTA (see page 123) is eventually expected to replace the paper I-94W form (see page 115) for travelers under the Visa Waiver Program (source: US Customs and Border Protection).

B-1 BUSINESS VISAS

Anyone who wishes to visit the US on business who doesn't qualify for visa-free travel (see **Visa Waiver Program** on page 1230) or, if he does, wishes to remain longer than 90 days, must apply for a category B-1 visa. B-1 visas are valid for a maximum of ten years and allow the holder to enter and leave the US as often as he wishes during its ten-year validity period.

The general rule is that B-1 visas don't give business visitors the right to work for a US-based company, even if payment is made outside the country. This doesn't, however, apply to business conducted as a visiting businessman, e.g. as a representative of an overseas company, when no payment is received from a US source. The holder of a B-1 visa may

consult with business associates, lawyers or accountants; take part in business and professional conventions; negotiate contracts; settle an estate; and look for investment opportunities. A category B-1 visitor must have a permanent overseas residence.

In addition to completing form DS-160, you may need to provide supporting documentation, such as a letter from your employer, verifying your continued employment, the reason for your trip, and your itinerary (see **Applications** on page 211).

Persons admitted to the US on a B-1 nonimmigrant business visa are usually granted a six-month stay. The actual period is determined by the immigration officer at the port of entry and he has the right to approve a shorter stay on a case by case basis.

Applications (see below) for B-1 visas must be made through a US embassy or consulate and usually require an interview (see page 97). For information about visas applications, including application forms, interviews, visa processing, fees, extensions and changes, and visas refusals, see **Chapter 3**.

Representatives of the foreign press, radio, film, journalists or other information media, require a nonimmigrant media (I)

visa to work in the US, and cannot travel to the US on a visitor or business visa or under the Visa Waiver Program.

Business Visa Center

In 2005, the Department of State established a Business Visa Center (☎ 202-663 3198, ✉ businessvisa @state.gov, 🖳 www.travel.state. gov/visa/temp/types/types_2664. html) to provide information and assist businesses in the US and their partners, customers and colleagues around the world.

The Business Visa Center (BVC) is an information portal for US-based businesses and provides information about the application process for business (B-1) visitor visa travel to the US. The BVC explains the visa process when US companies invite employees or current and prospective business clients and partners to the US, and provides information to US conference and meeting organizers expecting a large number of foreign visitors. Additionally, where visa services has received notification by the US organizer of the event, the Bureau of Consular Affairs maintains a list of 'Upcoming Conferences' to be held in the US on their internal Department of State Intranet. However, having an event listed on the upcoming conferences web page doesn't guarantee visa approval.

The BVC cannot expedite interview appointments or the processing of visa applications, guarantee the issue of a visa or decide the merits of an application for a visa. The consular officer at the US embassy or consulate overseas makes these decisions during the application process.

Permitted Business Activities

There are strict guidelines as to what constitutes business activities which are permitted with a B-1 visa. Permitted business activities include, but aren't limited to, the following:

♦ Consult with business associates;

♦ Attend a scientific, educational, professional or business convention, or a conference on specific dates;

♦ Settle an estate;

♦ Negotiate a contract;

♦ Participate in short-term training.

An overview of key groupings of temporary business-related travel permitted on business visitor visas is shown in the table below:

Business Visitors

Purpose of Travel	Permitted Activities/Guidelines
Athletes	You must receive no salary or income from a US based company or entity, other than prize money for participation in a tournament or sporting event. This includes a trial for a professional team, but doesn't include playing on the team. Athletes or team members who seek to enter the US as members of a foreign-based sports team in order to compete with another sports team will be admitted provided: 1. The foreign athlete and the foreign sports team have their principal place of business or activity in a foreign country. 2. The income of the foreign-based team and the salary of its players are principally accrued in a foreign country. 3. The foreign-based sports team is a member of an international sports league or the sporting activities involved have an international dimension.
Business venture, investor seeking investment	To survey potential sites for a business and/or to lease premises in the US. It doesn't permit you to remain in the US to manage a business.
Conference, meeting, trade show or business event attendee	For business, educational, professional or scientific purposes. You must receive no salary or income from a US-based company or entity.
Exposition or trade show employees of foreign exhibitors at international fairs	To plan, assemble, dismantle, maintain or be employed in connection with exhibits at international fairs or expositions. You must receive no salary or income from a US-based company or entity.
Lecturer or speaker	You must receive no salary or income from a US-based company or entity, other than expenses incidental to your visit. If an honorarium will be received, activities can last no longer than nine days at any single institution or organization.

Continued over >

Business Visitors (Cont)

Purpose of Travel	Permitted Activities/Guidelines
Researcher	Independent research. You must receive no salary or income from a US-based source or benefit to US institution.
Sales/selling	Exhibition, taking orders, negotiating and signing contracts for products made outside the US.
Service engineer (commercial/industrial)	To install, service or repair commercial or industrial equipment or machinery sold by a non-US company to a US buyer, when specifically required by the purchase contract. Installation cannot include construction work, except for the supervision or training of US workers to perform construction.
Training	Participation in a training program that isn't designed primarily to provide employment. You must receive no salary or income from a US-based company or entity, other than expenses related to your stay.

The above list isn't an all-inclusive list of allowable B-1 visa business-related activities. If you have specific questions about your qualifications for a business visa, contact the US embassy or consulate (where you'll apply for the visa) or a qualified US immigration lawyer.

Others who are eligible for B-1 visas include:

♦ Foreign physicians coming to the US to observe new procedures and offer consulting services without performing any patient care.

♦ Personal or domestic servants accompanying returning US citizens with a permanent home abroad or a foreign employer in the US with B, E, F, H, I, J, L, M, O, P, or Q nonimmigrant visa status.

♦ Professional entertainers coming to the US to participate in a cultural program sponsored by their home country to perform before a non-paying audience or participate in a competition for which there's no remuneration, other than a prize (monetary or otherwise) and expenses.

♦ Volunteers and missionary workers coming to the US to perform missionary work on behalf of a religious denomination; engage in an evangelical tour; preach or exchange pulpits with their US counterparts; or participate in a voluntary service program which benefits a US local community. You must receive no remuneration other than an allowance or other reimbursement for expenses incidental to your stay.

♦ Foreign business people coming to the US in conjunction with litigation and those rendering professional services in the US that would otherwise qualify them for an H-1B visa, but who are paid for those services by a source outside the US.

♦ Personal or domestic employees (e.g. cooks, butlers, chauffeurs, housemaids, parlormaids, valets, footmen, nannies, au pairs, mothers' helpers, gardeners, and paid companions) who are accompanying or following to join an employer who seeks admission to, or who's already in, the US in nonimmigrant status.

Employees are required to submit a signed employment contract which contains statements that the employee is guaranteed the minimum or prevailing wage, whichever is greater (🖳 www.dol. gov), and free room and board, and that the employee will be the only provider of employment to the employee. The employee must show that he has been employed by the employer for at least one year or that the employer has regularly employed domestic help over a period of years, and that the employee has at least one year's experience as a personal or domestic servant.

Applications

As a general guideline, a business visitor should apply for a visa as soon as possible and no later than 60 days before the proposed date of travel. If the conference is scientific in nature or you have a scientific background, the visa application should be made no later than 90 days in advance of travel.

Business visa applicants must usually provide the following (the requirements may vary depending on the specific case):

◆ A completed form DS-160 (Nonimmigrant Visa Application – see **Chapter 3**);

◆ A copy of your passport, which must have at least one blank page and be valid for the duration of your trip (if the issuing country automatically extends a passport's validity for an additional six months after expiration – see 🖳 www.state.gov/documents/organization/104770.pdf.) or at least

six months beyond the period of your planned stay in the US;

◆ Two color photographs (2x2in/5x5cm) showing full face without head covering against a light background (you may wear a headdress if it's required by a religious order of which you're a member);

☑ SURVIVAL TIP

The US requirements for 'passport photographs' (see page 95) are different from the requirements in other countries. Usually, you cannot use photographs taken in DIY booths, but must go to a photographer familiar with the requirements.

◆ Information describing the company such as brochures, catalogs or annual reports;

◆ A copy of your itinerary in the US;

◆ Documentation demonstrating your ability and intention, or that of your employer, to support your travel and other expenses while in the US (see below);

◆ The visa application fee, which is payable when the application is made. There may also be a visa issue fee for some countries (see page 99).

Supporting documentation should be in the form of a letter from your employer and/or the inviting organization in the US, stating your name, date and place of birth and foreign address, and containing information regarding the purpose, location, duration and source of funding for the business trip. The letter should address, in some detail, the specific duties/activities to be undertaken by the employee in the US. If you qualify under the VWP, you must convince the consular official why you need to remain in the US for longer than 90 days. There are specific requirements for anyone who'll be performing services on a vessel in the Outer Continental Shelf (OCS).

If you have an APEC Business Travelers Card (ABTC – see 🖥 www. apec.org) you still need a visa to travel to the US (unless you qualify for the Visa Waiver Program). Possession of an ABTC doesn't alter your visa requirements, your visa status, or the visa process for travel to the US. However, holders of an ABTC are eligible to participate in US embassy or consulate business facilitation programs,

which offer expedited visa interview appointments.

If you've been refused a B-1 business visa in the preceding two years, you can re-apply after at least three working days from the date of the refusal through the Interview process.

Extensions & Changes

Travelers with B-1 visas are usually allowed to stay in the US for a period of up to six months, with the possibility of an extension for up to six additional months. Applications for extensions should be made between 15 to 45 days of the date of expiry of your I-94 form by submitting a form I-539 (Application to Extend/Change Nonimmigrant Status – see 🖥 www.uscis. gov/files/form/i-539.pdf) to the nearest USCIS office. Only those who are already in the US on a B-1 business visa may file an application for the extension of stay.

There's no guarantee that an application for an extension will be approved – and there's no appeal – by the USCIS, which takes into consideration factors such as the reason for the extension (a common reason is an unforeseen delay in conclusion of a business matter); your intention to depart the US at the end of the proposed extension period; and whether you're deemed to have a desire to remain in the country indefinitely. You must also provide evidence of financial support.

Individuals who enter the US with a B-1 business visa may be eligible to change their status to a permanent resident (Green Card holder) provided they qualify, or to another nonimmigrant status, including a temporary worker or student. However, you must prove that you had no preconceived intent to change your status. The option to change status is one of the advantages of a nonimmigrant visa, compared with entering the US under the Visa Waiver Program (see page 120).

B-2 VISITOR VISAS

Anyone who wishes to visit the US as a tourist or for medical treatment and who doesn't qualify for visa-free travel (see **Visa Waiver Program** on page 120) or, if he does, wishes to remain longer than 90 days, must apply for a category B-2 visitor visa (also called a holiday or tourist visa).

B-2 visas are valid for a maximum of ten years and allow the holder to enter and leave the US as often as he wishes during this period. However, you're usually permitted to remain in the US for a maximum of six months per visit (the actual period is decided by an immigration officer). Most visitors have their I-94 cards stamped with a six-month stay, although the immigration officer has the right to issue a shorter stay on a case by case basis. Factors which affect the validity period and the likelihood of admission with a B-2 visa include the number of entries made, the expiration date of your passport, and your history of travel to the US. You can request an extension of your visa once you're in the US (see below).

A B-2 visa doesn't give you the right to work in the US, even if payment is made outside the country.

In addition to completing form DS-160, you may need to supply supporting documentation in the form of an invitation from the person you're visiting or staying with in the US, evidence substantiating the purpose of your trip and your intention to depart the US after a temporary visit. Examples of the evidence required are listed on form DS-160.

In the case of pleasure trips, this includes documents outlining your plans in the US and stating the reasons why you're bound to return abroad after a short stay, such as family ties, employment (a self-employed person may require a letter from his accountant or solicitor confirming that he's known to them and stating how long he's been in business) or home ownership.

As a result of previous abuse by holders of B-2 visas, immigration officials may regard tourists as 'suspect' and make checks to ensure that you aren't planning to abuse the system.

Applications for B-2 visas must be made through a US embassy or consulate and require an interview (see page 97).

 Caution

If you make an application for a visitor's visa in a country other than your home country or country of residence, called an 'out-of-district' application, your application will be subject to increased scrutiny as it may be suspected that you're 'shopping around' for an easier port of entry.

It's possible for B-2 visas holders to apply for a change of status in the US, for example to F-1 student status, although the USCIS may decide that you misrepresented your intentions when coming to the US as a visitor and deny the change. If you wish to become a student in the US, it's best to apply for the appropriate student visa in your home country (see **Chapter 7**).

Medical Treatment

B-2 tourist visas are also issued to those coming to the US to undergo medical treatment. The application process is similar to that for a tourist visa, although there are additional documents that must be submitted to establish that you qualify for the visa. In addition to the documents listed below (under **B2 Visa Applications**), the following documentation is also required:

♦ **Medical diagnosis from a local physician** (in the applicant's home country or country of residence), explaining the nature of the ailment and the reason the applicant requires treatment in the US.

◆ **Appointment confirmation from a doctor or hospital in the US**. For example a letter from a physician or medical facility in the US, expressing a willingness to treat the specific ailment and detailing the projected length and cost of treatment (including doctors' fees, hospitalization fees and all medical-related expenses).

◆ **Evidence of ability to pay for the medical treatment.** For example a statement of financial responsibility from the individuals or an organization that will pay for the patient's transportation, medical and living expenses. The individuals guaranteeing payment of these expenses must provide proof of their ability to do so, often in the form of bank or other statements of income/ savings or certified copies of income tax returns.

The need for medical travel often arises suddenly and visas may need to be arranged quickly, therefore for urgent medical care you may need to make an interview appointment as quickly as possible, even if the documents listed above (or under **B-2 Visa Applications** below) aren't yet available. In urgent cases an embassy can initiate processing of the visa pending the arrival of the documents. In this case you may need to request an expedited or emergency appointment, which can be done via an embassy website or by telephone.

☑ SURVIVAL TIP

It's important to note that an individual suffering certain afflictions, e.g. a contagious disease, may be ineligible under the US Immigration and Nationality Act to receive a visa.

B-2 Visa Applications

As a general guideline, a visitor should apply for a visa as soon as possible and no later than 60 days before the proposed date of travel.

Visitor visa applicants must provide the following:

◆ A completed form DS-160 (Nonimmigrant Visa Application – see **Applications** on page 94).

◆ A copy of your passport, which must have at least one blank page and be valid for the duration of your trip (if the issuing country automatically extends a passport's validity for an additional six months after expiration – see 🖳 www.state.gov/documents/ organization/104770.pdf.), or at least six months beyond the period of your planned stay in the US;

◆ One color photograph (2x2in/5x5cm) showing full face without head covering against a light background (you may wear a headdress if required by a religious order of which you're a member). For information, see page 95. When using the form DS-160, the photo is uploaded via the online application system.

◆ The visas application fee, which is payable when the application is made. There may also be a visa issue fee in some countries (see page 218).

You will also need to provide evidence regarding the purpose of your trip and of the funds to support yourself (and any dependants) while in the US, or evidence that you have a sponsor in the US who's willing to support you, e.g. a letter of invitation from friends or relatives. Your sponsor in the US who will be providing support may need to complete a form I-134 (Affidavit of Support) and have it notarized.

You may also need to prove that you have compelling social and economic ties abroad and a residence outside the US, as well as other binding ties that will insure your return abroad at the end of your visit. It's impossible to specify the exact form the documentation should take as applicants' circumstances vary greatly.

If you've been refused a B-2 visitor visa in the preceding two years, you can re-apply after at least three working days from the date of the refusal through the Interview process.

B-2 Visa Extensions & Changes

Travelers with B-2 visas are usually allowed to stay in the US for a period of up to six months, with the possibility of an extension for up to six additional months. Applications for extensions should be made between 15 to 45 days of the date of expiry of your I-94 form by submitting a form I-539 (Application to Extend/Change Nonimmigrant Status – see 💻 www.uscis.gov/files/form/i-539.pdf) to the nearest USCIS office. Only those who are already in the US on a B-2 visitors visa may file an application for an extension of stay.

There's no guarantee that an application for an extension will be approved by the USCIS – and there's no appeal – which takes into consideration factors such as the reason for the

extension; your intention to depart the US at the end of the proposed extension period; and whether you're deemed to have a desire to remain in the country indefinitely. You must also provide evidence of financial support.

Individuals who enter the US on a B-2 visa may be eligible to change their status to a permanent resident (Green Card holder) provided they qualify, or to another nonimmigrant status, including a temporary worker or student. However, you must prove that you had no preconceived intent to change your status. The option to change status is one of the advantages of a nonimmigrant visa, compared with entering the US under the Visa Waiver Program (see page 120).

Technically you can leave the US after six months, return the following day and stay for a further six months, but you're unlikely to get away with this many times. Some people use a B visa to remain in the US for a year or two, but most eventually get caught and are deported/removed and refused re-admission.

5.

TEMPORARY EMPLOYEES

I f you wish to work in the US and don't qualify for an immigrant visa (see Chapter 8), you may qualify for a nonimmigrant visa as a temporary worker, which could lead to permanent residence. Visas for temporary workers can be confusing as there are many different categories, depending on the reason and type of work involved. However, those wishing to work in the US must usually apply and be approved for a visa for a temporary worker, which as the name implies, are valid for a limited period only.

☑ SURVIVAL TIP

Most visas can be renewed and your US employer may be willing to sponsor you for permanent residence, if applicable. Don't, however, expect your employer to sponsor you for a Green Card at the earliest opportunity, which – in any case – can take a very long time to be approved.

Nonimmigrant visas for temporary workers are divided into a variety of categories, each designed for specific groups depending on the type of work involved. With the exception of some permanent categories for those with extraordinary or exceptional ability (e.g. internationally-renowned artists and musicians who are self-employed), those wishing to live and work in the US need to be in possession of a guaranteed, permanent full-time job offer from a US-based company. In most cases the prospective US employer must file a petition (see below) with the USCIS before

you apply for a visa, and some also need labor certification and/or a Labor Condition Application (see page 137).

Each visa for temporary workers has a different set of qualification criteria which you'll need to meet. For example, an H-1B visa requires you to be employed in a specialist occupation and have higher education qualifications or the equivalent qualifying experience, while an H-2B visa is for seasonal jobs. Some temporary work visas have an annual quota.

Working in the US usually gives you the right to a US driver's license (provided you already have a valid foreign license or pass a US driving test!), a state ID card, bank account, credit card (depending on your credit rating), eligibility for a US mortgage to buy a home and many other 'privileges.' You can also travel freely to and from the US and your spouse and children usually also qualify to live in the US and attend school, although they cannot usually work.

Visas for temporary workers include those in the table shown overleaf, details of which are included in this chapter unless indicated by an asterisk (see the note below the table):

Nonimmigrant Visas

Visa	Application
E-1*	Treaty trader
E-2*	Treaty investor
E-3	Work visa for Australians
F-1*	Students in the OPT/CPT program
H-1B	Specialty occupations
H-2A	Temporary agricultural workers
H-2B	Temporary workers other than agricultural
H-3	Trainee and special education exchange
I	Representatives of foreign media
J*	Cultural exchange
O-1	Extraordinary ability
P-1	International athletes
P-2	Exchange artists/entertainers
P-3	Culturally unique education program
Q	International cultural exchange
R-1	Religious workers
TN	Canadian and Mexican professionals

* These visas aren't covered in this chapter, but in chapters 6 (E-1, E-2) and 7 (F-1, J).

PETITIONS

If you want to work in the US temporarily as a nonimmigrant, under US immigration law you need a specific visa based on the type of work you'll be doing. Most temporary worker categories require a prospective employer or agent to file a petition with the USCIS, which must be approved before you can apply for a visa. In addition, in order to be considered as a nonimmigrant under some temporary worker categories, a prospective employer or agent must also obtain a labor certification (see below) or other approval from the Department of Labor. Once that's received, the prospective employer or agent can file a form I-129 (Petition for Nonimmigrant Worker), which can be filed electronically with the USCIS.

If there's a chance that the beneficiary will need to obtain a visa at a US embassy or consulate after a change, extension or petition amendment, it's advisable to file a duplicate petition set with original signatures on the forms.

In some cases the prospective employer must file an Application for Alien Employment Certification or a Labor Condition Application (see **Labor Certification & LCAs** below) with the Department of Labor and/or obtain certain consultation reports from labor organizations **before** filing a petition with the USCIS.

It's important for prospective employers to file the petition as soon as possible (but not more than six months before the proposed employment is due to begin) in order to provide adequate time for it to be approved and subsequent visa processing. If you need the petition to be processed faster, you may be eligible to apply for premium processing. The Premium Processing Service is available for certain employment-based petitions **(H, L, O, P, Q and R categories)** and applications with a guaranteed 15-day processing period (rather than a number of months) for an additional fee of $1,000. A form I-907 (Request for Premium Processing Service) must be filed with the USCIS, who will determine whether they can meet the 15-day processing period. Once a petition has been filed, you can check the processing time via the USCIS (☎ 1-800-357-2099, 🖥 www.uscis.gov).

The petition (form I-129) must be approved by the USCIS before the prospective employee can apply for a visa at a US embassy or consulate abroad. When the petition is approved, the employer or agent is sent a form I-797 (Notice of Action), the notification of petition approval. However, the I-797 is

no longer required for the visa applicant's interview, as petition approval is now verified in the Department of State's system, called the Petition Information Management Service (PIMS). In order to verify the petition approval, you need your approved I-129 petition receipt number. Note that the approval of a petition doesn't guarantee that a visa will be issued if you're found to be ineligible under the Immigration and Nationality Act.

Those applying for a temporary worker (H), intra-company transferee (L), alien of extraordinary ability (O), athlete/artist/entertainer (P), international cultural exchange visitor (Q), or a religious worker (R) visa, must provide the receipt number of the approved I-129 petition. This number is provided by the USCIS after the petition is filed by the prospective employer. Applicants are also required to provide a copy of the petition and its supporting documents.

If an employee is required for longer than the period for which he was originally admitted, the employer may be able to file a new I-129 petition on behalf of the employee, which should be done well before it expires. Note, however, that if the employee has already stayed for the maximum period allowed, an extension may not be granted. If an employer applies for an extension and hasn't received a decision by the time the employee's visa expires, the employee can continue to be lawfully employed for a period of up to 240 days or until the USCIS makes a decision, whichever comes first. If the extension is denied and the employee's visa has expired (i.e. he's 'out of status'), he must cease employment immediately and leave the US.

Employers must keep the USCIS informed of any firings, termination of employment or changes in the employee's eligibility by submitting a letter to the USCIS office with jurisdiction over the application/petition. US employers are required by law to verify the employment eligibility of all workers employed in the US, irrespective of their immigration status. This is done via form I-9 (Employment Eligibility Verification) or the E-verify program, an online electronic system. Judging by the number of illegal workers in the US, this requirement is often ignored!

See also **Petitions** for immigrant visas on page 207.

LABOR CERTIFICATION & CONDITION APPLICATIONS

In some cases the employer must file an Application for Alien Employment Certification or a Labor Condition Application (LCA) with the Department of Labor and/or obtain certain consultation reports from labor organizations **before** filing a petition with the USCIS. Foreign Labor Certification (FLC) programs permit US employers to hire foreign workers on a temporary or permanent basis to fill jobs essential to the US economy. Certification may be obtained in cases where it can be demonstrated that there are insufficient qualified US workers available and willing to perform the work at wages that meet or exceed the prevailing wage paid for

that occupation in the area of intended employment.

Since 2005, applications for labor certification have been filed using the Program Electronic Review Management (PERM) system, to streamline the labor certification application.

The Department of Labor issues LCAs/FLCs for permanent and temporary employment under the following programs:

Category	Application
H-1B	Specialty (professional) workers – require an LCA only
H-1C	Nurses in disadvantaged areas
H-2A	Temporary labor certification (seasonal agricultural)
H-2B	Temporary labor certification (non-agricultural)

Although each foreign labor certification program is unique, there are similar requirements that the employer must complete prior to the issue of a labor certification. In the case of permanent labor certification, the employer must prepare a recruitment report in which it categorizes the lawful job-related reasons for the rejection of US applicants and the number of US applicants rejected in each category.

The labor certification procedure includes the following rules that employers must follow:

♦ Ensure that the position meets the qualifying criteria for the requested program.

♦ Complete the Employment and Training Administration (ETA) form designated for the requested program. This may include the form and any supporting documentation, e.g. job description, applicant's résumé, etc.

♦ Ensure that the wage offered equals or exceeds the prevailing wage for the occupation in the area of intended employment.

♦ Make sure that the compliance issues effected upon receipt of a foreign labor certification are completely understood.

♦ Ensure that the completed ETA form is submitted to the designated Department of Labor office for the requested program, e.g., SWA, regional office or the national office.

The employer will be notified of the decision by the Department of Labor.

Foreign labor certification programs are designed to assure that the admission of foreign workers into the US on a permanent or temporary basis won't adversely affect the job opportunities, wages, and working conditions of US workers. Regulations require that the wages attested to on foreign labor certification applications must be equal to or higher than the average wage paid to similarly qualified workers in the relevant occupation in the area of intended employment. This average wage is referred to as the prevailing wage. The employer isn't precluded from paying nonimmigrant(s) more than the prevailing wage.

Approval by the DOL doesn't guarantee a visa will be issued. Once the application is certified (approved), the prospective employer may submit an employment based petition to the USCIS.

In addition to FLC, a Labor Condition Application (LCA) is sometimes required by an employer to support the petition for a nonimmigrant visa and/or labor attestation (whereby an employer attests that they have attempted to find labor within the US). For example, an employer must file a Labor Condition Application (LCA) with the Department of Labor before he can 'sponsor' someone for an H-1B visa.

The prevailing wage for that position in the locality must be obtained from the Department of Labor or another source. The required wage for the position is the higher of the 'actual wage' paid to other employees (at the sponsoring organization) in the same position or the 'prevailing local wage'. There are various wage surveys that can be utilized, including the employer's own wage survey. In general, most LCAs are approved, provided that they aren't incomplete or obviously inaccurate.

VISA CATEGORIES FOR TEMPORARY WORKERS

The visas categories described below are issued to temporary workers. Note that category E (treaty traders & investors), category F (academic or language students entitled to work) and category J (exchange visitors) are listed below, but are described in detail in chapters 6 (category E) and 7 (categories F and J).

Category E: Treaty Traders & Investors

Category E visas are termed Treaty Trader (E-1) and Treaty Investor (E-2) and are

issued to people wishing to invest in or trade with a company in the US. (There are also E-3 visas – see below.) They're issued subject to certain conditions, but there's no restriction on the number issued each year. As the name suggests, category E visas are available only to citizens of countries with which the US has a commerce treaty. For more information, see **Chapter 6**.

It's also possible for investors who are investing a minimum of $500,000 in a commercial enterprise to obtain an immigrant (Green Card) EB-5 visa. For information, see page 169.

Category E-3 Visas

The E-3 treaty professional visa was introduced in 2005 and was created by an Act of Congress as a result of the Australia-United States Free Trade Agreement (AUSFTA), although it isn't formally a part of the AUSFTA. The E-3 visa applies only to Australian citizens who are employed in a specialty occupation, which means that Australians are no longer required to compete with other nationalities for H-1B visas.

The definition of a 'specialty occupation' is one that requires a theoretical and practical application of a body of specialized knowledge; and the attainment of a bachelor's or higher degree in the specialty (or its equivalent). (The definition is the same as for H-1B visas.) It isn't sufficient that an E-3 applicant holds a particular degree, but the job itself must also require a bachelor-level or higher qualification or its equivalent in terms of experience, or a combination of experience and bachelor level credits.

There's no definitive list of occupations eligible for an E-3 visa, although a useful general guide is to check the Occupational Information Network (🖥 http://online. onetcenter.org) and the Occupational Outlook Handbook (🖥 www.bls.gov/oco). If a special license is required or other official permission to practise in the specialty occupation, it must be obtained before you can commence employment.

If your degree and higher-level qualifications are from an Australian institution, you don't usually need to provide certified copies or evidence of their US equivalent, but you should bring the original certificates to your visa interview, and if possible, transcripts for your course of study. If your qualification(s) aren't from an Australian institution, a certified copy of the foreign degree and evidence that it's equivalent to the required US degree could be used to satisfy the 'qualifying credentials' requirement. It's advisable to have an evaluation of your foreign qualifications by a qualified academic evaluator.

You should produce certified copies of certificates and evidence of US equivalence at your interview. A certified copy of a US baccalaureate or higher degree, as required by the specialty occupation, would meet the minimum evidentiary standard. In the absence of an academic or other qualifying credential(s), evidence is required of education and experience that's equivalent to the relevant US degree.

You need a job offer from a US-based employer before you can apply for an E-3

visa; the prospective employer must apply for a form 9035/9035E (Labor Condition Application), although a petition isn't required. Change of visa status to E-3 isn't possible if you entered the country under the Visa Waiver Program and you must be outside the US when the application (form DS-160) is made. If you're applying in a country other than Australia, you should contact the nearest US embassy or consulate to check that they accept applications from non-residents. They will also be unfamiliar with Australian education institutions and therefore proving eligibility may be more difficult.

An E-3 visa is usually issued for two years at a time but can be extended indefinitely in two-year increments. You can change your employer when you're in the US, but your new employer must lodge a new Labor Condition Application (LCA), and the gap between jobs must be ten days or less.

The E-3 visa is similar in many respects to the H-1B (see page opposite). Important differences include the fact that the spouse of an E-3 visa holder may work or study in the US without restrictions (unlike other US nonimmigrant visas). The spouse and children (under age 21) of the main applicant aren't required to be Australian citizens and spouses of E-3 visa holders are entitled to an E-3D (dependant) visa and work authorization, which doesn't need to be in a specialty occupation. E-3 spouses can apply for a form I-765 (Employment Authorization Document) through the USCIS.

The annual quota for E-3 visas is 10,500 for a fiscal year (from October 1 to September 30), which is huge when you consider that fewer than 950 Australians succeeded in obtaining H-1B work visas in 2004, the year before E-3 visas were introduced.

Category F: Academic or Language Students

Qualified international students with an F-1 visa who have been accepted for a full-time course of study at an approved school can work under the Optional Practical Training (OPT) and Curricular Practical Training (CPT) schemes. If F-1 students meet the requirements for OPT, they can work in the US for one year after they finish their program of study, while CPT allows students to be paid for a required internship.

An F-2 visa is issued to the spouse and children of F-1 visa holders who wish to visit or accompany a foreign national studying in the US.

For more information, see page 179.

Category H Visas

If you wish to work in the US for a few years, you may qualify for a category H visa, some of which are valid (with extensions) for up to six years. In general, these visas are based on a specific offer of employment from a US-based employer. The employment must be approved in advance by the USCIS on the basis of a petition, form I-129H (Petition for Nonimmigrant Worker), filed by the prospective US employer. Australians should also see the E-3 visa (above).

There are six sub-categories of H visas:

An employer should use an experienced immigration lawyer when applying for a category H visa, as the procedure is complicated and constantly changing.

Quotas or Cap

The word 'cap' refers to annual numerical limitations (quotas) set by Congress on certain nonimmigrant visa classifications, e.g., H-1B and H-2B. Caps control the number of workers that can be issued a visa in a given fiscal year for a particular nonimmigrant classification. Caps also control the number of aliens already in the US that may be authorized to change status to a cap-subject classification. The annual numerical limitations generally don't apply to those who have already been counted against the cap in a particular nonimmigrant classification and are seeking to extend their stay in that classification.

H-1B Visas

H-1B visas are issued to workers in specialized occupations and the professions, e.g. accountants, architects, computer specialists, doctors of medicine, engineers, lawyers, specialist nurses, professors/teachers and scientists. The position applied for must usually require a bachelor's or higher degree or equivalent experience; applications made by those without a degree are subject to greater scrutiny and are much more difficult to obtain.

The H-1B visa program also includes certain fashion models of distinguished merit and ability and up to 100 people who will be performing services of an exceptional nature in connection with Department of Defense (DOD) research and development projects or coproduction projects.

Category H Visas

Category	Description
H-1B	workers in specialized occupations
H-1C	registered nurses in areas where there are shortages
H-2A	seasonal agricultural workers
H-2B	workers filling jobs that cannot be filled by US citizens or residents
H-3	trainees in a program that isn't primarily for employment
H-4	immediate families of H-1, H-2 and H-3 visa holders

Each of the above sub-categories is covered in detail below.

Many professions in the US are licensed and controlled by individual states, resulting in 50 different licensing procedures for each profession. Where a license is an essential prerequisite, then it must be obtained by the applicant prior to the employer submitting a petition on his behalf. However, in most states, professionals such as accountants, architects, engineers and lawyers who work for a company rather than in the public sector, don't require a license,

An employer must file a Labor Condition Application (LCA) with the Department of Labor before he can 'sponsor' someone for an H-1B visa. The prevailing wage for the position in the locality must be obtained from the Department of Labor or another source. The required wage for the position is the higher of the 'actual wage' paid to other employees in the same position or the 'prevailing local wage', which can be determined using one of the various wage surveys available, including the employer's own wage survey. In general, almost all LCAs are approved, provided they aren't incomplete or obviously inaccurate.

Various problems have been encountered by employers since LCAs were fully incorporated into the Department of Labor's web-based I-Cert Portal system in 2009, such as an LCA being denied because the Federal Employer Identification Number (FEIN) specified wasn't recognized by the DOL as a valid FEIN registered with the Internal Revenue Service. On a number of occasions, employers have complained about having to submit further documentation to the DOL (such as taxation documentation) in order to establish that their FEIN number is indeed registered with the IRS. This means that when the FEIN validity is finally proven to be valid by the DOL, the employer must reapply for the LCA, as the DOL must approve or deny an LCA application within seven working days. If an application is denied the employer can re-apply, but must wait a further seven days for the new application to be processed.

Contrary to popular myth, there's no requirement that employers must prove they couldn't find a US worker before hiring an H-1B worker. In the case of 'H-1B-dependent employers' (e.g. those with over 15 per cent of workers with H-1B visas), the law requires them to recruit US workers in 'good faith', but there's no effective enforcement mechanism.

H-1B petitions require prospective employers to provide certain information and documents including the employer's need for a professional to fill the position, and the applicant's professional abilities, educational qualifications and résumé/CV.

Form I-129W (H-1B Data Collection & Filing Fee Exemption) must also be completed and is used to collect information about the H-1B applicant and petitioner. It's also used to determine whether the H-1B petitioner is exempt from an additional filing fee ($750 for employers with fewer than 25 employees and $1,500 for employers with more than 25 employees).

H-1B visas are issued for up to three years, although citizens of certain countries receive visas for shorter periods – from one month to two years. Extensions of up to three years may be granted, making a maximum of six years. It's possible for an H-1B visa holder to change his status ('adjust status') to that of a permanent resident (Green Card) while in the US, provided an employer will act as a sponsor.

As a general rule, a person who's in one nonimmigrant status may not change status or change employers in that status until he applies to the USCIS for such a change, although such changes are usually granted. However, a provision called 'H-1B portability' permits certain individuals already in the US in H-1B status to commence employment for a new employer once the new employer has filed an H-1B petition with the USCIS.

Under immigration law, a US employer is liable for the reasonable costs of return transportation abroad for a foreign employee in the H-1B (and H-2B) category if the employer dismisses the employee before the end of the period of authorized admission, i.e. your employer must pay for your flight home if you're fired.

H-1B Quotas

US law currently limits the number of H-1B visas to 65,000 per annum, plus 20,000 which are issued to foreign nationals who obtained a masters degree or doctorate in the US. Because they are exempt from the 65,000 cap, H-1B visas issued to advanced degree foreign nationals beyond the first 20,000 are counted against the 65,000 cap.

> There's a vast gulf between the H1-B visa quota and the requirements of US employers, which is starkly illustrated by the fact that the quota for fiscal year 2009 was exhausted on the very first day on which applications could be submitted!

Up to 6,800 visas are reserved from the annual cap of 65,000 for the H-1B1 program under the terms of the US-Chile and US-Singapore Free Trade Agreements. Unused numbers in this pool are made available for H-1B use for the next fiscal year.

H-1B visa renewals and extensions of stay don't count towards the annual quotas (cap) and H-1B nonimmigrants who work at (but not necessarily for) universities and non-profit research facilities are also exempt from the quotas. Transfers of H-1B visas among US employers only count against the quota when the foreign national is changing jobs from a US employer who's exempt from the limits (i.e. academia or research) to one that isn't exempt (a for-profit business).

H-1B Filing Dates

The first day of filing for H-1B visas for fiscal year 2011 was April 1, 2010. If the foreign national is already in the US, he must stay in lawful nonimmigrant status until October 1, 2010, when the H-1B visa becomes effective. A review of past years (2004-2009) shows a rapid depletion of the H-1B quota each year, e.g. in fiscal year 2009 the entire 65,000 H-1B visa quota was met on the very first day of filing! For fiscal year 2010, the entire 20,000 advanced-degree H-1B quota exemption was also exhausted in just one day, although for fiscal year 2011 the quota was filled more slowly.

In order to be considered, your application must contain all the appropriate documentation and be sent to the correct USCIS service center. If the number of petitions received by the USCIS in the first five business days of April reaches or exceeds the quota (for both the 65,000 quota and the 20,000 advanced-degree quota), then a 'lottery' (often termed a 'mini lottery' so as not to be confused with the Green Card lottery – see page 196) is conducted. If the If H-1B quota isn't reached in the first five business days of April, then the USCIS continues to receive and accept petitions until the quota is reached.

Advanced degree holders have a better chance of being selected in the H-1B lottery than individuals who are seeking a regular H-1B visa, because the government first holds the lottery for the 20,000 advanced degree visas. Applications that aren't drawn as part of that selection process are then added to the pool of applications for the 65,000 regular H-1B visas, giving the first-time losers a second chance of getting an H-1B visa. If there's a lottery, receipts are issued only for petitions selected in the lottery process.

The USCIS will deny or revoke all petitions filed by an employer for the same H-1B worker if more than one filing is discovered. If multiple petitions are discovered, whether one or more such petitions are approved, the USCIS will retain all fees and either deny the petitions or, if a petition was approved, revoke it.

H-1C Visas

H-1C visas were introduced (Nursing Relief for Disadvantaged Area Act of 1999) in September 2000 for registered nurses (RNs) coming to the US to work in positions in 'health professional shortage areas' determined by the Department of Health and Human Services (DHHS). To be eligible for an H-1C visa, nurses must be fully trained and qualified; there are strict requirements and only a handful of hospitals are qualified to petition for nurses under this program. H-1C visas are valid for three years with no extensions.

Only 500 visas were available for H-1C visas and the program expired at the end of 2009 and is now dormant. There's currently no specific nurse visa available in the US, although they can qualify under other visas categories, such as H-1B or in immigrant categories such as the EB-3

for Schedule A workers. However, RNs don't usually qualify for H-1B visa status, although certain specialized nursing occupations that require a bachelor's or higher degree have a better chance of satisfying the H-1B visa requirements.

H-2A Visas

H-2A visas are for temporary or seasonal agricultural workers coming to the US, usually to pick crops or do other short-term jobs on farms or ranches. The H-2A temporary agricultural program establishes a means for farmers (who anticipate a shortage of domestic workers) to bring nonimmigrant foreign workers to the US to perform agricultural labor or services of a temporary or seasonal nature.

The approval of H-2A (and H-2B) petitions applies only to nationals of certain countries designated as participating countries by the Secretary of Homeland Security, published annually in the *Federal Register*. In 2010, the list of eligible countries was extended and included 39 counties (see box). The DHS may allow (on a case-by-case basis) a worker from a country that isn't on the list to be eligible for an H-2A visa.

Countries Eligible for H-2A & H-2B Visas		
Argentina	Guatemala	Norway
Australia	Honduras	Peru
Belize	Indonesia	Philippines
Brazil	Ireland	Poland
Bulgaria	Israel	Romania
Canada	Jamaica	Serbia
Chile	Japan	Slovakia
Costa Rica	Lithuania	South Africa
Croatia	Mexico	South Korea
Dominican Republic	Moldova	Turkey
Ecuador the	Netherlands	Ukraine
El Salvador	New Zealand	United Kingdom
Ethiopia	Nicaragua	Uruguay

Employers anticipating a shortage of agricultural workers need to apply at least 45 days before certification is necessary and can petition for multiple, unnamed agricultural workers. Before the USCIS approves an employer's petition for H-2A workers, the employer must file an application with the Department of Labor stating that there are insufficient workers who are able, willing, qualified and available, and that the employment of aliens won't adversely affect the wages and working conditions of similarly employed US workers. An employer who's been certified for a specific number of H-2A jobs must have initially attempted to find US workers to fill these slots, and even after H-2A workers are recruited, employers must continue to engage in the 'positive recruitment' of US workers.

The H-2A certification is valid for up to one year. Temporary or seasonal agricultural employment is performed during certain seasons only or for a limited period of less than one year, at times when an employer can show that the need for the foreign worker is truly temporary. Before filing a petition (form I-129H), with the USCIS, an employer is required to obtain labor certification (see page 137) from the Department of Labor, confirming that there are no qualified US workers eligible for the employment on which the petition is based.

H-2A Employment Conditions

An employer who files an application to employ H-2A workers must meet many specific conditions, including those concerning recruitment, wages, housing, meals, transportation, workers' compensation insurance, tools and supplies, certification fees, labor disputes and other conditions. Employers must provide each worker with a copy of their work contract or the job order on or before the first day of employment.

Workers must be provided with a statement on each pay day, detailing the hours worked, offered and refused, and the pay for each type of crop and the basis of pay, i.e. whether it's by the hour, by the piece, 'task' pay, etc. The statement must indicate their total earnings for the pay period and all deductions from wages, along with a statement why deductions were made.

The statute and departmental regulations provide for numerous worker protections and employer requirements with respect to wages and working conditions, which don't apply to non-agricultural programs. When employing a worker, employers must guarantee to provide employment for at least three-quarters of all contracted workdays during the term of the contract period. If the employer provides less employment, then he's obligated to pay the amount which employees would have earned if they had worked for the contracted period.

Employers must maintain records concerning any worker who was terminated (i.e. made redundant or fired) and the reason for such termination. In order to negate a continuing liability for wages and benefits to workers, the employer must notify the USCIS of any abandonment or abscondment. The employer should also indicate if replacements will be sought for such workers. An H-2A worker may change employers and can begin work with a new employer when he files the H-2A petition, provided the employer participates in the USCIS E-verify program (see **Petitions** on page 136).

An H-2A worker may remain in the US for a maximum of 30 days following the expiration of his visa. If he has spent three years in the US, he must reside (and be physically present) outside the US for at least three months before being eligible for another H-2A visa.

H-2B Visas

H-2B visas are for temporary workers (skilled and unskilled) who are coming to the US to perform a job which is temporary or seasonal in nature, and for which there's a shortage of US workers. The definition of 'temporary or seasonal' has been extended to allow US employers and eligible foreign workers the maximum flexibility to complete projects which could be for a specific one-time need of up to three years, without demonstrating extraordinary circumstances.

The approval of H-2B (and H-2A) petitions applies only to nationals of certain countries designated as participating countries by the Secretary of Homeland Security, published annually in the *Federal Register*. For a list of participating countries in 2010 see the table above. The DHS may allow (on a case-by-case basis) a worker from a country that isn't on the list to be eligible for an H-2B visa.

Before filing a petition (form I-129H), with the USCIS, an employer is required to obtain labor certification (see page 137) from the Department of Labor, confirming that there are no qualified US workers eligible for the employment on which the petition is based. A petitioner need specify only the number of positions sought and isn't required to name the individual workers except when a worker is already present in the US, or where a worker is from a country that isn't eligible for participation in the H-2B program (and a waiver is sought).

There are no educational requirements, and experience and qualifications depend on the job. The H-2B visa allows employers in industries with peak load, seasonal or intermittent needs to augment their labor force with temporary workers, or when necessary due to a one-time occurrence which necessitates a temporary increase in workers. A typical H-2B applicant is a skilled technician employed by a foreign company and coming to the US to install machinery or train US staff. H-2B workers are common in sectors such as construction, health care, landscaping, lumber, manufacturing, food service/processing

and resort/hospitality services. H-2B visas are also issued to entertainers who don't meet the criteria for category O or P visas.

There's an annual quota (cap) of 66,000 H-2B visas, half (33,000) of which are allocated for employment starting in the first half of the fiscal year (October 1 to March 31) and 33,000 allocated for employment commencing in the second half of the fiscal year (April 1 to September 30).

Visas are initially issued for one year and may be extended for an additional two years (one year at a time), up to a maximum of three years; nationals of certain countries are issued visas for up to six months only. Generally, an H-2B worker who extends his/her stay in H-2B status isn't counted against the quota, while a worker who changes his nonimmigrant status from another category of nonimmigrant visas to H-2B is counted against the annual H-2B cap.

An application must be filed more than 120 days before the date of the actual need for the H-2B worker's services, as shown on the labor certification; the employment start date on the petition (form I-129H) must be the same as stated on the approved temporary labor certification. It can take considerably longer to obtain an H-2B visa than, for example, an H-1B visa, usually several months, depending on the state where the employer is located.

Employers must notify the USCIS when H-2B workers fail to show up for work, complete work more than 30 days ahead of schedule, are terminated (fired) or abscond from the worksite.

An H-2B worker who has spent three years in the US must reside, and be physically present, outside the US for at least three months before he's eligible for another H-2B visa.

H-3 Visas

H-3 visas are for trainees coming to the US for on-the-job training or work experience in any field (e.g. agriculture, commerce, communications, finance, government,

technology, transportation or the professions), other than graduate education or training and medical training programs. The training must be to further the trainee's career in his home country and training cannot be used to provide productive employment in the US.

The employer is required to file a petition (form I-129H) with the USCIS in order to obtain approval for the training and must provide a statement describing the kind of training offered and the position for which the trainee is being trained. He must also explain why the training cannot be obtained in the trainee's own country.

There's no annual cap on the number of H-3 visas that can be issued. Spouses and unmarried children aged under 21 of H-3 visa holders are eligible for H-4 visas (see below). Dependants may remain in the US and travel to and from the US, but aren't permitted to work.

H-3 visas are usually issued for the duration of the training program (up to two years) and extensions may be granted, but only up to the two-year limit.

H-4 Visas

H-4 visas are issued to the spouse and unmarried children aged under 21 of H-1B, H-1C, H-2 and H-3 visa holders, who wish to accompany or join the principal visa holder in the US for the duration of his stay. You cannot work with an H-4 visa, for which the appropriate work visa is required.

Spouses and/or children who don't intend to reside in the US with the principal visa holder, but visit for vacations only, may be eligible to apply for visitor (B-2) visas – which allows stays of up to six months at a time – or, if qualified, travel visa-free under the Visa Waiver Program (see page 120) which allows stays of up to three months.

The spouse and/or children of an H-1 visa holder don't need to apply for student (F-1) visas if they wish to study in the US, and can study on an H-4 visa. However, if qualified they may apply for an F-1 visa. If you have school-age children, you should refer to the regulations governing the issue of F-1 visas (see **Chapter 7**).

Category I: Foreign Media Representatives

Category I visas are issued to representatives of foreign information media, representatives of a foreign tourist bureau or film crew members holding professional journalism credentials and planning to work on news or non-commercial documentaries. I category visas are issued only to those involved in the newsgathering process, and those involved in associated activities, such as research, aren't eligible. Freelance journalists are only considered for an I visa when they're under contract to a media organization.

> ☑ SURVIVAL TIP
>
> All journalists must have an I visa when entering the US to work, even if they're from a Visa Waiver Program (see page 120) country and staying for less than 90 days. They also cannot work on a B-1 business visa.

Visas are issued on the basis of reciprocity and include spouses and unmarried children under 21. They're issued for up to five years at a time and are renewable. It isn't possible for a foreign journalist to change employers in the US without prior permission from the USCIS.

Members of the media engaged in the production or distribution of film, including employees of independent production companies, qualify for I category visas only if the material being filmed will be used to disseminate information or news. Definition of the term 'representative of the foreign media' includes, but isn't limited to, members of the press, radio or film whose activities are essential to the foreign media function, such as reporters, film crews, editors and those in similar occupations.

Foreign journalists working for an overseas branch of a US TV network, newspaper or other media outlet, aren't excluded from applying for an I visa, provided they're coming to the US solely to report on US news events for a foreign audience, and they'll continue to be paid by the foreign based office. If the journalist is to replace or augment an American journalist reporting on events in the US for a US audience, then the appropriate employment-based (O or H) visa is required.

It's important to note that only those whose activities are generally associated with journalism qualify for the I visa and those involved in associated activities such as proofreaders, librarians, set designers, etc. require the appropriate H, O or P visa. The final determination on the appropriate classification of employment-based visa is made by the USCIS when the petition is filed.

The spouse and/or children of an I visa holder don't need to apply for a student (F-1) visa if they wish to study in the US, and can study on an I visa. However, if qualified they may apply for an F-1 visa. If you have school-age children, you should refer to the regulations governing the issue of F-1 visas. However, the holder of a derivative I visa may not work in the US without an appropriate visa.

Category J: Exchange Visitors

Category J-1 visas (known as nonimmigrant cultural exchange visas) are issued to foreign exchange visitors including students, scholars, trainees, teachers, professors, medical graduates, research assistants, specialists or leaders in a field of specialized knowledge or skill, who wish to enter the US temporarily as a participant in an approved program. The kind of work that may be performed includes teaching, instructing or lecturing, studying, observing, conducting research, consulting, demonstrating special skills or receiving training. Programs also allow those aged between 18 and 25 to work as au pairs for up to a year.

Foreign students may also be eligible for an F-1 or M-1 visa (for information, see **Chapter 7**).

Category O: People of Extraordinary Ability

Category O-1 visas are for people of extraordinary ability in the fields of science, art, education, business and athletics, and workers in film and television whose work has earned them 'sustained national or international acclaim'. O-2 visas are issued to the support staff and crew of O-1 visa holders, e.g. a film or television production crew, but only if they possess skills and experience that isn't available in the US and the relationship is of long standing. Typical examples of proof of extraordinary ability may include contracts, awards, nominations, prizes, published material or similar documentation reflecting the nature of the individual's achievement. In order for a group to qualify, each member must meet the extraordinary ability test.

A US sponsor is required to file a petition (form I-129) on your behalf with the USCIS. In the case of someone who's traditionally self-employed or who uses agents to arrange short-term employment with numerous employers, a US agent may file the petition with the USCIS. A US agent may also file a petition on behalf of a foreign employer. If you don't apply well in advance, it may be necessary to apply for premium processing in order to obtain a visa in good time.

An O-1 visa is issued for up to three years with an indefinite number of one-year renewals permissible. Holders of O visas can apply for an adjustment of status and obtain an immigrant visa (Green Card).

Spouses and children under the age of 21 who wish to accompany or join a principal O visa holder in the US for the duration of his stay require an O-3 visa or can visit the US with a B-2 visitor visa (see page 131) or, if qualified, travel visa-free under the Visa Waiver Program (see page 120), which allows stays of up to three months. The spouse and children of an O-1 or O-2 visa holder can study in the US on an O-3 visa, but cannot work without an appropriate visa.

Under immigration law, the US employer and petitioner are jointly and severally responsible for the reasonable costs of return transportation abroad for a foreign employee in the O (and P) category if employment is terminated for reasons other than voluntary resignation.

Category P: Athletes & Entertainers

P category visas are for internationally recognized athletes, individually or part of

Pierce Brosnan

a team, or a member of an internationally recognized entertainment group. Individual members of the entertainment industry aren't eligible for a P-1 visa (they need an O-1 visa), but individual athletes are.

The qualifications necessary for P visas aren't as stringent as for O visas (see above), although there's a significant overlap between the uses and qualifications for O and P visas. P visa holders are required to have a residence abroad that they don't intend to abandon, but not O visa holders.

The P visa consists of four sub-categories: P-1, P-2, P-3 and P-4, as described below:

♦ **P-1:** individual athletes and teams;

♦ **P-2:** individuals or groups involved in a reciprocal exchange program between the US and one or more foreign countries (necessary documentation includes formal reciprocal exchange agreements, descriptions of the exchange program, and evidence of qualifying skills);

♦ **P-3:** performers (individuals or groups) to perform, teach, or coach under a program that's culturally unique;

♦ **P-4:** the spouses and unmarried children aged under 21 of those granted P-1, P-2 and P-3 visas.

A US sponsor is required to file a petition (form I-129) on your behalf with the USCIS. Petitions may only be filed by a US employer, a US sponsoring organization, a US agent or a foreign employer through a US agent. P-1 visa holders may work for multiple employers, but each employer must file a separate petition. Evidence is required that applicants and groups have been established and performing regularly for a period of at least one year in order to qualify for a P category visa. If you don't apply well in advance, it may be necessary to apply for premium processing (see page 98) in order to obtain a visa in good time.

For members of the entertainment industry, visas are issued for a specific event only. However, individual athletes may be admitted for five years (which can be extended for up to ten years) and a team for a period of six months. Holders of P visas can apply for an adjustment of status and obtain an immigrant visa (Green Card).

Spouses and children under the age of 21 who wish to accompany or join a principal P visa holder in the US for the duration of his stay, require an P-4 visa or can visit the US with a B-2 visitor visa (see page 131) or, if qualified, travel visa-free under the Visa Waiver Program (see page 120), which allows stays of up to three months. The spouse and children of a principal P visa holder can study in the US on an P-4 visa, but cannot work without an appropriate visa.

Under immigration law, the US employer and the petitioner are jointly and severally responsible for the reasonable costs of return transportation abroad for a foreign employee in the P (and O) category if employment is terminated for reasons other than voluntary resignation.

David Beckham

Category Q: Cultural Exchange Visitors

Category Q visas are for participants in international cultural exchange programs designed to provide practical training, employment, or opportunities for sharing with US citizens the history, culture and traditions of your home country. Before a petition can be filed with the USCIS, the following criteria must be met:

♦ the culture-sharing must take place in a school, museum, business or other establishment where the public is exposed to aspects of a foreign culture as part of a structured program;

♦ the cultural component must be an essential and integral part of the participant's employment and training, and must be designed to exhibit the attitude, customs, history, heritage, philosophy and/or tradition of the alien's country of nationality;

♦ the alien's employment and training may not be independent of the cultural component.

The organization must demonstrate that it has the ability to conduct a responsible international cultural exchange program **and** has the financial ability to remunerate the participant and offer him wages and working conditions comparable to those of local US workers similarly employed. **Applicants** must be aged at least 18, be qualified to perform the stated service or labor or receive the specified type of training, and have the ability to communicate effectively in English about their culture.

The US sponsor is required to file a petition (form I-129) with the USCIS on behalf of applicants. A Q visa petition is approved for the length of the program or for 15 months, whichever is shorter, and cannot be extended. The holder of a Q visa who has spent 15 months in the US may not be issued a visa or be re-admitted under the Q visa classification unless he has lived abroad and been physically present outside the US for at least one year.

There's no derivative visa category for the spouse and children of a Q visa holder and spouses and/or children who wish to accompany a Q visa holder to the US for the duration of the program must qualify for visas in their own right. If they wish to visit the US they can do so with a B-2 visitor visa (see page 131) or, if qualified, travel visa-free under the Visa Waiver Program (see page 120), which allows stays of up to three months. However, if they wish to study or work in the US they require the necessary nonimmigrant visa.

Fir more information, see 🖥 www.uscis.gov (>Working in the United States >Temporary Workers >Q Cultural Exchange).

Category R: Religious Workers

Category R-1 visas are for workers who have been members of recognized religious groups for at least two years and are coming to the US to work for an affiliated religious organization in any capacity. The term 'worker' includes clergy, counselors, social workers, health-care workers for religious hospitals, missionaries, translators and religious broadcasters.

☑ SURVIVAL TIP

Some R-1 visas applicants, particularly from third world countries, come under intense scrutiny as it's fairly common for bogus religious workers to try to use an R visa to obtain a nonimmigrant visa and then apply for a Green Card.

Religious workers include individuals authorized by a recognized employing entity to conduct religious worship and to perform other duties usually performed by authorized members of the clergy of that religion, and workers engaging in a religious vocation or occupation. The following conditions apply:

♦ the applicant must be a member of a religious denomination with a bona fide non-profit religious organization in the US;

♦ the religious denomination and its affiliate, if applicable, must be exempt from taxation or the religious denomination must qualify for tax-exempt status;

♦ the applicant must have been a member of the denomination for the two years immediately preceding the application for religious worker status.

There's no requirement that individuals applying for R-1 visas have a residence abroad that they have no intention of abandoning. However, they must intend to depart the US at the end of their lawful status. An applicant must have resided and been physically present outside the US for the year immediately prior to an application if he's previously spent five years in this (Q visa) classification.

The US sponsor is required to file a petition (form I-129) on your behalf with the USCIS. The initial admission period for ministers and religious workers entering the US in R status is limited to 30 months. Extensions may be granted for a maximum stay of five years. Religious workers may apply for a Green Card under the 'special' immigrant category (see **Chapter 8**).

Spouses and children under the age of 21 who wish to accompany or join a principal R-1 visa holder in the US for the duration of his stay require an R-2 visa or can visit the US with a B-2 visitor visa (see page 131) or, if qualified, travel visa-free under the Visa Waiver Program (see page 120), which allows stays of up to three months. The spouse and children of an R-1 visa holder can study in the US with an R-2

visa, but cannot work without an appropriate visa.

Category TN: NAFTA Work Visas

TN NAFTA work visas are temporary work visas available only to citizens of Mexico and Canada. There's no annual cap on TN work permits. Under the North American Free Trade Agreement (NAFTA), a citizen of a NAFTA country may work in a professional occupation in another NAFTA country, provided the applicant meets certain requirements, including the following:

♦ the profession must be on the NAFTA list;

♦ the prospective employee must possess the credentials required and meet the specific criteria for that profession;

♦ the position must require someone in that professional capacity;

♦ the position must be with a US employer.

A TN visa cannot be used to engage in self-employment in the US or to render services to a corporation or other entity in which the visa holder is a controlling owner or shareholder.

Canadians may apply for TN-1 classification directly at a US Class A port-of-entry, at a US airport handling international traffic or at a US pre-flight/pre-clearance station in Canada. Applicants require a letter from the US employer (or a sending employer in Canada) describing the nature and duration of professional employment and the salary in the US. No visa is required.

The procedures for Mexican citizens applying for TN status are more complex than for Canadians, although they have been significantly simplified. At one time, Mexicans were subject to an annual quota and to procedures similar to an H-1B visa. However, since January 1, 2004, a Mexican citizen follows a similar procedure to Canadians, but they must first obtain a TN-2 visa at a US embassy or consulate (generally in Mexico). Once the TN-2 visa is obtained they may enter the US in TN status in a similar manner to a Canadian citizen.

TN visas are issued for a maximum of three years and can be extended indefinitely provided the temporary purpose of the employment continues.

The spouse and unmarried minor children of the principal applicant are entitled to derivative status (called a TD visa), but they're unable to work in the US. They can be included on the application of the TN principal (no separate filing fees) and admitted for the same duration of stay. TD visa holders may study in the US but cannot work without an appropriate nonimmigrant visa. Canadian dependants' eligibility to work may, however, be adjudicated at a US port-of-entry.

6.

DOING BUSINESS

There are specific visas for entrepreneurs and investors, i.e. those wishing to invest or buy an existing business, or establish a new business or a branch office in the US, including E-1, E-2 and L-1 nonimmigrant visas, and the EB-5 immigrant visa, each of which is described in this chapter. The E-1/E-2 and L-1 nonimmigrant visas are easier and quicker to obtain than an EB-5 immigrant visa, but don't automatically allow for permanent residence, although this is an option after a business has been in operation for at least a year.

It isn't absolutely necessary to engage an immigration lawyer to make a visa application as an entrepreneur or investor – or any other visa – but the documentation required is usually substantial and the process can be complicated. For this reason, most people use a specialist immigration lawyer to file the application on their behalf. Always obtain a quotation in writing from an immigration lawyer and shop around a number of lawyers (but check their credentials and references), as fees can run into many thousands of dollars, depending on the amount of work involved.

A summary of the options for foreign business investors in the US – and the most important considerations – is shown in the table overleaf.

DOING BUSINESS IN THE US

One of the main attractions of buying or investing in a business in the US is that it offers a relatively easy method of obtaining a visa, as the US government is keen to encourage foreign entrepreneurs.

However, the US can be a minefield for foreigners with little or no knowledge or experience of American business methods. Whatever people may tell you, starting your own business isn't easy, particularly in a foreign country. It's advisable to anticipate spending your first few months (at year) learning the ropes and the ground rules for doing business in the US.

It requires a lot of hard work; a sizeable investment and operating funds (many businesses fail due to lack of capital); good organization (e.g. bookkeeping and planning); excellent customer relations (in America the customer is always right – even when he's wrong!); and a measure of luck – although generally the harder you work, the more 'luck' you'll have!

The key to buying or starting a successful business is exhaustive research, research and yet more research; choosing the location for a business is of paramount importance. Always thoroughly investigate an existing or proposed business before investing a cent and be extremely wary of businesses you know

Categories of Business Visas

Subject	E-1/E-2	L-1	EB-5 Individual	Regional Center
Investment Sum	Not fixed Usually $100,000+	Any amount	$500,000 or $1m	Minimum of $500,000
Job Creation	Minimal	No set minimum	10 direct jobs	10 direct or indirect jobs
Investors' Skills	Manager or essential skills, unless investor	Executive/Manager or specialized knowledge	Policy making	Limited partner
Procedure	Can go direct to consul	USCIS first unless a blanket application	USCIS, then consul or form I-485	USCIS, then consul or form 1-485
Visa Processing	Minimum of 1-2 months	Less than 30 days with premium processing	Around one year	Around one year
Can visa be expedited	depends on country & Premium process	Yes, premium process	No	No
Initial visa Validity	up to five years	one year for start-ups	two-year conditional Green Card	two-year conditional Green Card
Permanent Residence	Possible EB-1 after one year	Possible EB-1 after one year	Yes, after two-year conditional period	Yes, after two-year conditional period
Maximum Period	Unlimited extensions	5 or 7 years	permanent residence	permanent residence
Working Spouse	Yes	Yes	three months after I-485	three months after I-485
Employment Authorization	Around 90 days	Around 90 days	Usually 6 months	Usually 6 months

Categories of Business Visas (Cont.)

Subject	E-1/E-2	L-1	EB-5 Individual	EB-5 Regional Center
School Attendance	Yes	Yes	In-state tuition sooner	In-state tuition sooner
Investment Funds Loan Collateral	The enterprise cannot be loan	Yes	The enterprise cannot be loan collateral	The enterprise cannot be loan collateral
Country	Only treaty Countries	Not relevant	Source of funds could be an issue	Source of funds could be an issue
Buy Existing Company	Yes	Yes	Must add 10 jobs	No
Need Overseas Company	No	Yes	No	No
Prior Overseas employment	No	Yes, one year	No	No
Geographical Area	Any	Any	Rural/high unemployment for $500,000	Rural/high unemployment for $500,000

nothing about. Ideally, you should only invest in highly-developed parts of the US, where there's money, prospective clients and a wealth of qualified specialists.

It's usually better to buy a going concern than start from scratch, which will be much more expensive in the long run and the documentation required to convince the authorities is more extensive for a start up in terms of cashflow/employment projections, business plans and research data.

Before buying a company you need to carry out extensive due diligence and an audit, no matter how attractive an offer may appear. This applies even when you're buying a business from friends or relatives – which isn't usually recommended – who may not even be aware of the true state of a business and its prospects. Finally, you should visit the US personally and investigate a business you're planning to buy at first hand, meet the people involved and ask lots (and lots) of questions.

CATEGORY E: TREATY TRADER & TREATY INVESTOR VISAS

The US has treaties with most countries, particularly so-called treaties of 'Friendship, Commerce and Navigation (FCN)', which are designed to promote trade and investment between the US and other countries, thereby encouraging good relations and peace. More recently the US has entered into a number of bilateral Investment treaties with mainly former communist states, designed to promote investment but which don't generally confer any trade-related immigration privileges. Potential investors may seek out investment opportunities, sign contracts, and take other steps to purchase or establish a business while traveling to the US on a B1 or B2 visa (see **Chapter 4**) or under the Visa Waiver Program (see page 120).

An applicant for an E-1 or E-2 visa first needs to establish that the trading enterprise or investment enterprise meets the legal requirements and complies with the rules for an E visa. Then applicants must register the enterprise with the treaty visa office at your nearest US embassy or consulate. Both owners and employees of Treaty Trader and Treaty Investor businesses receive the same category of visa (E-1 or E-2) and the law makes no distinction between them. However, investors and employees go through different processes to obtain their visas. Investors must submit a file of supporting documents (a list is provided on some US embassy websites, e.g. see the London US embassy website (🖥 www.usembassy.org.uk/cons_new/visa/niv/enew2.html), which are reviewed by the consular officer.

There are no educational requirements for E visa applicants and neither a job offer or relevant experience are required. However, proof of relevant work and/or business experience may prove to be pertinent by showing that you have the necessary expertise to manage the enterprise successfully.

Application Procedure

It isn't possible to specify the exact documentation required as circumstances vary considerably for different applicants and business enterprises. Applicants for an E-1 or E-2 visa need to file form DS-160 (Nonimmigrant Visa Application) and form DS-156E (Nonimmigrant Treaty Trader/Investor Application) on their own behalf at a US embassy or consulate in the country where they're resident, plus other forms as required. Forms can be downloaded from the USCIS website (🖥 www.uscis.gov/forms) free of charge and can be completed online using Adobe Reader®.

The procedure varies, but in general you submit the registration documents for review by the embassy, which then issues an invitation for an interview, usually coupled with a request for further documents or forms. On the day of the interview the consular official either rejects or approves the visa application.

It's possible to change your status to that of a Treaty Trader or Investor if you're already in the US, and also to change your status from E-1 or E-2 to another nonimmigrant visa or to an immigrant visa. It can take a number of months to process an E visa application, depending on the country, although once the principal applicant has obtained registration as a Treaty Investor or Trader, it's relatively straightforward to obtain E visas for qualifying employees.

An E visa is usually granted for two or five years, with two-year or five-year extensions. The initial visa is normally issued for two years only, as many small businesses are volatile and often don't succeed, although when a visa is renewed after two years it's generally for the maximum five years. In the case of large companies with a high turnover employing many Americans, the first visa may be issued for five years. There's no limit to the number of extensions you can obtain, therefore you can remain in the US indefinitely with an E visa provided you maintain your status with the enterprise or business and it continues to be viably operated. However, should you sell the business or it ceases trading, you and your family will be required to leave the US.

Investors who have changed status in the US with the USCIS must follow the steps for all first-time investors. The change of status remains valid only while you remain in the US and once you've left the country you require an E-visa to return and resume the running of your business. A change of status doesn't guarantee the issue of a visa, nor does it exempt you from the normal process of filing documents in advance with a US embassy or consulate. Note also that the application of the regulations for E visas can vary considerably between the USCIS and US Embassies, and some embassies tend to be stricter than others in the application of the rules.

It may be possible for an E visa holder to qualify for immigrant status, e.g. on the basis of a multinational manager application after the US business has traded for at least one year. The size of the foreign and US companies will also have a bearing on your eligibility.

The spouse and unmarried children (aged under 21) of Treaty Traders, Treaty Investors or employees of qualifying enterprises may also receive derivative E visas. Dependants aren't required to have the same nationality as the principal applicant. Spouses may work in the US when they have obtained employment authorization (form I-765) from the USCIS after arrival. Dependent children may not work (even in the 'family' business, unless they apply for an E-2 specialist/key employee visa), although they may study until the age of 21, when they must qualify for a visa in their own right. They can obtain F-1 visas if they're attending college, which would continue for the duration of their course of study, or they could become investors in a business and qualify for E-2 investor visas in their own right.

While Canadians are exempt for most categories of visas, a Canadian seeking admission as a Treaty Trader or Investor under the provisions of NAFTA must be in possession of a nonimmigrant visa issued by a US consular officer (only two consular posts in Canada process E visas: Toronto and Vancouver).

Category E-1: Treaty Trader Visas

Category E-1 Treaty Trader visas permit foreign nationals of eligible countries to live in the US in order to engage in trade of a substantial nature between the US and the applicant's country of nationality. The trade involved must be an international direct exchange of 'items' between the US and a treaty country, and can be in goods or services. E-1 visas are issued subject to certain conditions, but there's no restriction (quota) on the number issued each year.

To qualify for an E-1 visa, a company or individual must plan to establish an office in the US. The volume of trade must be sufficient to justify the trader or his employee(s) being in the US to manage the trade, and must constitute the majority of the trader's international trade, i.e. at least 50 per cent of the trader's exports/imports must be to/from the US. There's no set minimum level of trade, but obviously the lower the volume of trade the less likely you are to qualify as a Treaty Trader. Smaller businesses are expected to yield income sufficient to support the Treaty Trader and his family. The trading company must already be in existence when the application is made.

An example of a Treaty Trader business would be a clothing business located in a European country that designs and manufactures clothes and sells many of its products in the US, but has no retail stores of its own or any manufacturing facilities there. If the volume of its transatlantic trade is significant and continuous, and the Europe-US trade comprises over 50 per cent of its total international trade, then the business could qualify for Treaty Trader status and the owner of the business or some of its employees may be eligible for E-1 visas.

E visas aren't intended to serve as a means for foreigners to retire or merely reside in the US.

Treaty Trader Countries

As the name suggests, E-1 visas are available only to citizens of countries with which the US has a trade treaty. Most major countries have both trader and investment treaties with the US, the exceptions being Brunei, Greece and Israel, which have only Treaty Trader agreements. With the exception of these three countries (marked with an asterisk in the table) the countries shown in the table have BOTH trader and investment treaties with the US.

Countries With Treaty Trader & Treaty Investment Agreements

Argentina	Greece*	Pakistan
Australia	Honduras	Paraguay
Austria	Iran	Philippines
Belgium	Ireland	Poland
Bolivia	Israel*	Serbia
Bosnia & Herzegovina	Italy	Singapore
Brunei*	Japan	Slovenia
Canada	Jordan	Spain
Chile	Korea (South)	Suriname
China (Taiwan)	Kosovo	Sweden
Colombia	Latvia	Switzerland
Coast Rica	Liberia	Thailand
Croatia	Luxembourg	Togo
Denmark	Macedonia	Turkey
Estonia	Mexico	United Kingdom
Ethiopia	Montenegro	Yugoslavia
Finland	Netherlands	
France	Norway	*Nationals of Brunei, Greece and Israel qualify only for E-1 visas.
Germany	Oman	

Treaty Trader Requirements

An E-1 visa holder must be a principal owner who controls at least 50 per cent of the company, or a key employee (with the same nationality as the principal owner), i.e. a manager, an executive or a person with skills essential to the business.

The requirements for E-1 Treaty Trader visas include the following:

♦ The applicant must be a national of a treaty country.

♦ The trading company for which the applicant is coming to the US must have the nationality of the treaty country. At least 50 per cent of the ownership of the company must have the nationality of the treaty country.

♦ The international trade must be 'substantial' in the sense that there's a sizable and continuing volume of trade.

♦ The trade must be principally between the US and the treaty country, which is defined to mean that over 50 per cent of the international trade involved must be between the US and the applicant's country of nationality.

♦ The applicant must be employed in an executive or supervisory capacity or possess specialized skills essential to the efficient operation of the company. Ordinary skilled or unskilled workers don't qualify.

Trade means the international exchange of goods, services, and technology, where title of the trade items must pass from one party to the other.

Category E-2: Treaty Investor Visas

An E-2 visa is granted to the principal owner or a key employee of a company that has invested a 'substantial sum of money' in a business enterprise in the US. Like the E-1 visa, there's no set minimum level of investment which may qualify for E-2 status, but the lower the investment the less likely you are to qualify. The level of investment must be sufficient to justify the treaty national (or his employees) presence in the US. The investment must be in a fully operating business and you're expected to be actively engaged in developing and directing it; passive investments, such as simply buying property or stocks and bonds, don't qualify. You'll need to demonstrate that the business in which you're investing will generate more than enough income to support you and your family, and will contribute to the economy, usually by employing US workers and paying US taxes.

If you have $500,000 or more to invest in a business, you may wish to consider the EB-5 immigrant visa (see page 165) which offers a Green Card.

The actual amount of the investment depends on the kind of business and there's no minimum sum. The investor must be the source of the invested funds, although personal loans from relatives or friends can be considered part of your investment, provided the business isn't collateral for the loan. Gifts of funds for the investment are also permitted.

There are limitations on the percentage of financing (borrowing) permitted, which depends on the value of the business, but the cash investment must usually be from 30 per cent for an enterprise costing over $3m, to 70-75 per cent for an enterprise costing $500,000 or less. A business can be jointly owned with a spouse or a partner (who can be a US citizen), but only two co-investors with equal 50 per cent shares are permitted as they each must have negative control. This can be, for example, husband/wife, father/mother or son/daughter, or two unrelated business partners may also both be able to obtain E-2 work visas. E-2 investors are permitted to work only in their own business. The spouse of an E-2 investor can apply for work authorization when in the US, which will allow him to work for any employer.

More important than the amount of money invested is whether the business is likely to be profitable and whether it will employ Americans. The business must generate significantly more income than what's required to provide a living for the investor and his family. It's generally easier to obtain an E-2 visa for an existing business than a new business. Funds must usually be irrevocably committed to the investment (i.e. at the very least placed in an escrow account) and contingent only upon the issue of the visa. Investment funds may come from any country, including the US, provided they're controlled by the investor.

An example of what may constitute an acceptable Treaty Investor business is a foreigner who purchases 75 per cent of a restaurant in say New York, which makes a profit and employs over 20 people, most of whom are US citizens. If all other conditions for the visa are met, the investor could obtain an E-2 Treaty Investor visa to enter the US in order to operate the business and oversee his investment. He would also be able to send qualified employees who are foreign citizens to work in the business, provided they meet certain specific requirements.

The following countries (in the table shown below) have ONLY treaty investor status with the US.

Treaty Investor Requirements

The requirements for E-2 treaty investor visas include the following:

◆ The investor, either a real or corporate person, must be a national of a treaty country.

◆ The investment must be substantial and sufficient to ensure the successful operation of the enterprise. The percentage of investment for a low-cost business enterprise must be higher than the percentage of investment for a high-cost enterprise.

◆ The investment must be a real operating enterprise. Speculative or idle investment doesn't qualify. Uncommitted funds in a bank account or similar security aren't considered an investment.

◆ The investment may not be marginal. It must generate significantly more income than simply to provide a living for the investor and his family, or it must have a significant economic impact in the US.

◆ The investor must have control of the funds and the investment must be at risk in the

Countries With US Investment Treaties

Albania	Ecuador	Morocco
Armenia	Egypt	Panama
Azerbaijan	Georgia	Romania
Bahrain	Grenada	Senegal
Bangladesh	Jamaica	Slovak Republic
Bulgaria	Kazakhstan	Sri Lanka
Cameroon	Kyrgyzstan	Trinidad & Tobago
Congo (Brazzaville)	Lithuania	Tunisia
Congo (Kinshasa)	Moldova	Ukraine
Czech Republic	Mongolia	

commercial sense. Loans secured with the assets of the investment enterprise aren't permitted.

♦ The investor must be coming to the US to develop and direct the enterprise. If the applicant isn't the principal investor, he must be employed in a supervisory, executive or highly specialized skill capacity. Ordinary skilled and unskilled workers don't qualify.

Anyone planning to buy a business in the US should enquire about the likelihood of obtaining an E-2 visa before signing a purchase contract and should make the contract contingent on obtaining a visa.

There may be a fee for issuing an E-2 visa (e.g. $105 in the UK), in addition to the application fee (see page 99), which increased to $390 on June 4, 2010.

CATEGORY L: INTRA-COMPANY TRANSFEREES

Category L-1 visas are granted to intra-company transferees, who are people employed abroad who are transferred to a branch, subsidiary affiliate or joint venture partner of the same company in the US (it can be a US or foreign company). A 'subsidiary' is defined as a company, corporation or other legal entity of which a parent owns (directly or indirectly) over half the entity and controls the entity, or owns (directly or indirectly) 50 per cent of a 50-50 joint venture and has equal control and veto power over the entity. It may also include an entity where the parent owns less than half of it, but in fact controls the entity.

L-1 visas can also be obtained for start-up (new) companies in the US. For a variety of tax and legal reasons, it may be advisable that companies establish a US corporation rather than a US branch office. It's wise to consult an American CPA or tax attorney regarding taxation issues. There's no quota for L-1 visas.

To qualify, you must have served in a managerial or executive capacity (L-1A visa) or possess specialized knowledge (L-1B visa) necessary to the US business, and be transferred to a position within the US company at one of these levels, although not necessarily in the same position as held previously. You must have been employed outside the US by the international company continuously for at least one year in the three years immediately preceding the application.

An L-1 visa is also the appropriate visa classification for a qualified employee of an international company who's coming to the US to establish a parent, branch, affiliate or subsidiary, i.e. commence business. When filing the petition, the company is required to show that premises to house the new business have been secured and that within one year of the approval of the petition, the intended US operation will support an executive or managerial position. In the case of a person with specialized knowledge, the petitioner is required to show that it has the financial ability to remunerate the beneficiary and to start doing business in the US.

actions (such as promotion and leave authorization), or if no employees are directly supervised, function at a senior level within the organizational hierarchy or with respect to the function managed;

♦ exercise discretion over the day-to-day operations of the activity or function for which the employee has authority.

To qualify as a specialized knowledge transferee (L-1B), the employee must possess knowledge of the company products and their application in international markets or have an advanced level of knowledge of processes and procedures of the company. An employee has specialized knowledge if it's different from that generally found in the particular industry. Possible characteristics of an employee who possesses specialized knowledge include:

♦ knowledge that's valuable to the employer's competitiveness in the market place;

♦ knowledge of foreign operating conditions as a result of special knowledge not generally found in the industry;

♦ experience of working abroad in a capacity involving significant assignments which have enhanced the employer's productivity, competitiveness, image or financial position;

♦ knowledge which normally can be gained only through prior experience with that employer;

♦ knowledge of a product or process which cannot be easily transferred or taught to another individual.

Application Procedure for Category L Visas

The US employer or international company must file a petition (form I-129) at the USCIS service center with jurisdiction over the place of employment in the US. Labor certification isn't required for an L visa. After the petition has been approved, the individual can apply

To qualify as an international executive (L-1A), the employee must meet the following requirements:

♦ direct the management of the organization or a major component or function;

♦ establish the goals and policies of the organization, component or function;

♦ exercise wide latitude in discretionary decision-making;

♦ receive only general supervision or direction from higher-level executives, the board of directors or stockholders of the organization.

♦ To qualify as an international manager, the employee must meet the following requirements:

♦ manage the organization or department, subdivision, function or component of the organization;

♦ supervise and control the work of other supervisory, professional or managerial employees, or manage an essential function within the organization, or a department or subdivision of the organization;

♦ have the authority to hire and fire, or recommend hire/fire and other personnel

for a visa from his nearest US embassy or consulate. If an applicant is already in the US, a change of status may be possible.

> If your a Canadian applying for an L-1 visa under the North American Free Trade Agreement (NAFTA), the petition can be filed at the port of entry when applying for admission.

A petition for a qualified employee of a new office (i.e. a start-up company) will initially be approved for a period of one year only, after which the petitioner must demonstrate that it's doing business as described in order for the visa to be extended. The reason is that start-up companies often fail and in the past many have been established primarily to obtain a Green Card. One way around this is to ensure that the company has sufficient funds to cover operations for at least a year, plus a detailed budget plan for the first two to three years.

Multinational corporations (for whom the L-1 visa was created) can benefit from a 'blanket' L-1 rule, whereby they aren't required to file an individual petition each time they need to transfer employees to the US. The blanket petition (form I-129S) provision is reserved for relatively large established companies with multi-layered structures and numerous related business entities. The blanket petition provision is available only to managers, executives and specialized knowledge professionals who'll be based in an established US office. *Applicants (or their employer) must pay an additional $500 'anti-fraud' fee prior to their visa interview.*

Companies can provide the approval notice and form I-129S petition and submit an application for a visa to their nearest US embassy or consulate. To benefit, a company must have had at least ten intra-company transferees approved in the last year or have combined annual sales of a minimum of $25m or a US workforce of at least 1,000.

Validity of Category L Visas

L-1A visas are valid for up to seven years and L-1B visas for up to five years. It's possible to change to another nonimmigrant visa at the end of the maximum validity period, such as E-1 or E-2. If this isn't done, you must leave the US for one year, during which you must work for a parent, subsidiary, affiliate or branch of the US company abroad before becoming eligible to reapply for an L-1 visa. One advantage of an L-1 visa is that executives and managers usually qualify for a Green Card (permanent residence) as a multi-national manager after one year of doing business, although conversion of an L-1 visa to a Green Card isn't automatic. L-1 visa applicants cannot be denied a visa on the basis that they are intending immigrants (so-called 'dual intent') or that they don't have a residence abroad which they don't intend to abandon.

An L-2 visa is granted to an L-1 visa holder's spouse and unmarried children aged under 21. The spouse of an L-1 visa holder can work in the US without restriction, but children cannot accept paid employment without an appropriate visa. The spouse and children of an L-1 visa holder don't require an F-1 (student) visa to study in the US and can study with an L-2 visa up to the age of 21. At the age of 21, a child must apply for his own visa, e.g. an F-1 visa (see page 179) to study at a US university.

EB-5 INVESTOR IMMIGRANT VISAS

Foreigners who are planning to make a considerable investment in a commercial enterprise in the US may qualify for an EB-5 immigrant visa (officially called an 'employment creation' immigrant), created in 1990. The EB-5 visa provides a flexible path to a Green Card based on a US investment and doesn't require you to actively manage the day-to-day affairs of a business (e.g. unlike a nonimmigrant E-2 visa). EB-5 regulations require 'involvement' in management or policy making, although simply being a limited partner in the organization that owns the business qualifies as an active role.

For many people, it's the fastest and most secure way to obtain a Green Card, but it's also the most expensive. To qualify, you must invest $1m, or $500,000 when investing in a designated 'targeted employment area' (which includes most Regional Centers) or a troubled business.

There are no investor 'suitability' standards, points system, or language or business experience requirements. Investors may invest in an existing business or a new business, and more than one person can invest in the same business (but each must invest $500,000 or $1m, as applicable). An EB-5 investor can also be a minority owner of the business and although the investor's role cannot be completely passive, he doesn't have to be involved in the day-to-day management of the business (unless he wants to be). The spouse and unmarried children under the age of 21 are admitted to the US with the investor. The initial Green Card is provisional for the first two years and is made permanent when the USCIS are satisfied that the investment proceeds have been made (and not withdrawn) and the requisite jobs have been created.

A maximum of 10,000 EB-5 immigrant visas are available annually, not less than 3,000 of which are reserved for investors in a targeted rural or high unemployment area, plus 3,000 set aside for investors in Regional Centers (see below). Immediate family members (spouse and unmarried children aged under 21) of EB-5 visa applicants also receive EB-5 visas, and are counted against the 10,000 annual cap. The number of EB-5 investor visas issued annually is usually well below the quota, although it has risen in recent years. The pilot program was scheduled to end in 2009, but has been extended until September 30, 2012.

Types Of EB-5 Investment

There are three ways in which you can qualify for an EB-5 visa: by investing in a new business enterprise, a troubled business or through the Regional Center Pilot Program, each of which is described opposite.

EB-5: Types of Investment

1. New Business Enterprise	2. Troubled Business	3. Regional Center Pilot Program

◆ **New Business Enterprise:** This option is for someone who primarily wants to start or manage a business and have control over their investment. Note, however, that there are more hurdles to be overcome than with the Regional Center investment.

◆ **Troubled Business:** A troubled business is one with substantial losses as quantified in the regulations. There may be an opportunity to qualify for a visa based on preserving existing employees as opposed to adding new ones.

◆ **Regional Center Pilot Program:** A Regional Center investment is an investment in a business in a 'targeted employment area'. It's often the quickest option as the immigration process is usually quicker and there are fewer legal issues to overcome. However, the investor isn't running his own business and the rate of return may be lower than for a successful individual investment.

New Business Enterprise

A new business enterprise must be a commercial enterprise, i.e. a for-profit business, and in addition to new, original businesses, includes existing businesses that have been restructured or expanded.

To qualify for an EB-5 visa by investing in a new business enterprise you must:

◆ Invest or be in the process of investing at least $1,000,000. If your investment is in a designated targeted employment area (see below) then the minimum investment requirement is $500,000.

◆ Benefit the US economy by providing goods or services to US market.

◆ Create full-time employment for at least ten US workers. This includes US citizens, Green Card holders (lawful permanent residents) and other individuals lawfully authorized to work in the US, but doesn't include you (the immigrant) or your spouse, sons or daughters.

◆ Be involved in the day-to-day management of the new business or directly manage it through formulating business policy, for example as a corporate officer or board member.

A targeted employment area is defined by law as 'a rural area or an area that has experienced high unemployment of at least 150 per cent of the national average.' These may be listed on state websites such as California (http://business.ca.gov > Additional Resources > International Trade > EB-5 Investor Visa program > Targeted Employment Area > List of Identified High Employment Areas).

Troubled Business

To qualify for an EB-5 visa by investing in a troubled business, i.e. a loss-making business, the business must:

♦ have existed for at least two years and have incurred a net loss (based on generally accepted accounting principles), for the 12 to 24 month period before you filed the form I-526;

♦ have made a loss for the preceding 12 to 24 month period that must be at least equal to 20 per cent of the business's net worth before the loss;

♦ maintain the number of jobs at no less than the pre-investment level for a period of at least two years;

♦ be involved in the day-to-day management of the troubled business or directly manage it through formulating business policy, for example as a corporate officer or board member;

♦ make the same investment as for a new business enterprise (see above), i.e. $1,000,000 or $500,000 in a targeted employment area.

Regional Center Pilot Program

A Regional Center is an area designated by the USCIS as eligible to receive immigrant investor capital. It's defined as any economic unit, public or private, that's involved with the promotion of economic growth, improved regional productivity, job creation (whether directly or indirectly), and increased domestic capital investment. Most Regional Centers are situated in targeted employment areas where $500,000 is the required investment.

The organizers of a Regional Center seeking the Regional Center designation from the USCIS must submit a proposal showing:

♦ how the Regional Center plans to focus on a geographical region within the US and how it will achieve the required economic growth within this area;

♦ that the Regional Center's business plan can be relied upon as a viable business model grounded in reasonable and credible estimates and assumptions for market conditions, project costs, and activity timelines;

♦ how in verifiable detail (using economic models in some instances) jobs will be created directly or indirectly through capital investments made in accordance with the Regional Center's business plan;

♦ the amount and source of capital committed to the project and the promotional efforts made and planned for the project.

To qualify for an EB-5 visa by investing in a Regional Center pilot program you must:

♦ Invest at least $1,000,000 or $500,000 in a Regional Center affiliated new commercial enterprise or a troubled business located within the area of the Regional Center.

♦ Create at least ten new full-time jobs either directly or indirectly.

There are around 80 approved Regional Centers, a list of which (by state) is available on the USCIS website (🖳 www.uscis.gov >Working in the US > Permanent Workers > Employment-Based Immigration: Fifth Preference EB-5 – left column > Immigrant Investor Regional Centers – top of right-hand column).

Choosing a Regional Center

Before choosing a Regional Center investment it's important to do your homework and due diligence and ask the right questions and ensure that you get them answered to your satisfaction. You should treat this as you would any other investment and seek independent professional investment advice.

The following list of questions is intended to help you choose the best Regional Center for your investment and fulfill the conditions to obtain a permanent Green Card after two years. The list isn't conclusive.

◆ When was the Regional Center approved by the USCIS and when did it start taking funds for the current project?

◆ How many I-526 petitions have been filed by investors in the Regional Center? How many have been approved and denied?

◆ How many I-829 condition removal approvals have the Regional Center investors received? How many denials? From an immigration point of view, the safest Regional Center investments are those in centers with the most condition removal approvals. Some Regional Centers have a 100 per cent record of success.

◆ How much more capital does the Regional Center need to complete their project and when might that be forthcoming?

◆ What income does the Regional Center offer. What has been the historic rate of return to investors?

◆ Will the Regional Center have any borrowing (which could be a danger)?

◆ How many years of experience does the general partner or principal in the investment project have in working with immigrant investor programs, and how much experience do the principals involved in the Regional Center have in job creation?

◆ Is the Regional Center affiliated with any government entity (which could be advantageous)?

◆ What provisions are made regarding the security of the investment?

◆ What use is made of the investor's funds? What is the type or types of projects?

◆ What is the form of the investment, e.g. limited partnership, LLC or other?

◆ Does the Regional Center provide regular reports of the status of the investment to investors, and, if so, at what intervals?

◆ Does the Regional Center investment include direct or indirect job creation or both? What precautions are taken to monitor job creation and what steps are taken if the requisite job creation doesn't happen according to plan?

◆ How much in total is the investor required to pay in Regional Center fees?

◆ Is payment made into an escrow account and is the investment refunded if the I-526 is not approved?

◆ What is the exit strategy? Can the investor redeem his investment following condition removal?

You should also ask for the contact details of previous investors (the earliest ones preferably) and ask them about their investment and whether they would recommend it.

EB-5 Application Procedure

The application procedure for an EB-5 visa is as follows:

1. File form I-526 (Immigrant Petition by Alien Entrepreneur – see below) with the appropriate USCIS Service Center, which requests the USCIS to certify the applicant and the investment are eligible for EB-5 visa status. Applicants must also include a business plan which details the amount and source of funds and demonstrates how the business will support at least ten employees.

2. Upon approval of the I-526 petition, if you live outside the US you must wait for notification from your nearest embassy or consulate in your home country (or country of residence) to prepare documents for the visa interview. You and your family members (including children) must undergo medical, police, security and immigration history checks before visas are issued. If you're in the US on a nonimmigrant visa, you can file form I-485 (Application to Register Permanent Residence or Adjust Status) plus supporting documents at the USCIS regional processing center serving your US residence.

3. Upon approval after the visa interview, you'll receive a form as evidence and a travel document. You'll also receive your temporary Green Card in the mail. If you're outside the US, you must enter the country within six months of the date of the visa approval.

4. Upon arrival in the US you must establish residency there. Evidence of intent to reside includes opening bank accounts, obtaining a driver's license and social security number, paying state and federal income taxes, and renting or buying a home. You may work overseas if required, depending upon the nature of your business or profession.

5. A form I-829 (Petition by Entrepreneur to Remove Conditions) must be filed with the USCIS 90 days prior to the two-year anniversary of the granting of your conditional Green Card. When this petition is approved you're issued with a new 'permanent' Green Card with no conditions and are permitted to live and work in the US without any restrictions or time limit.

Processing times for EB-5 visas vary considerably depending on the state where you'll be investing, the complexity of your application and the documentation provided. After you've submitted your visa application, you can expect processing to take from 6 to 18 months and to be on the safe side you should allow at least 12 months.

☑ SURVIVAL TIP

All forms can be downloaded from the USCIS website (💻 www.uscis.gov/forms) free of charge and can be completed online using Adobe Reader®.

Filing Form I-526

New Commercial Enterprise

The following supporting documentation is required:

◆ evidence that you have established a 'for profit' new commercial enterprise;

◆ evidence that your business has been established in a targeted employment area (if applicable);

◆ evidence that you have invested or are in the process of investing the amount required ($1,000,000 or $500,000);

◆ evidence that the investment funds (see also **Proof & Source of Funds** below) were obtained through lawful means,

which may be demonstrated by the following:

- foreign business registration records;

- personal and business tax returns, or other tax returns of any kind filed anywhere in the world within the previous five years;

- documents identifying any other source of money;

- certified copies of all pending civil or criminal actions and proceedings, or any private civil actions involving money judgments against the investor within the past 15 years.

♦ Evidence that the new commercial enterprise will create at least ten full-time positions – not including yourself, your spouse, sons or daughters, or any temporary/nonimmigrant workers. You'll need to submit a comprehensive business plan showing that, due to the nature and projected size of the new commercial enterprise, the need for not fewer than ten employees will result, including approximate dates, within the next two-years, and when each employee will be hired.

♦ Evidence that you'll be actively involved in the management of the new commercial enterprise (day-to-day or through policy).

Troubled Business

The same documentary evidence which is listed above for investors in a new commercial enterprise apply, except that instead of evidence that the business will create at least ten new jobs, you must submit evidence that the number of existing jobs (at least ten) will be maintained at no less than the pre-investment level for a period of at least two years. Photocopies of tax records, forms I-9 (tax forms) or other relevant documents for the qualifying employees, and a comprehensive business plan must be submitted in support of the petition.

Regional Center Program

The following supporting documentation is required:

♦ Evidence that you have invested in a designated Regional Center according to the approved Regional Center business plan. A letter from legacy INS or the USCIS should be attached with form I-526 designating the Regional Center. Your investment must be in a business enterprise within the geographical area specified in this letter.

♦ Evidence that your business has been established in a targeted employment area (if applicable).

♦ Evidence that you have invested or are in the process of investing the amount required ($1,000,000 or $500,000).

♦ Evidence that the investment funds were obtained through lawful means.

♦ Evidence that your investment in the Regional Center will create at least ten direct or indirect full-time jobs.

EB-5 Fees

In addition to the minimum capital contribution of $500,000, you should expect to pay expenses for company formation, agency fees, marketing expenses, and visa, medical examination and legal fees. You shouldn't invest any money until you're certain that you investment will be refunded in full if the conditional Green Card isn't granted. Obviously some expenses won't be refunded, such as your visa application fee, but you should try to keep your losses to the absolute minimum.

The EB-5 visa filing fee is $1,435 per applicant family and the fee payable to the National Visa Center (NVC) is $380 per applicant; the fee for medical examinations varies and in the UK is £200 for adults and £95 for children aged under 15. Fees charged by some investment companies are very high, e.g. $25,000 to $50,000 payable up front, with no guarantee of receiving a Green Card. In addition, a passive investment company – such as a real estate investment – may take the first $50,000 of profit from an investment. Legal fees will vary depending on the work involved, but are likely to be $10,000 to $15,000. There's also a further filing fee of $2,850 for form I-829 – see below – in order to obtain your permanent Green Card.

Therefore the fees for a family of two adults and two children can easily reach $50,000 or more, in addition to your investment of at least $500,000. Also bear in mind that the amount you're paying for the company is 'only' your primary investment. You'll also need working capital and you may need to invest in upgrading equipment (plant) and, premises, and in marketing and sales.

Proof & Source of Funds

The USCIS requires that you have invested or be in the process of investing. Although it specifically states that the investor may be 'in the process of investing', the USCIS may require that the entire investment

EB-5 Fees	
Item	**Fee**
Minimum capital contribution	$500,000
Regional Center fee (if applicable)	$25,000-50,000 (variable)
Legal fees	$15,000 (maximum)
EB-5 visa filing fee (I-526)	$1,435 (per family)
National Visa Center fee	$380 (per person)
Medical examinations	£200 (adult), £95 (child under 15) in the UK
I-829 filing fee	$2,850 (per family)

If you're investing in a Regional Center you should allow around $50,000 for the total fees for a family of four.

be invested and at risk in the commercial enterprise before the I-526 immigrant petition is approved. However, in practice, investors can place funds in a trust or

---

An escrow account is permissible provided the following standards are met:

♦ the escrow agreement must state that the required initial capital contribution is actually committed to the new commercial enterprise, where it will be available and put to use for job creation purposes immediately and irrevocably upon approval of the petition and issue of the visa or adjustment of status.

♦ the escrow holder must be a bank or similar entity that has no relationship other than that of escrow holder with you (the investor), the new commercial enterprise or their legal representatives.

♦ the escrow agreement must permit you the return of your money upon either the denial of the petition or its withdrawal.

escrow account pending visa approval and the funds may only be released upon visa approval. If for some reason, you don't receive your Green Card the contract is null and void and your money is refunded. Note, however, that the USCIS may look more favorably on petitions based on a completed investment rather than a pending one where the finds are in escrow.

If necessary, an additional statement may be required stating that the petitioner won't enter into any agreements that would prevent the escrow funds from being irrevocably committed to the investment enterprise for job creation purposes.

Some companies insist on payment up front, but you need to ask yourself whether they really need the money before the visa is issued. For example, the argument with regard to a real estate investment is that if your capital sits in escrow or trust pending the results of a visa application, the target investment which formed the basis of your visa petition may have been sold to other investors by the time the visa is approved. **While this may be true, what happens to your investment if the Green Card application is refused? Can you get it back if required?**

Each investor must provide complete biographical information and the principal applicant must prove the source of the investment funds. To prove the source of investment funds, INS requires five years of tax returns and bank records, proof of ownership in any businesses, financial statements for each business and business licenses. This is designed to present a track record of honest dealing. If your capital came from a specific transaction, such as the sale of a house, inheritance or gift, you must provide evidence of the transaction via an official document, such as a closing statement or contract or other official documents. This isn't an exhaustive list and other documents may be required which may vary on a case by case basis.

The most common problem area if often insufficient documentation of the source of funds. Some people try to disclose the least possible information, only to have the file returned with a request for further information. It's better to provide too much information rather than too little.

Obtaining Your Permanent Green Card

In order to obtain your permanent Green Card, you must file form I-829 (Petition by Entrepreneur to Remove Conditions, see below) during the 90 days prior to the second anniversary of the date you obtained your conditional permanent resident status. Filing form I-829 automatically extends your conditional permanent residence for six months. **The filing fee for form I-829 is an eye-watering $2,850!**

The USCIS will examine the business at the end of the two-year period to determine whether you've complied with the requirements, after which your permanent Green Card will be issued (usually after two to three months). Five years after the initial grant of conditional permanent residence, you can apply for US citizenship (see **Chapter 9**).

Once you have your permanent Green Card, you're free to sell your investment in the business.

Filing Form I-829

You must submit form I-829 (Petition by Entrepreneur to Remove Conditions) within the 90-day period immediately before the second anniversary of your admission to the US as a conditional permanent resident, along with the following supporting documentation:

♦ Evidence that you in fact established a new commercial enterprise. This evidence may include, but isn't limited to, copies of the business's organizational documents, and federal tax returns.

♦ Evidence that you have invested the total amount of required funds.

♦ Evidence that you have sustained your investment in the new commercial enterprise throughout your two-year period of conditional permanent residence. This evidence may include, but isn't limited to, the following:

 - business invoices and receipts;
 - bank statements;
 - contracts;
 - business licensees;
 - audited or reviewed financial statements;
 - complete copies of federal or state income tax returns or quarterly tax statements.

♦ Evidence of the number of full-time employees at the beginning of your business and at present. Such evidence may include but isn't limited to:

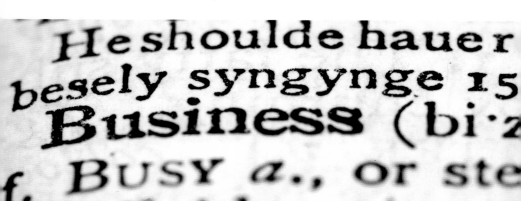

- business payroll records;
- relevant tax documents;
- employee tax form I-9's.

The same documentary requirements for an investor in a new commercial enterprise apply to an investor in a troubled business, except that the investor must show that he or she has maintained (not created) at least ten jobs. Those who have invested in a Regional Center must show that the capital investment was made in accordance with the Regional Center's business plan in order to be credited with the creation of indirect jobs.

EB-5 Benefits & Risks

There are a many advantages to obtaining an EB-5 visa compared with other potential Green Card options. Notably obtaining an EB-5 visa doesn't require labor certification to demonstrate there's a shortage of US workers to perform the potential job. Moreover the EB-5 visa doesn't require you to maintain an existing home country business or show extraordinary ability in business.

⚠ **Caution**

Bear in mind that an EB-5 investment could fail and you could lose your money and still not receive a Green Card. Investors need to be very careful before investing in a 'troubled business' or in a targeted employment area, i.e. an area with high unemployment.

The EB-5 visa is one of the most complicated areas of US immigration law and has a chequered history. There are two main concerns for investors: the risk to the investment capital and the risk that you won't receive your Green Card. There are many successful EB-5 projects, but there are also projects that have failed due to mismanagement, miscalculated risk, fraud and scams. You need to start or buy a company or invest in a project that's fully in compliance with the EB-5 program requirements.

Bear in mind that a company that employs ten or more people is already a serious business and, if it's profitable, it's likely to cost a lot more than a million dollars. It may make more sense to buy a barely profitable or an unprofitable company which will be many times cheaper, provided you're aware of its shortcomings and problems, **and you (or your management team) know how to fix them and add value within a reasonable period (months rather than years).**

You also need to take care when choosing a Regional Center – the more an investment program promises, the more you should investigate its claims. **Never accept claims at face value but demand evidence!** You also need to know the right questions to ask. Websites and brochures tend to emphasize the pros rather than the cons. Many sites that appear to be independent and to provide impartial and useful information, are just sales' promotions for a particular Regional Center. Also bear in mind that if you invest in a program that's dependent on job creation, then irrespective of the return on investment, if the project fails to create the required number of jobs within two years, you won't receive your permanent Green Card.

7.

STUDENTS & EXCHANGE VISITORS

There are a number of nonimmigrant visas for students who wish to study in the US or participate in an exchange program. These include the F-1 or student visa, for those planning to study at an accredited US college or university, or study English at a university or language institute; the J-1 or exchange visitor visa for those participating in an educational or cultural exchange program; and the M-1 or student visa for those enrolled in non-academic or vocational programs.

Those who are coming to the US to pursue full-time academic or vocational studies are usually admitted in the F-1 or M-1 nonimmigrant categories. The F-1 category includes academic students in colleges, universities, seminaries, conservatories, academic high schools, other academic institutions and language schools, while the M-1 category includes vocational students. Before applying for a visa, all student and exchange visitor applicants must be accepted and approved for a course at an approved school. When accepted, educational institutions and program sponsors provide applicants with the necessary approval documentation, which needs to be submitted when applying for a visa.

Information about studying in the US and exchange programs is available from the Bureau of Educational & Cultural Affairs websites (🖥 http://educationusa. state.gov and http://exchanges.state.gov). Enquiries about F-1 or M-1 student visas or J-1 exchange visitor visas, can also be made to the Student/Exchange Visitor Visa Center (✉ fmjvisas@state.gov).

Prospective students can visit the US as tourists (see **Chapter 4**) to vet schools, although if you've been admitted on a B-1 or B-2 visa and apply for a change of status form I-539 (Application to Extend/ Change Nonimmigrant Status) to a student, you cannot begin your studies until your application for a student visa has been approved. If you're going to the US primarily for tourism, but wish to take a short course of study (less the 18 hours per week) which is recreational or vocational, you may be able to do so with a visitor's visa or the Visa Waiver Program. However, if a course of study is for 18 hours or more a week, you'll need a student visa.

STUDENT & EXCHANGE VISITOR PROGRAM (SEVP)

Before schools can offer places to foreign students and issue a form I-20 (Certificate of Eligibility for Student Status) to prospective students, they must be SEVP-certified. An SEVP-certified school is a college, university, seminary, conservatory, high school, private elementary school, other academic or vocational institution, or language training program that has applied for and received certification, which allows them to enroll F or M category nonimmigrants.

SEVP acts as the bridge for varied government organizations which have an interest in information about foreign students and employs the Student and Exchange Visitor Information System (SEVIS – see below), to track and monitor schools and programs, students, exchange visitors and their dependants throughout the duration of their approved participation within the US education system. SEVP collects, maintains and provides the information so that only legitimate foreign students or exchange visitors gain entry to the country.

The following schools are considered to be academic institutions and may be approved for attendance by nonimmigrant students:

♦ a college or university, i.e., an institution of higher learning which awards recognized bachelor's, master's doctor's or professional degrees;

♦ a community college or junior college that provides instruction in the liberal arts or professions and awards recognized associate degrees;

♦ a seminary;

♦ a conservatory;

♦ an academic high school;

♦ a private elementary school;

♦ an institution which provides language training, instruction in the liberal arts, fine arts or the professions, or instruction or training in more than one of these disciplines.

Students & Exchange Visitor Information System (SEVIS)

In 2003, the Homeland Security USICE department (💻 www.ice.gov/sevis) established the Student and Exchange Visitor Information System (SEVIS); a centralized database designed to track visa holders engaged in academic and vocational studies, as well as participants in exchange programs and fellowships.

SEVIS has been a high priority issue for the DHS, due to the fact that most of the terrorists who carried out the September 11, (9/11) 2001 attacks had gained entry to the country using student visas for flight training schools. The manual system in place for tracking students was notorious for losing track of those who had never shown up for classes, dropped out of their programs or simply failed to go home after completing them. SEVIS is designed to track the activity of students and exchange participants from the time they arrive in the US until they return to their home country. More information is available on the ICE website (💻 www.ice.gov/sevis/index.htm).

All schools, universities and exchange programs that are approved to admit foreigners must participate in the SEVIS network – most public and accredited private colleges, universities and vocational schools are approved. A change of school or academic program is permitted, but prior consent must be obtained from the USCIS.

☑ SURVIVAL TIP

Not all educational establishments are approved under SEVIS, therefore you need to check.

You must be proficient in the English language or must be taking a course in English to reach the necessary standard (unless all courses are taught in your native language). You must also show that you can pay for your studies and support yourself for the period of your proposed stay, and you may also require private health insurance. You'll also need to provide evidence of a residence abroad to which you'll return at the end of your studies.

When you're admitted to a study or exchange program that qualifies for a visa (category F, J or M), you'll be registered in the SEVIS system and a form confirming this will be sent to you. The confirmation form and proof of payment of the SEVIS fee are a necessary part of the documentation required at your visa interview. The fee varies according to the type of study or exchange program and the type of visa that you're applying for, and may be paid by your school or sponsor. The fee for F-1, J-1 (with the exception of those applying for the au pair, camp counselor and summer work/travel programs, for which the fee is $35) and M-1 visas is $140. The SEVIS fee is in addition to the visa fee.

Those entering the US under a SEVIS visa category aren't permitted to enter the country more than 30 days before the official start of their classes, course or program (shown on form DS-2019). In fact, Immigrations and Customs Enforcement recommends that you don't arrive more than ten days in advance unless you have a good reason for your early arrival.

If you wish to enter the US more than 30 days before your studies are due to start, you'll need a visitor's visa (see **Chapter 4**), after which you'll need to apply for a change of status (see page 100). The 30-day limitation doesn't apply to visa holders who have left the US for a period after starting a study or exchange program and are returning to continue their studies. Visa holders can usually remain in the US for up to 30 days after the completion on their studies or exchange program.

Bear in mind that being accepted by a school doesn't guarantee you a student visa.

CATEGORY F: ACADEMIC OR LANGUAGE STUDENTS

A student wishing to attend a university or other academic institution in the US, including primary and secondary schools or a language training program, requires an F-1 visa.

F-1 visas are for full-time foreign students studying at US language schools, high schools, universities and other institutions of higher education (henceforth referred to simply as 'schools'). Thousands of schools are approved by the USCIS to accept foreign students, and it's also possible to change schools with an F-1 visa without leaving the country.

F-1 visas aren't issued for attendance at public (state) elementary schools (from grades K to 8) or publicly-funded adult education programs such as foreign language classes (see **Attending Public Schools** below). Students may obtain an F-1 visa for public high school for a maximum of 12 months, but must show proof that payment has been made for the full, unsubsidized cost of education before the visa can be issued. This rule doesn't apply to the dependants of individuals in other visa categories, who wish to study at public schools. Visitors who take a few classes for recreational purposes and students who have a spouse or parent in the US with a nonimmigrant A, E, G, H, J, L or NATO visa don't require a student visa.

The criteria used to determine whether a course qualifies as full-time are the number of hours or credits scheduled during each term (semester) for post-secondary studies, and the period required to complete a course of study. F-1 visas are issued for the length of time it's estimated it will take you to complete your studies up to a maximum of five years, although citizens of certain countries are issued visas for shorter periods, e.g. from two months to four years. You must continue in full-time education for a visa to remain valid.

One of the key differences between an F-1 visa and an M-1 visa is that an F-1 visa holder can change his status to an H-1B nonimmigrant visa, while an M-1 visa holder cannot. A masters degree or doctorate in the US can also be a stepping stone to an H-1B temporary (nonimmigrant) work visa (see page 143), 20,000 of which are issued annually to foreign nationals who have obtained a masters degree or doctorate in the US.

Attending Public Schools

The Immigration and Nationality Act (INA) prohibits the issue of F-1 visas to students attending US public elementary schools (grades K through 8 – approximate ages 5 to 14) and publicly-funded adult education programs such as foreign language classes. Publicly-funded adult education is defined as education, training or English-as-a- second-language (ESL) programs operated by, through or for a local public school district, system, agency or authority, irrespective of whether such a program charges fees or tuition. Programs under this definition cannot accept students in F-1 status, even if a tuition fee is charged.

Students applying for F-1 visas to attend public secondary schools (grades 9 through 12, approximate ages 14 to 18) are limited to a maximum of 12 months public high school (plus a 60-day grace period) in F-1 status and must show proof that payment has been made for the full, unsubsidized cost of education before a visa is issued. This rule doesn't apply to dependants of individuals in other visa categories, who wish to study at public schools. Visitors who take a few classes for recreational purposes and students who have a spouse or parent in the US with a nonimmigrant A, E, G, H, J, L or NATO visa don't require a student visa.

Foreign students who wish to attend public secondary school (high school) must pay the full cost of education, the amount of which is listed under 'tuition' on form I-20 (Certificate of Eligibility for Student Status). If the form I-20 doesn't include the cost of tuition, the student must have a notarized statement, signed by the designated school official who signed the form I-20, stating the full cost of tuition and that the student has paid the tuition in full. The full, unsubsidized cost of education is the cost of providing education to each student in the school district where the public school is located. Annual fees are usually between $3,000 and $10,000.

The student secondary school cost reimbursement requirement is mandatory and school systems cannot waive this. A US organization or individual can, however, pay the full tuition costs for a student, but payment cannot come from public funds. The student must still show that he has sufficient funds to cover his education and living expenses while in the US. Foreign students can also come to the US to live with a US citizen relative while attending public school, but the restrictions noted above still apply (for both primary and secondary schools).

Application Procedure

The first step for a prospective nonimmigrant student is to be accepted for enrolment at an SEVP-certified (see page 177) school. The following conditions apply in order to be accepted at a school:

◆ You must have successfully completed a course of study normally required for enrolment and be prepared to provide transcripts and diplomas from previous institutions attended, and results from examinations such as the TOEFL, SAT, GCSE, A Levels, IB, etc., as applicable.

◆ You must have been accepted for a full course of study by an educational institution approved by the USCIS. The institution sends you a form I-20 A-B – Certificate of Eligibility for Nonimmigrant (F-1) Student Status – For Academic and Language Students – and an acceptance letter.

◆ You must be sufficiently proficient in English to pursue the planned course of study or the school you plan to attend must have made special arrangements to teach you English or conduct the course in your native language (you're exempt from this requirement if you plan to come to the US to participate exclusively in an English language training program). You may need to take a TOEFL test.

◆ You've sufficient funds to cover the first year of study and access to sufficient funds to cover subsequent years. This may mean that you need a guarantor or you'll need to apply for financial aid. If you'll have any dependants with you, you must also provide evidence that you can support them. See **Financial Support & Evidence** below.

◆ You must have a permanent residence in your home country that you don't intend to abandon.

◆ You must intend to depart the US upon completion of the course of study. You can establish this by presenting evidence of economic, social and/or family ties in your home country sufficient to induce you to leave the US upon completion of your studies.

◆ Your proposed education in the US should be useful in your homeland and therefore induce you to leave the US upon completion of your studies.

Bear in mind that the busiest time to apply for a nonimmigrant visa interview in some countries is during the summer vacation period, particularly before the beginning of the fall semester, therefore you may need to plan well ahead to avoid delays. An F-1 visa can be issued up to 120 days before you need to register for your studies, although you're only permitted to enter the US 30 days before your course commences.

Financial Support & Evidence

As a foreign student in the US, you must be able to prove that you'll be able to pay for your studies before you can obtain a visa. When applying for an F-1 visa, you'll need to provide evidence that you have sufficient funds to cover the first year of study and access to sufficient funds to cover subsequent years (as applicable). Parents, guardians or benefactors need to provide an Affidavit of Support (form I-134) and proof of sufficient funds to support you for the duration of your studies. If you've applied for financial aid (see below), then this must have been approved before your visa is issued. If you'll have any dependants with you in the US, then you must also provide evidence that you can support them.

If you don't have access to your own funds, you'll need to show that your parents or other sponsors have sufficient funds to cover your tuition and living expenses during the period of your intended study. For example, if you or your sponsor is a salaried employee, you'll need income tax documents and original bank books and/or statements. If you or your sponsor owns a business, you'll need evidence of business registration, licenses and tax documents,

etc., as well as original bank books and/or statements.

Fees & Financial Aid

Financing a US college degree is expensive, even for most Americans, and it can be even more expensive for foreign students who must also pay to travel to the US and don't usually have the option of staying with their family while studying. Over two-thirds of foreign students use their own resources and/or help from their families to fund their US education, while some 20 per cent receive most of their funding in financial aid from a US college or university.

In addition to accommodation, living costs (e.g. food and incidental expenses) and books – the cost of which varies widely from $15,000 to $60,000 per annum – you'll also need to pay tuition costs. The cost of tuition varies depending on the educational institution and the type of course, ranging from $15,000 to $40,000+ a year (and rising!). State-supported schools – rather than private colleges – tend to offer much lower tuition fees (with up to 75 per cent discount) to foreigners who are resident in the state. The College Board website contains a useful 'College Cost Calculator'

(🖥 http://apps.collegeboard.com/fincalc/college_cost.jsp).

Many private US schools, colleges and universities provide financial aid to overseas students. If this is important, you should ask institutions that you're planning to apply to whether they provide aid for international students. Although many US schools provide little or no aid for foreign students (except for exceptional athletes or brilliant child prodigies), some schools offer scholarships or have special programs to help foreign students pay their fees.

☑ SURVIVAL TIP

Note that many scholarships apply only to US citizens, so the first thing you need to check is whether a grant or scholarship applies to non-resident foreign students.

Grants & Scholarships

You can obtain information about US grants and scholarships from numerous websites, including 🖥 www.college-scholarships.com, http://directory.edvisors.com, www.scholarships.com and www.studentscholarshipsearch.com. All major colleges and universities have a financial office, links to many of which are listed on Yahoo (🖥 http://dir.yahoo.com/Education/Financial_Aid/College_and_University_Aid_Offices). The US Journal of Academics has a useful search facility for international students wishing to study in the US (🖥 www.usjournal.com/en/students/info/study-usa.html).

Other sources include the College Board (🖥 www.collegeboard.com/student/pay/index.html), eduPASS (🖥 www.edupass.org/finaid), fastweb (🖥 www.fastweb.com) – a free scholarship service – International Education Financial Aid (🖥 www.iefa.org), the International Student Loan Center (🖥 www.internationalstudentloan.

com), International Scholarships (🖥 www.internationalscholarships.com), Mach25 (🖥 www.collegenet.com/mach25) and NAFSA: Association of International Educators (🖥 www.nafsa.org – the original name was National Association of Foreign Student Advisers). Scholarship Experts (🖥 www.scholarshipexperts.com) maintain a current database of college scholarships and graduate school scholarships for international students, and although its services aren't free, they may save you a lot of time.

You can also research grants or loans in your own country for study in the US, such as the Fulbright Program UK (🖥 www.educationusa.info/fulbright-uk), which is part of EducationUSA, a global network of over 400 advice centers supported by the Bureau of Educational and Cultural Affairs at the US Department of State (🖥 http://exchanges.state.gov). Some international agencies, such as the United Nations and the World Council of Churches, also provide financial aid for students wishing to study in the US, although competition is fierce.

Schools are more likely to offer grants and scholarships to foreigners who prove themselves superior in their fields of study. Graduate students usually have more success in finding aid, as graduate and teaching assistantships and fellowships are offered to students with proven academic records, irrespective of whether they're foreign or US citizens. Note, however, that even if you're applying for graduate studies, some schools won't consider you for a fellowship or assistantship until your second year of study.

A useful website for prospective foreign students is Foreign Born (🖥 http://foreignborn.com, >study in the US>Paying for school: Financial Aid), which contains comprehensive advice and information about financial aid for foreign students in the US. A useful book for foreign students seeking financial aid is 'Funding for United

States Study', an annual guide published by the Institute of International Education (💻 www.iiebooks.org/funforunstat.html).

Entry & Length of Stay

When you enter the US on a student visa – a maximum of 30 days before the commencement of your studies – you're usually admitted for the duration of your student status, often abbreviated in your passport or on your I-94 card (see page 112) as 'D/S'. This means that you're allowed to stay in the US for as long as you're enrolled as a full-time student in an educational program and making normal progress toward completion of your course of study.

Your I-94 card contains your admission number to the US, which will also be written on your form I-20 A-B (see above) by the Immigration officer, who will then send pages one and two of this form to your school as a record of your legal admission into the US. You need to retain pages three and four, known as the I-20 ID, which is proof that you're allowed to study in the US as an F-1 student. You must also keep your form I-94 in a safe place – it's usually stapled into your passport – as it proves that you legally entered the country.

As an example regarding duration of status, if you have a visa that's valid for five years that will expire on January 1, 2011, and you're admitted into the US for the duration of your studies, you can stay in the US as long as you're a full time student. Even if January 1, 2011 passes and your student visa expires while in the US, you'll still be in legal student status. However, if you depart the US with an expired visa, you'll need to obtain a new one before being readmitted to resume your studies.

At the end of your studies or practical training, you're given 60 days to prepare to leave the country or transfer to another school. If approved, you'll also be allowed to stay in the country for up to 12 additional months beyond the completion of your studies to pursue practical training. If you wish to remain longer, you must apply for an adjustment of status or extension of stay from the USCIS office with jurisdiction over your place of residence in the US.

If you need to leave the US for any reason, you should obtain an endorsed form I-20ID, which verifies that you're still in school and making satisfactory progress in your studies; without the I-20 ID you risk being denied entry. You may visit Canada or Mexico for up to 30 days without a visa, provided you have a valid I-94 and an endorsed I-20 ID. All other destinations require a visa to re-enter the US. Students (in or outside the US) who have been absent from classes for more than five months may need a new visa to enter the US.

Many prospective students drop out of school, never attend classes or 'disappear' and work illegally, which leads the USCIS to carefully monitor student visa applications. Good students (with good academic records) planning to attend top schools rarely experience difficulties, while students with poor or average grades come under greater scrutiny.

Changing Schools

In order to change schools with an F-1 visa, you must be a full-time student in good academic standing. You need to notify your current school of your intention to transfer to another school and ask the new school to provide a new form I-20 A-B. You then complete this form and give it to your new designated school official (DSO) within 15 days of the transfer. The DSO will give you the last two pages, known as form I-20 ID, and forward a copy of the first two pages to the USCIS and your previous school.

Dependants

The F-2 dependant visa is a derivative nonimmigrant visa that allows dependant spouses and children aged under 21 of F-1 student visa holders to enter the US. Dependants may stay in the US as long as the principal F-1 visa holder maintains his status. If your spouse or children are following you at a later date, they should provide the consular official with a copy of your passport and form I-20 ID (Certificate of Eligibility for Nonimmigrant F-1 Student Status – for Academic and Language Students) and provide proof of their relationship to you, i.e. marriage and birth certificates.

As an F-2 spouse, you may not work but can study and an F-2 child may only engage in full-time elementary or secondary school study (kindergarten through twelfth grade). If a dependant spouse wishes to work in the US, he or she must apply to the USCIS for a change of status to a work-related status, e.g. H-1B. Spouses and children who don't intend to live in the US with an F-1 visa holder, but visit for holidays only, can apply for a visitor's visa or travel without a visa under the Visa Waiver Program (see page 120), if applicable.

The F-2 status of your family is dependent upon your status as an F-1 student, therefore if you change your status, your family must change theirs also, and if you lose your status, your family will also lose theirs.

Working with an F-1 Visa

Students with F-1 and J-2 visas are permitted to work up to 20 hours a week under certain circumstances. In the first year, work during term-time must be on-campus (many colleges and universities have 'student help' jobs available), but after this period students may be able to obtain authorization to work off campus.

On-campus jobs may include working in the library, cafeteria, bookstore, family & childcare center, computer center, gym, media center, printing services, the college newspaper or even mowing the campus lawns. Payment for campus jobs is usually low (e.g. less than $10 an hour), but for most students every dollar helps when it comes to buying textbooks or living on more than breakfast cereal or popcorn! You can usually work unlimited hours during holidays and summer vacation.

You shouldn't depend on finding work during term time as you'll have to compete with many other students and shouldn't rely on it to help pay your living expenses.

After you've been studying in the US for a year you can obtain forms from your school's international student's or registrar's office to apply to work off campus. Note that only the USCIS can grant you work permission, but your school can help you apply. If you're approved, you'll still be limited to working no more than 20 hours a week during term time, but you can work full-time during holidays or school vacations. Being able to work off-campus during the summer not only helps with pocket money, but also gives you the opportunity to gain valuable work experience.

Students who have an unforeseen change in their economic situation such as substantial fluctuations in the value of currency or exchange rate, unexpected changes in the financial condition of the student's source of support, medical bills, or other substantial and unexpected expenses, may be eligible for severe economic hardship work authorization. To qualify you must have maintained F-1 status for a full academic year and work authorization must be approved by the USCIS.

Students who drop out of school, work in violation of their student visa or otherwise violate the terms of their visa, may be expelled from the US and barred from entry for five years.

If you don't have a Social Security Number, you must apply for one based on your work authorization. In general, F-1 students who've been in the US for less than five years are exempt from social security taxes. However, you should bring this to the attention of your employer as many aren't familiar with this provision of the tax laws. Students in F-1 status are subject to all other taxes that may apply, including federal, state and local taxes.

For more information, consult with a tax professional or the Internal Revenue Service (📖 www.irs.gov).

In addition to on-campus term jobs and off-campus jobs during vacation periods, there are two practical work programs for students: Curricular Practical Training (CPT) and Optional Practical Training (OPT), which are described below.

Curricular Practical Training (CPT)

Curricular Practical Training (CPT) for F-1 students is intended to provide work experience in situations where the work serves as an integral part of a student's academic program. CPT must be 'an integral part of an established curriculum' and is defined as 'alternate work/study, internship, cooperative education, or any other type of required internship or practicum offered by sponsoring employers through cooperative agreements with the school'. You may apply for CPT to gain work experience in your field of study while a full time student and be paid for a required internship.

You can do up to 364 days of CPT without it affecting your eligibility for OPT, but if you do 365 days or more of CPT, you'll lose your eligibility for OPT (see below).

You must have been enrolled full-time and in status for a full academic year to be eligible for CPT, although there's an exception for graduate students whose programs require *immediate* participation in an internship, a practicum or other employment. Training must be approved by you instructional department as an integral part of the established curriculum, fulfilling graduation requirements for your field of study. Work isn't

required for an AA or AS degree. Optional internships aren't approved for CPT and it isn't available for students in intensive English-language programs. You may work up to 20 hours a week while school is in session and 40 hours a week during breaks and vacation periods. CPT is approved for one quarter at a time and you must obtain approval before the start of each quarter if employment continues.

You may qualify for curricular practical training if any of the following apply:

♦ you're required to take an academic course with concurrent work experience or work which follows the course;

♦ you're given course credit for employment – possibly even if the course is an elective;

♦ you aren't given credit for the employment, but the internship or practicum is a mandatory requirement for graduation.

During the school year while classes are in session, you can engage in CPT on a part-time basis for up to a maximum of 20 hours a week. If you're eligible, there's no limit on the length of time you may participate in part-time CPT, but you must maintain lawful F-1 status. You can engage in full-time CPT during official school breaks and vacation periods, and also during a dissertation or thesis stage. However, CPT authorization ends when your dissertation or thesis finishes.

To apply for CPT you need the following:

♦ A copy of your official employment offer letter on the company letterhead signed by the prospective employer. A photocopy is acceptable. The letter should include the employer's name, address and dates of employment.

♦ A CPT recommendation form completed by your academic advisor.

♦ Proof of registration for a CPT course if you're earning academic credit for the training.

USCIS approval isn't required for CPT which is approved by your international student advisor (ISA). If you're eligible, the advisor will then copy your I-20, complete form I-538 (Certification for Designated School), and send them to the local USCIS data processing center. Because CPT doesn't require official approval from the USCIS, the process of obtaining work authorization usually takes very little time and may be issued within just three business days.

You may engage in CPT employment only after you have received the I-20 with your CPT authorization, which is **valid only for the specific employer, location, time period and part-time or full-time basis, as approved and recorded** on your I-20. Note that you must be registered for a CPT course in the same semester during which the work will be done, e.g. you must be registered for a CPT course in the summer if you'll be working in the summer. **You may not continue employment beyond the date authorized unless you apply and are granted an extension.**

 Caution

Working without authorization is a serious offence and could end in your visa or form I-94 being cancelled and you having to leave the US.

Optional Practical Training (OPT)

Optional Practical Training (OPT) is temporary employment that's directly related to an F-1 student's major area of study. Under earlier rules, an F-1 student could be authorized to receive up to 12 months practical training either before (pre-) and/or after (post-) completion of studies (but see **STEM Students** below). However, the total period of practical training permitted is 12 months, therefore if, for example, you're authorized for three months of pre-completion OPT during the holidays, you'll only be eligible to nine more months of post-completion OPT after you've completed your degree. Furthermore, any time spent in Curricular Practical Training (see above) reduces the amount of time you may work in OPT. M-1 students are also permitted to engage in post-completion OPT and are entitled to one month of training for each four months of study, up to a maximum period of six months.

An F-1 student may be authorized to participate in pre-completion OPT after he has been enrolled for one full academic year. The pre-completion OPT must be directly related to the student's major area of study. Students authorized to participate in pre-completion OPT may only work part-time while school is in session, but may work full time when school isn't in session, i.e. during summer vacation.

Pre-completion optional practical training may be either of the following:

♦ A part-time or full-time job during an annual vacation.

♦ A part-time or full-time job after completion of all coursework, but while working on your thesis, dissertation or project.

During the academic year, while pursuing a full course load, only part-time jobs are allowable

For post-completion optional practical training, you may:

♦ work as a full-time employee;

♦ work for as many companies as you wish;

♦ work as an independent contractor.

The first step in applying for OPT is to complete the top portion of form I-538 (Certification by Designated School) and give it to your school's Designated School Official (DSO) – with your current I-20 ID. He'll certify that your employment is directly related to your major area of study and is appropriate for your educational level. You must then complete form I-765 (Application for Employment Authorization Document or EAD for short). The form I-538, copy of form I-20, form I-765, the fee, two photos and a signature card must then be submitted to the USCIS service center with jurisdiction over your school.

You don't need a job to be eligible for either pre- or post-completion Optional Practical Training. If you have F-1 status, you need permission for OPT employment, which can be filed up to 90 days before and up to 60 days after your degree completion. However, the application must be submitted to the USCIS within 30 days of the date the CIE enters the recommendation for OPT in SEVIS (see page 178).

☑ SURVIVAL TIP

Students are strongly advised to apply for OPT at the earliest opportunity; if you apply after completion of your degree you may end up with less than 12 months OPT due to the processing time.

Bear in mind that it can take up to 120 days for the USCIS to approve your application and you won't be eligible to work before it's approved. Therefore, you must plan ahead and apply at the earliest possible date. The start date of OPT is the date requested or the date OPT is approved by the USCIS, whichever is later.

Students who are authorized for OPT must have an I-20 form endorsed for OPT and provide a USCIS Employment Authorization Document (EAD). When the USCIS approves your OPT application, you'll be issued with an EAD card, usually within three to four months, which is the size of your driver's license with a picture and information about your OPT.

You may change employers any time after receiving authorization from the INS, if the new job is directly related to your field of study and is appropriate for someone with your level of education. You can also have as many jobs with as many companies as you wish or work as an independent contractor. You may not accrue more than 90 days unemployment during any post-completion OPT or 120 days unemployment during the total 29-month OPT period if you're granted a 17-month extension (see **STEM Students** below).

If you do a year of practical training after completing your degree, you cannot obtain another period of practical training upon completing another degree.

STEM Students

On April 4, 2008, the Department of Homeland Security (DHS) released an interim final rule extending the period of OPT from 12 to 29 months for qualified F-1 nonimmigrant students. The extension is available to students who are employed by businesses enrolled in the E-verify program (see 🖥 www.uscis.gov > E-Verify Homepage on the right of the screen), a free internet-based system operated by the USCIS in partnership with the Social Security Administration. E-verify allows participating employers to electronically verify the employment eligibility of prospective employees.

To be eligible for the 17-month OPT extension, a student must have a STEM degree (Science, Technology, Engineering, or Mathematics) in one of the following fields:

- Actuarial Science
- Biological & Biomedical Science
- Computer Science Applications
- Engineering
- Engineering Technologies
- Life Sciences
- Mathematics & Statistics
- Medical Science
- Military Technologies
- Physical Sciences
- Science Technologies

To qualify for the OPT 17-month extension, you must fulfill the following criteria:

- have a bachelor's, master's, or doctorate degree included in the STEM-designated degree program list;
- currently be in an approved post-completion OPT period based on a designated STEM degree;
- apply on time, i.e., before the current post-completion OPT expires;
- not have previously received a 17-month OPT extension;
- pay the application fee of $340 with the application;

◆ have a job offer from an employer enrolled in E-verify.

If your post-completion OPT expires while the 17-month extension application is pending, you'll receive an extension of employment authorization, provided the STEM extension application was filed in good time. The extension of employment authorization is for a maximum of 180 days.

The OPT extension provides a permanent solution to the H-1B 'cap-gap', whereby an academic foreign student's F-1 status and work authorization expires during the current fiscal year before the student can start approved H-1B employment (see page 141) during the next fiscal year (beginning on October 1). Previous cap-gap provisions extended only the stay but not the employment authorization, therefore an F-1 student often had to leave the US for several months and return when his H-1B status became effective. The extension of the OPT period for STEM degree holders gives US employers two chances to recruit graduates through the H-1B process, as the extension allows for H-1B petitions to be filed in successive fiscal years.

CATEGORY J: EXCHANGE VISITORS

The Exchange Visitor Program (EVP) is carried out under the provisions of the Mutual Educational and Cultural Exchange Act of 1961, as amended. The purpose of the act is to increase mutual understanding between the people of the US and other countries by means of educational and cultural exchanges. At the conclusion of their EVP, participants are expected to return to their home countries to utilize the experience and skills they have acquired in the US. The EVP is administered by the Office of Exchange Coordination and Designation in the Bureau of Educational and Cultural

Affairs (🖥 http://exchanges.state.gov/jexchanges/index.html).

Category J-1 visas, known as nonimmigrant cultural exchange visas, are issued to foreign exchange visitors including students, scholars, trainees, teachers, professors, medical graduates, research assistants, and specialists or leaders in a field of specialized knowledge or skill. Applicants must enter the US temporarily as a participant in an approved program through a designated sponsoring organization. The activities that may be performed include teaching, instructing, lecturing, studying, observing, conducting research, consulting, demonstrating special skills or receiving training. In addition, there are several exchange visitor programs for young people, including summer employment, internship for university students and au-pair programs.

The categories of people and professions covered under the EVP include the following, each of which has specific requirements and regulations:

◆ Alien Physician

◆ Au Pair & Educare

◆ Camp Counselor

◆ Government Visitor

◆ Intern (see below)

◆ International Visitor (reserved for Department of State use)

◆ Professor & Research Scholar

◆ Short-term Scholar

◆ Specialist

◆ Student, college/university

◆ Student, secondary

◆ Summer work/travel

◆ Teacher

◆ Trainee & Flight Training

In order to perform services as a member of the medical profession or to receive graduate medical education in the US, certain alien physicians are required to pass the National Board of Medical Examiners (NBME) Parts I and II, or an examination determined to be equivalent. For more information about the above categories, see 🖳 www.travel.state.gov/visa/temp/types/types_1267.html.

In 2007, an 'intern' category was created to distinguish non-professionals from professionals, and the regulations for a J-1 visa were revised in order to widen the available programs and prevent abuses. Interns must be pursuing a foreign post-secondary course or have graduated not more than 12 months before the start of the exchange program, while trainees must have graduated at least 12 months previously or have at least five years' work experience in their field outside the US. The maximum duration of the exchange is 12 months for interns and 18 months for trainees.

A form DS-2019 (Certificate of Eligibility for Exchange Visitor Status) must be provided by your program sponsor and registered with SEVIS (see page 178). You must also complete form DS-7002 (Training/Internship Placement Plan), which must be signed by you, the host company and the sponsoring organization. When you apply for a J-1 visa at a US consulate or embassy, you must submit forms DS-2019 and DS-7002 along with your other application forms and documents (information will be provided by your sponsor). The DS-2019 form doesn't guarantee that you'll receive a J-1 visa, but shows that a Department of State-designated visa sponsor supports your visa application.

Applicants must demonstrate that they meet the requirements for a J-1 visa, including the following:

◆ that they plan to remain in the US for a temporary, specific, limited period only;

◆ evidence of funds to cover their expenses in the US;

◆ evidence of compelling social and economic ties abroad and other binding ties, which will insure their return abroad at the end of their visit.

Applicants must have an adequate knowledge of English and establish that they have adequate financial resources to cover all their expenses (including tuition) while in the US. Finance may consist of your own or your family's private resources, scholarships or a salary that's part of the program. As most programs include scholarships or employment, this requirement isn't usually difficult to meet. You're also required to prove that you have a residence abroad to which you intend to return at the end of your stay. Medical graduates must pass parts I and II of the US National Board of Medical Examiners or the Foreign Medical Graduates examination.

Certain exchange visitors are subject to a two-year, home country physical presence requirement. This stipulates that on completion of your period as an exchange visitor, you aren't usually eligible for a Green Card or a temporary worker, trainee or intra-company transferee visa until you've spent at least two years outside the US in the country of your nationality or last residence. This applies to those on exchange programs that are financed in whole or in part, directly or indirectly, by a US government agency or by a foreign government; if you came to the US on a program to learn skills that are in short supply in your home country; or you're a medical graduate who entered the US to receive medical education or training.

It's possible to obtain a waiver that allows you to work in the US before the two-year qualification period has expired, but this can be difficult.

The spouse and unmarried children aged under 21 of a J-1 visa holder are issued with J-2 visas and are permitted to study in the US but aren't allowed to work without an appropriate work visa. The sponsor must approve the accompaniment of the spouse and/or children, who are each issued with their own form DS-2019.

Exchange Visitor Program Organizations

Information about international student exchange programs can be obtained from US schools, although you may find that exchange program information on US school websites primarily addresses the needs of American students. Contact schools directly to obtain information specific to your own situation. Alternatively you can contact the US Educational Advising Center in your home country (see 🖳 www.educationusa. info/centers.php).

There are numerous organizations that can help you find an appropriate exchange program in the US. Foremost among these is the Institute of International Education (🖳 www.iie.org > Programs Portal>Browse Programs>Non-US Student Programs), which is an independent nonprofit organization that's among the world's largest and most experienced international education and training organizations.

Others include the Association of International Practical Training (AIPT, 🖳 www.aipt.org), the Bureau of Educational and Cultural Affairs (🖳 http://exchanges. state.gov), CDS International (🖳 www. cdsintl.org), the Council for International Educational Exchange (CIEE, 🖳 www. ciee.org/wat/index.html), the Council for International Exchange of Scholars (CIES, 🖳 www.iie.org/cies), the Fund For American Studies (TFAS, 🖳 www.tfas.org/page. aspx?pid=216), the Fulbright Program for Foreign Students (🖳 www.foreign. fulbrightonline.org) and the International Association of Students in Economics and Business Management (AIESEC, 🖳 www. aiesec.org), the world's largest student organization.

CATEGORY M: NON-ACADEMIC STUDENTS

A student wishing to pursue a course of study which is principally vocational or non-academic (other than language training) at an established vocational or other recognized nonacademic institution, such as a post secondary vocational or business school, requires an M-1 visa. M-1 visas are issued for the estimated length of time it will take you to complete your proposed studies up to a maximum of five years, although visas aren't initially usually approved for longer than 18 months. An M-1 student may receive extensions up to three years for the total program.

Approval for the attendance of non-academic students may be solicited by a community or junior college that provides vocational or technical training and awards associate degrees; a vocational high school; a trade school or a school of non-academic training other than language training. It can also mean study at a post secondary vocational or business school which grants associate or other degrees. You must normally be enrolled for a full course of study, which means study with at least 12 semesters. Different educational institutions have different admission policies and will inform you of the documentation required in order to determine that you're academically eligible.

When you've been accepted for a full course of study by a vocational institution approved by the USCIS, the school will send you a certificate of eligibility for nonimmigrant (M-1) student status for vocational students (form I-20M-N). You must provide evidence that sufficient funds are immediately available to pay all tuition and living costs for the entire period of your intended stay. Other conditions are the same as for F-1 visas (see page 185).

All M-1 visa holders must be entered into the SEVIS system (see page 178) and must submit their copy of the registration form (I-20M) and payment of the SEVIS fee as part of their visa application. Students with an M-1 visa are permitted to attend only the specific school for which their visa has been approved and are prohibited from changing their course of study after six months' study, except under exceptional circumstances.

M-1 visa holders in technical and vocational programs aren't permitted to work during the course of their studies. You can apply for an extension of stay after the completion of your studies to pursue practical training. M-1 visa holders are allowed to work only if it's a required part of their training and the employment has been approved in advance by the USCIS. If approved, you'll be allowed to undertake one month of practical training for each four months of study that you've completed up to a maximum of six months total practical training.

The spouse and unmarried children aged under 21 of an M-1 visa holder are issued with M-2 visas. The spouse is permitted only vocational or recreational study and isn't allowed to study full-time or work without an appropriate visa. Children may study full-time in an elementary or secondary school (kindergarten through twelfth grade).

On completion of your studies, you must return to your home country (you aren't allowed to continue on to the university level).

8.
PERMANENT RESIDENCE (IMMIGRANT VISAS)

If you want to live and/or work in the US permanently and eventually become a US citizen, then you'll need an immigrant visa. In general, to apply for an immigrant visa a foreign citizen must be sponsored by a US citizen relative, a US lawful permanent resident or a prospective US employer, and be the beneficiary of an approved petition (see page 200).

There's also an annual 'Green Card Lottery', officially called 'Diversity Immigrants' (see page 204), targeted at immigrants from under-represented countries. It's also possible to become an immigrant through refugee or asylum status, and through the Legal Immigration Family Equity (LIFE) Act, which enables certain individuals in the US who wouldn't normally qualify to apply for 'adjustment of status' (see **Extensions & Change of Status** on page 100) and obtain a Green Card.

An immigrant visa bestows upon the holder the status of a permanent resident and consists of a stamp or label in your passport inserted by a US embassy or consulate outside the US (as with nonimmigrant visas), which allows you to enter the US to take up permanent residence. Permanent residents, officially termed 'lawful permanent residents' (LPRs), are issued with a Permanent Resident Card, commonly referred to as a Green Card due to its original color (although it's now white), consisting of a plastic identification card with your photo, thumb print and signature on the front. See **Permanent Resident (Green) Card** below.

There are two ways most people can obtain a Green Card: through blood ties (or marriage), i.e. as an immediate or close relative of a US citizen or permanent resident, and through employment; some nonimmigrant visas also allow you to apply for immigrant status.

Most Green Cards (other than those for immediate relatives) are issued on a preferential basis and applications can take up to ten years to be approved, depending on the category. As a consequence, it's common practice for prospective immigrants to enter the country with a nonimmigrant visa, such as an H-1B visa, and then get your employer to sponsor you for a Green Card.

The US is one of the only countries in the world that doesn't allow the spouses and dependant children of **permanent** residents to live together (in the US) without restriction. For example, the spouse of a Green Card holder may have to wait up to five years to

been a misnomer since the '60s, when the US switched to various hues of blue and, most recently, white, although the name has stuck. The latest version is white plastic (similar in size to a credit card) with a thick green stripe on the back. The card features holograms and microdot portraits of US Presidents – intended to make it more difficult to forge – and incorporates an optical memory stripe containing encrypted information which can be read by a scanner. It also contains a digital photograph of the holder and his thumbprint.

Most of the information on the card is self-evident, with the exception of the computer and human readable signature at the bottom, which contains the following data:

1. First line, characters:

♦ 1–2: C1 or C2; C1 = Resident within the USA, C2= Permanent Resident commuter (Living in Canada or Mexico).

♦ 3–5: USA (issuing country).

♦ 6–14: 9-digit number (A#, alien number).

♦ 15: not documented, assumed to be a check-number.

♦ 16–30: immigrant case number that resulted in the approved Green Card. The '<' symbol represents a blank space.

2. Second line, characters:

♦ 1-6: birth date (YY/MM/DD).

join her spouse – by which time the resident sponsor will have qualified to become a US citizen. **If any other country had such restrictions it would be considered an outrage – especially by Americans!**

Furthermore, this puts Green card holders in a uniquely disadvantaged position, vis-à-vis nonimmigrants, such as temporary workers, businessmen and students with a nonimmigrant visa (e.g. H-1, F-1 J-1 or L-1), whose spouses and children can apply for derivative beneficiary visas to accompany them or follow later to join them in the US.

PERMANENT RESIDENT (GREEN) CARD

The Permanent Resident Card, commonly referred to as a 'Green Card', is an identification card attesting to the Legal Permanent Resident (LPR) status of an alien in the US. The term 'Green Card' has

◆ 7: not documented, assumed to be a check digit.

◆ 8: gender.

◆ 9-14: expiration date (YY/MM/DD).

◆ 15: not documented, assumed to be a check digit.

◆ 16-29: country of birth.

◆ 30: not documented, assumed to be a check digit.

3. Third line, characters:

◆ last name, first name, middle name, first initial of father, first initial of mother (this line is spaced with '<<' between the last name and first name). Depending on the length of the name, the father's and mother's initials may be omitted.

Your Green Card must be in your possession at all times and you must show it to a USCIS officer or other authorized official, when requested. (US citizens aren't required to carry any citizenship identification, although they can be arrested for being unable to show ID!) Prior to September 11, 2001 (the attack on the World Trade Center in New York), an alien's status was checked when the permanent resident returned from foreign travel, but the requirement to carry the Green Card was almost never enforced when residents traveled domestically. However, since 9/11 officials from the US Department of State occasionally ask people if they're US citizens and if they aren't they're required to produce their Permanent Resident Card or other proof of legal status.

The US Citizenship and Immigration Services (USCIS) is responsible for issuing Green Cards. If your Green Card expires, is lost, mutilated or destroyed, you must contact the USCIS for a replacement ASAP (🖳 www.uscis.gov).

Obtaining a Green Card

The procedure for obtaining a Green Card is a three step process:

◆ An immigrant petition is filed by the sponsor, a US citizen, Legal Permanent Resident or a prospective employer.

◆ With the exception of immediate relatives (for whom there are no quotas), prospective immigrants must wait for an immigrant visa number to be issued, which may take many years.

◆ When an immigrant visa number becomes available you can apply for an immigrant visa at your nearest US embassy or consulate. This include an Affidavit of Support, if applicable.

If you're already in the US, you may be able to apply for an adjustment of status (AOS) from nonimmigrant to immigrant. After you've filed form I-485 (Application to Register Permanent Residence or Adjust Status), you can obtain two important permits. The first is a temporary work permit – form I-765 (Employer Authorization Document or EAD) – which allows you to work in the US. The second is a temporary travel document – form I-131 (Advance Parole) – which permits you to re-enter the US as an LPR while waiting for your Green Card to be issued. Both permits confer benefits that are independent of your existing status.

Obligations & Rights of Residents

An immigrant visa gives you the right to live and work in the US (and change jobs freely) on a permanent basis and confers eligibility for US citizenship (see **Chapter 9**) after three years (for the spouse of a US citizen) or five years for all others. Green Card holders also have the right to petition for a Green Card for their spouse and unmarried children under 21 years of age.

The main difference between the rights of a permanent resident and those of a

US citizen is that a permanent resident, although having all the responsibilities of a US citizen, is ineligible for certain welfare benefits, including some Medicaid and Social Security insurance benefits, and cannot vote in federal elections or serve on a jury.

> Green cards are valid for ten years and cannot be withdrawn, provided you don't abandon your US residence for more than a year or commit certain crimes (see **Departing the US & Abandoning Permanent Residence** on page 220).

A Green Card serves as a US entry document for permanent residents returning to the US after a period abroad.

A Lawful Permanent Resident can apply for US citizenship or naturalization (see **Chapter 9**) after five years of residency, which is shortened to three years if you're married to a US citizen or four years if permanent residency was received through asylum. Citizens are entitled to more rights (and obligations) than permanent residents (who are still classified as aliens in this respect). Lawful Permanent Residents generally

don't have the right to vote, the right to be elected in federal and state elections, the ability to bring family members to the US (permanent residents are allowed to sponsor certain family members, but this often isn't practical due to the long approval delays), or eligibility for federal government jobs.

Male permanent residents between the ages of 18 and 26 are subject to registration in the Selective Service System, whereby the US government maintains information on those potentially subject to military conscription (there's currently no conscription in the US). All men aged between 18 and 25 are required to register within 30 days of their 18th birthday.

Permanent residents who reside in the US must pay taxes on their worldwide income, like US citizens. Certain conditions that may result in a legal permanent resident being deported don't apply to US citizens.

Conditional Permanent Residence

Those who apply for permanent residence based on either a recent marriage to a US citizen or as an investor (EB-5) are granted permanent residence on a conditional basis for two years. An exception to this rule is the case of a US citizen legally sponsoring a spouse in which the marriage at the time of the adjustment of status (form I-485) is

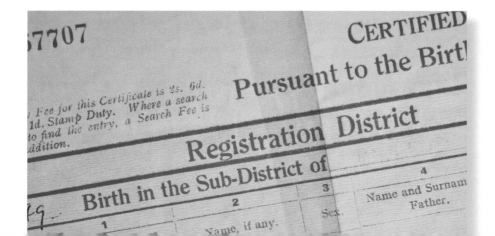

more than two years old. In this case, the conditional status is waived and a ten-year Permanent Resident Card is issued after USCIS approval. A permanent resident under the conditional clause may receive an I-551 stamp as well as a Permanent Resident Card. The expiration date of the conditional period is two years from the approval date and the immigrant visa category is CR (conditional resident).

When this two-year conditional period is completed, the permanent residence automatically expires and you're subject to deportation and removal. To avoid this, you must file form I-751 (Petition to Remove Conditions on Residence) with the USCIS up to 90 days before your conditional residence expires (if conditional permanent residence was obtained through marriage) or form I-829 (Petition by Entrepreneur to Remove Conditions) if conditional permanent residence was obtained through investment, to have the conditions removed.

Once the application is filed, permanent residence is extended for 1-year intervals until the request to remove conditions is approved or denied. The USCIS requires that you provide both general and specific supporting evidence that the basis on which you obtained conditional permanent residence wasn't fraudulent. For an application based on marriage, birth certificates of children, joint financial statements, and letters from employers, friends and relatives are examples of evidence that's accepted. A follow-up interview with an immigration inspector is sometimes required, but usually waived if the evidence is sufficient. This is to ensure that the marriage was in good faith and wasn't fraudulent with the sole intention of obtaining a Green Card. Both husband and wife must usually attend interviews. You receive an I-551 stamp in your passport upon approval of your case and are then free from the conditional requirement.

Your new Permanent Resident Card is sent to you within the next few months and replaces the two-year conditional residence card. The Green Card must be renewed after ten years, however permanent resident status is granted for an indefinite period provided that residence conditions are complied with.

The USCIS may renew your Green Card before it's expiry date, due to security enhancements or as a part of a revalidation campaign to exclude counterfeit cards from circulation.

The two-year conditional residence period counts towards time as a permanent resident for all purposes, including naturalization. However, the application for the removal of conditions must be adjudicated before naturalization can be granted.

IMMIGRANT VISA CATEGORIES

People emigrating to the US are divided by immigration law into categories, such as immediate relatives, family-sponsored and employment-based immigrants, investors and 'diversity' immigrants, as described below. Some categories have annual numerical limitations (quotas) – known as 'preference categories' – including family-sponsored immigrants and employment-based immigrants.

The US immigration 'year' runs from October 1 to September 30 and isn't the calendar year.

Immediate Relatives

The immediate relatives of US citizens are entitled to permanent residence, without any limitation on their numbers, i.e. there are no quotas and some 300,000-500,000 immediate relatives are admitted annually. Immediate relative immigrant visas are based on a close family relationship with a US citizen, including spouses, children, and parents. A US citizen can also sponsor

Visas for Immediate Relatives

Relationship	Notes
Spouse of a US citizen (IR-1)	For information about nonimmigrant visas for a fiancé(e), see page 108.
Unmarried child (aged under 21) of a US citizen (IR-2)	An immigrant visa can be processed for a child only if he has no claim on US citizenship. Children must be aged under 21 when they enter the US.
An orphan adopted abroad by a US citizen – (IR-3) or an orphan to be adopted in the US by a US citizen (IR-4)	Adopted children must be aged under 16 see ⌨ http://adoption.state.gov
Parent of a US citizen (IR-5)	The US citizen (petitioner) must be aged 21 or over.
Step-parent or step-child of a US citizen	The step-parent, step-child relationship must have occurred before the child's 18th birthday; foreign children adopted before their 16th birthday are also eligible.
Spouse of a deceased US citizen	The petition must be filed within two years of the death of the US citizen.

a child adopted or to be adopted from abroad, provided the child meets the definition of orphan under immigration law. Family members of US citizens (not Legal Permanent Residents) can file Immediate relative petitions (see below).

The table above shows immediate relatives of US citizens are eligible to qualify for an immigration visa in the immediate relative category.

Family-sponsored Immigrants

Family-sponsored immigrants are specific, more distant (e.g. than immediate relatives above) family relationships with a US citizen and include some relationships with a Lawful Permanent Resident (Green Card holder). Under immigration law, there are fiscal year numerical limitations (quotas) for family-sponsored immigrants as shown below. As a consequence, there's a huge backlog of applicants (shown below) in all categories, ranging from two to over ten years.

The latest priority dates are issued by the Department of State in the Visa Bulletin (see ⌨ http://travel.state.gov/visa/bulletin/bulletin_1360.html). Visa availability information is also available via a recorded message (☎ 202-663-1541), which is updated in the middle of the month with information regarding cut-off dates for the following month.

The availability of visa numbers for family-sponsored immigrants in July 2010 are shown in the table below. A date indicates that the class is oversubscribed (the date is the priority date when numbers will be issued); 'C' means current, i.e., numbers are available for all qualified applicants; and 'U' means unavailable, i.e., no numbers are available. Numbers are available only for applicants whose priority date is earlier than the cut-off date listed opposite.

Family	All Areas Except Those Listed (right)	China-mainland born	Dominican Republic	India	Mexico	Philippines
1st	01APR05	01APR05	01APR05	01APR05	01NOV92	01SEP95
2A	01JUL08	01JUL08	01JUN07	01JUL08	01JUN07	01JUL08
2B	01MAY03	01MAY03	01MAY03	01MAY03	15JUN92	01MAR00
3rd	01SEP01	01SEP01	01SEP01	01SEP01	01MAR92	01MAY93
4th	01JAN01	01JAN01	01JAN01	01JAN01	01MAR95	01APR89

Relatives of US citizens and of permanent resident aliens (referred to as preference relatives) are limited to a minimum of 226,000 visas per year, though an additional 55,000 visas a year are allocated to relatives of amnesty recipients.

Preference relatives are divided into the following four preference categories (annual quotas for each category are shown):

♦ **F-1 (First Preference):** unmarried sons and daughters of US citizens aged over 21 and their children; the quota is 23,400 plus any unused by the fourth preference. In July 2010, visa numbers were being allocated to individuals with a priority date of April 2005, for all countries except Mexico and the Philippines.

♦ **F-2 (Second Preference):** spouses, minor children and unmarried sons and daughters (aged over 20) of lawful permanent residents, i.e. Green Card holders. At least 75 per cent of all visas in this category go to spouses and children, the remainder being allocated to older unmarried sons and daughters. The family second preference category is divided into two sub-categories: F-2A and F-2B. Category F-2A includes spouses and children and comprises 77 per cent of the overall second preference limitation, of which 75 per cent are exempt from the per-country limit. Category F-2B includes unmarried sons and daughters (aged 21 or older) and comprises 23 per cent of the overall second preference limitation. The total allocation is 114,200 plus the number (if any) by which the worldwide family preference level exceeds 226,000, and any unused first preference numbers.

In July 2010, visa numbers for F-2A visas were being allocated to individuals with a priority date of July 2008 for all countries except the Dominican Republic and Mexico. For F-2B visas, numbers were being allocated to individuals with a priority date of May 2003 for all countries except Mexico and the Philippines.

♦ **F-3 (Third Preference):** married sons and daughters (of any age) of US citizens and their spouses and children; the quota is 23,400 plus any unused by first and second preferences. In July 2010, visa numbers were being allocated to individuals with a priority date of September 2001 for all countries except Mexico and the Philippines.

♦ **F-4 (Fourth Preference):** brothers and sisters of US citizens and their spouses and children, provided the US citizen is aged at least 21; the quota is 65,000 plus any unused by the first three preferences. In July 2010, visa numbers were being allocated to individuals with a priority date of January 2001 for all countries except Mexico and the Philippines.

☑ SURVIVAL TIP

Grandparents, aunts, uncles, in-laws and cousins cannot sponsor a relative for immigration.

You must be aged at least 18 and have a domicile in the US before you can sign the Affidavit of Support (form I-864), which is required for an immigrant visa for spouses and other relatives of US sponsors (see **Petitions** below). Minor US citizen children cannot file a petition for a parent until they reach the age of majority, i.e. 21.

Whenever there are more qualified applicants for a category than there are available numbers, the category is considered oversubscribed, and immigrant visas are issued in the chronological order in which the petitions were filed, until the numerical limit for the category is reached. The filing date of a petition becomes your priority date. Immigrant visas cannot be issued until your priority date is reached. In certain heavily over-subscribed categories, there are waiting lists of up to ten years before a priority date is reached.

There are separate waiting lists for family and employment based applicants, as well as sub-categories within those main classifications. Once an applicant has established a priority date through the approval of a form I-130, I-140, or I-360, he should refer to the monthly 'Visa Bulletin' to determine his visa availability (see 🖥 http://travel.state.gov/visa/bulletin/bulletin_1360.html). The bulletin is available free via email by sending an email to ✉ istserv@calist.state.gov with the following message in the body type: 'Subscribe Visa-Bulletin first name/last name' (example: 'Subscribe Visa-Bulletin John Doe').

Employment-Based Immigrants

In order to become an employment-based immigrant, you must be sponsored by a prospective US employer, which is a three-step process:

1. **Labor Certification:** labor certification proves that there are no suitable (what 'suitable' means is decided by the Department of Labor) qualified US citizens or LPRs available for the position that has been offered to you (see **Labor Certification & LCAs** on page 137.

2. **Green Card employment petition:** The petition – when approved – confirms that you qualify for a Green Card and that a job has been offered to you.

3. **Green Card employment visa application:** The Green Card visa application.

A total of at least 140,000 immigrant visas a year are available in this category, with 40,000 (28.6 per cent of the total) being allocated to each of preferences one to three. A maximum of 7 per cent (9,800) can be allocated to people born in any one country (not citizenship). A per-country limit (cap – not a quota, to which any particular country is entitled) for preference immigrants is set at 7 per cent of the total annual family-sponsored and employment-based preference limits, i.e. 7 per cent of 366,000 = 25,620. Currently, individuals from China (mainland), India, Mexico and the Philippines are subject to per-country quotas in most categories, and waiting times may be longer. In July 2010, in some categories the USCIS was still processing applications filled in 2001!

Employment-based (EB) immigrants are divided into the following five groups, each of which is subject to an annual quota (shown below):

◆ **EB-1 first preference (Priority Workers):** people of extraordinary ability in the sciences, arts, education, business, or athletics; outstanding professors and researchers; and certain multinational executives and managers. The annual quota is 40,000 (or 28.6 per cent of the worldwide employment-based preference level) plus any numbers not required for fourth and fifth preferences. Most people would like to file their Green Card application in this category because the priority dates are current most of the time, while there's often a long wait in other employment based categories. However, few people qualify for EB-1 visas and applications are strictly scrutinized.

◆ **EB-2 second preference (Members of the Professions):** professionals holding advanced degrees or equivalent, or baccalaureate degrees plus at least five years' experience in their field, and people of exceptional ability in the sciences, arts and business, e.g. professors and researchers. The annual quota is 40,000 plus any numbers not required by the first preference. It's easier to obtain approval under EB-3 than EB-2, as the job requirements in EB-2 are carefully scrutinized. However, it's advantageous for those born in over-subscribed countries (such as China and India) to apply in EB-2 if they qualify, as processing (although slow) is faster than in EB-3. In July 2010, all countries were current except for China and India.

◆ **EB-3 third preference (Professionals, Skilled & Unskilled Workers):** professionals holding baccalaureate degrees, skilled workers with at least two years' training or experience, and other workers whose skills are in short supply in the US. Unskilled workers are subject to a limit of 10,000, which is included in the annual quota of 40,000, plus any numbers not required by the first and second preferences. Visa numbers are currently being allocated to individuals with a priority date of August 2003 for all areas except India and Mexico.

◆ **EB-4 fourth reference (Special Immigrants):** certain religious workers and ministers of religion; employees of certain international organizations and their immediate family members; specially qualified and recommended current and former employees of the US government; and returning residents. The annual quota is 10,000 or 7.1 per cent of the worldwide level.

♦ **EB-5 fifth preference (Investors):** people who create employment for at least ten full-time US workers (not family members) by investing capital in a new commercial enterprise in the US. The minimum investment is $500,000, depending on the employment rate in the geographical area. The annual quota is 10,000 (7.1 per cent of the worldwide level), not less than 3,000 of which are reserved for investors in a targeted rural or high-unemployment area, plus 3,000 set aside for investors in regional centers.

The EB-5 visa provides a flexible path to a Green Card based on a US investment and doesn't require you to actively manage the day-to-day affairs of a business (unlike a nonimmigrant E-2 visa). EB-5 regulations require 'involvement' in management or policy making, although simply being a limited partner in the organization that owns the business qualifies as an active role. For many people, it's the fastest and most secure way to obtain a Green Card, but it's also the most expensive.

For further information, see **EB-5 Investor Immigrant Visas** on page 165.

In addition to the above quotas, there are limits on certain sub-preferences, some of which are based on formulas which change each year. Contact a US embassy or consulate for the current regulations.

Diversity Immigrants

The Immigration Act 1990 created a new category, Diversity Immigrants – commonly referred to as the 'visa lottery' – with the aim of providing immigration opportunities to people born in countries which have had the lowest numbers of immigrants in recent years (selection is based on country of birth and not residence or citizenship). A maximum of 55,000 DV-1 visas are available each fiscal year through the scheme, which are allocated by lottery (hence 'visa lottery') – or rather by random computer selection. There were 13.6m applicants in the 2010 program!

The Nicaraguan and Central American Relief Act (NACARA) passed by Congress in November 1997 stipulates that beginning with DV-99, and for as long as necessary, up to 5,000 of the 55,000 annually-allocated diversity visas will be made available for use under the NACARA program. This has resulted in the DV-2011 annual limit being effectively reduced to 50,000.

DV visas are divided among six geographic regions and no one country can receive more than 7 per cent (3,500) of the available visas in any one year. To be eligible, a country must have had fewer than 50,000 immigrant visas, excluding diversity visas, issued to it during the previous five years.

Natives of the following countries weren't eligible to apply for the DV-2011 lottery because their countries sent more than 50,000 immigrants to the US over the previous five years: Brazil, Canada, China (mainland-born), Colombia, Dominican Republic, Ecuador, El Salvador, Guatemala, Haiti, India, Jamaica, Mexico, Pakistan, Peru, the Philippines, Poland, South Korea, the United Kingdom (except Northern Ireland) and its dependant territories, and Vietnam. Those born in the Hong Kong Special Administrative Region (SAR), Macau SAR and Taiwan are eligible.

Applicants require a high school diploma (or equivalent) or a proven job skill requiring at least two years' training and two years' experience in that job within the last five years. Theoretically there's no age limit, but the education and experience requirements mean that applicants must usually be aged at least 18.

No fee is payable on application, but successful applicants must pay a $375 'surcharge'. The application period for DV-1 visas varies each year but usually lasts for two months only; for example, the application period for the 2009 lottery (DV-2011 – termed 2011 because the visas will be issued in 2011) ran from noon, Eastern Daylight Time (EDT), on Friday October 2, 2009, until noon, Eastern Standard Time (EST) on Monday November 30, 2009.

Applications must be submitted online via the Diversity Lottery website (🖳 www.dvlottery.state.gov), using the Electronic Diversity Visa Entry Form (E-DV Entry form DS-5501), including the submission of all photos and any supporting documents required. One photo of each application is required (only digital or scanned photos are accepted). Applications take around 30 minutes to complete and no professional help is necessary. Only one application is permitted per person, although a husband and wife can each submit an application, even when only one spouse qualifies. If more than one application is submitted, the applicant is disqualified for that year.

After a successful application is submitted, you receive a confirmation number, with which you can check online whether your entry was selected (🖳 http://travel.state.gov/visa/immigrants/types/types_1318.html). The results of the DV-2011 lottery were available online from July 1, 2010 and winners are also notified directly by mail by the US Department of State. If selected, you and your spouse and unmarried children aged under 21 can apply for permanent resident status in the US. You should apply for your visas as soon as possible after receiving written notification of your selection. After the immigrant visas have been issued, you have six months to enter the US.

Note that selection in the lottery doesn't guarantee that an immigration visa will be issued. There are several additional immigration forms and documents that must be submitted and approved before you receive your visa.

Information about DV-1 visas and the application procedure can be obtained from US embassies and consulates, via the Diversity Lottery website (🖳 www.dvlottery.state.gov) or the US State Department's visa information website (🖳 http://travel.state.gov/visa/immigrants/types/types_1318.html). Instructions are available on the latter website in a number of languages.

⚠ **Caution**

No assistance is necessary from a lawyer or immigration expert to apply for a DV-1 visa – which is straightforward – and you don't need an 'application guide'. There are a wealth of online companies offering information or assistance with visa lottery applications, most of which are scams. Some websites even pose as official US government websites – apply only via 🖳 www.dvlottery.state.gov. **No outside service can improve you chance of being selected in the visa lottery.**

There have been arguments by long-term temporary US legal residents concerning the fairness of the DV program. For example, many highly skilled (H1-B) workers remain on temporary visas in the US for years with no clear path to becoming permanent residents, while 50,000 random people are picked around the world and handed permanent resident status. Several attempts have been made by Congress over the last five years to end the lottery and its future is uncertain.

BEFORE MAKING AN APPLICATION

Before applying for an immigrant visa, you must establish that you fulfill the criteria for whatever category of visa you're applying for. Provided you qualify, you may apply for an immigrant visa under more than one category. When applying for an immigrant visa (and many nonimmigrant visas) it's advisable to employ the services of a qualified and experienced immigration lawyer, although it isn't always necessary. It depends on the individual case and circumstances, although the procedure can be complicated and the rules and regulations change frequently.

Many visa applications are rejected because the paperwork is incorrect, e.g. the wrong information has been provided, a form hasn't been completed correctly, the wrong visa application has been made, or even because a lawyer hasn't made the correct approach to the authorities. If someone makes an application on your behalf, you should check that the information provided is correct in every detail.

You can apply for an immigrant visa while in the US, provided you're there legally and have a nonimmigrant visa that permits an adjustment of status to immigrant status, or from abroad. If you're in the US, you must apply to the USCIS for an adjustment of status (AOS) by filing a form I-485 (Application to Register Permanent Residence or Adjust Status), provided you're eligible. If you're outside the US,

your case is decided by a consular officer at a US embassy or consulate, after you've had a petition accepted (see below) and a immigrant visa number is issued.

☑ **SURVIVAL TIP**

If your application is rejected, you may be less likely to be granted a visa by appealing or re-applying, therefore it's important to get it right first time.

There are literally thousands of immigration lawyers in the US and abroad, many of whom deal with certain categories of immigrant only. Lawyers' fees depend on the complexity of the case and range from $250 for a simple consultation to between $5,000 and $10,000 (or more) for a complex application involving a lot of work. You should engage a lawyer who's been highly recommended or who has a good reputation, as incompetent and dishonest lawyers aren't unknown.

The most reliable source of information about US lawyers is said to be the Martindale-Hubbell list, which includes a rating of each lawyer (see 🖳 www.lawyers.com). It's advisable to ensure that a lawyer is a member of an immigration related organization, such as the American Immigration Lawyers Association (AILA). Ensure that you know exactly how much you must pay and the exact services you'll receive in return for your money. **No lawyer, however much you pay him, can guarantee that your application will be approved.** On the other hand, if you wish to appeal successfully against a refusal to grant you a visa or Green Card, it's almost essential to engage the services of an immigration lawyer.

If you're already in the US, a cheaper alternative to hiring an immigration lawyer is the 400 or so immigration agencies operating throughout the US, some of which, such as the recently accredited Irish Immigration Center in Boston (☎ 617-542-7654, 🖥 www.iicenter.org), charge no fees at all.

PETITIONS

The first step in the application for an immigrant visa is for the sponsor (a US citizen, legal permanent resident or prospective employer) to file a petition, e.g. when an applicant's qualification for an immigrant visa is based on his relationship to a US citizen, a permanent resident or an offer of employment. The person who files the petition is known as the petitioner (or sponsor) and must usually be either a US citizen, Green Card holder relative or a US employer. Some applicants, such as priority workers, investors, certain employment-based immigrants and diversity immigrants, can petition on their own behalf.

Petitions can only be filed with the USCIS and cannot be filed with the consular section of a US embassy or consulate. However, when a petition is filed abroad with a US embassy or consulate, the National Visa Center (see page 208) isn't involved in processing the application.

Family-sponsored immigrants who believe that they're entitled to immigrant status based on their relationship to a US citizen or resident alien, must ask their relative to file form I-130 (Petition for Alien Relative). Petitioners filing stand-alone forms and filing by courier/express delivery must submit their petitions to the USCIS Chicago Lockbox (USCIS Lockbox, Attn: SAI-130, 131 South Dearborn – 3rd Floor, Chicago, IL 60603-5517). Forms are then routed to, and adjudicated at, the USCIS Service Center with jurisdiction over their place of residence in the US. If in doubt contact the USCIS or see their website (🖥 www.uscis.gov). If you need to make an appointment with the USCIS, either abroad or in the US, you can do this online via Infopass (🖥 http://infopass.uscis.gov).

In certain cases, petitions for alien relatives can be filed abroad by US citizen petitioners who have been authorized to be continuously resident in their consular districts for at least the preceding six months. These include members of the US armed forces, emergency cases involving life and death or health and safety, and others determined to be in the national interest or in many cases simply US citizens living outside the US (see below). Petitions are filed with the USCIS abroad or at the nearest US embassy or consulate when there's no local USCIS presence. Refer to your local US embassy website for information (🖥 www.usembassy.gov).

There's a $355 filing fee for the I-130 form. In certain cases where the sponsor is resident abroad, petitions can be filed at a US embassy or consulate, but the sponsor must be in the process of moving back to the US with the alien being sponsored.

Employment-based immigrants who believe that they're entitled to immigrant status based on proposed employment in the US, require an approved form I-140 (Immigrant Petition for Alien Worker) from the USCIS. The filing fee for this petition is $475. Some people who qualify as priority workers may petition on their own behalf with the USCIS, but most

must have their prospective employer file the petition.

Before filing, sponsors of applicants for classification as members of the professions, professionals, skilled and unskilled workers (second and third preference employment-based immigrants, apart from those occupations classified as Schedule A) must obtain 'labor certification' (see page 137) from the US Department of Labor. This is a protracted process requiring the employer to prove that there are no qualified US workers available to take the job, e.g. by advertising the job vacancy in newspapers and at his offices for a certain period.

Investors (see page 165) must file form I-526 (Immigrant Petition by Alien Entrepreneur) with the USCIS, with a filing fee of $1,435.

Affidavit of Support

An Affidavit of Support is legally required for the petitioning sponsor for many family-based and some employment based immigrants, to show that the intending immigrant will have adequate means of financial support when planning to immigrate to the US. Sponsors must file form I-864 (Affidavit of Support) in which they agree to support the prospective immigrant and any dependants and to reimburse any government agency or private entity that provides the sponsored immigrant with federal, state or local public benefits (e.g. social security). The Affidavit of Support is a legally binding contract between the sponsor and the US government. Sponsors may be required to submit copies of their last three years' federal income tax returns, therefore you need to ensure that the relative sponsoring you has been filing them!

A 'petitioning sponsor' is a person who has filed an immigrant petition that has been approved by the USCIS. Generally speaking, the obligation to support an alien relative continues until the immigrant becomes a US citizen, leaves the US permanently or dies. There are so-called 'Poverty Guideline' tables

for petitioners and sponsors, which are the minimum income that they must demonstrate.

Upgrading a Petition

If you filed a petition for a family member when you were a lawful permanent resident (LPR) and have since become a US citizen, you must upgrade the petition from family second preference (F-2) to immediate relative (IR). You can do this by sending proof of your citizenship to the National Visa Center (NVC), i.e. a copy of the biodata page of your US passport or a copy of your certificate of naturalization.

IMPORTANT

If you become a US citizen, you must file separate immigrant visa petitions for each of your children. If you upgrade a family second preference (F-2) petition for a family member and you didn't file separate petitions for your children when you were a lawful permanent resident (LPR), you must do so now. A child doesn't have derivative status in an immediate relative (IR) petition, which is different from the family second preference (F-2) petition when a child is included in a parent's F-2 petition. A child isn't included in a parent's IR petition.

National Visa Center (NVC)

The National Visa Center (NVC), Portsmouth, NH, processes immigrant visa petitions after they have been approved by the USCIS, and retains them until the cases are ready for adjudication by a consular officer abroad. The NVC (among other responsibilities) provides instructions to petitioners and sponsors, processes form I-864 (Affidavit of Support), receives fees and other required documentation.

Consular posts are designated as either 'Standard Review' or 'Appointment Review' posts. For Standard Review posts, the NVC collects the DS-230 Part I, I-864 (Affidavit of Support), the fee and other basic initial documentation such as tax returns and W2s. The case is then forwarded to the consulate (provided the qualifying date is current), which schedules an interview appointment. For 'Appointment Review' posts, the NVC does a more extensive document collection and schedules the interview appointment.

In a Standard Review case in which some initial documentation is missing, the NVC will send a request for the missing documents. When this happens, the file is taken out of the normal stream of processing, which can result in delays to the case. Most petitions are scanned into the NVC database and given an NVC case number within 24 hours of receipt from the USCIS. This case number is used to track the case throughout its duration at the NVC.

Each month, the Visa Office (VO) establishes qualifying dates that determine if a petition will be eligible for processing. Qualifying dates are the latest priority dates that can be processed for certain visa categories. An immigrant visa petition can only become ready for further processing when the qualifying date in the appropriate visa category has advanced to the priority date of the petition (see below).

Petitions may remain at the NVC for several months or many years, depending on the visa category and the country of birth of the visa applicant.

> **IMPORTANT**
>
> The NVC provide notifications and instructions for both US sponsors and visa applicants. It's important that you submit forms and documentation only when requested by the NVC and follow the instructions carefully. Sending the NVC documentation (or paying fees) when they weren't requested is likely to result in a delay in processing.

When an applicant's priority date meets the most recent qualifying date, the NVC contacts the applicant and petitioner with instructions for submitting the processing fees. After the processing fees are paid, the NVC contacts the applicant and petitioner again to request that the necessary immigrant visa documentation be submitted,

If a child is about to turn 21 (termed 'age out'), the NVC will short-cut the normal process and send the file directly to the relevant embassy or consulate if a visa number is available. It's important to notify the NVC of such cases in order to expedite them, although the NVC doesn't guarantee that such cases will be processed in time.

Specific questions about a case should be sent to the National Visa Center, Attn: WC, 31 Rochester Ave. Suite 200, Portsmouth, NH 03801-2915, while forms, documents, and photographs should be sent to the National Visa Center, Attn: CMR, 31 Rochester Ave. Suite 100, Portsmouth, NH 03801-2914. **Don't send anything unless it has been specifically requested by the NVC.** You can also contact the NVC by telephone (☎ 603-334-0700, Monday through Friday 7.30-12am EST) or email (✉ NVCINQUIRY@state.gov).

Case Number

The NVC assigns each immigrant petition a case 'number' with three letters followed by ten digits (numbers). The three letters are an abbreviation for the overseas embassy or consulate that will process the immigrant visa case, e.g. GUZ for Guangzhou, MNL for Manila and CDJ for Ciudad Juarez. The digits signify exactly when the NVC created the case. For example, for case number MNL2009747003:

♦ MNL: the case is assigned to the US embassy in Manila;

♦ 2009: the year in which the NVC received the case from the USCIS;

♦ 747: the date the case was created, which is the day of the year (247) plus 500 – this case was created on September 4, 2009;

♦ 003: indicates that it was the third case created for Manila on that day.

☑ SURVIVAL TIP

This case number isn't the same as the USCIS receipt number, which is written on the 'Notice of Action' (form I-797) from the USCIS, and a US embassy won't be able to find a case if all you have is the USCIS receipt number.

Application Made Via a US Attorney

If you have made an application via a US attorney, you (or he) must have previously submitted form DS-3032 (Choice of Address and Agent) to appoint an agent or attorney to receive documentation about your application.

If you're working with an attorney, the NVC will take the following steps:

1. Assigns a case number (see below) to the petition.

2. Sends the Affidavit of Support processing fee and the immigrant visa fee bill to the attorney.

3. After the Affidavit of Support processing and immigrant visa application fees have been paid, the NVC sends the Affidavit of Support Process and the Applicant Document Process instructions to the attorney.

4. After the Affidavit of Support and applicant documents are submitted to the NVC, the NVC reviews the information submitted for correctness and completeness.

5. After reviewing the submitted documentation and determining that the file is complete with all the required documents, the NVC sends the petition to the embassy or consulate where you'll apply for a visa.

For certain embassies and consulates, the NVC will schedule your interview. Approximately one month before your scheduled interview appointment with a consular officer, all interested parties (applicant, petitioner and attorney) will receive an appointment letter containing the date and time of your visa interview, along with instructions for obtaining a medical examination.

Application Made Without a US Attorney

If you aren't working with an attorney, the NVC will take the following steps:

1. Assigns a case number (see below) to the petition.

2. Sends form DS-3032 (Choice of Address and Agent) to you and the Affidavit of Support processing fee bill to the petitioner.

3. After you select an agent the NVC sends the immigrant visa processing fee bill to

the agent (who doesn't need to be an attorney).

4. After the immigrant visa application processing fee has been paid, the NVC sends instructions to the agent explaining the Applicant Document Process.

5. After the applicant documents are submitted to the NVC, they review the information submitted for correctness and completeness.

6. After the Affidavit of Support processing fee is paid, the NVC sends an instruction letter to the petitioner, which explains the Affidavit of Support Process.

7. After the Affidavit of Support documents are submitted to the NVC, the NVC reviews the information submitted for correctness and completeness.

8. After reviewing the submitted documentation and determining that the file is complete with all the necessary documents, the NVC sends the petition to the embassy or consulate where you'll apply for a visa.

For certain embassies and consulates, the NVC will schedule your interview. Approximately one month before your scheduled interview appointment with a consular officer, all interested parties (the applicant, petitioner and third-party agent, if applicable) will receive an appointment letter containing the date and time of your visa interview, along with instructions for obtaining a medical examination.

Petition Approval

Once a petition has been approved, you're given a 'priority date'. When this date is reached, you're invited to submit an application for an immigrant visa to enter the US. In certain heavily oversubscribed categories, there's a waiting period of up to ten years or more before a priority date is reached!

The filing fee for a petition must be paid by certified check, dollar money order or international bank draft. Be wary of any prospective employer who asks you to reimburse him for the sponsor filing fees, especially before your arrival in the US. If the petition filed on your behalf is approved, the USCIS forwards it to the NVC, who in turn forward it to the consular section of your nearest US embassy or consulate when your priority date becomes current. The embassy will inform you of the steps to take to apply for a visa. If your petition is denied, the USCIS notifies you directly.

When your petition has been accepted (and you've received notification of this) you should receive an 'Instruction Package for Immigrant Visa Applicants' from your nearest US embassy or consulate.

VISA APPLICATION PROCEDURE

The application procedure and documentation for immigrant visas varies according to the category and the procedures of the nearest US embassy or consulate. Once your petition has been

accepted (and you've received notification of this) you should receive an 'Instruction Package for Immigrant Visa Applicants' from the applicable US embassy or consulate. Follow the instructions carefully, especially those related to how and where to pay the visa application fee.

The exact contents of the instruction package will depend on where you'll be interviewed for a visa, but it usually includes (but isn't limited to) the following documents:

♦ DS-2001 (formerly known as OF-169): 'Instructions for Immigrant Visa Applicants.' Instructions are different for Canada, Albania, Turkey, United Arab Emirates and Africa, with separate instructions for the rest of the world.

♦ DS-230 Part I: Application for immigrant visa and alien registration – biographic data.

♦ DS-230 Part II: Application for immigrant visa and alien registration – sworn statement (sent as part of the package only for Appointment Review consulates).

If you don't receive the above forms, you can download then from your local embassy website or from the USCIS website (💻 *www. uscis.gov/forms)*.

You must make your visa application within one year from the date that you're informed that it's possible to do so, e.g. when you receive notification from the NVC that a visa interview appointment has been made. If you fail to do so within one year from the date of the interview, the application and any visa petition approved will be cancelled.

Preparation

The Immigrant Visa Unit of your nearest embassy will inform you that they are processing your application for a visa and that you should prepare for your interview by taking the following steps:

1. Complete form DS-230 Part 1 for each family member applying for a visa. The form contains questions regarding specific biographical information required for the immigrant visa.

2. Assemble all the documents required in support of your application (see the **Document Checklist** below). When you have obtained all the necessary documents for you and your family, you need to complete form DS-2001 to attest to this and to notify the Immigration Visa Unit that you're ready for the immigrant visa interview.

3. Schedule a medical examination (see page 216). Visa applicants, regardless of age, require a medical examination prior to their interview and the issue of a visa.

The completed forms should be mailed to the Immigrant Visa Unit at the embassy or consulate dealing with your visa application. Don't send any documents to the embassy with these forms, which must be presented to the consular officer on the day of the visa interview.

On receipt of forms DS-230-I, DS-2001 and the document checklist, the Immigrant Visa Unit will complete all the necessary administrative processing of your visa application. You'll be required to provide additional information if you have incomplete or missing forms and will be contacted in writing if that's the case.

Approximately one month before your scheduled interview appointment with a consular officer, you're likely to receive an appointment letter containing the date and time of your visa interview. On the day of the visa interview, you'll be required to bring with you all your original documents or certified copies, plus a set of photocopied duplicates.

The embassy cannot guarantee when you're visa interview will be. You must notify the embassy if the circumstances of your application have changed, e.g. a change of address, change of marital status, the death of the petitioner, or the birth or adoption of additional children.

Document Checklist

Original documents or certified copies, photocopies, and translations of the following documents must be provided at your visa interview, plus one photocopy (it's advisable to make two copies in case the first set is lost or damaged) for the primary applicant and each family member who will accompany him to the US. All documents pertaining to your visa application are required, even if they were previously submitted to the USCIS with the petition, e.g. for family-based cases this includes all the documents used to establish the relationship between the petitioner and you.

◆ **Birth certificate:** obtain the original or certified copy of the birth record for each family member (yourself, your spouse, and all unmarried children under the age of 21), even if they aren't immigrating with you. If the children are deceased, state this and give the year of death. The certificate must contain the person's date of birth, the names of both parents, and an annotation by the appropriate authority indicating that it's an extract from the official records.

◆ If your birth record is unavailable, for example your birth was never officially recorded, your birth records have been destroyed or the appropriate government authority won't issue one, you need to obtain a certified statement from the appropriate government authority stating the reason your birth record isn't available. With the certified statement you must obtain secondary evidence which may include a baptismal certificate containing the date and place of birth, and both parent's names (providing the baptism took place shortly after birth); an adoption decree for an adopted child; or an affidavit from a close relative, preferably your mother, stating the date and place of birth, both parent's names, and the mother's maiden name.

◆ If you now use a different name from the one shown on your birth certificate, you must produce a document explaining the use of the name, such as baptismal, deed poll or school records, showing the early use of the name.

◆ Those born in certain countries, e.g. India or Pakistan, must present their registration certificate if their birth was registered. If it wasn't registered, either in the locality or, if a Christian, in church, sworn affidavits may be submitted. Such an affidavit must be executed before an official authorized to take oaths, i.e. a magistrate, commissioner of oaths, justice of the peace or similar, by the mother. If she's deceased the father may swear to the affidavit. The affidavit should state that the applicant's date of birth wasn't registered; the date of the applicant's birth; the full maiden name of the mother of the applicant; the full name of the applicant's father; and the place of the applicant's birth. If neither parent is alive, the next closest relative, who was old enough and of such relationship as to have personal knowledge of the birth at the time and place it occurred, may execute the affidavit.

◆ **Adoption certificate:** the certificate must show the date and place of adoption, along with the names of the adoptive parents, be issued by a public authority and show that a public record exists of the adoption.

◆ **Passports:** a passport must be valid for travel to the US and must have at least eight months' validity beyond the issue date of the visa. Children may be included on a parent's passport, but if they're over the age of 16 they must have their photographs attached to the passport.

◆ **Marriage certificate:** married applicants must obtain an original marriage certificate or a certified copy, bearing the appropriate seal or stamp of the issuing authority. If a person has been married or widowed previously, a divorce decree or death certificate must be provided.

◆ **Military records:** those who have served in the military forces of any country must obtain a copy of their military record. On the day of the visa interview you're required to furnish either your discharge papers or evidence of terminal leave from the forces. If you're unable to obtain a copy of your military records, contact the Immigrant Visa Unit at your local US embassy or consulate.

◆ **Affadavit of Support (form I-864):** a contractual affidavit of support, must be submitted for most family-based and employment-based applicants when a relative is the petitioner or has ownership interest in the petitioner's business. Employment based visa applicants must show a recent letter from their prospective employer confirming that the job offer upon which their application is based is still available. Qualified nurses must also present their 'Visa Screen Certificate'. All other applicants must show evidence that they're unlikely to become a public charge while in the US.

◆ **Police certificate:** police certificates are required for each visa applicant aged 16 years or older. See **Police Certificates** below for information.

◆ **Court & prison records:** Persons who have been convicted of a crime must obtain a certified copy of each court record and any prison record, regardless of the fact that he may have subsequently benefited from an amnesty, pardon or other act of clemency. Court records should show complete information

regarding the circumstance surrounding the crime of which the applicant was convicted and the disposition of the case, including the sentence or other penalty or fine imposed. (Court records, usually called a 'Memorandum of Conviction' in Britain and 'Certificates of Conviction' in Northern Ireland, must be obtained from the clerk of the court in which you were tried.)

◆ **Photographs:** two color photographs that meet the Department of State specifications (see page 95) are required for each applicant.

In addition to the above, employment-based applicants also need an appointment letter or a recent letter from their prospective employer confirming the essential elements of the job offer.

> **IMPORTANT**
>
> All documents that aren't in English must be accompanied by a certified English translation, which must include a statement signed by the translator that states that the translation is accurate and sworn to before a Notary Public.

Police Certificates

Police certificates are required for each applicant aged 16 years or over. The table below shows the police certificates required, based on where each applicant lives and has lived previously. Present and former residents of the US don't require any police certificates covering their residence in the US. The police certificate must cover the entire period of the applicant's residence in that area, and state what the appropriate police authorities records show concerning each applicant, including all arrests, the reason for the arrest(s) and the disposition of each case of which there's a record.

Police certificates from certain countries are unavailable or are obtained directly by the US authorities. Many countries require fingerprints to process police certificates for immigration purposes, including Australia, Canada and Nigeria, and police certificates completed without the required fingerprints aren't valid. However, many foreign police forces offer a fingerprinting service.

You need to pay close attention to the police certificate requirements; in some cases there are specific 'Police Certificate Request' forms that must be submitted in order to properly request and obtain the applicable police certificate(s) based on your residence history.

Police Certificates		
If the applicant...	**And...**	**Then the applicant needs a police certificate from...**
is living in their country of nationality at their current residence for more than 6 months	is 16 years old or older	the local police authorities
lived in a different country for more than 12 months	is 16 years old or older	the local police authorities
was arrested for any reason, regardless of how long they lived there	was any age at that time	the local police authorities

For example, a visa applicant who has resided in the United Kingdom for six months or longer since the age of 16 is required to obtain a police certificate from the Association of Chief Police Officers (see 🖥 www.acpo.poice.uk/certificates.asp).

☑ **SURVIVAL TIP**

Note that the US embassy Immigrant Visa Unit considers police certificates to be valid for 12 months from the date of issue, not six months as stated on the certificate.

Medical Examination

All immigrant visa applicants, regardless of age, require a medical examination and certain vaccinations prior to the issue of an immigrant visa. You need to bring your passport or photo driving license and present it to the examining physician to establish your identity. You may also need to complete a 'Medical Questionnaire' (available via US embassy websites) for each person requiring a medical, and bring it with you to the appointment.

The medical examination consists of a chest X-ray and blood test, which includes testing for HIV infection and venereal diseases. The blood test and X-ray aren't generally required of for those aged under 15 on the date of the appointment. Pregnant women may forgo the X-ray if they so wish, although they'll be required to have an X-ray in the US after the birth of the child.

On the day of the medical examination, the physician is required to verify that the immigrant visa applicant has met the vaccination requirement or that it's medically inappropriate for the applicant to receive one or more of the following vaccinations: Diphtheria Toxoids, Hepatitis A and B, Influenza and Influenza Type B (HIB), Measles, Meningococcal MCV, Mumps, Pertussis, Pneumococcal, Polio, Rotavirus, Rubella Tetanus and Varicella (the last isn't applicable in the UK).

In order to assist the physician and avoid delays in the processing of an immigrant visa, all immigrant visa applicants should have their vaccination records available for the physician's review at the time of the medical examination. A list of the required vaccinations and the ages at which they're required is contained on the US embassy, London website (🖥 www.usembassy.org.uk/cons_new/visa/iv/vaccinechart.html).

Visa applicants should consult their family doctor to obtain a copy of their immunization record, if one is available. If you don't have a vaccination record, the physician will explain which vaccinations you'll need to meet the requirement. Certain waivers of the vaccination requirement are available upon the recommendation of the physician.

If you aren't fully vaccinated or you have no record of your vaccinations, you're required to have the necessary vaccinations before the immigrant visa can be issued. The vaccinations may be performed by your own GP or a medical facility authorized to administer vaccines, and they may also be performed by the embassy's panel physician on the day of your medical examination, should you wish. A list of costs for vaccines performed by the embassy physician is available on demand or from your local embassy website (payment in the UK can be made in cash or by credit – Visa or MasterCard only – or debit card).

K visa applicants aren't required to meet the vaccination requirements at the time of their visa interview, but they'll be required to meet the requirements when applying for an adjustment of status (to immigrant status) with the USCIS. It's therefore prudent to have the required vaccinations at this stage in preparation for the adjustment of status stage.

The medical examination is usually performed at a designated medical center (it cannot be performed by the applicant's own physician) and must take place before the visa interview. The cost of the medical examination must be borne by applicants and varies according to the country, e.g. in the UK it's £200 for those aged 15 and over and £95 for those aged 14 and under. If you fail to keep an appointment or cancel/reschedule it with less than three days' notice, you'll be liable to a 50 per cent cancellation fee, i.e. £100 or £47.50. Fees are payable at the time of the medical examination in cash or by credit (Visa and MasterCard only) or debit card.

The medical results are couriered to the embassy within around five working days of the examination. If the results haven't been received by the time you attend the interview, provided the medical examination has taken place, action on your application will be suspended until such time that they are received. If you attend the embassy without having had a medical examination, the interview will be cancelled and you'll be required to reschedule for a later date.

Each US state requires school children to have a record of complete immunization at the time of their first enrollment in school. In most states this applies to transfer students entering any grade. Therefore, the US Public Health Services strongly recommends that children entering the country should have evidence of immunity consisting of physician documentation of prior disease or a record of immunizations.

INTERVIEWS

All immigrant visa applicants are required to have an interview with a consular official, which can take a number of hours when waiting time is included. The interviewing office will try to approve the issue of the visa on the day of the interview. However, if there are any complications, it's unlikely that you'll receive a decision on the day of the appointment, and you may have to return to the US embassy or consulate at a later date.

Approximately one month before your scheduled interview appointment, you (or your agent) will receive an appointment letter – which you must bring to your interview – containing the date and time of your interview (along with instructions for obtaining a medical examination, see above). If your interview is at an Appointment Review Consulate, you'll receive your original documents back at the time of the visa interview. At a Standard Review Consulate you'll need to bring all your original documents or certified copies with you to the visa interview.

The waiting period for scheduling visa immigrant interviews varies from a few weeks to several months. Applicants are required to swear or affirm to the truth and accuracy of their visa application (form DS-230), and to submit documentary evidence (see **Document Checklist** above) to establish their eligibility for an immigrant visa. You must have a medical examination prior to the interview and bring all your immunization records with you, plus (where applicable) receipts showing that the fees have been paid. During the interview process, an ink-free, digital fingerprint scan will be taken. Some visa applications require further administrative processing (which takes additional time) after your interview

If an applicant is 20 years old and his 21st birthday is prior to the appointment date, you should contact the US embassy/ consulate immediately as an earlier appointment may be possible. Visa applications are based upon the age of applicants at the time a visa is issued, rather than when the petition was filed, and failure to receive a visa prior to an applicant's 21st birthday may mean that he's no longer eligible for a derivative immigrant visa as a dependant child.

IMPORTANT

No assurance can be given in advance that a visa will be issued. A consular officer can make a decision only after your formal application and documents are reviewed, and you have been interviewed. You're advised NOT make any travel arrangements, dispose of any property or give up employment until a visa has been issued.

Visa Granted Or Denied

Once you've been issued with an immigrant visa, you must enter the US within six months of the issue date, otherwise it expires. However, you should note that the validity of the visa is limited to the validity of your medical examination, although this is usually valid for a year. If you apply to 'adjust status' while in the US, it's possible to obtain permission to travel abroad while waiting for a reply by applying for 'advance parole'. However, unless it's a matter of life

and death, it isn't recommended and in any case shouldn't be undertaken without legal advice.

If your application for an immigrant visa is denied and you believe that it hasn't been treated fairly, you can sometimes make an appeal. If this fails, you may have the option of a final appeal to the Board of Immigration Appeals in Washington. As a last resort, you can take your case to the federal court. However, an appeal should usually be made only with the assistance of an immigration lawyer.

FEES

Fees must be paid for each prospective immigrant regardless of age, and they aren't refundable. Local currency equivalents are acceptable when paid outside the US. Fees shouldn't be sent to the consular office unless requested specifically. When the sponsor resides in the US, the petition will be filed domestically, with the associated petition fee paid to the USCIS.

FEES

Application	Form	Fee
Affidavit of Support Review (domestic)	I-864	$70
Immigrant Visa Application	DS-230	$355
Immigrant Petition for Alien Worker	I-140	$475
Petition for Alien Fiancé(e)	I-129F	$455
Petition for Alien Relative	I-130	$355
Petition to Classify an Orphan as an Immediate Relative	I-600	$670 (see **note 1** below)
Petition to Classify Convention Adoptee as an Immediate Relative	I-800	see **note 2** below
Diversity Visa Lottery Surcharge		$375
Immigrant Visa Security Charge		$45
Biometric Services (fingerprinting)		$80 (see **note 1** below)
Medical Examination (e.g. UK)		£190 (child aged under 14, £95)

Notes

1. An $80 fee for biometrics is required for each person aged 18 or older who's living with an immediate relative applicant. No fee is required if you're filing based on an approved I-600A filed within the previous 18 months.

2. No fee is required for the first form I-800 filed for a child on the basis of an approved form I-800A. If more than one form I-800 is filed during the approval period for different children, the fee is $670 for the second and each subsequent form I-800. However, if the children are siblings before the proposed adoption, no additional filing fee is required.

Fees for petitions, immigrant visas and associated services are shown in the table above.

Medical examination and vaccination fees vary according to the country, e.g. an adult medical is £200 in London (UK) and vaccinations cost from £20 to over £100 each. Other costs may include fingerprinting, translation and photocopying charges, fees for getting the documents you require for the immigrant visa application (such as a passport, police certificates, birth certificates, etc.) and travel expenses to go to the embassy or consulate for the interview. Costs vary from country to country and case to case.

The NVC sends bills for certain fees at the appropriate time in the immigrant visa process, including bills for processing the I-864 Affidavit of Support (I-864W or I-864-EZ), where applicable (for the petitioner) and a bill for immigrant visa application processing (sent to the agent, if applicable). Bills are sent with an NVC addressed return envelope and it's important that you use it when paying them by check or money order. Don't forget to pay the correct postage when returning it. Don't pay any fees until the NVC asks you to do so and sends you a bill, and don't send payments to the NVC at Portsmouth, New Hampshire. Payments can also be made online (see below).

For more information about immigrant forms and fees, see the USCIS website (🖥 *www.uscis.gov/forms*).

Online Bill Payment

You can make fee payments online (where applicable) via the Consular Electronic Application Center's Immigrant Visa Invoice Payment Center (phew!). When paying online, you'll **need your case number and the invoice identification number, shown in the fee letter that you received from the NVC. You'll also need y**our bank's routing number and your bank account number (if you're *paying from your checking account, this information is available at the bottom of one of your checks).*

To pay bills online, go to the Immigrant Visa Invoice Payment Center's website (*see* 🖥 https://ceac.state.gov/CTRAC/Invoice/signon.aspx). To pay the Affidavit of Support or IV Application Fee, you must sign into the IV Fee Payment System, as follows:

1. Select one of the following roles that best describes your relationship to the case:

Principal Applicant, Attorney, Petitioner, or Third-party Agent, in the box provided.

2. Enter the NVC Case Number for which you're paying in the box provided. This information is located in the Online Payment Instructions that you received from the NVC.

3. Enter the Invoice Identification Number in the box provided. This information is located in the Online Payment Instructions that you received from the NVC.

4. Click on the **Sign In** button.

Follow the instructions on the screen.

DEPARTING THE US & REENTRY PERMITS

Green Card holders or applicants are entitled to depart the US on vacation or business as often as they wish. However, there are limitations on how long you can stay outside the US without losing your permanent resident status. If the absence is longer than one year but less than two years, a reentry permit is required to reenter the US. This permit is also issued to Lawful Permanent Residents who want to travel outside the US, but cannot get a national passport from their country of nationality.

To obtain a reentry permit you need to submit form I-131 (Application for Travel Document), for which there's a fee of $305.

Traveling outside the US without a reentry permit can have severe consequences for permanent or conditional residents, as it could be determined that you abandoned your resident status (see below). The benefit of having a valid reentry permit is that you aren't required to obtain a returning resident visa from a US embassy or consulate abroad. However, the permit doesn't relieve you of any of the requirements of US immigration law and possession of a reentry permit doesn't guarantee admission into the US, as you're still subject to immigration inspection at the port of entry to determine your admissibility. Reentry permits are usually valid for two years from the date of issue, although if after obtaining a Green Card you've been outside the US for more than four of the last five years, the permit is restricted to one year. Reentry permits cannot be extended.

Permanent residents must be physically present in the US when filing an application for a reentry permit, although leaving the US before a decision has been decided doesn't affect the application. However, the problem with leaving the country before the permit is approved is that the application document may be denied, hence creating a problem upon returning to the country. It may be possible to obtain a returning resident visa, but this isn't guaranteed.

You can request that your reentry permit be sent to a US embassy or consulate abroad or to a Department of Homeland Security (DHS) office abroad when you file the application. There's a place on the form I-131 to furnish the information necessary to receive the reentry permit outside the US.

Before a Green Card holder can apply for US citizenship through the naturalization process (see **Chapter 9**), he needs to fulfill a residency requirement and any time spent abroad doesn't count towards this requirement. Therefore, Green Card holders staying abroad for lengthy periods may disrupt their residency, as the time spent abroad doesn't usually count towards the residency requirement for naturalization (there are exceptions). However, it's possible to submit form N-470 (Application to Preserve Residence for Naturalization Purposes), for which there's a fee of $305.

If you remain abroad for more than a year without obtaining a reentry permit, you must apply at a US embassy or consulate for a visa as a returning resident and prove that you didn't intend to abandon your residence when you left the US (which can be difficult!).

> ☑ **SURVIVAL TIP**
>
> A reentry permit isn't an Advance Parole, which is issued to an alien who doesn't have Green Card status.

GREEN CARD UPDATES & RENEWALS

It's important to ensure that your Green Card doesn't expire, particularly while you're abroad, otherwise you may be considered 'out of status' and could be denied reentry to the US. If your Green Card was issued over ten years ago, you should check its expiry date, and if it has expired or is about to expire you should renew it immediately.

> ☑ **SURVIVAL TIP**
>
> Note that you should not submit form I-90 to report a change of address.

You're required to inform the USCIS of an address change or change of any data on your Green Card. This is particularly important if you change your name due to marriage or for other reasons. A name change requires the Green Card to be replaced and updated as soon as possible. Several documents must be submitted to update the name on the Green Card. It's a misdemeanor to willfully fail to inform the USCIS in writing of a change in the details on your Green Card, a change of your permanent address or a name change, which must be notified within ten days.

If your biographic data has been legally changed, you must submit a **copy of the original court order** or a **certified copy** of your marriage certificate showing the new name with your application. To replace a card due to a change of any other biographical data, you must submit copies of documentation verifying that the new data is correct.

Green Card Replacement

If you need to replace your Green Card due to a lost, damaged or destroyed card, you need to complete form I-90 (Application to Replace Permanent Resident Card). You can download the application form from the USCIS website (🖳 www.uscis.gov/files/form/i-90.pdf).

All paper-based I-90 applications **along with all supporting documentation** must be filed at: USCIS, PO Box 21262, Phoenix, AZ 85036 or when mailing via USPS express mail or courier to the USCIS, Attention: I-90, 1820 Skyharbor, Circle S Floor1, Phoenix, AZ 85034. You can also file it electronically (see 🖳 www.uscis.gov).

If you choose to file a paper version of the form, you must include a check or money order with the application for the appropriate fee **payable to US Department of Homeland Security** (don't use the initials 'USDHS' or 'DHS'). In addition, you must submit **all** required evidence with your application, including a copy of your current Green Card or other evidence of identity, and any supporting documentation.

The fee for a replacement Green Card is $290; a fee of $80 for biometrics (fingerprinting) may be included. There's no fee if the card wasn't received from the USCIS (e.g. it was lost in the mail) or it was wrongly issued due to a USCIS error. If you're filing to register at age 14, your existing card won't expire before your 16th birthday and you're filing within 30 days of your 14th birthday, there's also no fee.

After filing your application, the USCIS will inform you in writing when to go to your local USCIS Application Support Center (ASC) for your biometrics appointment.

ABANDONING PERMANENT RESIDENCE

A Green Card holder may abandon permanent residence voluntarily by filing form I-407 (Abandonment of Lawful Permanent Resident Status), along with the Green Card, at a US embassy. Under certain conditions, permanent residence status can be lost involuntarily, such as committing a criminal act that makes a person removable from the US.

A person may also be found to have abandoned their status if he or she moves to another country to live there permanently, stays outside the USA for more than 365 days (without obtaining a reentry permit before leaving), or doesn't file an income tax return. Permanent resident status can also be lost if it's found that the application or grounds for obtaining permanent residence was fraudulent. However, failure to renew a Green Card doesn't result in the loss of status, except in the case of conditional permanent residents.

A person who loses permanent residence status is immediately removable from the US and must leave the country as soon as possible or face deportation and removal. In some cases, you may be banned from entering the country for three or seven years, or even permanently.

Golden Gate Bridge, San Francisco

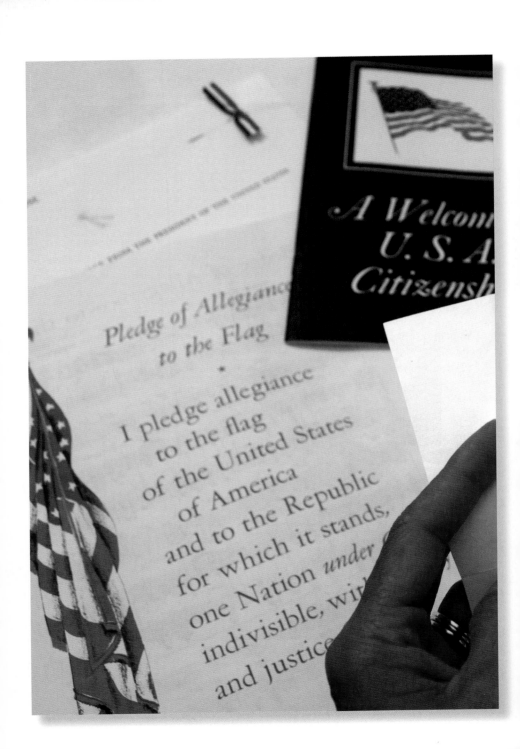

9.

CITIZENSHIP

T he concept of citizenship wasn't mentioned in the original US constitution and was only legally defined in 1868 when the 14th Amendment described citizens as those who were either born in the US or who had become citizens by a process of naturalization. (The Supreme Court has never explicitly ruled on whether children born in the US to illegal immigrant parents are entitled to birthright citizenship via the 14th Amendment, although it has generally been assumed that they are.) There are exceptions even to this simple definition; for example those born in the US to foreign diplomats or to enemy aliens in times of war are excluded. A birth certificate issued by a US state or territorial government is evidence of citizenship and is usually accepted as proof.

> The US citizenship laws have spawned 'birth tourism', whereby foreign expectant mothers come to the US to give birth, thus ensuring that their offspring are entitled to US citizenship.

CITIZENSHIP THROUGH PARENTS OR ADOPTION

Whether someone born outside the US to a US citizen parent or parents qualifies as a US citizen depends on the law in effect when the person was born. The law has changed over the years, but usually requires a combination of at least one parent being a US citizen when the child was born and having lived in the US or its possessions for a period of time. Additionally, children born outside the US may become citizens after birth based on their parent's citizenship or naturalization.

A child living in the US automatically becomes a US citizen when the following conditions have been met:

♦ at least one parent is a US citizen, whether by birth or naturalization;

♦ the child is aged under 18;

♦ the child is residing in the US in the legal and physical custody of the US citizen parent based on a lawful admission for permanent residence;

♦ an adopted child may automatically become a citizen if the child satisfies the requirements applicable to adopted children.

Biological or adopted children who regularly reside outside the US may also qualify for naturalization if they must meet the following requirements:

- at least one parent is a US citizen or, if deceased, the parent was a US citizen at the time of death;

- the US citizen parent or his US citizen parent has (or had at the time of death) been physically present in the US or its outlying possessions for at least five years, at least two of which were after the age of 14;

- the child is aged under 18;

- the child is residing outside the US in the legal and physical custody of the US citizen parent (or, if the citizen parent is deceased, an individual who doesn't object to the application);

- the child is temporarily present in the US after having entered lawfully and is maintaining lawful status.

For more information, see the USCIS website (🖥 www.uscis.gov > Citizenship > Citizenship Through Parents).

> The easiest and most popular way of becoming a US citizen is to marry a US national, although it's prohibited to do so purely in order to obtain US citizenship (or residence in the US) – a situation light-heartedly explored in the film Green Card, featuring Gerard Depardieu.

CITIZENSHIP THROUGH NATURALIZATION

An immigrant aged 18 or older can become a US citizen under a process called naturalization, which involves living in the US for a minimum of five years (three years when married to a US citizen) and passing a naturalization test (see below). Except in extremely rare cases, it's impossible for an alien to become a naturalized US citizen

without first obtaining a Green Card (see Chapter 8).

Citizenship is conferred by a judge in a 'naturalization or oath ceremony', when an 'oath of allegiance' is taken. US law permits dual nationality (see page 231) for naturalized citizens, who have virtually the same rights as native-born Americans (but cannot become President or Vice President). There's no compulsion for immigrants (Green Card holders) to become US citizens and they're free to live in the US for as long as they wish, provided they abide by the laws of the land.

The main official source of information about naturalization is the USCIS website (🖥 www.uscis.gov), from where all the necessary forms can be downloaded and printed free of charge. The USCIS also operates a 'Genealogy Program', a fee-charging service that helps people looking into their family history to find historical immigration and naturalization records

The naturalization process has been speeded up in recent years and should take from six to nine months. To qualify you must have:

- lived in the US as a permanent resident for a minimum of five years (or three years if married to a US citizen);

- have a period of continuous residence and physical presence in the US;

- be of 'good moral character' with no felony convictions;

- be able to read, write and speak basic English, with the exception of someone who:

  - is aged 55 and has been a permanent resident for at least 15 years; or

  - is aged 50 and has been a permanent resident for at least 20 years; or

  - has a permanent physical or mental impairment that makes someone unable to fulfill these requirements.

- a basic knowledge of US history and government.

Except in rare cases, it's impossible to become a naturalized US citizen without first obtaining a Green Card (see Chapter 3). Green Cards were previously issued for life but must now be renewed after ten years (to help prevent fraud). Citizenship is conferred by a judge in a naturalization ceremony when an oath of allegiance is taken.

Naturalized citizens have virtually the same rights as native-born Americans (but cannot become President or Vice President). There's no compulsion for immigrants to become US citizens and while they have a valid Green Card they're free to live in the US for as long as they wish, provided they abide by the laws of the land. However, many immigrants prefer to become US citizens, although fewer (under 10 per cent) than a generation ago, when as many as 80 per cent became citizens.

A record 1,046,539 aliens were naturalized as US citizens in 2008, when the most common countries of birth were Mexico, India and the Philippines.

APPLYING FOR NATURALIZATION

If you believe that you qualify to apply for naturalization, the first step should be to visit the USCIS website (🖳 www.uscis.gov/n-400), where you can download a 'Guide to Naturalization' (form M-476) and an Application Form (N-400) – see the links at the bottom of the page. The guide provides comprehensive information about how to complete the application form.

The questions you may be asked in the naturalization examination and other information about naturalization are listed in a free booklet, *Guide to Naturalization*, available from USCIS offices or the Superintendent of Documents (US Government Printing Office, Washington, DC 20402-9325) or can also be downloaded from the USCIS website (🖳 *www. uscis.gov/natzguide*).

Naturalization forms can be ordered by phone (☎ 1-800-870-3676) or be downloaded from the USCIS website (🖳 www.uscis.gov > FORMS > Citizenship and Naturalization Based Forms).

Application Procedure

The application procedure for naturalization is as follows:

1. **Complete and file form N-400:** Once you have read and understood the 'Guide to Naturalization' (see above) you should print and complete form N-400 (Application for Naturalization). The USCIS website (Application for Naturalization) also lists the address where you need to file the completed form, which depends on where you reside in the US. The form N-400 is free, but there's a $675 fee ($595 filing fee plus a biometrics fee of $80 for applicants aged under 75) for most applicants (exceptions include some military applicants). Processing can take anything from three months to a year, although the average has been less than five months in recent years.

2. **Have your fingerprints taken at a USCIS facility:** After you've filed form

N-400, you'll receive a letter telling you where and when to have your fingerprints taken (biometrics). Usually this is in a nearby Application Support Center, but in some areas of Alaska and Hawaii a mobile service may be provided. You'll need to take with you the letter summoning you to the session, your Permanent Resident Card (Green Card) and another form of identity, e.g. your driver's license. Your fingerprints are usually taken electronically and will be checked by the FBI to determine whether you have a criminal record. At this stage you may also be asked to submit further documentation.

3. **Prepare for and take the naturalization test:** You'll be notified by mail about where and when your naturalization interview will take place, therefore it's important to keep the USCIS informed of a change in your address. If you cannot make the appointment you need to send a letter of explanation and a new appointment will be scheduled. You should arrive 30 minutes before the appointed time; note that offices can be crowded and therefore you're requested not to take anyone with you.

The Naturalization Test

The naturalization test is an essential part of the naturalization process, as it's where you demonstrate that you're able to read, write and speak basic English, and show that you have a basic knowledge of US history and government (also know as 'civics').

The civics test doesn't contain any trick questions and the pass rate since it was revised in 2009 is over 90 per cent.

Passing the English requirement of the test won't be a problem if you can read this book and consists of simply reading and writing one of three sentences correctly in English. Your ability to speak English is also

judged during your naturalization interview by the way you answer questions asked by the USCIS officer regarding the information on your naturalization application form (N-400).

Finally, you must answer six out of ten civics (history and government) questions correctly out of a possible 100 questions (see **Civics Test** below). If you fail any part of the interview you can be retested (on the part you failed) between 60 and 90 days later.

Study Materials

There are a number of study materials and resources on the USCIS website (🖥 www.uscis.gov > Citizenship) to help you pass the naturalization test, shown on the right side of the screen on the 'Citizenship' page. These include:

♦ How Do I Apply for Citizenship

♦ A Guide to Naturalization

♦ Naturalization Self Test

♦ Study Materials for the Naturalization Test

♦ Citizenship & Naturalization Based Resources

♦ Naturalization Information Sessions

There are also two videos:

♦ Becoming a US Citizen: An Overview of the Naturalization Process

♦ The USCIS Naturalization Interview and Test

Civics Test

As part of the naturalization test, you're asked up to ten civics questions selected from the 100 questions shown in **Appendix D** (with answers). These range from general knowledge ('What is the name of the current US president?') to the more obscure, to a non-American at least, 'What territory was bought from the French in 1803?' They are all matters which native-born US citizens would (or should) have learned at school or while growing up, and which immigrants should learn and be aware of out of respect to their new country.

There's a useful 'Naturalization Self Test' on the USCIS website (💻 www.uscis.gov/teststudymaterials > Tools > Naturalization Self Test, at right of screen). It's only a sample test and there may be additional correct answers to the questions contained in this self test. If you can answer most of the questions correctly, you'll have no trouble passing the test. Note that the actual test **isn't** a multiple choice test but an oral test. The USCIS Officer will ask you up to 10 of the 100 civics questions and you must answer six out of the ten questions correctly in order to pass.

When you're ready to begin the self test, click the 'Generate Questions' button at the bottom of the page to see the first set of four questions. Answer each question and then click the 'Review Answers' button at the bottom to show the correct answers to the displayed questions. When you're ready to see more questions, click 'Generate Questions' again.

Oath of Allegiance

I hereby declare, on oath, that I absolutely and entirely renounce and abjure all allegiance and fidelity to any foreign prince, potentate, state, or sovereignty of whom or which I have heretofore been a subject or citizen; that I will support and defend the Constitution and laws of the United States of America against all enemies, foreign and domestic; that I will bear true faith and allegiance to the same; that I will bear arms on behalf of the United States when required by the law; that I will perform non-combatant service in the Armed Forces of the United States when required by the law; that I will perform work of national importance under civilian direction when required by the law; and that I take this obligation freely without any mental reservation or purpose of evasion; so help me God.

DUTIES & PRIVILEGES OF CITIZENSHIP

Once you have passed the naturalization test, the final step is to take the oath of allegiance (see the box). This consists of swearing to obey the laws and US constitution, renounce any foreign allegiance, and agreeing to serve in the armed forces if required. The good news for those with memories of the US draft (conscription) – whereby citizens were compelled to serve in the armed forces (as happened during the Vietnam war) unless exempted – is that US military personnel are now all volunteers. Most of the other obligations of citizenship, such as obeying the law and paying taxes, will already have been experienced by applicants during their qualifying period of residence in the US. One of the few negatives of becoming a US citizen is that you can be selected to perform jury duty.

Becoming a US citizen is generally advantageous for permanent residents, particularly if you wish to sponsor family members to come to the US. Citizens have a legitimate right to stay in the US and live and work there, and are no longer required to qualify for or renew a visa or Green Card to do so. They also have the option to vote and play a part in the political process, although they aren't eligible to become the President or Vice President of the United States of America, although they can run for state governor (see the box).

Other advantages are less tangible. US citizens can request government support while traveling; the days of gunboat diplomacy may be over, but those who are arrested while abroad may find it reassuring to know that the world's greatest military power is on their side. US citizens can also make use of federal government services, from free education to welfare payments.

However, perhaps one of the your most important rights as a US citizen is that it enables you to make use of their freedom of speech and action without living in fear of losing your residence status as a consequence. A citizen also cannot be deported, but a permanent resident can. For example, possession of a small quantity of cannabis (for personal use) may involve just a $100 fine for a US citizen, but for a foreign national, even one with a Green Card, it has been known to result in a jail sentence followed by deportation.

As an Austrian-born US citizen, Arnold Schwarzenegger will probably have to satisfy his political ambitions with being Governor of California, even though he married into the Kennedy clan (which is considered by many as political royalty) – his wife, Maria Shriver, is the niece of John F. and Robert F. Kennedy.

APPLYING FOR A US PASSPORT

Passports are issued by the Department of State, and information about obtaining a passport is available from their website (⌨ http://travel.state.gov > Passports > Apply for a U.S. Passport). Those applying for their first US passport must apply in person at an acceptance facility or passport agency (see ⌨ http://iafdb.travel.gov), which include post offices, clerk of courts, public libraries and other local government offices.

To apply for a passport you need to complete form DS-11 (Passport Application), which can be completed online or you can print a copy and complete it by hand in black ink. The documentation and steps to apply for a US passport are as follows:

♦ Complete and submit form DS-11: Application for a U.S. Passport.

♦ Submit evidence of US citizenship, i.e. one of the following:

- naturalization certificate;

- certificate of citizenship;

- previously issued, undamaged US passport;

- certified birth certificate issued by a city, county or state;

- consular report of birth abroad or certification of birth.

♦ Provide identification, i.e. a naturalization certificate; previously issued, undamaged US passport; driver's license; or current government or military ID.

♦ Provide a photo copy of the identification in 3. above.

♦ Pay the fee ($100 for first-time applicants or $120 with a passport card – see below).

♦ Provide two passport photos (see page 95.

For further information about the above steps, see 🖥 http://travel.state.gov/passport/get/first/first_830.html.

You can check on the processing time required to issue a passport online (🖥 http://travel.state.gov/passport/processing/processing_1740.html), which in July 2010 was between four and six weeks. If you need a passport sooner, an expedited service is available for an extra $60 plus overnight delivery costs, which is estimated to take two to three weeks door-to-door. You need to make an appointment to be seen at a Regional Passport Agency, but only if the passport is required in **less than two weeks** for international travel or **within four weeks** to obtain a foreign visa. Contact the National Passport Information Center to make an appointment or locate a Passport Agency (🖥 http://travel.state.gov/passport/npic/agencies/agencies_913.html).

To check on the status of an online passport application, ☎ **1-877-487-2778** between 8am and 10pm EST to speak with a representative or visit 🖥 http://travel.state.gov/passport/npic/npic_896.html.

Passport Card

A passport card was introduced in 2008 and is, as the name implies, a credit-card sized personal proof of identity. Compared to a 'book' passport it's relatively inexpensive, at $45 for a first time applicant or $20 if you order one at the same as a regular book passport. However, it's of limited use to most people as it can be used only to enter the US at land border crossings or sea ports-of-entry from Canada, Mexico, the Caribbean and Bermuda. **It cannot be used for international travel by air.**

Dual Nationality

The concept of dual nationality means that a person is a citizen of two countries at the same time, which is prohibited by some countries. However, the US government permits its citizens to hold dual nationality (or even, in principle, be a citizen of three countries), but doesn't encourage it as it's a potential cause of confusion and means that technically a person is subject to the laws of two countries and may also have divided loyalties. It may, for example, involve someone owing tax in two countries or even being liable for national service outside the US. Although naturalized citizens are required to undertake an oath renouncing previous allegiances, the oath has never

been enforced to require the actual termination of the original citizenship.

One circumstance where dual citizenship may run counter to the expectations of government agencies, is in matters of security clearance. For example, a person with Presidential access requires 'Yankee White' security vetting and must be absolutely free of foreign influence, and for other security clearances one of the grounds that may result in a rejected application is an actual or potential conflict of national allegiances.

The Supreme Court has ruled that citizenship of a foreign country is a constitutional right which cannot be taken from someone against their will, and therefore holding dual nationality is protected by law. The US Supreme Court also ruled that a naturalized US citizen has the right to return to his native country and to resume his former citizenship, and also to remain a US citizen, even if he never returns to the US.

A person who's automatically granted another citizenship doesn't risk losing US citizenship, but if someone acquires a foreign citizenship by applying for it, they may lose their US citizenship. In order to lose US citizenship, the law requires that you must apply for the foreign citizenship voluntarily, by free choice and with the intention of giving up your US citizenship. A person with dual US nationality can choose to renounce their foreign or US nationality at any time.

If you're a US citizen with dual nationality, you must use your US passport to enter and leave the US (and may also be required to use the passport of the dual nationality country to enter that country).

For further information about dual nationality, see 🖥 http://travel.state.gov/travel/cis_pa_tw/cis/cis_1753.html.

Physicist Albert Einstein became a US citizen in 1940 and retained his Swiss Citizenship (he was also a citizen of Austria and his native Germany).

New York CIty

10.

MISCELLANEOUS

This chapter contains miscellaneous information of general interest to anyone planning to live or work in the US.

CRIME

The purpose of this section isn't to scare you, but to warn you about the high level of crime and violence in the US, which in the major cities is much higher than in many other countries, especially those in western Europe.

⚠ Caution

The 'ground rules' aren't the same in the US, as in many other countries, and you need to aware of your surroundings and avoid 'risky' areas at all time. However, if you follow the rules your chances of being a victim are as low as in most European cities – but break them and they rise dramatically.

The US generally has a high crime rate, due in no small measure to the vast number of guns (over 200m) in circulation (Canada, which has much stricter gun control, has relatively few murders). Every day on average, 25 people are killed by guns and a further 600 or more are robbed or raped at gunpoint. Most Americans support gun registration, although few favor a complete ban on the sale and possession of guns (Americans cannot understand why foreigners fail to grasp their obsession with guns).

However, owning a gun is little deterrent against crime, as you must be ready and able to use it. Most people could never react quickly enough to a threatening incident, and statistics show that a gun is over 20 times more likely to kill a family member, friend or acquaintance than to kill an intruder. Many children accidentally kill themselves or their playmates with guns that are left lying around homes (half the guns in US households aren't kept under lock and key). Despite the statistics, the National Rifle Association (NRA) insists that any connection between gun ownership and crime is purely coincidental!

The crime rate varies considerably according to the region (the west has the most crime, the Northeast the least) and city (see below), although the recent application of a 'zero tolerance' policing policy (i.e. imprisoning an increasing number of offenders – the prison population has swollen to over 2.3m, compared with just 300,000 in 1970) in many major cities has resulted in a dramatic reduction in crime rates, which are currently at their lowest for 25 years. In recent years, the right wing view has held sway, the majority believing that crime will go away if only they get tough, build more prisons, lock offenders away longer and execute more murderers.

According to figures published by the FBI in December 2009, there was a decrease of 4.4 per cent in the number of violent crimes (e.g. murder, forcible rape, robbery, and aggravated assault) for the first six months of 2009 compared with the same period in 2008. The number of property crimes (including burglary, larceny-theft and motor vehicle theft) in the US from January to June of 2009 decreased 6.1 per cent compared with 2008.

In November of 2009, Forbes compiled a list of the most dangerous cities in the US. By analyzing FBI crime data from cities with more than 500,000 residents, Forbes ranked each city in terms of murder, forcible rape, robbery, aggravated assault, and other violent crimes. It will come as no surprise (at least to Americans) that Detroit, Michigan was rated the most dangerous city in the country. The top 15 cities were: Detroit (MI), Memphis (TN), Miami (FL), Las Vegas (NV), Stockton (CA), Orlando (FL), Little Rock (AR), Charleston (SC), Nashville (TN), Baltimore (MD), New Orleans (LA), Baton Rouge (LA), West Palm Beach (FL), Charlotte (NC) and Philadelphia (PA).

Black-on-black crime is the biggest problem in the US and the middle-class US has largely ignored the urban warfare raging in inner-city areas. Most whites live in rural areas and communities hermetically sealed from the trigger-happy chaos of the US's black urban life (some 8m Americans live in 'gated communities' with high fences, security floodlights and bullet-proof guard boxes). However, there are increasing signs that the horror of the US's romance with the gun is spreading to small town, white America. One of the most worrying aspects is the increase in violent crime committed by children: in recent years there have been a number of high-profile 'massacres' perpetrated by children aged as young as eight. Schools routinely check children for weapons (using metal detectors), and many inner-city schools have armed security guards and a prison-like regime in order to reduce crime.

Despite the statistics, the vast majority of Americans manage to get through the day without being molested, mugged, knifed or shot (or even witnessing such events), and most live to a ripe old age and die natural deaths (if over-consumption and sloth are considered natural!). Although crime and violence are among the most disturbing aspects of life in the US, it's important to maintain a sense of perspective, as heightened anxiety or paranoia about crime can be just as bad or worse than being a victim (and is a complete waste of time and effort). Nevertheless, anyone coming to live in the US would be wise to choose a low-crime, middle class suburb and avoid 'high-crime' areas (e.g. most inner cities) at all times.

GOVERNMENT

The US is a federal republic consisting of 50 states and the federal District of Columbia (known locally as 'the district'). Although it's geographically situated in Maryland, DC is a separate autonomous area, chosen to be the nation's capital and seat of government.

The US system of government is based on the Constitution of 1787, a concise document comprising just a few thousand words but containing a number of checks and balances to ensure that power isn't concentrated in a few hands. The Constitution lays down the division of power between the executive, the legislature (see below) and the judiciary (see **Legal System** on page 241). A unique feature of the US political system is that the executive and the legislature are elected, housed and function separately. Power is also split between federal, state and local governments. Each state has its own semi-autonomous government headed by a governor, who's elected for four years.

The Executive

The executive branch of government is responsible for administering the laws passed by Congress (the legislature – see below). It's presided over by the President, who is the head of state and chief executive of the government, and whose official residence is the White House in Washington, DC. He (there have been no female presidents) is elected for a term of four years and can be re-elected for a further term, making a total of eight years. He and his Vice President (veep) are the only members of the government elected by a nationwide vote. The Vice President has just two official constitutional duties: presiding over the Senate and assuming the presidency if the President dies, is unable to perform his duties or is removed from office. However, everyone knows the veep's real job is to make the President look good and to act as a deterrent against assassination. The President's main job is to veto bills originated by Congress.

There are usually just two candidates for the presidency, one from each of the two major parties, the Democrats and the Republicans, the latter also being called the Grand Old Party (GOP). There are few major differences between the parties, although the Democrats are to the left of the Republicans and considered liberals (a dirty word to many Americans). Democrats are usually in favor of increased public spending and taxation, to expand the economy and increase welfare. In contrast, Republicans are more conservative, strongly in favor of big business and private enterprise, and opposed to the welfare state. The Democrats traditionally garner most of their support from blue-collar workers and ethnic and religious minority groups, while the Republicans are supported by the large middle class, big business and farming interests.

The US presidential election process is long, complicated and expensive, costing hundreds of millions of dollars, with campaigning beginning in earnest almost two years before the election.

The spring and summer of a presidential election year are dominated by the battle for party nominations, beginning with primary elections (or primaries) in February, in which voters choose their party's presidential candidate. The list of candidates put forward by a party, e.g. for President and Vice President, is called the 'ticket'. Final nominations are supposed to be decided at the parties' national conventions in July or August, although increasingly the nomination has already been decided months earlier based on the results of a few early primaries. After his first term of office, a President is almost never challenged for his party's nomination and rarely fails to be elected for a second term (unless he has made an almighty mess of things and is unpopular, and sometimes even that doesn't stop his re-election!).

There's no system of proportional representation and elections are based on the 'winner takes all' system (not unlike American society). This system guarantees that minor 'third' parties are excluded from the political system as most people are reluctant to 'waste' their vote on someone who cannot win (Americans hate losers). Presidential elections are based on an electoral 'college' system of voting, where voters cast their votes for electors (not for the presidential candidate) who are pledged to one party and its candidate on the ballot. Each state has as many electors as it has senators and representatives, a total of 538 (100 senators, 435 representatives, plus three electoral votes for the District of Columbia). The electoral votes assigned to each state go to the party polling the most votes, and the party's candidate who receives the majority of the 538 votes becomes the President elect. There has been talk of changing or doing away with the electoral college system, although this would need a constitutional amendment, something which is difficult to do and which would take several years to complete.

When voters select their President, they're in effect choosing an entire administration or government. On taking office, the President makes more than 2,000 appointments, from his Cabinet down to key officials in the myriad government departments and agencies. The Cabinet is comprised of the heads (or secretaries) of the 15 executive departments: agriculture, commerce, defense, education, energy, health and human services, homeland security, housing and urban development, interior, justice, labor, state, transport, the treasury, and veterans' affairs. Apart from key political appointments, government departments are manned by permanent civil servants.

Although the office of President has enormous prestige and symbolic significance, the President's authority is limited by Congress, particularly when the presidency and the majority in Congress are held by different parties. The President has no authority to make laws himself, although as head of the executive he's expected to ensure that laws are faithfully executed. He can veto legislation passed by Congress, although a two-thirds majority in both houses overrides a presidential veto. However, although Congress can throw out or amend legislation, it's often the President who provides the initiative. A bill must be passed by both houses of Congress and signed by the President before it becomes law.

The Legislature

Congress is the legislative branch of government responsible for making laws. It consists of two houses, the Senate and the House of Representatives (referred to as 'the House'), both with their seat in the Capitol building in Washington, DC. The Senate is the senior house and consists of 100 senators, two from each state.

Capitol, Washington DC

The House has a total of 435 members or congressmen (only a few of them are women, who represent electoral 'districts'. The number of congressmen per state is based on each state's population, e.g. California has 52 representatives while 16 other western states have a total of 50 between them. Senators are elected for six years, which means that around a third of the seats are up for election every two years. Congressmen are elected for a two-year period and voting is held for the entire House of Representatives at the same time as the Senate elections (elections held between presidential elections are called 'mid-term' elections).

Each house has specific duties. For example, the Senate's duties include confirming or rejecting presidential appointments (including those of supreme court judges) and the ratification of foreign treaties, while laws concerning the raising of revenue originate in the House of Representatives. The real power of Congress lies in the numerous standing, select and special committees, the most important of which are 'rules' committees, whose job is to decide which bills will be considered. Both houses initiate legislation that begins as a bill and is sent to the appropriate committee.

One of the most unusual features of the political system is the thousands of lobbyists and pressure groups. These have considerable influence in Washington, particularly those representing business and commercial interests. Powerful corporations, associations, organizations and myriad special-interest groups employ professional lobbyists (often with large numbers of employees), whose job is to coordinate financial support and disburse funds to suitable members of Congress (as lampooned in the film *The Distinguished Gentleman* with Eddie Murphy). In some countries, this is called bribery, although in the US 'buying' votes is an accepted and

traditional part of politics. Consequently, it's practically impossible to get Congress to enact legislation going against the interests of any powerful lobby group (unless a more powerful group outbids them).

> One of the failings of the US political system is that members of Congress spend most of their time arguing for local interests (with a wary eye on the next election), while neglecting more important issues.

Self-preservation and self-interest are at the root of all US politics, and when it comes to the crunch hardly any American politicians have the courage to cast unpopular votes. Every vote on Capitol Hill comes down to the same question: 'Will my vote lose me votes in my own backyard?' (the amount of federal money politicians get for their district is called pork-barrel spending). A vote on any issue possibly adversely affecting local issues is immediately recorded and used as ammunition by opponents. Congressmen and senators spend most of their time in office fund-raising, much of which is spent on TV advertisements savaging the records of their political opponents. The US has the most entertaining and expensive political campaigns in the world and American politicians never stop campaigning. No tricks are too cheap or dirty for American politicians on the campaign trail.

The federal government is responsible for foreign trade and commerce between states, borrowing and minting money, foreign relations, the post office, federal highways, defense, internal security, immigration and naturalization, and customs and excise.

State Governments

The states have a large degree of autonomy to control their own affairs, including setting their own taxes (in addition to federal taxes) and drafting state laws with regard to trade and commerce, education, state highways and driving, marriage, divorce, licensing, weapons, social services (e.g. health and welfare), wages, and criminal justice. Like the federal government, each state government consists of three branches: the executive, legislature and the judiciary. Each state also has its own great seal, flag, song, motto, flower, bird and tree.

States are subdivided into counties, municipalities, towns, school districts and special districts, each with its own 'government'. Municipalities include cities, boroughs, towns and villages. In most large cities, local government consists of a mayor and a city council, although some have administrative managers and a board of 'selectmen' or a commission. Mayors aren't ceremonial figures, but chief executives with broad powers. Counties may be governed by a council-commission, council-administrator or a council-elected executive, the powers of which vary widely.

Local Government

There are some 500,000 elected officials in the US, mostly at the local level where local governments establish policy and set laws in their communities. Their responsibilities include primary and secondary education (school district governments), police, fire and ambulance services, libraries, health and welfare, public transport subsidies, parks and recreation, waste disposal, highways and road safety, and trading standards. Local laws, e.g. licensing and trading laws, are often decided at county level, rather than by individual towns.

Voting

Only US citizens and naturalized citizens are permitted to vote, which is a major source of contention among the millions of immigrants who are permanent residents of the US and who vainly clamor for 'no taxation without representation'. It's also illegal for foreigners without permanent resident status to make financial contributions to political parties (although why any of them would want to beggars belief!).

Even among those eligible to vote, many aren't registered, and participation in local, state and federal elections is less than in most other democratic countries (around 30 per cent of the population, some 65m people, don't bother to vote or register). The voter turnout for presidential elections is usually around 50 per cent and even lower for state and local elections (only a quarter of Americans under 35 vote in presidential elections). Voter turnout in 2008 was the highest (56.8 per cent) since 1968 and much higher than in 2004 (just 37.1 per cent). Midwestern and western cities have the highest voter turnout, the south the lowest. Not surprisingly, voter apathy is at its highest in poor areas, where experience has taught people that whoever is in power their prospects remain the same: zero.

Like all wise people, most

Americans distrust politicians (who they consider to be corrupt) and have a negative view of politics, although paradoxically most are proud of their political system. Political scandals are common and widely publicized. Americans make a point of washing their dirty linen in public and many Americans are more interested in a politician's sex life than his policies (some politicians are evidently well aware of this!). Corruption is rife and local politics are inherently criminal (Americans have a saying that a person is 'so crooked he could run for public office'). Not surprisingly, many politicians are also lawyers! (Bear in mind that although Americans criticize and complain about their politics and politicians, they aren't so keen for ignorant foreigners to join in!)

LEGAL SYSTEM

The US legal system is based on federal law, augmented by laws enacted by state legislatures and local laws passed by counties and cities. Most rights and freedoms enjoyed by Americans are enshrined in the first ten amendments of the US Constitution (written in 1787) and popularly known as the 'Bill of Rights'. American law and the US Constitution apply to everyone in the US, irrespective of citizenship or immigration status, and even illegal immigrants have most of the same basic legal rights as US citizens. Under the US Constitution, each state has the power to establish its own system of criminal and civil laws, resulting in 50 different state legal systems, each supported by its own laws, prisons, police forces, and county and city courts.

The US judiciary is independent of the government and consists of the Supreme Court, the US Court of Appeals and the US District Courts. The Supreme Court, the highest court in the land, consists of nine judges, who are appointed for life by the President. Its decisions are final and legally binding on all parties. In deciding cases, the Supreme Court reviews the activities of state and federal governments and decides whether laws are constitutional. The Supreme Court has nullified laws passed by Congress and even declared the actions of some US Presidents unconstitutional. Momentous judgments in recent years have involved the Watergate scandal, racial segregation, abortion and capital punishment. However, when appointing a Supreme Court judge, the President's selection is based on a candidate's political and other views, which must usually correspond with his own. The Supreme Court was for many years made up of members with a liberal or reformist outlook, although this trend has been reversed in recent years with the appointment of conservative judges by Republican presidents.

☑ SURVIVAL TIP

There's a wide variation in state and local laws, making life difficult for people moving between states. Never assume that the law is the same in different states (Conflict of State Laws is a popular course in American law schools).

A separate system of federal courts operates alongside state courts and deals with cases arising under the US Constitution or any law or treaty. Federal courts also hear disputes involving state governments or between citizens resident in different states. Cases falling within federal jurisdiction are heard before a federal district judge. Appeals can be made to the Circuit Court of Appeals and in certain cases to the US Supreme Court.

There's a clear separation and distinction between civil courts, which settle disputes between people (such as property division after a divorce), and criminal courts that prosecute those who break the law. Crimes are categorized as minor offences ('misdemeanors') or serious violations of the law ('felonies'). Misdemeanors include offences such as dropping litter, illegal parking or jay-walking, and are usually dealt with by a fine without a court appearance. Felonies, which include robbery and drug dealing, are tried in a court of law and those found guilty are generally sentenced to prison (jail). In many counties and cities, there are often eccentric local laws, usually relating to misdemeanors rather than felonies.

People who commit misdemeanors may be issued with a summons (unsuspecting foreigners who violate local by-laws may be let off with a warning), while anyone committing a felony is arrested. An arrest almost always involves being 'frisked' for concealed weapons, handcuffed and read your rights. You must be advised of your constitutional (Miranda) rights when arrested. These include the right to remain silent, the right to have a lawyer present during questioning, and the right to have a free court-appointed lawyer if you cannot afford one. You'll be asked if you wish to waive your rights. This isn't recommended, as any statement you make can then be used against you in a court of law. It's better to retain your rights and say nothing until you've spoken with a lawyer.

If you're arrested, you'll be charged and have the right to make one telephone call. This should be to your embassy or consulate, a lawyer or the local legal aid office, or (if necessary) to someone who will stand bail for you. You're then put into a cell until your case comes before a judge, usually the same or next day, who releases you (if there's no case to answer) or sets bail, which may be a cash sum or the equivalent property value. For minor offences you may be released without bail, although in serious cases a judge may oppose bail altogether.

In many areas, lawyer (or attorney) referral services are maintained by local (e.g. county)

bar associations, whose members provide legal representation for a 'reasonable' fee. Before retaining a lawyer, ask exactly what legal representation costs, including fees for additional services such as medical experts, transcripts and court fees. Most importantly, hire a lawyer who's a specialist and experienced in handling your type of case. If you cannot afford a lawyer and your case goes to court, a court-appointed lawyer represents you.

An unusual feature of the US legal system is plea bargaining, which involves the prosecution and the defence making a deal where the defendant agrees to plead guilty to a lesser charge, thus saving the court time and leading to a reduced sentence. This has made the US legal system something of a lottery, often with victims' lives at stake, and in high profile cases (such as the O.J. Simpson case) a media circus.

In the US, you're normally considered guilty until proven innocent, at least in the eyes of the general public and law enforcement officers, and you may be tried and convicted by the media (there are virtually no reporting restrictions), long before your trial comes to court. Penalties are often harsh, particularly for less serious crimes, while professional and white-collar criminals who can afford the best defence often get off with a light sentence or a fine. Many American judges are elected, rather than appointed from qualified members of the legal profession, which often results in bad legal decisions and a lack of consistency in sentencing (at the lower court levels, corrupt judges aren't unknown).

In the '90s new 'three-strikes-you're-out' (the name come from baseball) laws were introduced in many states response to the clamor for longer sentences, whereby anyone convicted three times of violent federal crimes automatically receives a longer or even life sentence.

Litigation

Litigation is an American tradition and national sport, and every American has a right to his day in court (as well as to his 15 minutes of fame). There are 15 to 20m civil suits a year, which leads to a huge backlog of cases in all states and even the Supreme Court. One of the most unusual aspects of US law is that lawyers are permitted to work on a contingency fee basis, whereby they accept cases on a 'no-win, no-fee' basis. If they win, their fee is as high as 50 per cent of any damages. If you must hire a lawyer on a non-contingency basis, the cost is usually prohibitive. Many people believe this system helps pervert the cause of justice, as a lawyer's only concern is winning a case, often irrespective of any ethical standards or the facts of the matter. The contingency-fee system is responsible for the proliferation of litigation cases, which lawyers are happy to pursue due to the absurdly high awards made by US courts.

The litigation system is primarily designed to make lawyers rich, while ensuring that almost everyone else ends up a loser. Not only must individuals have liability insurance to protect against being sued, but everyone from doctors to plumbers must have expensive malpractice insurance to protect themselves against litigious patients or customers. The whole US economy and legal system is underpinned by litigation in which it seems half the population are directly employed and the other half are plaintiffs or defendants! Everyone (except lawyers) agrees that litigation is out of control and is seriously undermining the US's competitiveness. Nobody, however, seems to know what to do about it. Meanwhile, lawyers spend their time dreaming up new and lucrative areas of litigation. (They even follow ambulances in an attempt to be first in line to represent accident victims, hence the term 'ambulance chasers'.)

In many states, there are hair-raising product liability, personal liability and consequential loss laws. Some of these have limited liability, while others don't, meaning that multiple warnings are printed on the most unlikely articles. In fact, most companies attempt to anticipate the most ridiculous and implausible events in order to protect themselves against litigation. Taken to ridiculous extremes a bottle of beer would have warnings about drinking and driving, choking on the stopper, breaking the glass and cutting yourself or someone else, swallowing broken glass, taking alcohol where it's prohibited, drinking under age or giving a drink to someone under age, alcoholism, carrying alcohol in your car or over certain state borders, being mugged or falling over while drunk, etc, etc. – and this is hardly an exaggeration!

In fact, alcohol does carry a number of health warnings regarding the risk of cancer and other health problems, birth defects, driving and operating machinery. In Colorado, a barman must insure himself against being sued for serving someone who is later involved in a car accident. In the US, you can sue a tobacco company for causing your cancer, a car manufacturer for causing an accident, a ski firm for contributing to your ski accident, or a computer software company for fouling up your tax return. In fact anything that can

(however remotely) be blamed on someone else will be!

If you're the victim of an accident, you must never discuss your injuries with anyone connected with the other party and must never sign any documents they present to you without legal advice. Put the matter in the hands of an experienced litigation lawyer and let him handle everything. And in case you might forget, there are television adverts advising you of your rights to sue in accident situations, by attorneys claiming special competence at winning huge settlements.

Most companies and professionals are so frightened of the courts that many cases don't go to trial, e.g. personal injury and medical malpractice cases, which, apart from the cost of losing, are bad for business. This adds to the proliferation of law suits, as it's expensive to fight a legal battle even if you win, and litigants know that most companies are happy to settle out of court. If you're in business and not being sued by at least 100 people, it's usually a sign that you're broke and therefore not worth suing. If someone sues you for your last dime, don't take it personally – it's simply business.

Not surprisingly there are a lot of lawyers in the US (more than 500,000, i.e. one for every 600 Americans, e.g. compared with one for every 10,000 people in Japan. The chief role of lawyers is to make themselves (very) rich and to make business as difficult as possible for everyone else. Never forget that lawyers are in business for themselves and nobody else and, although they may be representing you, their brief never strays far from the bottom line, i.e. how much they will be paid.

☑ SURVIVAL TIP

If you have a dispute with a person, company or government agency involving a sum of from $100 to $5,000 (depending on the state), you can use the small claims court, which doesn't require a lawyer (hurrah!).

Obtaining Legal Help

Many social service agencies provide free legal assistance to immigrants (legal and illegal), although some may serve the nationals of a particular country or religion only. There are help lines and agencies offering free legal advice in most towns and cities, many with legal aid societies (offering free advice and referral on legal matters), Better Business Bureaus (dealing with consumer-related complaints, shopping services, etc.) and departments of consumer affairs (which also handle consumer complaints). See also **Crime** on page 235 and **Police** on page 247.

MILITARY SERVICE

There's no conscription (draft) in the US (it was last used during the Vietnam war) and all members of the armed forces are volunteers. Nevertheless, all male permanent residents and US citizens aged 18 to 25 must register for military service with their local board of the Selective Service System (SSS, see notices at US post offices) or online (🖳 www.sss. gov). Resident, 18-year-old men must register within 30 days of their birthday. All qualifying immigrant men are required to register within six months of entering the US, but may be exempt if they've served at least one year in the armed forces of another country. SSS registration is a requirement of eligibility for state-funded higher education, state jobs and training, and citizenship. Failure to register can result in a fine of up to $25,000 and/or a five-year prison sentence.

There have been constant rumours in recent years concerning the resurrection of the draft, particularly since the beginning of the various campaigns in the War on Terror. The Bush Administration has repeatedly denied all such rumours, and in October 2004, a potential law to resurrect the draft was resoundingly defeated in the House of Representatives. The armed forces in the US consist of the Army, Navy, Air Force, Marines, Coast Guard,

Merchant Marines and the National Guard. Until the start of the War on Terror, the National Guard were considered 'weekend warriors', keeping their civilian jobs while training one weekend a month and for a few weeks during the summer. Active duty for the National Guard normally consisted of domestic service after a natural disaster or major accident, but increasingly, the National Guard units are being called into active combat roles in the Middle East and elsewhere for periods of up to a year or more.

Homosexuals are officially prohibited from serving in the armed services and acknowledged homosexuals are discharged. The US prohibits lesbian, gay, bisexual and transgender (often referred to by the acronym, LGBT) service members from serving openly under its 'Don't ask, don't tell' policy. Service members who remain closeted are allowed to serve, but investigation into a member's sexuality without suspicion is prohibited.

There are around 200,000 women in the military (some 10 per cent of the total) and women are permitted to serve in combat roles, although they aren't required to register for military service. Despite the number of servicewomen, sexual harassment and prejudice against women is rife throughout the military. A veteran is an ex-serviceman of either sex and any age. Veterans are entitled to a number of benefits, including tuition grants and assistance for attending university (a common motivation for enlisting in the armed forces).

Prior to 9/11, the federal government was reducing defence spending and manpower in recent years, although expenditures has increased with the War on Terror launched shortly after the September 11 attacks on the World Trade Center in 2001. The military budget for fiscal year 2010 was $680bn, rising to almost £1 trillion when defense-related spending outside the Department of Defense is added.

PETS

The import of all animals and birds into the US is subject to health, quarantine, agriculture, wildlife and customs regulations. Pets, particularly dogs, cats and turtles, must be examined at the first port of entry for possible evidence of disease that can be transmitted to humans. Pets excluded from entry must be re-exported or destroyed. Dogs, cats and turtles may be imported free of duty, although duty may be payable on other pets, the value of which can be included in your customs exemption if they accompany you and aren't for resale.

Dogs must be vaccinated against rabies at least 30 days before their entry into the US. Exceptions are puppies less than three months old and dogs originating or located for six months or longer in areas designated by the Public Health Service as being rabies-free. All domestic cats must be free of evidence of diseases communicable to man when examined at the port of entry and vaccination against rabies isn't required (though it's highly recommended). Birds must be quarantined upon arrival for at least 30 days in a facility operated by the US Department of Agriculture (USDA) at the owner's expense.

For regulations concerning the import of other animals, contact your nearest US embassy or consulate or write to the US Public Health Service (Center for Disease Control, Foreign Quarantine Program, Atlanta, GA 30333, ☎ 404-491-515, 🖥 www.cdc.gov). A leaflet, *Pets, Wildlife: US Customs*, is available from the US Customs and Border Protection Service (Office of Public Information, 1300 Pennsylvannia Avenue, N .W. Washington DC 20229, ☎ 202-344-2050, 🖥 www.cbp.gov, then follow the links for 'Travel' and 'Pets'). The publication number is 0000-0509 and it can be downloaded from the Travel section of the CBP website.

If you're traveling with pets within the continental US, they must have a valid Interstate Health Certificate and be fully vaccinated (documentation is required).

All but four states require dogs to be inoculated against rabies and some also require it for cats. To take a dog, cat or bird to Alaska or Hawaii, you need a valid Interstate Health Certificate, signed by an accredited veterinarian and issued no more than ten days before shipping. Hawaii has strict anti-rabies laws and all dogs and cats (including those from the continental US) must be quarantined for 120 days, with the exception of those coming from a rabies-free area (e.g. Australia, the UK and New Zealand). Alaska requires a written statement from a veterinarian certifying that your pet is free of rabies. Further

information about interstate pet transportation can be obtained from the USDA's information hotline (☎ 202-720-2791) or in the Travel section of the USDA website (🖥 www.usda.gov).

Mexico and the US enforce stringent regulations regarding pets, and visitors to Mexico usually find it more convenient to leave their pets at veterinary boarding facilities in the US. When pets are taken into Mexico and returned to the US, owners must present a rabies vaccination certificate dated not less than one month or more than 12 months previously. A booklet, *Traveling With Your Pet*, is available from the ASPCA (see the address below) and contains inoculation requirements by territory and country.

You can take your dog or cat to a veterinary surgeon for a course of vaccinations, some of which (e.g. rabies) are mandatory. Some municipalities provide free rabies shots for cats and dogs. After vaccination your pet must wear a rabies tag attached to its collar. (In most areas, all dogs are required to wear collars and those without are considered to be strays.) If you live in a rabies area, don't let your pets run free and don't allow your children to play with or approach strange or wild animals, as if they're bitten by an unknown animal they may require a series of anti-rabies injections. You can also take your dog or cat to a vet for neutering (recommended by the ASPCA), the cost of which varies according to the region and the vet. Shop around and compare veterinarian fees. It's possible to take out health insurance for your pets in order to reduce veterinary bills. The American Animal

Hospital Association (☎ 800-883-6301, 💻 www.healthypet.com) provides help in finding vets near your home. Tattooing of dogs and cats for identification purposes isn't commonly done (except for valuable show animals), although the ASPCA encourages the use of a small tattoo (at the site of the incision) to identify neutered animals. Chipping (the insertion of a small electronic chip under the skin) isn't commonly used except for pedigree pets or those likely to travel overseas to countries where chipping is more commonly used.

Many Americans aren't content with just keeping a cat or a dog like 'normal' people, but keep exotic pets such as leopards, cougars or boa constrictors. Although most states have strict regulations regarding the keeping of wild animals as pets, many Americans keep them illegally, particularly in Florida, one of the main gateways for the import of illegal animals.

Some cities and suburbs require dogs and cats to be licensed, therefore you should check.

Animal lovers can join the American Society for the Prevention of Cruelty to Animals (ASPCA, 424 East 92nd Street, New York, NY 10128-6804, ☎ 212-876-7700, 💻 www.aspca.org) for $25 per year (members receive the quarterly *Animal Watch*). The ASPCA campaigns vigorously against the killing of wildlife and the destruction of their habitats and publishes a wealth of free information for pet owners.

POLICE

There's no national police force in the US, where policing is organized on a state and local basis. The country has around 500,000 police officers and a total of 40,000 separate police forces, over half of which are simply one or two-man sheriffs' offices in small towns (sheriffs are normally locally elected officials with no formal training). Police forces include city police (possibly with separate departments to deal with schools, traffic and even refuse), county police, transport police, sheriffs' departments, state police (state troopers) and highway forces such as the California Highway Patrol. An ordinary policeman is usually called a patrolman. In addition to regular full-time police officers, many towns have auxiliary, part-time police officers, special duty and volunteer sheriff's posses (which assist sheriffs' offices in some areas). The US response to increasing crime is usually to put more cops on the beat.

The division between federal and state law can be confusing; for example murder is classified as a state crime, while less serious crimes such as taking a woman across state lines for immoral purposes is a federal crime (although it may be dealt with by a local police force). City police are concerned with local crime, and offences outside their jurisdiction are usually dealt with by state police or federal investigators (the FBI). With the increased emphasis on fighting and preventing terrorism, more and more responsibility has fallen on local police forces and many jurisdictions are being stretched to the limit, with promised federal funds for fighting terrorism proving inadequate for the measures proposed.

All police are armed and popular weapons include .38 specials and shotguns. Police officers also carry truncheons (night-sticks), and some forces are issued with an electronic tazer gun administering a charge of 50,000 volts for around eight seconds (originally a cattle prod), used to knock out aggressive drug addicts.

In many areas, police wear bullet-proof vests, although even these are no defence against the Teflon-coated bullets (known as cop-killers) used by some criminals. Police officers also carry mace, a riot gas similar to CS gas. Police officers are among the most frightening looking Americans you're likely to meet, with their carefully developed tough-men looks, truncheons and guns. In some states, police can legally shoot suspected criminals trying to evade arrest, so don't even think about it!

As in most countries, the efficiency, honesty and politeness of police officers vary from city to city and state to state. Police corruption is reportedly widespread, particularly in the major cities such as New York, where many officers are involved in criminal activities such as selling drugs seized from pushers.

⚠ Caution

Although some people claim to present their driving license to a traffic cop along with a $50 bill, you should never attempt to bribe a police officer, even if he gives you an open invitation.

As in many countries, most complaints against the police are dismissed out of hand by police review boards, and most people consider it a waste of time reporting cases of bad cops.

If you're stopped by a policeman, either in a car or when walking, don't make any sudden moves and keep your hands where they can be seen. Some policemen are extremely jumpy (often justifiably so) and may interpret any movement as an attempt to reach a concealed weapon. Always be courteous and helpful. It may not do any harm to emphasize that you're a foreigner (depending on your nationality) or to tell the officer you're a visitor or newcomer. If you've broken the law, you should apologize and stress that it was innocently and inadvertently done (although they may not be convinced if you've just held up a bank with an AK-47).

In addition to federal and state police forces, there are around 75 federal law enforcement agencies such as the Federal Bureau of Investigation (FBI), which deal with interstate crime. The FBI has some 20,000 plain clothes agents who normally concern themselves with major offences such as murder, kidnapping and robbery. It publishes a list of the 'ten most wanted fugitives' and provides state and local police forces with information. In the last few years, however, the FBI has had its role expanded to include 'homeland security' and there's talk of merging or at least coordinating the activities of the FBI with those of the Central Intelligence Agency (CIA).

Each state also has a reserve national guard under the command of the state governor that can be called on to deal with civil unrest such as riots, as well as dealing with natural catastrophes, e.g. earthquakes, fires, floods and hurricanes. The National Guard has had its role vastly increased in recent years (see **Military Service** on page 244).

See also **Crime** on page 235 and **Legal System** on page 241.

RELIGION

The US has a tradition of religious tolerance and residents has total freedom of religion without hindrance from the state or community. The establishment and free exercise of religion is enshrined in the First Amendment of the US Constitution. For this reason, prayer isn't permitted in schools or at the start of sports games and was ruled unconstitutional by the US Supreme Court (although you may privately pray for your team to prevail). Although the influence of religion declined in most western societies in the latter part of the 20th century, the US has remained solidly religious (it's one of the world's most deeply religious nations).

The national motto 'In God We Trust' is inscribed upon US coins, and the pledge of allegiance to the American flag still refers to the US as 'One Nation Under God' despite

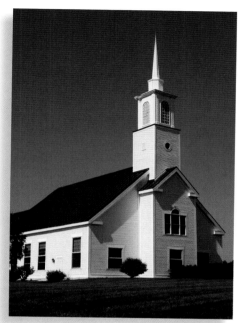

New England Church

Astonishingly, around a third of Americans claim to be 'Born Again Christians', so called because they believe life starts anew when you commit yourself to Jesus Christ (being born again doesn't, however, guarantee you a longer life!). They, and other fundamentalists, contend that every word in the bible is literally true and that Darwin's theory of evolution is baloney. The central states (especially Kansas and Missouri) are known as the 'bible belt' because of the prominence of fundamentalist Protestants. In many parts of the US, there's a relentless determination by religious zealots to impose their views on non-believers, often through so-called street preachers.

The most famous (or infamous) evangelists conduct their business via radio and TV (the 'electronic' church). A staggering 1,300 radio and TV stations (television ministries) are devoted full-time to religion. Although TV religious broadcasts may look like game shows, they're a deadly serious, multi-million dollar business (God is BIG business in the US). The chief aim of TV ministries is to encourage viewers to donate pots of money to pay for their salvation (or the preacher's high life). Enterprising readers should note that one of the fastest ways to get seriously rich in the US is to start a religious organization, which enjoy tax-exempt status.

Many religious groups have considerable influence in US society and politics, locally and nationally. (The backing of religious organizations was credited in part with President Bush's victory in the 2004 election.) Religion pervades political life and prominent politicians (and sportsmen) often praise or call on God in public or share their religious beliefs with millions of TV viewers (atheism is bad for business). Often sportsmen state that they won 'with God's help', although losers don't usually blame divine intervention.

The US, particularly California, is also the birthplace of many of the world's most

sporadic legal attempts to have the words removed. Religion is conspicuous in the US, where it's a part of everyday life (only sport is taken more seriously). More than 90 per cent of Americans claim to believe in God (and Mammon), two-thirds are members of a local church or temple and around 45 per cent attend religious services at least once a week. Some 60 per cent of Americans are Protestant, 25 per cent Roman Catholic, 2 per cent Jewish, 1 per cent Orthodox and 4 per cent belong to other religions such as Buddhism, Hinduism or Islam (the remaining 8 per cent claim no religion). Not surprisingly, more Americans believe in heaven (around 80 per cent) than hell (65 per cent), and 70 per cent believe in life after death (they hope they can take their pile with them or at least come back and enjoy it in their next life). As a consequence of the diverse religions, Americans refer to 'first' or 'given' names, rather than 'Christian' names.

bizarre religious organizations, including Hare Krishna, the Moonies, the Rajneeshies, Scientology and Transcendental Meditation (TM). Many 'cults' seek the total commitment and involvement of their members, which means giving up their worldly possessions or donating a large percentage of their salaries to the cult. Some cults have a fundamentalist outlook, while others are based on oriental religions or philosophies. Many Americans consider cults to be dangerous, as they appear to indulge in brain-washing techniques (which is why some have been banned in a number of countries).

Churches and religious meeting places representing a multitude of faiths can be found in every town (often outnumbering bars), and Sunday traffic jams are common, as people commute to church (some even have drive-in services). Recent years have seen the advent of mega-churches (known as 'God's shopping malls') with seating for up to 6,000 worshippers or more than 30,000 a week. They generally offer a computerized, pulsating, video-age service packaged as big-time entertainment and dished up with a variety of added attractions. In some towns, practically everyone attends church or Sunday school, when people dress in their Sunday best.

The bible remains the nation's best-selling book and most bookshops have a section for religious books. In smaller towns and communities, churches are often the main centers of social and community life.

Most churches organize a wide range of social activities, including sports events, dances, coffee hours, dinners and suppers, discussion groups and outings. Many also operate nursery schools and after-school and youth programs for older children. Most

colleges and universities have 'campus ministries' affiliated with churches. Many of the US's largest charities are administered by religious groups, which run hospitals, homeless shelters, canteens, workshops for the disabled, refugee and youth centers, special schools, and many other establishments and projects. In many cases, these charities have now become eligible for federal government funding under programs developed to encourage 'faith-based' initiatives to replace social services previously cut back due to budgetary constraints.

For information about local religious centers and service times, contact your local library or telephone religious centers for information (listed in the yellow pages under 'Religious Organizations' or 'Churches'). Many religious centers hold services in a number of languages. In some areas, a church directory is published and local religious services are usually listed in tourist guides and published in local weekend newspapers, where a whole page may be devoted to religious news.

SOCIAL CUSTOMS

All countries have their social customs and peculiarities, and the US is no exception. Good manners, politeness and consideration for others are considered important by most people. Americans are generally informal in their relationships and won't be too upset if you break the social rules, provided your behavior isn't outrageous. As a foreigner you may be forgiven if you accidentally insult your host (although you may not be invited again). On the other hand, you may consider normal American behavior occasionally shocking. Here are a few American customs you may like to familiarize yourself with:

◆ Americans often greet total strangers, particularly in small towns and communities. This may vary from a formal 'good morning' to a more casual 'Hi!'; it's considered polite to respond likewise. On parting, it's customary to say 'Have a nice day' (don't, however, say it to the bereaved at a funeral), although this habit is reportedly dying out as Americans become weary of ritual insincerity. Americans often reply 'You're welcome' or something similar when somebody thanks them, and they may think you're impolite if you don't do likewise. If someone asks 'How are you?', it's usual to reply 'Fine thanks' (even if you feel dreadful).

♦ When introduced to someone, it's common to follow the cue of the person performing the introduction, e.g. if someone is introduced as George, you can usually call him George. Americans generally dislike formality or any sort of social deference due to age or position, and most quickly say 'Please call me Rick (or Rita)'. To Americans, informality shows no lack of respect. Because of the rise of women's liberation in America, women may be introduced with the title 'Ms' (pronounced 'mizz') and some women object to being addressed as 'Miss' or 'Mrs'. In some social circles, women are introduced after their husbands, e.g. Mrs Chuck Whizzkid, although you shouldn't address her as Chuck! Some American women retain their maiden (family) names after marriage. Many American first names can be confusing and it's often difficult to know whether a name refers to a man or a woman (or the difference between a family and give/Christian name.)

♦ After you've been introduced to someone, you usually say something like, 'Pleased to meet you' or 'My pleasure' and shake hands.

♦ When saying goodbye, it isn't customary to shake hands again, although some people do. Among friends, it's common for men to kiss ladies on one or both cheeks. Men don't usually kiss or embrace each other, although this depends on their nationality or ethnic origin (or sexual proclivity).

♦ Americans don't have status or inherited titles (e.g. Sir or Lord) but do defer to people with a professional title which has been earned. These include foreign diplomats (e.g. Sir), members of the Senate (Senator) or Congress (Congressman/Congresswoman), judges, medical doctors and others with a doctorate, military officers (e.g. General, Colonel), professors, priests and other religious ministers (e.g. Father, Rabbi, Reverend). Retired people usually retain their military, political and professional titles for life.

♦ If you're invited to dinner, it's customary to take along a small present, e.g. flowers, a plant, chocolates or a bottle of wine (but nothing extravagant or ostentatious). Flowers can be tricky, as to some people carnations mean bad luck, chrysanthemums are for cemeteries and roses signify love. Maybe you should stick to plastic, silk or dried flowers (or a nice bunch of weeds). Wine can also be a problem, particularly if you bring a bottle

Thank you

of Italian plonk and your hosts are wine connoisseurs or members of a religious group that considers alcohol consumption a sin. If you stay with someone as a guest for a few days, it's customary to give your host or hostess a small gift when you leave.

♦ A wedding or baby 'shower' is a party organized by female friends to shower presents on a prospective bride or new mother. Presents may be of a particular kind, as in a china or linen shower or you may be directed to the gift registry at a local department store.

♦ Although many foreigners have the impression that Americans are relaxed and casual in their dress, they often have strict dress codes. In the puritanical New England states, people usually dress conservatively and more formally than in most other regions. This is particularly true of office workers, who are usually expected to wear a suit and tie (and have short hair). In the east, casual wear (jeans or casual trousers, open-necked shirt) is acceptable for the beach or the garden but is unacceptable in many restaurants. In the south and west, casual dress is more acceptable, both in the office and socially, and only the most expensive restaurants insist on ties and formal dress.

Many offices have introduced a 'dress-down' day on one day a week (usually Friday), when employees may wear casual attire (although jeans may still be off limits).

♦ When going anywhere that could be remotely formal (or particularly informal), it's wise to ask in advance what you're expected to wear. Usually when dress is formal, such as evening dress or dinner jacket, this is stated in the invitation (e.g. 'black tie'), and you won't be admitted if you turn up in the wrong attire. On the other hand, at some informal gatherings you may feel out of place if you aren't wearing jeans and a T-shirt. If you're invited to a wedding, enquire about dress (unless you want to stick out like a sore thumb). Black or dark dress is almost always worn at funerals.

♦ Guests are normally expected to be punctual, with the exception of certain society parties, when late arrival is *de rigueur* (provided you don't arrive after the celebrity guest). It's usual to arrive half an hour to an hour after the official start of a dance. Invitations to cocktail parties or receptions may state 5pm to 7pm, in which case you may arrive at any time between these hours. Dinner invitations are often phrased as 8pm for 8.30pm. This means you should arrive at 8pm for drinks and dinner will be served (usually promptly) at 8.30pm. Anyone who arrives late for dinner or, horror of horrors, doesn't turn up at all, should expect to be excluded from future guest lists, unless he has a good excuse (e.g. he has been murdered or kidnapped). On the other hand, you must never arrive early (unless you plan to help with the cooking). You should never be late for funerals, weddings (unless you're the bride, who is always late) or business appointments.

♦ Many families say grace before meals, so follow your host's example before tucking in. If you're confused by a multitude of knives, forks and spoons, don't panic but just copy what your neighbor is doing (the rule is to start at the outside and work in). You'll notice that most Americans don't eat with a knife and fork like 'normal' people. When not eating with their hands they usually eat everything with a fork held in the right hand (unless left-handed). If anything cannot be broken up into bite-size pieces with a fork (e.g. steak), you're permitted to use a knife, but must dispense with it afterwards (knives are generally reserved for killing people!).

Even desserts are eaten with a fork, and a spoon is usually for your coffee.

◆ Don't overstay your welcome. This becomes obvious when your host starts looking at his watch, talking about his early start the next day, yawning, or in desperation, falling asleep.

For more information about US customs and culture, obtain a copy of our sister publication, *Culture Wise America* (Survival Books) see below.

America needs you... (possibly)

APPENDICES

APPENDIX A: USEFUL ADDRESSES

Embassies & Consulates

A selection of foreign embassy addresses in Washington DC is shown below (for others see 🖥 www.embassy.org/embassies). In addition to their embassies in Washington DC, many countries have consulates in a number of other US cities (see local telephone directories). Links to US embassy websites can be found at 🖥 www.usembassy.org.

Algeria: Kalorama Road, NW, Washington, DC 20008 (☎ 202-265-2800, 🖥 www.algeria-us.org).

Antigua & Barbuda: 3216 New Mexico Avenue, NW, Washington, DC 20016 (☎ 202-362-5122).

Argentina: 1600 New Hampshire Avenue, NW, Washington, DC 20009 (☎ 202-939-6400, 🖥 www.embassyofargentina.us).

Australia: 1601 Massachusetts Avenue, NW, Washington, DC 20036 (☎ 202-797-3000, 🖥 www.usa.embassy.gov.au).

Austria: 3524 International Court, NW, Washington, DC 20008-3035 (☎ 202-895-6700, 🖥 www.austria.org).

Bahamas: 2220 Massachusetts Avenue, NW, Washington, DC 20008 (☎ 202-319-2660).

Barbados: 2144 Wyoming Avenue, NW, Washington, DC 20008 (☎ 202-939-9200).

Belgium: 3330 Garfield Street, NW, Washington, DC 20008 (☎ 202-333-6900, 🖥 www.diplobel.us).

Brazil: 3006 Massachusetts Avenue, NW, Washington, DC 20008 (☎ 202-238-2700, 🖥 www.brasilemb.org).

Bulgaria: 1621 22nd Street, NW, Washington, DC 20008 (☎ 202-387-0174, 🖥 www.bulgaria-embassy.org).

Canada: 501 Pennsylvania Avenue, NW, Washington, DC 20001 (☎ 202-682-1740, 🖥 www.canadianembassy.org).

Chile: 1732 Massachusetts Avenue, NW, Washington, DC 20036 (☎ 202-785-1746, 🖥 www.chile-usa.org).

China: 2300 Connecticut Avenue, NW, Washington, DC 20008 (☎ 202-328-2500, 🖥 www.china-embassy.org).

Costa Rica: 2114 S Street, NW, Washington, DC 20008 (☎ 202-234-2945/2946, 🖥 http://costarica-embassy.org).

Cuba: 2630 & 2639 16th Street, NW, Washington, DC 20009 (☎ 202-797-8518, 🖥 http://embacu.cubaminrex.cu/default.aspx?tabid=1025).

Cyprus: 2211 R Street, NW, Washington, DC 20008 (☎ 202-462-5772, 🖥 www.cyprusembassy.net).

Czech Republic: 3900 Spring of Freedom Street, NW, Washington, DC 20008 (☎ 202-274 9100, 🖥 www.mzv.cz/washington).

Denmark: 3200 Whitehaven Street, NW, Washington, DC 20008 (☎ 202-234-4300, 🖥 www.ambwashington.um.dk/en).

Ecuador: 2535 15th Street, NW, Washington, DC 20009 (☎ 202-234 7200, 🖥 www.ecuador.org).

Egypt: 3521 International Court, NW, Washington, DC 20008 (☎ 202-895-5400, 🖥 www.egyptembassy.net).

Finland: 3301 Massachusetts Avenue, NW, Washington, DC 20008 (☎ 202-298-5800, 🖥 www.finland.org).

France: 4101 Reservoir Road, NW, Washington, DC 20007 (☎ 202-944-6000, 🖥 www.info-france-usa.org).

Germany: 4645 Reservoir Road, NW, Washington, DC 20007 (☎ 202-298-4000, 🖥 www.germany-info.org).

Greece: 2221 Massachusetts Avenue, NW, Washington, DC 20008 (☎ 202-939-1300, 🖥 www.greekembassy.org).

Hungary: 3910 Shoemaker Street, NW, Washington, DC 20008 (☎ 202-362-6730, 🖥 www.huembwas.org).

Iceland: 1156 15th Street, NW, Suite 1200, Washington, DC 20005-1704 (☎ 202-265-6653, 🖥 www.iceland.org/us).

India: 2107 Massachusetts Avenue, NW, Washington, DC 20008 (☎ 202-939-7000, 🖥 www.indianembassy.org).

Iran: 2209 Wisconsin Avenue, NW, Washington, DC 20007 (☎ 202-965-4990, 🖥 www.daftar.org/eng/default.asp?lang=eng).

Ireland: 2234 Massachusetts Avenue, NW, Washington, DC 20008 (☎ 202-462-3939, 🖥 www.embassyofireland.org).

Israel: 3514 International Drive, NW, Washington, DC 20008 (☎ 202-364-500, 🖥 www.israelemb.org).

Italy: 3000 Whitehaven Street, NW, Washington, DC 20008 (☎ 202-612-4400, 🖥 www.ambwashingtondc.esteri.it/ambasciata_washington).

Jamaica: 1520 New Hampshire Avenue, NW, Washington DC 20036 (☎ 202-452-0660, 🖥 www.embassyofjamaica.org).

Japan: 2520 Massachusetts Avenue, NW, Washington, DC 20008 (☎ 202-238-6700, 🖵 www.embjapan.org).

Jordan: 3504 International Drive, NW, Washington, DC 20008 (☎ 202-966-2664, 🖵 www.jordanembassyus.org).

Kenya: 2249 R. Street, NW, Washington, DC 20008 (☎ 202-387-6101, 🖵 www.kenyaembassy.com).

Korea: 2450 Massachusetts Avenue, NW, Washington, DC 20008 (☎ 202-939-5600, 🖵 www.koreaembassyusa.org).

Luxembourg: 2200 Massachusetts Avenue, NW, Washington, DC 20008 (☎ 202-265-4171, 🖵 www.luxembourg-usa.org).

Malaysia: 3516 International Court, NW, Washington, DC 20008 (☎ 202-572-9700, 🖵 http://myperwakilan.mfa.gov.my/am/washington).

Malta: 2017 Connecticut Avenue, NW, Washington, DC 20008 (☎ 202-462-3611, 🖵 www.foreign.gov.mt/pages/main.asp?sec=17).

Mexico: 1911 Pennsylvania Avenue, NW, Washington, DC 20006 (☎ 202-728-1600).

Morocco: 1601 21st Street, NW, Washington, DC 20009 (☎ 202-462-7979).

Netherlands: 4200 Linnean Avenue, NW, Washington, DC 20008 (☎ 1-877-388-2443, 🖵 www.netherlands-embassy.org)

New Zealand: 37 Observatory Circle, NW, Washington, DC 20008 (☎ 202-328-4800, 🖵 www.nzembassy.com).

Nigeria: 1333 16th Street, NW, Washington, DC 20036 (☎ 202-986-8400, 🖵 www.nigeriaembassyusa.org).

Norway: 2720 34th Street, NW, Washington, DC 20008 (☎ 202-333-6000, 🖵 www.norway.org).

Pakistan: 3517 International Court, NW, Washington, DC 20008 (☎ 202-243-6500, 🖵 www.pakistan-embassy.org).

Peru: 1700 Massachusetts Avenue, NW, Washington, DC 20036 (☎ 202-833-9860, 🖵 www.peruvianembassy.us).

Philippines: 1600 Massachusetts Avenue, NW, Washington, DC 20036 (☎ 202-467-9300, 🖵 www.philippineembassy-usa.org).

Poland: 2640 16th Street, NW, Washington, DC 20009 (☎ 202-234-3800, 🖵 www.polandembassy.org).

Portugal: 2125 Kalorama Road, NW, Washington, DC 20008 (☎ 202-328-8610, 🖵 www.portugalemb.org).

Romania: 23rd Street, NW, Washington, DC 20008 (☎ 202-332-4848).

Russia: 2650 Wisconsin Avenue, NW, Washington, DC 20007 (☎ 202-298-5700, 🖵 www.russianembassy.org).

St. Kitts and Nevis: 3216 New Mexico Avenue, NW, Washington, DC 20016 (☎ 202-686-2636, 🖵 www.embassy.gov.kn/default.asp?pageidentifier=88).

St. Lucia: 3216 New Mexico Avenue, NW, Washington, DC 20017 (☎ 202-364-6792).

St. Vincent and the Grenadines: 3216 New Mexico Avenue, NW, Washington, DC 20016 (☎ 202-364-6730).

Singapore: 3501 International Place, NW, Washington, DC 20008 (☎ 202-537 3100, 💻 www.mfa.gov.sg/washington).

South Africa: 3051 Massachusetts Avenue, NW, Washington, DC 20008 (☎ 202-232 4400, 💻 www.saembassy.org).

Spain: Pennsylvania Avenue, NW, Washington, DC 20037 (☎ 202-452-0100, 💻 www.spainemb.org/ingles/indexing.htm).

Sweden: 2900 K Street NW, Washington, DC 20007 (☎ 202-467-2600, 💻 www.swedenabroad.se/pages/start____6989.asp).

Switzerland: 2900 Cathedral Avenue, NW, Washington, DC 20008 (☎ 202-745-7900, 💻 www.swissemb.org).

Thailand: 1024 Wisconsin Avenue, NW, Suite 401, Washington, DC 20007 (☎ 202-944-3600, 💻 www.thaiembdc.org).

Trinidad and Tobago: 1708 Massachusetts Avenue, NW, Washington, DC 20036 (☎ 202-467-6490, 💻 www.ttembassy.org).

Tunisia: 1515 Massachusetts Avenue, NW, Washington, DC 20005 (☎ 202-862-1850).

Turkey: 2525 Massachusetts Avenue, NW, Washington, DC 20008 (☎ 202-612-700).

United Arab Emirates: 3522 International Court, NW, Washington, DC 20008 (☎ 202-243-2400, 💻 http://uae-embassy.org).

United Kingdom: 3100 Massachusetts Avenue, NW, Washington, DC 20008 (☎ 202-588 6500, 💻 www.britainusa.com).

Uruguay: 1913 I Street, NW, Washington, DC 20006 (☎ 202-331-1313, 💻 www.uruwashi.org).

Venezuela: 1099 30th Street, NW, Washington, DC 20007 (☎ 202-342-2214, 💻 www.embavenez-us.org).

Vietnam: 1233 20th Street, NW, Suite 400, Washington, DC 20036 (☎ 202-861-0737, 💻 www.vietnamembassy-usa.org).

Zimbabwe: 1608 New Hampshire Avenue, NW, Washington, DC 20009 (☎ 202-332-7100, 💻 www.zimbabwe-embassy.us).

Government Departments

Information about the federal government is available from the Federal Information Center via state and regional toll-free telephone numbers (see your local telephone book or ask information) or by contacting the Federal Information Center, PO Box 600, Cumberland, MD 21502 (☎ 1-800-333-4636, 🖥 www.firstgov.gov), whose Internet site has links to most government department sites.

Department of Agriculture (USDA): 1400 Independence Avenue, SW, Washington, DC 20250 (☎ 202-720-2791, 🖥 www.usda.gov).

Department of Commerce (DOC): 1401 Constitution Avenue, NW, Washington, DC 20230 (☎ 202-482-2000, 🖥 www.commerce.gov).

Department of Defense (DOD): 1400 Defense Pentagon, NW, Washington, DC 20301-1400 (☎ 703-571-3343, 🖥 www.defense.gov).

Department of Education (ED): 400 Maryland Avenue, SW, Washington, DC 20202 (☎ 1-800-872-5327, 🖥 www.ed.gov).

Department of Energy (DOE): 1000 Independence Avenue, SW, Washington, DC 20585 (☎ 202-586-5000, 🖥 www.energy.gov).

Department of Health and Human Services (HHS): 200 Independence Avenue, SW, Washington, DC 20201 (☎ 1-877-696-6775, 🖥 www.hhs.gov).

Department of Homeland Security (DHS): Washington, DC 20528 (☎ 202-282-8000, 🖥 www.dhs.gov).

Department of Housing and Urban Development (HUD): 451 7th Street, SW, Washington, DC 20410 (☎ 202-708-1112, 🖥 www.hud.gov).

Department of the Interior (DOI): 1849 C Street, NW, Washington, DC 20240 (☎ 202-208-3100, 🖥 www.doi.gov).

Department of Justice (DOJ): 950 Pennsylvania Avenue, NW, Washington, DC 20530-0001 (☎ 202-514-2000, 🖥 www.usdoj.gov).

Department of Labor (DOL): 200 Constitution Avenue, NW, Washington, DC 20210 (☎ 1-866-4-USA-DOL, 🖥 www.dol.gov).

Department of State (DOS): 2201 C Street, NW, Washington, DC 20520 (☎ 202-647 4000, 🖥 www.state.gov).

Department of Transportation (DOT): 1200 New Jersey Avenue, SE, Washington, DC 20590 (☎ 202-366-4000, 🖥 www.dot.gov).

Department of the Treasury: 1500 Pennsylvania Avenue, NW, Washington, DC 20220 (☎ 202-622-2000, 🖥 www.treasury.gov).

Department of Veterans' Affairs (VA): 810 Vermont Avenue, NW, Washington, DC 20420 (☎ 202-273-5400, 🖥 www.va.gov).

Internal Revenue Service (IRS): 500 N. Capitol Street, NW, Washington, DC 20221 (☎ 1-800-829-1040, 🖥 www.irs.gov).

Social Security Administration (SSA): 6401 Security Blvd., Baltimore, Maryland 21235-0001 (☎ 1-800-772-1213, 💻 www.ssa.gov).

State Governments

Alabama: 3 South Jackson Street, Suite 200, Montgomery, AL 36104 (☎ 1-866-353-3468, 💻 www.alabama.gov).

Alaska: State Capitol Building, Third Floor, P.O. Box 110001, Juneau, AK 99811-0001 (☎ 1-907-465-3500, 💻 www.alaska.gov).

Arizona: Governor's Office, 1700 West Washington, Phoenix, AZ 85007 (☎ 1-602-542-4331, 💻 www.az.gov).

Arkansas: State Capitol Room 250, Little Rock, AR 72201 (☎ 1-501-682-2345, 💻 www.state.ar.us/government.php).

California: State Capitol Building, Sacramento, CA 95814 (☎ 1-916-445-2841, 💻 *www.ca.gov).*

Colorado: The Governor's Office, 136 State Capitol, Denver, CO 80203 (☎ 1-303-866-2471, 💻 *www.colorado.gov).*

Connecticut: Office of the Governor, State Capitol, 210 Capitol Avenue, Hartford, CT 06106 (☎ 1-860-566-4840, 💻 www.ct.gov).

Delaware: Dover Government Office, Tatnall Building, William Penn Street, 2nd Floor, Dover, DE 19901 (☎ 1-302-744-4101, 💻 www.delaware.gov).

Florida: Governor's Office, PL-05 The Capitol, Tallahassee, FL 32399 (☎ 1-850- 488-4441, 💻 www.myflorida.com).

Georgia: State Capitol, 206 Washington Street, Downtown, Atlanta, GA 30334 (☎ 1-404-656-2844, 💻 www.georgia.gov).

Hawaii: State Capitol, Room 415, Honolulu, HI 96813 (☎ 1-808-586-0222, 💻 www.hawaii.gov).

Indiana: Government Office, 999 Main Street, Suite 910, Boise, ID 83702 (☎ 1-208-332-0102, 💻 www.accessidaho.org).

Illinois: Office of the Governor, 207 Statehouse, Springfield, IL 62706 (☎ 1-217-782-0244, 💻 www.illinois.gov).

Indiana: State Government Center, 402 West Washington Street, Indianapolis, IN 46204 (☎ 1-317-233-0800, 💻 www.in.gov).

Iowa: State Capitol, 1007 East Grand Avenue, Des Moines, IA 50319 (☎ 1-515-281-5211, 💻 www.iowa.gov).

Kansas: Office of the Governor, Capitol, 300 SW 10th Avenue, Suite 2128, Topeka, KS 66612 (☎ 1-785-296-3232, 💻 www.kansas.gov).

Kentucky: Governor's Office, 700 Capitol Ave, Suite 100, Frankfort, KY 40601 (☎ 1-502-564-2611, 💻 www.kentucky.gov).

Louisiana: Governor's Office, PO Box 94004, Baton Rouge, LA 70804 (☎ 1-225-342-7015, 🖳 www.louisiana.gov).

Maine: Office of the Governor, #1 State House Station, Augusta, ME 04333 (☎ 1-207-287-3531, 🖳 www.maine.gov).

Maryland: The Governor's Office, 100 State Circle, Annapolis, MD 21401 (☎ 1-410-974-3901, 🖳 www.maryland.gov).

Massachusetts: Office of the Governor, Massachusetts State House, Room 280, Boston, MA 02133 (☎ 1-617-725-4005, 🖳 www.mass.gov).

Michigan: Governor's Office, P.O. Box 30113, Lansing, MI 48909 (☎ 1-517-373-3400, 🖳 www.michigan.gov).

Minnesota: Office of the Governor, 130 State Capitol, 75 Rev. Dr. Martin Luther King Jr. Boulevard, Saint Paul, MN 55155 (☎ 1-651-296-3391, 🖳 www.governor.state.mn.us).

Mississippi: Governor's Office, P.O. Box 139, Jackson, MS 39205 (☎ 1-601- 359-3150, 🖳 www.mississippi.gov).

Missouri: Office of the Governor, P.O. Box 720, Jefferson City, MO 65102 (☎ 1-573-751-3222, 🖳 www.mo.gov).

Montana: Office of the Governor, Montana State Capitol Bldg, P.O. Box 200801, Helena, MT 59620 (☎ 1-406-444-3111, 🖳 www.governor.mt.gov).

Nebraska: Office of the Governor, P.O. Box 94848, Lincoln, NE 68509 (☎ 1-402-471-2244, 🖳 www.nebraska.gov).

Nevada: Office of Governor, State Capitol, 101 N. Carson Street, Carson City, NV 89701 (☎ 1-775-684-5670, 🖳 www.nv.gov).

New Hampshire: Office of the Governor, State House, 25 Capitol Street, Concord, NH 03301 (☎ 1-603-272-2121, 🖳 www.nh.gov).

New Jersey: Office of the Governor, 125 West State Street, Trenton, NJ 08608 (☎ 1-609-292-6000, 🖳 www.state.nj.us).

New Mexico: Office of the Governor, 490 Old Santa Fe Trail, Room 400, Santa Fe, NM 87501 (☎ 1-505-476-2200, 🖳 www.newmexico.gov).

New York: Office of the Governor, State Capitol, Albany, NY 12224 (☎ 1-518-474-8390, 🖳 www.state.ny.us).

North Carolina: Office of the Governor, 20301 Mail Service Center, Raleigh, NC 27699 (☎ 1-919-733-4240, 🖳 www.ncgov.com).

North Dakota: The Governor's Office, 600 East Boulevard Avenue, Bismarck, ND 58585 (☎ 1-701-328-2200, 🖳 www.nd.gov).

Ohio: Governors' Office, Riffe Center, 30th Floor, 77 South High Street, Columbus, OH 43215 (☎ 1-614-466-3555, 🖳 www.ohio.gov).

Oklahoma: Office of the Governor, State Capitol Building, 2300 N. Lincoln Blvd, Room 212, Oklahoma City, OK 73105 (☎ 1-405-521-2342, 🖳 www.ok.gov).

Oregon: Governor's Office, 160 State Capitol, 900 Court Street, Salem, OR 97301 (☎ 1-503-378-4582, 💻 www.oregon.gov).

Pennsylvania: Governor's Office, Room 225, Main Capitol Building, Harrisburg, PA 17120 (☎ 1-717-787-2500, 💻 www.state.pa.us).

Rhode Island: Office of the Governor, State House Room 115, Providence, RI 02903 (☎ 1-401-222-2080, 💻 www.ri.gov).

South Carolina: Governor's Office, 1301 Gervais Street, Suite 710, Columbia, SC 29201 (☎ 1-803-734-9900, 💻 www.sc.gov).

South Dakota: Office of the Governor, 500 E. Capitol Avenue, Pierre, SD 57501 (☎ 1-605-773-3212, 💻 www.sd.gov).

Tennessee: Governor's Office, Tennessee State Capitol, Nashville, TN 37243 (☎ 1-615-741-2001, 💻 www.tennesseeanytime.org).

Texas: Office of the Governor, P.O. Box 12428, Austin, TX 78711 (☎ 1-512-463-2000, 💻 www.texasonline.com).

Utah: Government Office, 30 East Broadway, Suite 300, Salt Lake City, UT 84111 (☎ 1-801-983-0275, 💻 www.utah.gov).

Vermont: Governor's Office, 109 State Street, Pavilion, Montpelier, VT 05609 (☎ 1-802-828-3333, 💻 www.vermont.gov).

Virginia: Government Office, East Main Street, Suite 901, Richmond, VA 23219 (☎ 1-804-796-4718, 💻 www.virginia.gov).

Washington: Office of the Governor, P.O. Box 40002, Olympia, WA 98504 (☎ 1-360-902-4111, 💻 access.wa.gov).

Washington DC: Executive Office of the Mayor, 1350 Pennsylvania Avenue NW, Suite 316, Washington, DC 20004 (☎ 1-202-727-2980, 💻 www.dc.gov).

West Virginia: Governor's Office, 1900 Kanawha Boulevard E, Charleston, WV 25305 (☎ 1-888-438-2731, 💻 www.wv.gov).

Wisconsin: Office of the Governor, 115 East State Capitol, Madison, WI 53702 (☎ 1-608-266-1212, 💻 www.wisconsin.gov).

Wyoming: Governor's Office, State Capitol, 200 West 24th Street, Cheyenne, WY 82002 (☎ 1-307-777-7434, 💻 www.wyoming.gov).

Other US Government Resources

Bureau of Consular Affairs, 2100 Pennsylvania Avenue, NW, Washington DC 20037-3202 (☎ 202-663 2468, 🖥 http://travel.state.gov/visa). Provides a wealth of information about US visas for both immigrants and Americans (plus lots of other useful information).

Customs and Border Protection (CBP), 1300 Pennsylvania Avenue, NW, Washington, DC 20229-0002 (☎ 703-526 4200, 🖥 www.cbp.gov). The front line agency of the Department of Homeland Security (see below) responsible for securing and facilitating trade and travel while enforcing hundreds of US regulations, including immigration and drug laws.

Department of Homeland Security (DHS): Washington, DC 20528 (☎ 202-282 8000, 🖥 www.dhs.gov). The Department of Homeland Security is responsible for security, both internally and externally, ranging from aviation and border security to emergency response, cyber-security analysis to chemical facility inspections.

Department of State (DOS): 2201 C Street, NW, Washington, DC 20520 (☎ 202-647 4000, 🖥 www.state.gov). News about all aspects of government, including embassies and consulates, travel, education, careers, current issues and more.

Immigration and Customs Enforcement (ICE), 500 12th Street, SW, Washington, DC 20536 (☎ 202-732 4242, 🖥 www.ice.gov). Part of the Department of Homeland Security, ICE's mission is to protect the security of the American people and homeland by vigilantly enforcing the nation's immigration and customs laws.

US Citizenship and Immigration Services (USCIS), 20 Massachusetts Ave., NW, Washington, DC 20529 (☎ 1-800-375 5283, 🖥 www.uscis.gov). The USCIS is responsible for the approval of immigrant and nonimmigrant petitions, the authorization of permission to work in the US, the issuance of extensions of stay, and the change or adjustment of an applicant's status while he's in the US, and more.

USCIS Service Centers:

- **California:** USCIS, California Service Center, 24000 Avila Road, 2nd Floor, Room 2326, Laguna Niguel, CA 92677.

- **Nebraska:** USCIS, Nebraska Service Center, 850 S Street, Lincoln, NE 68508.

- **Texas:** USCIS, Texas Service Center, 4141 St. Augustine Road, Dallas, TX 75227.

- **Vermont:** USCIS, Vermont Service Center, 30 Houghton Street, St. Albans, VT 05478-2399.

US Government, General Services Administration, Office of Citizen Services and Communications, Suite G-142, 1800 F Street, NW, Washington, DC 20405 (☎ 1-800-333 4636, 🖥 www.usa.gov). Disseminates US government information on a wide range of topics, including information for visitors to the US.

APPENDIX B: FURTHER READING

Newspapers & Magazines

American Heritage magazine, 416 Hungerford Drive, Suite 216, Rockville, MD 20850-4127 (☎ 240- 453-0900, 💻 www.americanheritage.com).

American Lifestyle magazine, 1100 First Avenue, Suite 200, King of Prussia, PA 19406 (☎ 610-878-5000, 💻 www.americanlifestylemag.com).

Essentially America magazine, 120-126 Lavender Avenue, Mitcham, Surrey, UK (☎ 020-7243-6954, 💻 www.essentiallyamerica.com).

Florida Monthly magazine, Florida Media, Inc., 801 Douglas Ave., Suite 100, Altamonte Springs, FL 32714 (☎ 407-816-9596, 💻 www.floridamagazine.com).

Florida Travel & Life magazine, Florida Media, Inc., 401 N Orlando Avenue, Suite 200, Winter Park, FL 32789, 💻 www.floridatravellife.com).

Los Angeles magazine, 5900 Wilshire Blvd., 10th Floor, Los Angeles, CA 90036 (☎ 323-801-0100, 💻 www.lamag.com).

Magazines of America, 650 Peter Jefferson Parkway, Suite 190, Charlottesville, VA 22911 (☎ 866-271-7582, 💻 www.magazinesofamerica.com).

New York magazine, 75 Varrick Street, New York, NY 10018 (☎ 212-508 0700, 💻 www.nymag.com).

The New Yorker magazine, 4 Times Square, New York, NY 10036-6592 (☎ 515-243-3273, 💻 www.newyorker.com).

Time Out New York magazine, 475 Tenth Avenue, 12th floor, New York, NY 10018 (☎ 646-432-3000, 💻 www.timeout.com/newyork).

Many local 'lifestyle' magazine are published in the US for states, regions and cities (see 💻 http://en.wikipedia.org/wiki/Category:American_magazines_by_state).

Books

There are numerous publications written about America. The following is just a brief selection. Books are listed under subject in alphabetical order, with the title followed by the author's name and the publisher (in brackets).

Business

American Business Values, A Global Perspective, Gerald F Cavanagh (Prentice Hall)

Business Protocol: Contemporary American Practice, David Robinson (Atomic Dog)

Business Travel Guide to United States of America: East Coast (Mercury Business Books)

Speak Business English like an American: Learn the Idioms and Expressions You Need to Succeed on the Job!, Amy Gillett (Language Success PR)

Culture

101 American Customs: Understanding Language and Culture through Common Practices, Harry Collis & Joe Kohl (McGraw-Hill)

American Ways: A Guide for Foreigners in the United States, Gary Althen (Intercultural Press)

American Ways: An Introduction to American Culture, Maryanne Kearny Datesman, JoAnn Crandall & Edward N Kearny (Pearson Education)

Brit-think, Ameri-think: A Transatlantic Survival Guide, Jane Walmsley (Penguin)

Culture Wise America, David Hampshire & Anthony Poulton-Smith (Survival Books)

Made in America, From Levis to Barbie to Google, Nick Freeth (Motor Books)

Oxford Guide to British and American Culture (Oxford University Press)

Xenophobe's Guide to the Americans, Stephanie Faul (Oval Books)

History

A History of the American People, Paul Johnson (Weidenfeld & Nicolson)

American Colonies: The Settling of North America, Alan Taylor (Penguin)

A People's History of the United States: 1492 – Present, Howard Zinn (Harper Perennial)

Bury My Heart at Wounded Knee: An Indian History of the American West, Dee Brown (Vintage)

Letter from America, Alistair Cooke (Penguin)

The American Civil War, Stephen D Engle, Gary W Gallagher, Joseph T Glatthaar & Robert Krick (Osprey)

The American Future: A History, Simon Schama (Bodley Head)

The Limits of Liberty: American History 1607-1992, Maldwyn A Jones (Oxford University Press)

The Penguin History of the United States of America, Hugh Brogan (Penguin)

Language

American-English, English-American: A Two-way Glossary of Words in Daily Use on Both Sides of the Atlantic, Anthea Bickerton (Abson Books London)

Bum Bags and Fanny Packs: A British-American American-British Dictionary, Jeremy Smith (Carroll & Graf)

Divided by a Common Language: A Guide to British and American English, Christopher Davies (Houghton Mifflin Company)

Made in America: An Informal History of the English Language in the United States, Bill Bryson (Black Swan)

Speak American, Dileri Borunda Johnston (Random House)

Webster's American English Dictionary, Merriam-Webster (Federal Street Press)

Literature

An American Dream, Norman Mailer (Harper Perennial)

Breakfast of Champions, Kurt Vonnegut (Vintage)

Gone with the Wind, Margaret Mitchell (Pan)

Invisible Man, Ralph Ellison (Essential Penguin)

To Kill a Mockingbird, Harper Lee (Arrow)

The Adventures of Huckleberry Finn, Mark Twain (Penguin Classics)

The Grapes of Wrath, John Steinbeck (Penguin Classics)

The Great Gatsby, F Scott Fitzgerald (Penguin Modern Classics)

The Red Badge of Courage, Stephen Crane (Wordsworth Classics)

The Sound and the Fury, William Faulkner (Vintage Classics)

Uncle Tom's Cabin, Harriet Beecher Stowe (Wordsworth Classics)

Living & Working

Buying or Renting a Home in New York, Graeme Chesters and Bev Laflamme (Survival Books)

Legal US Immigration, Adam Edward Rothwell (Booklocker)

Living & Working in America, David Hampshire (Survival Books)

U.S. Immigration Made Easy, Ilona Bray, Jeptha Evans & Ruby Lieberman (Nolo)

Tourism

Discover America (Reader's Digest)

DK Eyewitness Travel Guide: USA, Collectif (Dorling Kindersley)

Let's Go USA, Sergio Ibarra et al (Let's Go)

Lonely Planet USA, Sara Benson (Lonely Planet Country Guide)

National Parks – The Family Guide: A Complete Family Travel Guide to All America's National Parks, Monuments, Memorials, Battlefields, Seashores, Dave Robertson & June Francis (On Site)

The Comprehensive Guide to Train Travel in North America, Jack Swanson & Jeff Karsh (Rail Ventures)

The Rough Guide to the USA, Greg Ward, Samantha Cook et al (Rough Guides)

Unauthorized America: A Travel Guide to the Places the Chamber of Commerce Won't Tell You About, Vince Staten (Harper Perennial)

United States of America (Berlitz Pocket Travel Guides)

USA by Rail, John Pitt (Bradt)

Where to Stay in the United States of America (Frommer's Family Travel Guides)

Wild West: A Traveler's Guide, Michael McCoy (Globe Pequot Press)

Travel Literature

A Walk in the Woods: Rediscovering America on the Appalachian Trail, Bill Bryson (Black Swan)

Blue Highways: A Journey into America, William Least Heat-Moon (Fawcett)

Drive thru America, Sean Condon (Lonely Planet Journeys)

Notes from a Big Country, Bill Bryson (Black Swan)

On the Road, Jack Kerouac (Penguin Modern Classics)

River Horse: The Logbook of a Boat across America, William Least Heat-Moon (Houghton Mifflin)

Stephen Fry in America, Stephen Fry (Harper Collins)

The Lost Continent: Travels in Small-Town America, Bill Bryson, (Abacus)

Travels with Charley: In Search of America, John Steinbeck (Penguin)

Miscellaneous

American Mania: When More is Not Enough, Peter Whybrow (Norton)

American Popular Music: From Minstrelsy to MTV, Lawrence Starr & Christopher Waterman (OUP USA)

Beyond Light: American Landscapes, Robert Werling (Merrell)

Eccentric America: The Bradt Guide to All That's Weird and Wacky in the USA, Jan Friedman (Bradt Travel Guide)

Fast Food Nation: What the All-American Meal is Doing to the World, Eric Schlosser (Penguin)

Get Up and Go: The History of American Road Travel, Sylvia Whitman (Lerner)

Granta The Magazine of New Writing/77: What We Think of America, edited by Ian Jack (Grove Press, Granta)

Hollywood Babylon, Kenneth Anger (Bantam Doubleday Dell)

Only in America, Matt Frei (Fourth Estate)

The American Diner Cookbook: More Than 450 Recipes and Nostalgia Galore, Linda Everett & Elizabeth McKeon (Cumberland House)

The Everything American Presidents Book: All You Need to Know about the Leaders Who Shaped US History, Martin Kelly and Melissa Kelly (Adams Media Corporation)

The Oxford Companion to American Food and Drink, Andrew F. Smith (OUP USA)

The Wind is My Mother: The Life and Teachings of a Native American Shaman, Bear Heart and Molly Larkin (Berkley Publishing)

USA Cookbook, Sheila Lukins (Workman)

What's Cooking? The History of American Food, Sylvia Whitman (Lerner)

APPENDIX C: USEFUL WEBSITES

The following pages contain just a small selection of the many thousands of websites dedicated to the US.

Business

Better Business Bureaux (🖥 www.bbb.org). Links to local better business bureaux around the US.

Biz Buy Sell (🖥 www.bizbuysell.com). Businesses for sale listed by state

Business (🖥 www.business.gov/states). State and local business resources.

Business Nation (🖥 www.businessnation.com). Information about starting a business, business resources and businesses for sale.

Doing Business (🖥 www.doingbusiness.org/exploreeconomies/?economyid=197). Business regulations in the US compared with 183 other countries.

Employment Law (🖥 www.dol.gov/compliance/guide). Useful guide from the US Department of Labor.

Florida Business Broker (🖥 www.floridabusinessbrokers.com). One of Florida's largest business brokers with offices in Fort Myers, Naples and Port Charlotte.

I Think Bigger (🖥 www.ithinkbigger.com). Useful information for small businesses.

National Association of Self-Employed (🖥 www.nase.org). Excellent information source for those who want to work for themselves.

Resource Links (🖥 www.resourcelinks.net). Business directory.

Small Business Administration (🖥 www.sba.gov, click on 'Local Resources' and choose the state from the map). Programs and services to help you start, grow and succeed in business.

US Chambers of Commerce (🖥 www.uschamber.com). Provides links to each state and city's chamber of commerce.

Women Connect (🖥 www.uswc.org). An online networking website with connections to women's organizations across the US.

See also the business contacts for individual states in **Chapter 1**.

Culture & Entertainment

American Family Traditions (🖥 www.americanfamilytraditions.com). Cheesy, Waltons-style website; heavy on promoting family values but with some interesting cultural information.

American Jokes & Humour (🖥 www.thejokes.co.uk/american-humor.php). A broad selection of the type of jokes which allegedly make Americans laugh.

Culture & Ethnic Groups (🖥 www.usa.gov/citizen/topics/history_culture.shtml). Part of the vast www.usa.com website, with sections devoted to cultures and ethnic groups including African Americans and Hispanics.

Festivals & Events (🖥 www.2camels.com/festivals/usa.php). Articles and reports on the more unusual US festivals.

Native American Culture (🖥 www.greatdreams.com/native.htm). Huge resource with many links providing information about indigenous Americans, their languages, beliefs and culture, from Cherokee to Inuit.

Movie Tickets (🖥 www.movietickets.com). Allows you to purchase tickets for the latest films in advance.

Popular Culture (🖥 www.wsu.edu/~amerstu/pop). Washington State University provides links to sites on various forms of popular culture, including music, film, television, advertising, sports, fashion, toys, magazines and comic books.

Theatre (🖥 www.telecharge.com). Online box office with theatre news, ticket prices and a facility for booking tickets across the US.

Ticket Master (🖥 www.ticketmaster.com). Use this website to locate and purchase tickets for concerts, sports, arts, theatre and many other events.

Education

American Universities (🖥 www.usuniversities.com and 🖥 www.petersons.com). Two sites offering searchable listings of US universities, plus general information about selecting a school and information for foreign students.

American School Directory (🖥 www.asd.com). Facts about local schools. Requires a subscription to access information, but offers annual and monthly subscriptions.

Education America (🖥 www.educationamerica.net). Jobs in education.

Education USA (🖥 http://educationusa.state.gov). US Department of State official website for anyone wishing to study at a US college or university.

High Schools (🖥 www.high-schools.com). Lists every high school in the US, both private and public, with contact details.

National Center for Education Statistics (🖥 www.nces.ed.gov). Statistical information on the American education system, presented in many different ways.

US Department of Education (🖥 www.ed.gov). The official website of the US Department of Education, with tips for parents and students.

US Study Guide (🖥 www.usastudyguide.com). An international guide to education and study in the US, including schools, colleges, universities and even cooking schools

Government & Immigration

Administration on Aging (🖥 www.aoa.gov). Information about retirement and related issues.

Federal Citizen Information Center (🖥 www.info.gov). Official US government site with links to documents and consumer information.

Federal Trade Commission (🖥 www.ftc.gov). The premier consumer protection website, with information covering every possible issue you might encounter, from unhelpful store assistants to identity fraud.

Gov Spot (🖥 www.govspot.com). Offers information and links to state and federal government sites, publications and more.

Green Card Lottery (🖥 www.dvlottery.state.gov). Take your chance in the US Diversity Lottery online.

Immigration Support (🖥 www.usimmigrationsupport.org). This independent company's website contains exhaustive details about visas, Green Cards, social security and citizenship, as well as downloadable instructions and application forms.

Internal Revenue Service (🖥 www.irs.gov). Everything you ever wanted to know about US taxes.

National Center for Health Statistics (🖥 www.cdc.gov/nchs). Official health statistics.

US Census Bureau (🖥 www.census.gov). Government statistics on every aspect of life in the US; the next census is not until 2010 but many of the 2000 stats have been updated.

US Citizen and Immigration Services (🖥 www.uscis.gov). The official line on visas, Green Cards, work permits and more

US Department of Health & Human Rights (🖥 www.hhs.gov/ocr/index.html). State information on civil rights, health information privacy and health service users' rights.

US Department of State (🖥 www.state.gov). News on all aspects of government, including embassies and consulates, travel, education, careers, current issues and more.

US Department of State – Travel Information (🖥 http://travel.state.gov). Information related to travel to and from the US. Includes travel warnings, warnings about drugs, and a list of useful travel publications for foreigners coming to the US and Americans traveling abroad.

US Government (🖥 www.usa.gov). Everything from taxes to healthcare is included on the official website of the US government.

US Postal Service/USPS (🖥 www.usps.com/moversnet). A guide to moving house.

US Social Security Administration (🖥 www.ssa.gov). This government website includes contact details and application forms, and covers every aspect of social security in the US.

The White House (💻 www.whitehouse.gov). The official site of the US President's residence, providing information on current US policies and proposals, proclamations and press briefings.

Language

American-British and British-American Dictionaries (💻 www.travelfurther.net/dictionaries). Discover the differences between the American and British uses of the English language in a fun way.

American English A-Z (💻 www.americanaccent.com). Guide to American pronunciation with audio tips.

American Slang (💻 www.spraakservice.net/slangportal/american.htm). Surf for 57 varieties of slang, including local argot from Boston to New Orleans and from gangland slang to police terminology.

America Study Guide (💻 www.americastudyguide.com/dir/esl/index). State-by-state directory of English as a Second Language (ESL) programs across the US.

English Language Schools (💻 www.englishinusa.com). Comprehensive directory of American English language schools and internet tutoring programs.

Learn American English Online (💻 www.learnamericanenglishonline.com). Useful resource for speakers of languages other than English.

Slang (💻 www.englishdaily626.com/slang.php). A dictionary of commonly used American slang and sayings.

Spelling (💻 www.2.gsu.edu/~wwwesl/egw/jones/differences.htm). A handy set of tables illustrating the basic differences between English and American spelling.

Living & Working

Au Pair USA (💻 www.aupairusa.org). Everything the would-be au pair might need to know.

Bureau of Labor Statistics (💻 www.bls.gov). All the facts and figures about employment (and unemployment), inflation, pay and benefits, plus salaries for more than 800 occupations and over 400 industries.

Blue Collar Jobs (💻 www.bluecollarjobs.com). A resource for finding skilled and unskilled jobs in the US.

Career Builder (💻 www.careerbuilder.com). Vacancies in a variety of sectors, plus advice on careers and a place to upload your CV.

Consumer Reports (💻 www.consumerreports.org/cro/index.htm). Product reviews, consumer rights and more.

Find A Lawyer (💻 www.lawyers.com). Search facility for legal eagles (attornies) in every state.

Franchise Finder (🖳 www.ftc.gov). A resource to check out franchise opportunities in the US.

HomeGain (🖳 www.homegain.com). Find a real estate agent, obtain a valuation and search homes for sale online.

Housing and Urban Development (🖳 www.hud.gov). Information about home ownership, renting and more. Information can be accessed online or ordered in pamphlet form.

Insurance Information Institute (🖳 www.iii.org). Independent advice on insuring your home, car and health.

Life in the USA (🖳 www.lifeintheusa.com). The complete web guide to American life for immigrants and Americans, written by Americans, with subjects ranging from sympathy cards to soccer mums.

Monster (🖳 http://globalgateway.monster.com). General information about working in the US (part of the job hunting website, Monster.com).

My Money (🖳 www.mymoney.gov). The US government's website dedicated to teaching Americans the basics about financial education. Contains important information from 20 federal agencies.

Survival Books (🖳 www.survivalbooks.net). The website of the publisher of this book and other US books such as *Buying or Renting a Home in New York*, *Culture Wise America* and *Living and Working in America*.

US Law (🖳 www.uslaw.com). Collection of legal articles on all points of law, plus a find-a-lawyer resource and the chance to put your questions to a legal team.

Media

Google News (🖳 www.news.google.com). Constantly updated national and international news items from the world's favourite search engine.

Magazines (🖳 www.magazines.com). A wealth of US magazines available on subscription.

National Climatic Data Center (🖳 www.ncdc.noaa.gov). Links to every kind of weather forecast across the 50 states.

Radio Locator (🖳 www.radio-locator.com). Search US stations by zip code or call letters or find an internet feed from your favourite radio channel.

TV Guide (🖳 www.tvguide.com). Listings for all the US television channels, plus articles, previews, DVD picks and more.

USA Today (🖳 www.usatoday.com). An online version of the nation's most popular daily newspaper.

World Newspapers (🖳 www.newspapers24.com). Find a local US newspaper or catch up with news from your home town, with links to over 12,000 newspapers worldwide.

Travel & Tourism

American Automobile Association (💻 www.aaa.com). The umbrella website for America's automobile clubs with tips and advice for drivers and travellers.

Amtrak (💻 www.amtrak.com). Fares, routes and timetables for train travel across the US with America's national railway company.

Cars.com (💻 www.cars.com). Online dealer for trade and private care sales, plus research into different models and shopping advice.

Department of Motor Vehicles (💻 www.dmv.org). Not an official government site but one which gives all the information you need to know about driving legally in the US, presented state by state.

Discover America (💻 www.discoveramerica.com). The official travel and tourism website of the US.

Greyhound (💻 www.greyhound.com). All the information on timetables and fares on the numerous routes of America's famous long-distance bus service.

See America (💻 www.seeamerica.org). General travel information.

Travel Channel (💻 www.travelchannel.com). The website of the television channel of the same name.

US Department of Transport (💻 www.dot.gov). The official transportation website, giving details on travel documentation requirements, the latest security measures, car safety, legislation, and much more.

USA Tourist (💻 www.usatourist.com). Tips, links, photos, maps, events and lists, designed to make your journey easier, cheaper and trouble free.

Visit USA (💻 www.visitusa.org.uk). Tourist information from the Visit USA Association.

World Travel Guide (💻 www.wtgonline.com). A general website for travellers and expatriates with a wealth of information on destinations in America.

Miscellaneous

AARP (💻 www.aarp.org). The website of the American Association of Retired Persons contains useful information for retirees, baby boomers and older (and not so old) US residents, with tips on health, money and much more.

American Pet Association (💻 www.apapets.org). Fun facts and bizarre stats about America's relationship with its four-legged friends.

Bloomingdales (💻 www.bloomingdales.com). Online link to one of the world's best department stores.

Dating Diversions (💻 www.datingdiversions.com). Humorous site with tips on the dating behaviour of potential partners from Connecticut to California.

Ebay (💻 www.ebay.com). America's favorite online auction site.

ESPN: Sports (🖥 www.espn.go.com). All the sports news across the US from gridiron to basketball.

Foodies (🖥 www.foodies.com). Celebrating American cuisine with recipes, tips and more.

The Humane Society of the US (🖥 www.rentwithpets.org). Provides information about moving with pets and a list of rental accommodation which allows pets.

Junk Food Mecca (🖥 www.junkfoodmecca.com). Feast on links to the websites of every purveyor of junk food across the 50 states.

Mall of America (🖥 www.mallofamerica.com). Visit the biggest shopping mall in the US from the comfort of your home.

Smithsonian American Art Museum (🖥 http://americanart.si.edu/index3.cfm). An online ticket to view the world's largest art collection.

Symbols of the United States (🖥 http://govdocs.evergreen.edu/symbols.html). A resource with links to sites covering America's most enduring symbols, including the flag, anthem and others. Also lists the nicknames, flags, birds and flowers adopted by each state.

The USA Online (🖥 www.theusaonline.com). Comprehensive interactive website containing details on just about every aspect of American life including the 50 states, national parks, US history, the presidents, society, population and the economy.

Tightwad Central (🖥 www.tightwad.com). Credit crunch-friendly website dedicated to saving you cash, full of frugal tips and freebies.

US Geological Survey (🖥 http://earthquake.usgs.gov/eqcenter/eqarchives). The latest earthquake statistics; worth a read before you decide where to put down roots.

World Health Organization (🖥 www.who.int/countries/usa/en). Direct link to health advice and statistics across the US.

APPENDIX D: CITIZENSHIP QUESTIONS

The 100 civics (history and government) questions and answers for the naturalization test are listed below.

♦ The civics test is an oral test and the USCIS Officer will ask you up to ten of the 100 civics questions. You must answer six out of the ten questions correctly to pass the civics portion of the naturalization test.

♦ Some questions have more than one correct answer, in which case all the acceptable answers are shown below. (USCIS is aware that there may be additional correct answers to the 100 civics questions, but applicants are encouraged to give the answers provided).

♦ The questions are also available in audio on the USCIS website (💻 www.uscis.gov > Resources > Citizenship & Naturalization Based Resources > The 100 civic questions and answers for the naturalization test).

For more information about naturalization, see **Chapter 9**.

If you're 65 years old or older and have been a legal permanent resident of the US for 20 years or more, you may study just the questions shown in bold print.

AMERICAN GOVERNMENT

A: Principles of American Democracy

1. What is the supreme law of the land?

A: The Constitution

2. What does the Constitution do?

A: sets up the government
A: defines the government
A: protects the basic rights of Americans

3. The idea of self-government is in the first three words of the Constitution. What are these words?

A: We the People

4. What is an amendment?

A: a change (to the Constitution)
A: an addition (to the Constitution)

5. What do we call the first ten amendments to the Constitution?

A: The Bill of Rights

6. What is one right or freedom from the First Amendment?

A: speech
A: religion
A: assembly
A: press
A: petition the government

7. How many amendments does the Constitution have?

A: twenty seven (27)

8. What did the Declaration of Independence do?

A: announced our independence (from Great Britain)
A: declared our independence (from Great Britain)
A: said that the US is free (from Great Britain)

9. What are two rights in the Declaration of Independence?

A: life
A: liberty
A: pursuit of happiness

10. What is freedom of religion?

A: You can practice any religion, or not practice a religion.

11. What is the economic system in the US?

A: capitalist economy
A: market economy

12. What is the 'rule of law'?

A: Everyone must follow the law.
A: Leaders must obey the law.
A: Government must obey the law.
A: No one is above the law.

B: System of Government

13. Name one branch or part of the government.

A: Congress
A: legislative
A: President
A: executive
A: the courts
A: judicial

14. What stops one branch of government from becoming too powerful?

A: checks and balances
A: separation of powers

15. Who is in charge of the executive branch?

A: the President

16. Who makes federal laws?

A: Congress
A: Senate and House (of Representatives)
A: (US or national) legislature

17. What are the two parts of the US Congress?

A: the Senate and House (of Representatives)

18. How many US Senators are there?

A: one hundred (100)

19. We elect a US Senator for how many years?

A: six (6)

20. Who is one of your state's US Senators?

A: Answers will vary. For District of Columbia residents and residents of US territories, the answer is that DC (or the territory where the applicant lives) has no US Senators.

21. The House of Representatives has how many voting members?

A: four hundred and thirty-five (435)

22. We elect a US Representative for how many years?

A: two (2)

23. Name your US Representative.

A: Answers will vary. Residents of territories with non-voting Delegates or resident Commissioners may provide the name of that Delegate or Commissioner. Also acceptable is any statement that the territory has no (voting) Representatives in Congress.

24. Who does a US Senator represent?

A: all people of the state

25. Why do some states have more Representatives than other states?

A: (because of) the state's population
A: (because) they have more people
A: (because) some states have more people

26. We elect a President for how many years?

A: four (4)

27. In what month do we vote for President?

A: November

28. What is the name of the President of the United States of America now?

A: Barack Obama
A: Obama

29. What is the name of the Vice President of the United States now?

A: Joseph R. Biden, Jr.
A: Joe Biden
A: Biden

30. If the President can no longer serve, who becomes President?

A: the Vice President

31. If both the President and the Vice President can no longer serve, who becomes President?

A: the Speaker of the House

32. Who is the Commander in Chief of the military?

A: the President

33. Who signs bills to become laws?

A: the President

34. Who vetoes bills?

A: the President

35. What does the President's Cabinet do?

A: advises the President

36. What are two Cabinet-level positions?

A: Secretary of Agriculture
A: Secretary of Commerce
A: Secretary of Defense
A: Secretary of Education
A: Secretary of Energy
A: Secretary of Health and Human Services
A: Secretary of Homeland Security
A: Secretary of Housing and Urban Development
A: Secretary of the Interior
A: Secretary of Labor
A: Secretary of State
A: Secretary of Transportation
A: Secretary of the Treasury
A: Secretary of Veterans' Affairs
A: Secretary of Labor
A: Attorney General
A: Vice President

37. What does the judicial branch do?

A: *reviews laws*
A: *explains laws*
A: *resolves disputes (disagreements)*
A: *decides if a law goes against the Constitution*

38. What is the highest court in the US?

A: *the Supreme Court*

39. How many justices are on the Supreme Court?

A: *nine (9)*

40. Who is the Chief Justice of the US?

A: *John Roberts (John G. Roberts, Jr.)*

41. Under our Constitution, some powers belong to the federal government. What is one power of the federal government?

A: *to print money*
A: *to declare war*
A: *to create an army*
A: *to make treaties*

42. Under our Constitution, some powers belong to the states. What is one power of the states?

A: *provide schooling and education*
A: *provide protection (police)*
A: *provide safety (fire departments)*
A: *give a driver's license*
A: *approve zoning and land use*

43. Who is the Governor of your state?

A: *Answers will vary. Residents of the District of Columbia and US territories without a Governor should reply 'we don't have a Governor.'*

44. What is the capital of your state?

A: *Answers will vary. District of Columbia residents should answer that DC is not a state and does not have a capital. Residents of US territories should name the capital of the territory.*

45. What are the two major political parties in the US?

A: *Democratic and Republican*

46. What is the political party of the President now?

A: *Democratic (Party)*

47. What is the name of the Speaker of the House of Representatives now?

A: *(Nancy) Pelosi*

C: Rights and Responsibilities

48. There are four amendments to the Constitution about who can vote. Describe one of them.

A: *Citizens eighteen (18) and older (can vote).*
A: *You don't have to pay (a poll tax) to vote.*
A: *Any citizen can vote. (Women and men can vote.)*
A: *A male citizen of any race (can vote).*

49. What is one responsibility that is only for US citizens?

A: *serve on a jury*
A: *vote in a federal election*

50. Name one right only for US citizens?

A: *vote in a federal election*
A: *run for federal office*

51. What are two rights of everyone living in the US?

A: *freedom of expression*
A: *freedom of speech*
A: *freedom of assembly*
A: *freedom to petition the government*
A: *freedom of worship*
A: *the right to bear arms*

52. What do we show loyalty to when we say the Pledge of Allegiance?

A: *the United States*
A: *the flag*

53. What is one promise you make when you become a US citizen?

A: *give up loyalty to other countries*
A: *defend the Constitution and laws of the US*
A: *obey the laws of the US*
A: *serve in the US military (if needed)*
A: *serve (do important work for) the nation (if needed)*
A: *be loyal to the US*

54. How old do citizens have to be to vote for President?

A: *eighteen (18) or older*

55. What are two ways that Americans can participate in their democracy?

A: *vote*
A: *join a political party*
A: *help with a campaign*
A: *join a civic group*
A: *join a community group*
A: *give an elected official your opinion on an issue*
A: *call Senators and Representatives*
A: *publicly support or oppose an issue or policy*
A: *run for office*
A: *write to a newspaper*

56. When is the last day you can send in federal income tax forms?

A: *April 15*

57. When must all men register for the Selective Service?

A: *at age eighteen (18)*
A: *between eighteen (18) and twenty-six (26)*

AMERICAN HISTORY

A: Colonial Period & Independence

58. What is one reason colonists came to America?

A: *freedom*
A: *political liberty*
A: *religious freedom*
A: *economic opportunity*
A: *practice their religion*
A: *escape persecution*

59. Who lived in America before the Europeans arrived?

A: *American Indians*
A: *Native Americans*

60. What group of people was taken to America and sold as slaves?

A: *Africans*
A: *people from Africa*

61. Why did the colonists fight the British?

A: *because of high taxes (taxation without representation)*
A: *because the British army stayed in their houses (boarding, quartering)*
A: *because they didn't have self-government*

62. Who wrote the Declaration of Independence?

A: *(Thomas) Jefferson*

63. When was the Declaration of Independence adopted?

A: July 4, 1776

64. There were 13 original states. Name three.

A: New Hampshire
A: Massachusetts
A: Rhode Island
A: Connecticut
A: New York
A: New Jersey
A: Pennsylvania
A: Delaware
A: Maryland
A: Virginia
A: North Carolina
A: South Carolina
A: Georgia

65. What happened at the Constitutional Convention?

A: The Constitution was written.
A: The Founding Fathers wrote the Constitution.

66. When was the Constitution written?

A: 1787

67. The Federalist Papers supported the passage of the US Constitution. Name one of the writers.

A: (James) Madison
A: (Alexander) Hamilton
A: (John) Jay
A: Publius

68. What is one thing Benjamin Franklin is famous for?

A: US diplomat
A: oldest member of the Constitutional Convention
A: first Postmaster General of the US

A: writer of Poor Richard's Almanac
A: started the first free libraries

69. Who is the 'Father of Our Country'?

A: (George) Washington

70. Who was the first President?

A: (George) Washington
B: 1800s

B: 1800s

71. What territory did the US buy from France in 1803?

A: the Louisiana Territory
A: Louisiana

72. Name one war fought by the US in the 1800s.

A: War of 1812
A: Mexican-American War
A: Civil War
A: Spanish-American War

73. Name the US war between the North and the South.

A: the Civil War
A: the War between the States

74. Name one problem that led to the Civil War.

A: slavery
A: economic reasons
A: states' rights

75. What was one important thing that Abraham Lincoln did?

A: freed the slaves (Emancipation Proclamation)
A: saved (or preserved) the Union
A: led the United States during the Civil War

76. What did the Emancipation Proclamation do?

A: freed the slaves
A: freed slaves in the Confederacy
A: freed slaves in the Confederate states
A: freed slaves in most Southern states

77. What did Susan B. Anthony do?

A: fought for women's rights
A: fought for civil rights

C: Recent American History & Other Important Historical Information

78. Name one war fought by the US in the 1900s.

A: World War I
A: World War II
A: Korean War
A: Vietnam War
A: (Persian) Gulf War

79. Who was President during World War I?

A: (Woodrow) Wilson

80. Who was President during the Great Depression and World War II?

A: (Franklin) Roosevelt

81. Who did the US fight in World War II?

A: Japan, Germany and Italy

82. Before he was President, Eisenhower was a general. What war was he in?

A: World War II

83. During the Cold War, what was the main concern of the US?

A: Communism

84. What movement tried to end racial discrimination?

A: civil rights (movement)

85. What did Martin Luther King Jr. do?

A: fought for civil rights
A: worked for equality for all Americans

86. What major event happened on September 11, 2001 in the US?

A: Terrorists attacked the US.

87. Name one American Indian tribe in the US.

A: Cherokee
A: Navajo
A: Sioux
A: Chippewa
A: Choctaw
A: Pueblo
A: Apache
A: Iroquois
A: Creek
A: Blackfeet
A: Seminole
A: Cheyenne
A: Arawak
A: Shawnee
A: Mohegan
A: Huron
A: Oneida
A: Lakota
A: Crow
A: Teton
A: Hopi
A: Inuit

INTEGRATED CIVICS

A: Geography

88. Name one of the two longest rivers in the US.

A: Missouri (River)
A: Mississippi (River)

89. What ocean is on the West Coast of the US?

A: Pacific (Ocean)

90. What ocean is on the East Coast of the US?

A: Atlantic (Ocean)

91. Name one US territory.

A: Puerto Rico
A: US Virgin Islands
A: American Samoa
A: Northern Mariana Islands
A: Guam

92. Name one state that borders Canada.

A: Maine
A: New Hampshire
A: Vermont
A: New York
A: Pennsylvania
A: Ohio
A: Michigan
A: Minnesota
A: North Dakota
A: Montana
A: Idaho
A: Washington
A: Alaska

93. Name one state that borders Mexico.

A: California
A: Arizona
A: New Mexico
A: Texas

94. What is the capital of the US?

A: Washington, DC

95. Where is the Statue of Liberty?

A: New York (Harbor)
A: Liberty Island
(Also acceptable are New Jersey, near New York City, and on the Hudson River).

B: Symbols

96. Why does the flag have 13 stripes?

A: because there were 13 original colonies
A: because the stripes represent the original colonies

97. Why does the flag have 50 stars?

A: because there is one star for each state
A: because each star represents a state
A: because there are 50 states

98. What is the name of the national anthem?

A: The Star-Spangled Banner

C: Holidays

99. When do we celebrate Independence Day?

A: July 4

100. Name two national US holidays.

A: New Year's Day
A: Martin Luther King, Jr., Day
A: Presidents' Day
A: Memorial Day
A: Independence Day
A: Labor Day
A: Columbus Day
A: Veterans Day
A: Thanksgiving
A: Christmas

APPENDIX E: IMMIGRATION FORMS

Whether you're applying for a US visa, Green Card, citizenship, passport, or just need to renew your Green Card, it's important to file your application with the latest form, as applications submitted on an expired or outdated form may result in a delay or denial of your application. The latest forms can be downloaded from the USCIS website (🖥 www.uscis.gov/forms) free of charge with Adobe Reader® and can be completed (filled in) on your computer.

> ⚠ **WARNING**
>
> Avoid commercial websites – many of which masquerade as official government sites by styling themselves in the same way – that aren't affiliated with the USCIS and which offer to sell you forms that are available from the USCIS for free.

Form Number	Title	Filing Fee	Edition	Notes
AR-11	Change of Address	$0	10/06/08. Previous edition accepted.	
AR-11 SR	Alien's Change of Address Card	$0	10/06/08. Previous edition accepted.	
EOIR-29	Notice of Appeal to the Board of Immigration Appeals from a Decision of an Immigration Officer	$110	04-Sep	
G-1041	Genealogy Index Search Request	$20	04/30/09. Prior Versions Accepted.	
G-1041A	Genealogy Records Request	see note	04/30/09. Prior Versions accepted.	The fee for a copy from microfilm is $20 per request. The fee for a copy of a hard copy file is $35 per request.
G-1145	E-Notification of Application/Petition Acceptance	$0	09/14/09	
G-28	Notice of Entry of Appearance as Attorney or Accredited Representative	$0	04/22/09. Previous editions not accepted.	
G-28I	Notice of Entry of Appearance as Attorney in Matters Outside the Geographical Confines of the US	$0	04/22/09. Previous editions not accepted.	
G-325	Biographic Information	$0	06/12/09. Previous editions accepted.	
G-325A	Biographic Information	$0	06/12/09. Previous editions accepted.	
G-325B	Biographic Information	$0	06/12/09. Previous editions accepted.	
G-325C	Biographic Information	$0	06/12/09. Previous editions accepted.	
G-639	Freedom of Information Act/Privacy Act Request	$0	02/04/09. Previous editions are not accepted.	
G-845	Verification Request (Non-SAVE agencies)	$0	07/25/08. Prior versions accepted.	
G-845 Supplement	Document Verification Request Supplement	$0	07/25/08	

Form	Name	Fee	Edition	Notes
G-845S	Document Verification Request (SAVE Agencies)	$0	07/25/08. Prior versions may be used.	
G-884	Return of Original Documents	$0	11/17/09. Prior versions accepted.	
I-102	Application for Replacement/Initial Nonimmigrant Arrival-Departure Document	$320	01/13/10. Previous editions accepted.	
I-129	Petition for a Nonimmigrant Worker	$320	12/04/09. Previous editions accepted.	
I-129F	Petition for Alien Fiancé(e)	$455; see note	02/19/10. 07/30/07 and 11/24/06 editions can be used; no other editions accepted.	There's no fee for petitions for K-3 status based on an immigrant petition filed by the same US citizen.
I-129S	Nonimmigrant Petition Based on Blanket L Petition	$0	01/06/10, previous editions accepted.	
I-130	Petition for Alien Relative	$355	05/27/08. Previous editions accepted.	
I-131	Application for Travel Document	$305; see note	2/12/10. Previous editions accepted.	The biometric fee is $80 for applicants aged 14-79 who request a Refugee Travel Document or Reentry Permit, unless the applicant resides outside the US at the time of filing his or her form. The application fee and biometrics services fee may be paid with one $385 check. Checks must be made payable to the Department of Homeland Security or US Citizenship and Immigration Services.
I-134	Affidavit of Support	$0	10/30/2008. Prior versions are also acceptable.	
I-140	Immigrant Petition for Alien Worker	$475	01/06/10. Previous editions not accepted.	
I-191	Application for Advance Permission to Return to Unrelinquished Domicile	$545	07/30/07. Previous editions accepted.	

Form	Description	Fee	Notes
I-192	Application for Advance Permission to Enter as a Non-Immigrant	$545	01/06/10. Previous editions accepted.
I-193	Application for Waiver for Passport and/or visa	$545	06/20/08
I-212	Application for Permission to Reapply for Admission into the US After Deportation or Removal	$545	07/30/07. Previous editions accepted.
I-243	Application for Removal	$0	09/14/09. No previous editions accepted.
I-290B	Notice of Appeal or Motion	$585	02/10/09. Previous editions accepted.
I-360	Petition for Amerasian, Widow(er), or Special Immigrant	$375	12/30/09 N. Previous versions not accepted.
I-361	Affidavit of Financial Support and Intent to Petition for Legal Custody for Public Law 97-359 Amerasian	$0	04/28/2009. Previous editions accepted.
I-363	Request to Enforce Affidavit of Financial Support and Intent to Petition for Legal Custody for P.L. 97-359 Amerasian	$0	09/14/2009. 10/06/08 and 03/18/08 version are also acceptable.
I-485	Application to Register Permanent Residence or Adjust Status	$1,010; see note	12/03/09. Previous editions not accepted. $930 plus a biometrics fee of $80. Exceptions apply.
I-485 Supplement A	Supplement A to Form I-485	$1,000	12/16/08. Previous editions accepted.
I-485 Supplement B	NACARA Supplement to Form I-485 Instructions	N/A	03/01/1998
I-485 Supplement C	Instructions for I-485, Supplement C, HRIFA	See form I-485	07/07/08. Prior revisions may not be used.
I-485 Supplement E	Instructions for I-485, Supplement E	$0	10/30/08
I-508	Waiver of Rights, Privileges, Exemptions and Immunities (Under Section 247(b) of the INA)	$0	11/17/09. 10/06/08 and 05/27/05 editions also acceptable.
I-508F	Waiver of Rights, Privileges, Exemptions, and Immunities	$0	11/17/09. Prior versions accepted.
I-526	Immigrant Petition by Alien Entrepreneur	$1,435	01/06/10. Previous editions accepted.

Form	Description	Fee	Edition	Note
I-539	Application To Extend/Change Nonimmigrant Status	$300	06/12/09. Previous editions accepted.	
I-539, Supplement A	For persons seeking V nonimmigrant status while in the US or extension of V status.	N/A	10/28/08. Previous editions accepted.	
I-566	Interagency Record of Request -- A, G or NATO Dependent Employment Authorization or Change/Adjustment to/from A, G or NATO Status	$0	03/26/09. 02/28/08 revision also accepted.	
I-589	Application for Asylum and Withholding of Removal	No fee	04/05/2010. Previous editions accepted.	
I-600	Petition to Classify Orphan as an Immediate Relative	$670; see note	12/30/09 N. Previous editions not accepted.	An $80 fee for biometrics is required for each person aged 18 or older who's living with the applicant. No fee is required if you're filing based on an approved I-600A filed within the previous 18 months.
I-600A	Application for Advance Processing of Orphan Petition	$670	12/30/09 N. Previous editions not accepted.	
I-601	Application for Waiver of Ground of Inadmissibility	$545	01/06/10. Previous editions not accepted.	
I-602	Application By Refugee For Waiver of Grounds of Excludability	$0	01/06/10. Previous editions accepted.	
I-612	Application for Waiver of the Foreign Residence Requirement (under Section 212(e) of the Immigration and Nationality Act, as Amended)	$545	08/10/09. Previous editions accepted.	
I-643	Health and Human Services Statistical Data for Refugee/Asylee Adjusting Status	$0	10/29/09 Prior versions acceptable.	
I-687	Application for Status as a Temporary Resident Under Section 245A of the Immigration and Nationality Act	$710	09/09/09. Prior versions aren't accepted.	
I-690	Application for Waiver of Grounds of Inadmissibility Under Sections 245A or 210 of the Immigration and Nationality Act	$185	01/06/10. Previous editions accepted.	

Form	Title	Fee	Edition	Notes
I-693	Report of Medical Examination and Vaccination Record	$0	02/25/2010	
I-694	Notice of Appeal of Decision Under Sections 245A or 210 of the Immigration and Nationality Act	$545	09/09/09. Previous editions accepted.	
I-698	Application to Adjust Status from Temporary to Permanent Resident (Under Section 245A of Public Law 99-603)	$1,410	12/29/2009. Previous editions not accepted.	
I-730	Refugee/Asylee Relative Petition	No fee	01/06/10. Previous editions accepted.	
I-751	Petition to Remove the Conditions of Residence	$545 ($465 plus $80 biometric service fee)	12/30/09. Previous editions accepted.	
I-765	Application for Employment Authorization	$340; see note	02/12/10. Previous editions accepted.	Checks must be made payable to the Department of Homeland Security or US Citizenship and Immigration Services.
I-777	Application for Replacement of Northern Mariana Card	$15	11/17/09 Previous editions accepted.	
I-800	Petition to Classify Convention Adoptee as an Immediate Relative	see note	04/16/09. Prior edition accepted.	No fee is required for the first Form I-800 filed for a child on the basis of an approved Form I-800A. If more than one Form I-800 is filed during the approval period for different children, the fee is $670 for the second and each subsequent Form I-800. However, if the children are siblings before the proposed adoption, no additional filing fee is required.
I-800A	Application for Determination of Suitability to Adopt a Child from a Convention Country	$670 for form I-800A; see note	04/16/09. Prior edition may be used.	An $80 fee for biometrics is required for the applicant (and spouse, if any). Additionally, an $80 fee for biometrics is required for each person aged 18 or older who's living with the applicant. Form I-800A, Supplement 1 (Listing of Adult Member of the Household) must also be provided for each adult member of the household, excluding the applicant and applicant's spouse. $340 for Form I-800A, Supplement 3 (Request for Action on Approved Form I-800A), if applicable.

Form	Description	Fee	Edition	Note
I-817	Application for Family Unity Benefits	$440	02/03/09. Previous editions accepted.	
I-821	Application for Temporary Protected Status	$50; see note	10/17/07. No previous editions accepted.	The fee is $50 for first time applicants. There's no application fee for re-registration. An $80 per person fee for biometrics may be required.
I-824	Application for Action on an Approved Application or Petition	$340	12/11/09. Previous editions accepted.	
I-829	Petition by Entrepreneur to Remove Conditions	$2,850; see note	04/27/2009. Previous editions accepted.	In addition to the filing fee there's a biometrics fee of $80. An additional biometrics fee of $80 must be paid for each conditional resident dependent, listed under Part 3 or Part 4 of Form I-829.
I-854	Inter-Agency Alien Witness and Informant Record	$0	03/31/07. Previous versions accepted.	
I-864	Affidavit of Support Under Section 213A of the Act	see note	10/18/07, 11/01/06 editions can be used; no other edition accepted.	Although the USCIS doesn't charge a fee for this form, the Department of State charges a fee of $70 when the Affidavit of Support is reviewed domestically. This doesn't apply when the Affidavit of Support is filed abroad.
I-864A	Contract Between Sponsor and Household Member	$0	10/18/07. 11/01/06 edition can be used, no other edition accepted.	
I-864EZ	Affidavit of Support Under Section 213A of the Act	see note	10/18/07. 01/15/06 edition can be used, no other edition accepted.	Although the USCIS doesn't charge a fee for this form, the Department of State charges a fee of $70 when the Affidavit of Support is reviewed domestically. This doesn't apply when the Affidavit of Support is filed abroad.
I-864P	Poverty Guidelines	$0	02/13/09. No previous edition accepted.	
I-864W	Intending Immigrant's Affidavit of Support Exemption	see note	10/18/07. 11/01/06 edition can be used; no other editions accepted.	Although the USCIS doesn't charge a fee for this form, the Department of State charges a fee of $70 when the Affidavit of Support is reviewed domestically. This doesn't apply when the Affidavit of Support is filed abroad.

Form	Description	Fee	Revision	Note
I-865	Sponsor's Notice of Change of Address	$0	11/17/09. Previous editions accepted.	
I-881	Application for Suspension of Deportation or Special Rule Cancellation of Removal (Pursuant to Section 203 of Public Law 105-100 (NACARA))	$285	05/26/2009. Previous editions accepted.	
I-9	Employment Eligibility Verification	$0	Rev. 08/07/09. The revision date can be found on the lower right hand corner of the form. The 02/02/09 edition is also accepted.	
I-9 CNMI	Employment Eligibility Verification CNMI	$0	Rev. 11/12/09. The revision date can be found on the lower right hand corner of the form.	
I-90	Application to Replace Permanent Resident Card	$290; see note	04/16/09. Previous editions accepted.	A biometrics fee of $80 may be included.
I-905	Application for Authorization to Issue Certification for Health Care Workers	$230	08/07/09. Previous editions accepted.	
I-907	Request for Premium Processing Service	$1,000; see note	08/10/09. Previous editions not accepted.	If you're requesting Premium Processing on a form type and classification that's Premium eligible, the $1,000 Premium processing fee is required in addition to all other filing fees required by the application to be processed. Checks should be made payable to Department of Homeland Security.
I-914	Application for T Nonimmigrant Status	see note	03/30/09. Previous editions accepted only through June 6, 2009.	No fee. Biometrics services may be required at no cost to the applicant.
I-918	Petition for U Nonimmigrant Status	None; see note	08/31/07	Petitioners may have to pay an $80 biometrics fee.
I-929	Petition for Qualifying Family Member of a U-1 Nonimmigrant	$215	07/15/09; Prior version accepted.	
N-300	Application to File Declaration of Intention	$235	09/08/09. Previous editions accepted.	

Form	Description	Fee	Edition	Note
N-336	Request for a Hearing on a Decision in Naturalization Proceedings (Under Section 336 of the INA)	$605	01/06/10. Previous editions accepted.	
N-4	Monthly Report Naturalization Papers	$0	11/09/09. No previous edition accepted.	
N-400	Application for Naturalization	$675; see note	04/05/2010, 01/22/09, 10/15/07, 07/30/07, 11/01/06, 05/31/01 can be used. No other editions accepted.	The fee includes a biometrics fee of $80. Applicants aged 75 or older aren't charged a biometric fee; their total fee is $595. No fee is required for military applicants filing under Section 328 and 329 of the INA.
N-426	Request for Certification of Military or Naval Service	$0	03/24/09. Previous editions accepted.	
N-470	Application to Preserve Residence for Naturalization Purposes	$305	01/06/10. Prior revisions aren't accepted.	
N-565	Application for Replacement Naturalization/Citizenship Document	$380	07/30/07. Previous editions accepted.	
N-600	Application for Certificate of Citizenship	$460; see note	01/06/10. Previous editions accepted.	If you're filing on behalf of an adopted minor child, $420.
N-600K	Application for Citizenship and Issuance of Certificate under Section 322	$460; see note	09/06/07. Previous editions accepted.	If you're filing on behalf of an adopted minor child, the fee is $420.
N-644	Application for Posthumous Citizenship	No fee	09/08/09. Previous editions accepted.	
N-648	Medical Certification for Disability Exceptions	$0	07/01/09. 10/16/08 revision also accepted.	

APPENDIX F: GLOSSARY

This appendix contains a glossary of immigration terms and words used by the US immigration authorities. It isn't intended to be conclusive.

A

Accompanying: A type of visa in which family members travel with the principal applicant (in immigrant visa cases, within six months of issuance of an immigrant visa to the principal applicant).

Adjust Status: To change from a nonimmigrant visa status to a permanent resident (Green Card holder). Also called 'Adjustment of Status'.

Admission: Entry into the US is authorized by a DHS, Customs and Border Protection (CBP) officer or an Immigration and Customs Enforcement (ICE) officer.

Adopted Child: An unmarried child aged under 21, who was adopted while under the age of 16, and who has been in legal custody and lived with the adopting parent(s) for at least two years.

Advance Parole: Permission to return to the US after travel abroad granted by the DHS prior to leaving the US.

Advisory Opinion: An opinion regarding a point of law from the Office of Visa Services in the Department of State, Washington DC.

Affidavit of Support: A document (form I-134 0r I-864) promising that the person who completes it will support an applicant financially in the US.

Agent: In immigrant visa processing the applicant selects a person who receives all correspondence regarding the case and pays the immigrant visa application processing fee. The agent can be the applicant, the petitioner or another person selected by the applicant.

Alien: A foreign national who isn't a US citizen.

AOS: Affidavit of Support (form I-134 or I-864). A document promising that the person who completes it will support an applicant financially in the US.

Applicant (visa): A foreign citizen who's applying for a nonimmigrant or immigrant US visa. The visa applicant may also be referred as a beneficiary for petition based visas.

Application Fee: The fee for making a visa application.

Appointment Package: The letter and documents that tell an applicant the date of the immigrant visa interview.

Approval Notice: A USCIS immigration form, notice of action form I-797, which states that the USCIS has approved a petition or a request for an extension of stay or change of status.

Asylee: A person who cannot return to his home country because of a well-founded fear of persecution.

Arrival-Departure Card: Also known as Form I-94/I-94W, Arrival-Departure Record. The carrier or Customs and Border Protection official at the port-of-entry gives foreign visitors (all non-US citizens) an Arrival-Departure Record when they enter the US.

Authentication: A federal or state Secretary of State-issued stamp or attachment to any document that verifies the genuineness of the signatures on the document.

B

Beneficiary: The applicant for a visa (or change of status, extensions or adjustment of status) named in a petition to the USCIS.

Biometric Passport: A passport containing biometric details, such as fingerprints or face recognition data on a microchip.

Biometrics: Biologically unique information used to identify individuals.

C

Cancelled Without Prejudice: A stamp that an embassy or consulate puts on a visa when there is a mistake in the visa or the visa is a duplicate visa (two of the same kind).

Case Number: The National Visa Center assigns each immigrant petition a case 'number' with three letters followed by ten digits (numerals).

CBP: Customs and Border Protection.

Certificate of Citizenship: A document issued by the DHS as proof that someone is a US citizen by birth (when born abroad) or derivation (not from naturalization).

Certificate of Naturalization: A document issued by the DHS as proof that someone has become a US citizen (naturalized) after immigration to the US.

Change of Status (COS): Changing from one nonimmigrant visa status to another

nonimmigrant visa status (form I-539) while in the US.

Charge/Chargeable: There are numerical limits on the number of immigrant visas that can be granted to aliens from any one foreign country, which is the same for all countries. The limit is based on place of birth, not citizenship, and where the immigrant is 'charged' means that person is counted towards a given country's numerical limit.

Child: Unmarried child under the age of 21 years. A child may be natural born, stepchild or adopted.

Citizenship: The status of a citizen with rights and duties, who can be a native or a naturalized member of a state. Naturalized US citizens have all the rights of native-born US citizens except the right to become President of the US. See *Naturalization*.

Common-law Marriage: An agreement between a man and woman to enter into marriage without a civil or religious ceremony, which may not be recognized as a marriage for immigration purposes.

Conditional Residence Visa: If you have been married for less than two years when your spouse obtains lawful permanent resident status (receives a Green Card), then your spouse receives residence on a conditional basis. This also applies to investment immigrant (EB-5) visas holders, who receive conditional residence for two years.

Consulate: A Department of State sub-office in a larger foreign country, responsible for issuing immigrant and nonimmigrant visas to aliens for entry into the US. The Consul is the chief diplomatic officer in a consulate.

Current/Non-current: Refers to the priority date of a petition in preference immigrant visa cases in relationship to the immigrant cut-off date. If your priority date is before the cut-off date according to the monthly *Visa Bulletin*, your case is current, which means it can be processed. However, if your priority date is later/ comes after the cut-off date, you'll need to wait until your priority date is reached (becomes current).

Customs and Border Protection: The federal law enforcement agency of the US Department of Homeland Security that's responsible for regulating and facilitating international trade, collecting import duties, and enforcing US regulations, including trade, drug and immigration laws.

Cut-off Date: The date that determines whether a preference immigrant visa applicant can be scheduled for an immigrant visa interview in any given month. See *Current/Non-current*.

D

Department of Homeland Security (DHS): The DHS is comprised of three main organizations responsible for immigration policies, procedures, implementation and enforcement of US laws, and more. The DHS encompasses the US Citizenship and Immigration Services (USCIS), Customs and Border Protection (CBP) and Immigration and Customs Enforcement (ICE).

Department of Labor (DOL): A cabinet level ministry of the US government with responsibility for labor issues and deciding whether certain foreign workers can work in the US.

Department of State (DOS): Often referred to as the State Department, the DOS is the US federal executive department responsible for international relations (called the Foreign Office or Foreign Department in many other countries).

Deportation: The expulsion process whereby someone is physically removed from the US by a DHS Deportation Officer to his native country, usually as a result of a deportation or removal order from an Immigration Court.

Derivative Citizenship: Citizenship conveyed to children through the naturalization of parents or, under certain circumstances, to foreign-born children adopted by US citizen parents.

Derivative Status: Obtaining a status (visa) through another applicant, as provided under immigration law for certain visa categories. For example, the spouse and children of an exchange visitor (J Visa holder) are granted derivative status as a J-2 Visa holder.

DHS: See *Department of Homeland Security*.

Diversity Visa Program: An annual lottery for US immigration visas for people from countries with low rates of immigration.

DOL: See *Department of Labor*.

Domicile: Place where a person has his or her principal residence.

Dual Nationality: Where a person has the nationality of two countries. A person with dual US nationality must use his US passport when entering or departing the US.

Duration of Status (d/s): In certain visa categories, such as diplomats, students and exchange visitors, a person may be admitted into the US for as long as he's carries out the activity for which the visa was issued, rather than being admitted until a specific departure dates. This is called admission for 'duration of status'.

DV: See *Diversity Visa Program*.

E

EAD: See *Employment Authorization Document.*

Embassy: The principal office of the US Department of State in a foreign country, responsible for issuing immigrant and nonimmigrant visas to aliens for entry into the US. The US Ambassador is the chief diplomatic officer in an embassy.

Emigrant: Someone who quits his native country (or region) to settle in another country. See also *immigrant* and *migrant.*

Employment Authorization Document (EAD): Popularly known as a 'work permit', an EAD is a document issued by the USCIS that gives the holder a legal right to work in the US. Not to be confused with the Green Card.

ESTA: Electronic System for Travel Authorization (ESTA) is a free automated system that determines the eligibility of visitors to travel to the US without a visa under the Visa Waiver Program (VWP).

Exchange Visitor: A foreign citizen coming to the US to participate in a particular program in education, training, research or other authorized exchange visitor program.

Extension of Stay or Status (EOS): An application to extend the term of a nonimmigrant visa.

F

Family First Preference: A category of family immigration (F1) for the unmarried sons and daughters of American citizens and their children.

Family Second Preference: A category of family immigration (F2) for the spouses, children, and the unmarried sons and daughters of lawful permanent residents.

Family Third Preference: A category of family immigration (F3) for the married sons and daughters of American citizens and their spouses and children.

Family Fourth Preference: A category of family immigration (F4) for the brothers and sisters of American citizens and their spouses and children.

Fiancé(e): A person who plans to marry. The foreign fiancé(e) of an American citizen may enter the US on a K-1 visa to marry the American citizen.

First Preference: See *Family First Preference.*

Fiscal Year: The budget year for the US government, which begins on October 1st and ends on September 30th of the following year.

FLC: Foreign Labor Certification. See *Labor Certification.*

Following to Join: A type of derivative visa status where a family member receives a visa after the principal applicant.

Fourth Preference: See *Family Fourth Preference.*

Full and Final Adoption: A legal adoption in which the child receives all the rights of a natural born, legitimate child.

G

Green Card: A wallet-sized card showing that a person is a lawful permanent resident (immigrant) in the US. It's also known as a Permanent Resident Card (PRC), an Alien Registration Receipt card and I-551. It's so-called because it was formerly green in color.

Green Card Lottery: See *Diversity Visa Program.*

H

Homeless: Persons from countries that don't have an American embassy or consulate where they can apply for immigrant visas are classed as 'homeless.'

Household Income: The income used to determine whether a sponsor meets the minimum income requirements under Section 213A of the INA for some immigrant visa cases.

I

I-551 (Green Card): Permanent Residence Card, Alien Registration Receipt Card or Green Card. See also *Green Card* and *Lawful Permanent Resident.*

I-94/I-94W: See *Arrival-Departure Card.*

ICE: See *Immigration and Customs Enforcement.*

Illegal Alien: Also known as an 'undocumented alien.' An alien (foreigner) who entered the US illegally or who entered the US legally but is 'out of status' and is deportable.

Immediate Relative (IR): Spouse, widow(er) and unmarried children under the age of 21 of an American citizen, or a parent if the US citizen is 21 years of age or older.

Immigrant. A person who enters a country of which he isn't a native for the purpose of permanent residence. Someone who's a lawful permanent resident of the US is an immigrant. See also *emigrant.*

Immigrant Visa (IV): A visa that permits an alien to live indefinitely and permanently in the US.

Immigration and Customs Enforcement (ICE): Part of the Department of Homeland Security; ICE's mission is to protect the security of the American people and homeland by enforcing the nation's immigration and customs laws.

Immigration and Nationality Act (INA): American immigration statute. The Immigration and Nationality Act, or INA, was created in 1952, Public Law No. 82-414.

Immigration and Naturalization Service (INS): A branch of the Department of Justice that formerly had responsibility for immigration and naturalization. The INS was renamed the 'US Citizenship and Immigration Services' (USCIS) and became part of the Department of Homeland Security (DHS) on March 1 2003.

INA: See *Immigration and Nationality Act.*

Inadmissible: An alien seeking admission at a port of entry who doesn't meet the criteria for admission.

Ineligible/Ineligibility: Immigration law says that certain conditions and actions prevent a person from entering the US. These conditions and activities are called ineligibilities and the applicant is ineligible for a visa.

In Status: Each visa classification has a set of requirements that the visa holder must follow in order to maintain 'in status' and their eligibility to remain in the US. Those who don't follow the requirements violate their status and are considered 'out of status.'

Issuance Fee: A fee for issuing a visa, which is made on a reciprocal basis.

IV: Immigrant visa.

J

Joint Sponsor: A person who accepts legal responsibility for supporting an immigrant with an I-864 Affidavit of Support, along with the sponsor.

Jurisdiction: Authority to apply the law in a given territory or region.

K

Kentucky Consular Center (KCC): A US Department of State facility located in Williamsburg, Kentucky. It gives domestic (US) support to the worldwide operations of the Bureau of Consular Affairs Visa Office and manages the Diversity Visa (DV) Program.

L

Labor Certification: A prerequisite for certain immigrant and nonimmigrant employment petitions, whereby employers must establish that there are no suitably qualified US workers available to fill the position. The employer is responsible for obtaining labor certification from the Department of Labor.

Labor Condition Application (LCA): An application made to the Department of Labor by employers prior to submitting certain non-immigrant employment based petitions. The employer is required to attest that the employment won't adversely affect the wages and working conditions of similarly-employed US workers.

Lawful Permanent Resident (LPR): A person who has immigrated legally but isn't an American citizen, who has been admitted to the US as an immigrant and has a Permanent Resident Card, Form I-551 (Green Card). Also called a Legal Permanent Resident.

Legitimation: The legal process which a natural father can use to acknowledge legally his children who were born out of wedlock (outside of marriage).

LIFE Act: Legal Immigration Family Equity (LIFE) Act and amendments, which allows foreign spouses of American citizens, the children of foreign spouses, and spouses and children of certain lawful permanent residents (LPR) to come to the US to complete the processing for their permanent residence.

Lose Status: To stay in the US longer than the period of time which the DHS officer allocated when a person entered the US, or to fail to meet the requirements or violate the terms of the visa classification. The person may become 'out of status.'

Lottery: See *Diversity Visa Program*.

LPR or LPRA: See *Lawful Permanent Resident*.

M

Machine Readable Passport (MRP): A passport with the biographic information entered on the data page (below the photograph) according to international specifications, which allows it to be scanned by a computer. A MRP is required to travel without a visa on the Visa Waiver Program (see page 120).

Machine Readable Visa (MRV): A visa that allows the data contained therein to be scanned by a computer.

Maintain Status: To adhere to the requirements of your visa status and comply with any limitations on duration of stay.

Means-tested Public Benefits: Assistance from a government unit. Benefits include food stamps, Medicaid, Supplemental Security Income (SSI), Temporary Assistance for Needy Families (TANF), and State Child Health Insurance Program (CHIP).

Migrant: A person who leaves his native country to seek residence in another country.

MRP: See *Machine Readable Passport.*

MRV: See *Machine Readable Visa.*

Multiple-entry Visa: a visa that allows the holder to visit the US an unlimited number of times provided the visa remains valid.

N

National Interest Waiver: For physicians and doctors who work in an area without adequate health care workers or who work in Veterans Affairs' facilities.

National Visa Center (NVC): A Department of State facility located in Portsmouth, New Hampshire, which processes approved immigrant visa petitions received from the USCIS and retains them until the cases are ready for adjudication by a consular officer abroad.

Native: A person born in a particular country is a native of that country.

Naturalization: A citizen who acquires nationality of a country after birth, i.e. someone who didn't become a citizen by birth but through a legal procedure. The process whereby a Green Card holder becomes an American citizen.

Nonimmigrant: An alien who seeks temporary entry to the US for a specific purpose.

Nonimmigrant Visa (NIV): A US visa that allows foreigners to apply to enter the US temporarily for a specific purpose.

Notice of Action: A USCIS immigration form (I-797) which states that the USCIS has received a petition you submitted, taken action, and has approved or denied the petition.

Number of Entries: the maximum allowable number of times that a US visa holder can enter the US during the validity of a visa before having to obtain a new visa.

NVC: See *National Visa Center.*

O

Orphan: A child who has no parents because of the death, disappearance, desertion or abandonment of his or her parents.

Out of Status: A visa holder who has overstayed a visa (or I-94 card) expiration date or engaged in activities that aren't permitted for the particular type of visa issued and has violated his status.

Overstay: An 'overstay' occurs when a visitor stays longer than permitted, as shown on his Arrival/Departure card (I-94/I-94W). See also *Out of status.*

P

Panel Physician: Embassies and consulates which issue immigrant visas have selected certain doctors (a 'panel physician') to perform medical examinations for immigrant visa applicants,

Passport: an identity document that a country issues to its citizens for the purpose of facilitating international travel.

Permanent Resident Card (PRC): A wallet-sized card showing that someone is a lawful permanent resident (immigrant) in the US. Commonly referred to as a 'Green Card' after its original color.

Petition: A request made to the USCIS on approval of which the beneficiary may apply for a visa abroad or – if already in the US on valid status – apply to change, extend or adjust his status.

Petitioner: The American citizen, legal permanent resident or US corporation filing on behalf of an alien for immigrant or nonimmigrant status.

Physical Presence: The place where a person is actually (physically) located.

Port of Entry: Place (usually an airport) where a person requests admission to the US from a Customs and Border Protection officer.

Post: American embassy, consulate or other diplomatic mission abroad. Not all American embassies, consulates and missions are visa-issuing posts.

Poverty Guidelines: The Department of Health and Human Services publishes a list each year giving the lowest income acceptable for a family of a particular size so that the family doesn't live in poverty.

Preference Immigration: A system for determining which people (and when) can immigrate to the US within the immigration limits set by Congress. In family immigration, preference is based on the status of the petitioner (American citizen or lawful permanent resident) and his/her relationship to the applicant.

Principal Applicant/Beneficiary: The person named in a petition, for example, a company files a petition for a worker. The worker is the principal applicant and his family members receive derivative status. A derivative beneficiary, such as a spouse or minor child, is someone who obtains status through the principal beneficiary.

Priority Date: The priority date decides a person's turn to apply for an immigrant visa. In family immigration the priority date is the date when the petition was filed at a USCIS office or submitted to an embassy or consulate abroad.

Public Charge: Refers to becoming dependent upon the government for the expenses of living, e.g. food, shelter, clothing etc.

Q

Qualifying Date: The latest priority date that visas can be processed for certain visa categories.

R

Rank Order Number: The number that the Kentucky Consular Center gives to the entries of DV Program (lottery) as the computer selects them. See *Diversity Visa Program*.

Receipt Notice: A USCIS form 'Notice of Action' (I-797) which states that the DHS has received a petition.

Re-entry Permit: A travel document that the USCIS issues to lawful permanent residents (LPRs) who want to remain outside the US for more than one year and less than two years.

Refugee: A person who has a well-founded fear of persecution if he should return to his home country.

Request for Evidence: A letter that the USCIS uses to request additional information on a pending case.

Residence Permit: The US doesn't issue residence permits as such, but issues nonimmigrant and immigrant visas that permit aliens to live and/or work in the US, either temporarily or permanently

Resident Alien: A US permanent resident (not to be confused with the broader US tax law definition of a resident alien).

Retrogression: Visa retrogression occurs when demand exceeds supply and the annual numerical limit for a particular immigrant visa category has been reached. In this case an immigrant visa number becomes unavailable or a cut-off date is imposed.

Returning Residents: Lawful permanent residents who wish to return to the US after staying abroad for a period, usually more than one year, or beyond the expiration of their reentry permits.

Revalidation or Renewal of a Visa: Nonimmigrant visa applicants who currently have a visa and are seeking renewal or revalidation of their visa for future travel to the US must apply abroad, generally in their country of residence.

Revocation of a Visa: Cancellation of a visa.

S

Schedule 'A' Occupations: Occupations for which the Department of Labor has given the USCIS authority to approve labor certifications.

Second Preference: See *Family Second Preference.*

Section 213A: A section of the Immigration and Nationality Act (INA) which establishes that sponsors have a legal duty to support immigrants they want to bring (sponsor) to the US.

Service Center: There are four regional service centers in the US in California, Nebraska, Texas and Vermont, which process petitions and other applications for immigration related benefits.

Single-entry Visa: A visa that allows the holder to visit the US only once before it expires.

Son/daughter: In immigration law, a child becomes a son or daughter when he/she turns 21 or marries.

Special Immigrant: A special category of immigrant visas for those who lost their citizenship through marriage or serving in foreign armed forces, certain foreign medical school graduates, Panama Canal immigrants, plus some others.

Sponsor: Someone who completes and submits an immigration visa petition (also called a petitioner) or a person who completes an affidavit of support (I-864) for an immigrant visa applicant.

Sponsored Immigrant: An immigrant who has had an affidavit of support filed for him.

Spouse: A legally married husband or wife. A co-habiting partner doesn't qualify as a spouse for immigration purposes.

State Workforce Agency: The agency or bureau in each state that deals with employment and labor issues.

Status: Your immigration status, which is indicated on your I-94/I-94W immigration card along with the period that you're permitted to stay in the US. See *Arrival-Departure Card.*

Stepchild: A spouse's child from a previous marriage or other relationship.

Surviving Parent: A child's living parent when the child's other parent is dead, and the living parent hasn't remarried.

T

Temporary Worker: A foreign worker who's permitted to work in the US for a limited period of time. Nonimmigrant visas classes for temporary workers include H, L, O, P, Q and R.

Third Country National: Someone who isn't an American and also not a citizen of the country where he's applying for a visa.

Third Preference: See *Family Third Preference.*

Treaty Nationals (TN): Citizens of Canada and Mexico who are professionals can obtain temporary TN (NAFTA) work permits.

U

Upgrade a Petition: If you naturalize (become an American citizen) you can ask the USCIS to change the petitions you filed for family members when you were a lawful permanent resident (LPR) from one category to another. This is called upgrading.

USCIS: United States Citizenship and Immigration Services.

US National: A citizen of the US.

US-VISIT: The US Visitor and Immigrant Status Indicator Technology (US-VISIT) program. A DHS immigration and border management system that involves the collection and analysis of biometric data (such as fingerprints).

V

Validity: the period of time before (or date on which) a passport or visa expires.

Visa: A permit (stamp or certificate) in a passport that allows the holder to travel to a US port of entry and apply for entry from a Customs and Border Protection (CBP) officer. The US issues visas for temporary (nonimmigrant visa) and permanent residence (immigrant visa).

Visa Expiration Date: The visa expiration date is shown on a visa.

Visa Numbers: Congress establishes the number of immigrants permitted each year.

Visa Validity: This generally means a visa is valid or can be used from the date it's issued until the date it expires.

Visa Waiver Program (VWP): The program whereby citizens of participating countries meeting the VWP requirements are permitted to enter the US for up to 90 days as visitors for pleasure or business without first obtaining a visa.

W

Waiver of Ineligibility: In immigration law, certain foreign nationals are ineligible for visas to enter the US due to medical, criminal, security or other conditions and activities.

Work Permit: The US doesn't generally issue work permits, with the exception of the EAD (see *Employment Authorization Document*), but issues certain nonimmigrant and immigrant visas that permit aliens to work in the US.

APPENDIX G: WEIGHTS & MEASURES

America uses the metric system of measurement. Those who are more familiar with the imperial system of measurement will find the tables on the following pages useful. Some comparissons shown are only approximate, but are close enough for most everyday uses. In addition to the variety of measurement systems used, clothes sizes often vary considerably with the manufacturer. The website 🖳 www.onlineconversions.com allows you to make instant conversions between different measurement systems

Women's Clothes										
Continental	34	36	38	40	42	44	46	48	50	52
UK		8	10	12	14	16	18	20	22	24	26
US		6	8	10	12	14	16	18	20	22	24

Pullovers													
	Women's						Men's						
Continental	40	42	44	46	48	50	44	46	48	50	52	54
UK	34	36	38	40	42	44	34	36	38	40	42	44
US	34	36	38	40	42	44		sm	med		lg	xl

Men's Shirts										
Continental	36	37	38	39	40	41	42	43	44	46
UK/US	14	14	15	15	16	16	17	17	18	-

Men's Underwear						
Continental	5	6	7	8	9	10
UK		34	36	38	40	42	44
US		sm	med		lg	xl

NB: sm = small, med = medium, lg = large, xl = extra large

Children's Clothes						
Continental	92	104	116	128	140	152
UK	16/18	20/22	24/26	28/30	32/34	36/38
US	2	4	6	8	10		12

Children's Shoes
Continental 18 19 20 21 22 23 24 25 26 27 28 29 30 31 32
UK/US 2 3 4 4 5 6 7 7 8 9 10 11 11 12 13
Continental 33 34 35 36 37 38
UK/US 1 2 2 3 4 5

Shoes (Women's & Men's)												
Continental	35	36	37	37	38	39	40	41	42	42	43	44
UK	2	3	3	4	4	5	6	7	7	8	9	9
US	4	5	5	6	6	7	8	9	9	10	10	11

Weight			
Imperial	**Metric**	**Metric**	**Imperial**
1oz	28.35g	1g	0.035oz
1lb*	454g	100g	3.5oz
1cwt	50.8kg	250g	9oz
1 ton	1,016kg	500g	18oz
2,205lb	1 tonne	1kg	2.2lb

Area			
British/US	**Metric**	**Metric**	**British/US**
1 sq. in	0.45 sq. cm	1 sq. cm	0.15 sq. in
1 sq. ft	0.09 sq. m	1 sq. m	10.76 sq. ft
1 sq. yd	0.84 sq. m	1 sq. m	1.2 sq. yds
1 acre	0.4 hectares	1 hectare	2.47 acres
1 sq. mile	2.56 sq. km	1 sq. km	0.39 sq. mile

Capacity			
Imperial	**Metric**	**Metric**	**Imperial**
1 UK pint	0.57 litre	1 litre	1.75 UK pints
1 US pint	0.47 litre	1 litre	2.13 US pints
1 UK gallon	4.54 litres	1 litre	0.22 UK gallon
1 US gallon	3.78 litres	1 litre	0.26 US gallon
NB: An American 'cup' = around 250ml or 0.25 litre.			

Length			
British/US	**Metric**	**Metric**	**British/US**
1in	2.54cm	1cm	0.39in
1ft	30.48cm	1m	3ft 3.25in
1yd	91.44cm	1km	0.62mi
1mi	1.6km	8km	5mi

Temperature	
°Celsius	**°Fahrenheit**
0	32 (freezing point of water)
5	41
10	50
15	59
20	68
25	77
30	86
35	95
40	104
50	122

Temperature Conversion

Celsius to Fahrenheit: multiply by 9, divide by 5 and add 32. (For a quick and approximate conversion, double the Celsius temperature and add 30.)

Fahrenheit to Celsius: subtract 32, multiply by 5 and divide by 9. (For a quick and approximate conversion, subtract 30 from the Fahrenheit temperature and divide by 2.)

NB: The boiling point of water is 100°C / 212°F. Normal body temperature (if you're alive and well) is 37°C / 98.6°F.

Power			
Kilowatts	Horsepower	Horsepower	Kilowatts
1	1.34	1	0.75

Oven Temperature		
Gas	Electric	
	°F	°C
-	225–250	110–120
1	275	140
2	300	150
3	325	160
4	350	180
5	375	190
6	400	200
7	425	220
8	450	230
9	475	240

Air Pressure	
PSI	Bar
10	0.5
20	1.4
30	2
40	2.8

INDEX

A

B

C

D

E

R/S

Survival Books

Essential reading for anyone planning to live, work, retire or buy a home abroad

Survival Books was established in 1987 and by the mid-'90s was the leading publisher of books for people planning to live, work, buy property or retire abroad.

From the outset, our philosophy has been to provide the most comprehensive and up-to-date information available. Our titles routinely contain up to twice as much information as other books and are updated frequently. All our books contain colour photographs and some are printed in two colours or full colour throughout. They also contain original cartoons, illustrations and maps.

Survival Books are written by people with first-hand experience of the countries and the people they describe, and therefore provide invaluable insights that cannot be obtained from official publications or websites, and information that is more reliable and objective than that provided by the majority of unofficial sites.

Survival Books are designed to be easy – and interesting – to read. They contain a comprehensive list of contents and index and extensive appendices, including useful addresses, further reading, useful websites and glossaries to help you obtain additional information as well as metric conversion tables and other useful reference material.

Our primary goal is to provide you with the essential information necessary for a trouble-free life or property purchase and to save you time, trouble and money.

We believe our books are the best – they are certainly the best-selling. But don't take our word for it – read what reviewers and readers have said about Survival Books at the front of this book.

Order your copies today by phone, fax, post or email from:
Survival Books, PO Box 3780, Yeovil, BA21 5WX, United Kingdom.
Tel: +44 (0)1935-700060, email: sales@survivalbooks.net,
Website: www.survivalbooks.net

Buying a Home Series

Buying a home abroad is not only a major financial transaction but also a potentially life-changing experience; it's therefore essential to get it right. Our Buying a Home guides are required reading for anyone planning to purchase property abroad and are packed with vital information to guide you through the property jungle and help you avoid disasters that can turn a dream home into a nightmare.

The purpose of our Buying a Home guides is to enable you to choose the most favourable location and the most appropriate property for your requirements, and to reduce your risk of making an expensive mistake by making informed decisions and calculated judgements rather than uneducated and hopeful guesses. Most importantly, they will help you save money and will repay your investment many times over.

Buying a Home guides are the most comprehensive and up-to-date source of information available about buying property abroad – whether you're seeking a detached house or an apartment, a holiday or a permanent home (or an investment property), these books will prove invaluable.

For a full list of our current titles, visit our website at www.survivalbooks.net

Living and Working Series

Our Living and Working guides are essential reading for anyone planning to spend a period abroad – whether it's an extended holiday or permanent migration – and are packed with priceless information designed to help you avoid costly mistakes and save both time and money.

Living and Working guides are the most comprehensive and up-to-date source of practical information available about everyday life abroad. They aren't, however, simply a catalogue of dry facts and figures, but are written in a highly readable style – entertaining, practical and occasionally humorous.

Our aim is to provide you with the comprehensive practical information necessary for a trouble-free life. You may have visited a country as a tourist, but living and working there is a different matter altogether; adjusting to a new environment and culture and making a home in any foreign country can be a traumatic and stressful experience. You need to adapt to new customs and traditions, discover the local way of doing things (such as finding a home, paying bills and obtaining insurance) and learn all over again how to overcome the everyday obstacles of life.

All these subjects and many, many more are covered in depth in our Living and Working guides – don't leave home without them.

The Expats' Best Friend!

Culture Wise Series

O ur **Culture Wise** series of guides is essential reading for anyone who wants to understand how a country really 'works'. Whether you're planning to stay for a few days or a lifetime, these guides will help you quickly find your feet and settle into your new surroundings. **Culture Wise** guides:

- Reduce the anxiety factor in adapting to a foreign culture
- Explain how to behave in everyday situations in order to avoid cultural and social gaffes
- Help you get along with your neighbours
- Make friends and establish lasting business relationships
- Enhance your understanding of a country and its people.

People often underestimate the extent of cultural isolation they can face abroad, particularly in a country with a different language. At first glance, many countries seem an 'easy' option, often with millions of visitors from all corners of the globe and well-established expatriate communities. But, sooner or later, newcomers find that most countries are indeed 'foreign' and many come unstuck as a result. **Culture Wise** guides will enable you to quickly adapt to the local way of life and feel at home, and – just as importantly – avoid the worst effects of culture shock.

Culture Wise – The Wise Way to Travel

The essential guides to Culture, Customs & Business Etiquette

PHOTO

CREDITS

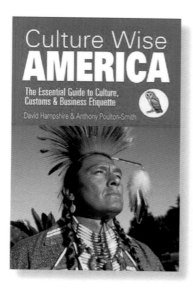